Setbacks and Advances in the Modern Latin American Economy

This volume explores several notable themes related to the economy in Latin America and offers insightful historical perspectives to understand national, regional, and global issues in the continent since the beginning of the 20th century to the present day. The collected essays focus on economic crises, the relationship of growth models to society and politics, the fluctuations of local economies, and regional protests. Other aspects of consideration in this area include the evolution of integrated regional trading blocs, the informal economy, and the destruction of the productive potential that has had a serious social, cultural, and environmental impact. The volume refuses to impose a traditional and uncritical linear historical narrative onto the reader and instead proposes an alternative interpretation of the past and its relation to the present.

Pablo A. Baisotti is currently a Research Assistant at the Department of Latin American Studies (ELA) at the University of Brasilia and an external Professor at the Institute of Iberian and Ibero-American Studies at the University of Warsaw.

Routledge Studies in the History of the Americas

For more information about this series, please visit:
https://www.routledge.com/Routledge-Studies-in-the-History-
of-the-Americas/book-series/RSHAM

Setbacks and Advances in the Modern Latin American Economy

Edited by Pablo A. Baisotti

Routledge
Taylor & Francis Group

NEW YORK AND LONDON

First published 2022
by Routledge
605 Third Avenue, New York, NY 10158

and by Routledge
2 Park Square, Milton Park, Abingdon, Oxon, OX14 4RN

Routledge is an imprint of the Taylor & Francis Group, an informa business

Library of Congress Cataloging-in-Publication Data
A catalog record for this title has been requested

ISBN: 978-0-367-49259-5 (hbk)
ISBN: 978-0-367-49309-7 (pbk)
ISBN: 978-1-003-04563-2 (ebk)

DOI: 10.4324/9781003045632

Typeset in Sabon
by KnowledgeWorks Global Ltd.

Contents

Figures

Graphs

Tables

Foreword

In late 2020, right in the middle of the COVID-19 pandemic, I met Dr Baisotti through a common colleague of ours, Dr Ronny Viales Hurtado from the University of Costa Rica's Central American Historical Research Centre (*Centro de Investigaciones Históricas de América Central* – CIHAC). In his introduction, Dr Viales explained that Dr Baisotti was a very active academic who had worked at several universities in Asia, Latin America, and Europe, and someone interested in intellectual history of inequality, solidarity economics, and impacts of natural resource extraction. I immediately wanted to know more about Dr Baisotti's work both because my work at Aarhus University's Global Studies Department touches on these areas as fields of research and as teaching subjects and also because my professional trajectory has taken me to several continents, so I thought we would have a lot to share.

Up until that time, Dr Baisotti had been a research fellow at the Costa Rican branch of the *Maria Sibylla Merian Center for Advanced Latin American Studies in the Humanities and Social Sciences*, the same place where I presented at one of its *Plataforma para el Diálogo* conference in 2019. When we finally met, we immediately started talking about our experiences as Latin American researchers in a globalized world, what it meant for our future careers, and the future of the continent we were born in. This led to a more focused conversation about research collaboration examining the nexus between natural resource extraction, disruption of community livelihoods, and reconstruction of local economies from the perspective of solidarity economics. This has become an ongoing discussion between Dr Baisotti and myself and members of our respective networks. I hope these early conversations bear fruit one day and lead to one or many forms of knowledge production about this combination of subjects.

I was also interested in the many books that Dr Baisotti was involved in as author, co-author, or editor. Back then, one project that caught my attention was the book you have in front of you: an edited volume

on "*Setbacks and Advances in the Modern Latin American Economy*",
part of Routledge Studies in the History of the Americas book series.
Initially, I was a bit hesitant to ask about the contents because, in the
past 10 years, many large publishing houses had already dealt with this
topic. Larrain, A. "*The Economics of Contemporary Latin America*"
published in 2017 by MIT, Yáñez, C. "*The Economies of Latin
America*" published in 2016 by Routledge and Holden, R. and Villars,
R. "*Contemporary Latin America: 1970 to the Present*" published in
2012 by Wiley-Blackwell are all good examples of publications dealing
with recent economic developments in the region.

   Still, I asked Dr Baisotti to tell me a bit about this particular project
and he kindly shared a pre-publication copy. Now that I have read the
chapters, I can see why this book is different from many of the others in
the market. To begin with, more than half of the authors contributing
to this volume are resident Latin Americans working in Latin American
research institutions. This is important because it provides the reader a
local perspective from researchers stationed on the ground where economic developments are taking place and not from a distant location,
dissociated from everyday economic realities.

   Relying on many Latin American authors based in southern institutions also gives this book credibility in terms of contributing to redress
the large imbalance that exists in academia where most knowledge
production occurs in northern institutions. This is specially the case
with Area Studies and studies of economies about the Global South.
Dr Baisotti is well aware of this imbalance and I think that he has done
a very good job at operationalizing post-colonial arguments about epis-
temic inequalities.

   Dr Baisotti has managed a collection of chapters that complement
each other and is not confined to a single methodology. The book does
not rely solely on case studies but also contends with theoretical problems such as the re-feudalization of Latin American societies and the
contribution of *Cepalismo* to economic thought. A few chapters touch
on the impact of the COVID-19 pandemic, which is a feature that many
publications before 2019 simply do not have and could not have foreseen. It also seems that many authors focus on one particular country or
an industrial sector within a country without ignoring the regional and
international dynamics of capitalist markets and global inequalities. I
can also see that Dr Baisotti was able to attract some fairly well-known
authors in the field of economic development but there are also a number of emerging authors, which is refreshing. Most important of all is
that the various chapters capture not only the problems that besiege the
region but also the advances that were achieved during the last two decades and this feature alone provides invaluable insights into the topic of
economic development in the region.

With all of the above in mind, I can only add that Dr Baisotti has put together a very engaging and coherent set of chapters for this volume and I hope that readers find it a good source of knowledge about Latin America and its economies.

Vladimir Pacheco-Cuevas
Professor, Global Studies Department, Aarhus University

Contributors

María Paula M. Aguilar Romero is an external Research Assistant in the Geo-economics and Geopolitics of emerging economies project coordinated by Dr Juan Carlos Gachúz. She holds a Bachelor in International Relations, and she is a Master Candidate in International Management. She was International Presidential Fellow in the Center for the Study of the Presidency and Congress in Washington DC, conducting research on bilateral National Security cooperation between Mexico and the United States. Her research interests are international security and geopolitics and geo-economics of Asia. She is currently Global Compliance and Reporting consultant at EY.

Pablo A. Baisotti holds two interdisciplinary MA degrees, one in International Relations Europe-Latin America (University of Bologna, 2006–2008) and the other in Law and Economic Integration (University Paris I Pantheon Sorbonne and University del Salvador, Argentina, 2005–2007). Also, he holds an interdisciplinary PhD from the Faculty of Political Science of the University of Bologna in Politics, Institutions, and History (2012–2015). He received his Bachelor's degree in History from the University of Salvador in 2004. He was a Calas-Costa Rica postdoctoral researcher at the Maria Sibylla Merian Center, University of Costa Rica. Besides, he is affiliated with different research groups such as the Latin American Social Science Council (CLASCO) and the Latin (and Hispanic American) Academic Network of Sinology Studies at the University of Costa Rica. He has served as a researcher and educator in the Centre for Latin American Studies at the School of International Studies, Sun Yat-sen University. He is currently a Research Assistant at the Department of Latin American Studies (ELA), University of Brasilia.

Noemí Brenta is an Economist, Researcher, and Professor of Economics at the University of Buenos Aires. She is Deputy Director of the Research Center for Economic, Social and International Relations History and Professor of these subjects at the School of Economics at the University of Buenos Aires and other national universities. She also is a Research Coordinator at the Institute of Historical, Economic, Social and International Studies (CONICET). She has directed and participated in numerous research projects, published articles in specialized magazines, and has several books including *Historia de las relaciones entre Argentina y el FMI* (Eudeba) and *Historia de la deuda externa argentina. De Martínez de Hoz a Macri, Capital Intelectual* (Capital Intelectual, 2019).

Veridiana Domingos Cordeiro holds a Bachelor, Master, and a PhD in Sociology from the University of São Paulo (partially completed at the University of Chicago). She researches on social memory, identity, narratives, and social theory. She published *Sociology in Brazil: A brief Institutional and Intellectual History* (Palgrave McMillan).

Loreto Correa Vera holds a Bachelor and Master in History from the University of Chile, Master in Latin American History from the International University of Andalucia, and a PhD in International Relations from the Universidad San Pablo CEU in Madrid. She is a Senior Researcher and Reader in History and International Relations at the National Academy of Political and Strategic Studies (ANEPE, Chile).

John Edmunds is a Professor of Finance at Babson College. He has taught extensively at overseas MBA programs, including Instituto de Empresa in Madrid, Spain, INCAE in Central America and La Universidad Católica Madre y Maestra in the Dominican Republic, and two universities in Chile. He has also taught at other schools in the Boston area, including the Arthur D. Little School of Management, Boston University, the Fletcher School of Law and Diplomacy, Harvard University, Hult International Business School, and Northeastern University. He is a member of the Golden Key Society, and at Hult as well as Arthur D. Little, he was voted Professor of the Year. He is the author of over 300 articles and cases published both in academic and practitioner journals. He has published five books. Over 150 of his articles are about Latin American capital markets and have been published in Spanish. He has consulted with the Harvard Institute for International Development, the Rockefeller Foundation, Stanford Research Institute, and numerous private companies.

Monserrat Espinach Rueda holds a degree in Business Administration with emphasis on Production from the State Distance University, Costa Rica. She is a Master in Business Administration with emphasis in International Business and has a Master Degree in Banking and Finance, both from Fundepos University, Costa Rica. She is a PhD Candidate in Economics and Administrative Sciences from the University for International Cooperation, Mexico. She is a professor, writer, and researcher of Administration Sciences at the Universidad Estatal a Distancia, Costa Rica.

Ricardo Ffrench-Davis is a Member of the Department of Economics, Faculty of Business and Economics, University of Chile, and was awarded Chile's National Prize of the Humanities and Social Sciences. He holds a PhD in Economics from the University of Chicago. His most recent paper (co-authored by Miguel Torres) is "Neo-structuralism" in *The New Palgrave Dictionary of Economics*, Springer, 2021.

Juan Carlos Gachúz Maya is a full-time Professor in the Department of International Relations and Political Science at the Universidad de las Américas Puebla and a Professor at the Colegio de Defensa Nacional de México. He is Bachelor and Master in International Relations from the Faculty of Political and Social Sciences of the UNAM and Master and Doctor in Government from the University of Essex, England. He received the Alfonso Caso medal by the UNAM and the MacArthur-Ford-Hewlett scholarship to carry out master's studies in Government. He received the Essex University-CONACYT scholarship to carry out doctoral studies in Government. He was an Asia Fellow at Harvard Kennedy School of Government and Puentes Visiting Scholar at Rice University. He has participated as an analyst in national and international media such as El Financiero Bloomberg, CNN, and the newspaper El Economista. He has been a lecturer at the College of National Defense. He is a member of the International Studies Association (ISA). It belongs to the National System of Researchers of I CONACYT.

Élio Gasda holds a PhD in Theology from the Pontifical University Comillas (Madrid) and a Post-doctorate in Political Philosophy from the Catholic University of Portugal. He is a Professor of Theological Ethics at the FAJE – Jesuit College (Brazil). He is a member of the research groups Christian Social Thought Studies Group (Organization of Catholic Universities in Latin America and the Caribbean – ODUCAL) and the Future of Work and Common House Group (Latin American Council of Social Sciences – CLACSO). His research areas are Social Ethics, Capitalism, Workers, and Human Rights. His recent books are *Christianity and Economics: Rethinking Work beyond Capitalism* (Cristianismo y Economía. Repensar el trabajo más allá del capitalismo. 1. ed. Madrid: Ediciones HOAC, 2017) and *The Social Doctrine: Economy, Labor and Politics* (La Doctrina Social: economía, Trabajo y Política. 1. ed. Ciudad de México: Ediciones Dabar, 2019).

Olaf Kaltmeier is a Professor of Ibero-American History at Bielefeld University and the Director of the Maria Sibylla Merian Center for Advanced Latin American Studies (CALAS). He is editor of the Routledge Series "InterAmerican Research: Contact-Communication-Conflict", and general editor of the Routledge Handbooks on the

Americas (History and Society; Political Economy and Governance, Media and Culture.). He recently published with Routledge, *Sonic Politics. Music and Social Movements in the Americas* (Routledge, 2019) and *Entangled Heritages. Postcolonial Perspectives on the Uses of the Past in Latin America* (Routledge, 2019).

Felipe Lagos-Rojas holds a PhD in Sociology from Goldsmiths College, University of London, UK. He is the Coordinator of the Program on Latin American Critiques at the International Institute for Philosophy and Social Studies, IIPSS, and general editor of *Pléyade. Revista de Humanidades y Ciencias Sociales*. He also works as Instructor in different tertiary institutions in Chile, Bolivia, and the United States. He is the author of several papers on Latin American Marxism, and co-editor of *Latin American Marxisms in Context. Past and Present* (Cambridge Scholar Publishing, 2019). He has also published articles in the journals *Postcolonial Studies, Cuadernos Americanos*, and *Theory, Culture and Society* (online), among others.

Colin Lewis is a Professor Emeritus of Latin American Economic History at the London School of Economics and Political Science. His recent books include *Historical Dictionary of Argentina*, with Bernardo Duggan (Langham: Rowman & Littlefield, 2019); *British Railways in Argentina, 1857–1914* (London: Bloomsbury Press, 2015); *Argentina: A Short History* (Oxford: One World, 2002); and *Exclusion and Engagement: Social Policy in Latin America*, edited with Christopher Abel (London: Institute of Latin American Studies, 2002).. Recent articles and chapters include "CEPAL and ISI: Reconsidering the debates, policies and outcomes" Revista de Estudios Sociales (2019), "Post-colonial South America: nineteenth-century laissez faire governance" in Pía Riggirozzi and Christopher Wylde (eds.) *Handbook of South American Governance* (2018), among others. In Latin America, he has held visiting professorships and/or taught short course on economic history and development at UBA, UNESPE (Araraquara), USP, UFMF and UFPe, and lectured in Colombia and Mexico. He has also held visiting professorships at universities in Germany, India, Japan, Spain, and the United States.

Federico Li Bonilla holds a Bachelor in Business Administration with emphasis on Cooperatives and Associations, a Master in Strategic Management, and a PhD in Administrative Sciences. He is an expert in dairy production, with studies in banking, finance, and accounting. He has lectured at universities in Europe and America (North, Central, and South America). He is the author of several articles on many topics: social economy, labor economy, cooperativism, solidarism, agro-industrial models, management models, self-perception, EVA, working capital in finance, electricity tariff model, as well as articles on SMEs and entrepreneurship, disruptive technologies, artificial intelligence, teleworking, among others. Li Bonilla is the Coordinator of Professional Career (Academic) of the UNED, Costa Rica, and Dean of the School of Administration Sciences, at UNED.

Ivan Daniel Müller holds a PhD in Sociology from the Universidade Federal do Rio Grande do Sul (UFRGS, Brasil). He also holds a Master in Diversity and Social Inclusion from the Universidade Fedevale. His areas of interest are social movements, participation, and participatory budgeting.

Gustavo Oliveira is a PhD Candidate in Social Science from the Universidade do Vale do Rio dos Sinos (UNISINOS, Brasil). He holds a Master in Social Science from the same university, and his areas of interest are social movements, society-state interactions, and autonomies.

Mario Rapoport has a degree in Political Economy from the University of Buenos Aires, and a PhD in History from the University of Paris I-Sorbonne, France. He is a Professor Emeritus of the UBA and of the ISEN (Institute of the National Foreign Service) that belongs to the Ministry of Foreign Affairs. He is Senior Researcher of the Conicet, and currently he is the Director of the National Fund for the Arts. He has worked as a professor, researcher, and director in prestigious institutions in Argentina and abroad, and was awarded national and international prizes. He is also a Fellow of the International Wilson Center of Washington DC. He has published more than 30 books.

Andrés Ruggeri is a social anthropologist from the University of Buenos Aires, and since 2002 has directed the Facultad Abierta program in the same university, that supports, advises, and researches with the companies recovered by the workers. He is the author and co-author of several specialized books on the subject, and has given talks and courses in several countries in Latin America, Europe, and Asia. Since 2007, he coordinates the organization of the International Meeting "The Economy of Workers" which has two editions in Argentina, one in Mexico and another in Brazil, along with a European meeting in France. He is also the author of the book *Del Plata a La Habana. America on a Bicycle* (Ediciones Colihue, 2001).

Pierre Salama is Professor at the University Paris XIII, France. He is a recognized Latin Americanist, winner of the Julio Cortázar Chair. Salama has published numerous books, many of which have been translated into Spanish and Portuguese. He is a member of the editorial board of several foreign journals, he was the Scientific Director of the Revue Tiers Monde and of the Research Group on the State, the Internationalization of Techniques and Development (GREITD).

The dynamics of underdevelopment and the mode of financialization of emerging countries are his main fields of research. He is also a specialist in drug economy.

Edward L. Tapia is an independent Marxist political economist living in Chicago. He graduated from the Evergreen State College in Olympia, Washington. He was part of the editorial board of New Politics. Author of *Remembering Dependency Theory: A Marxist-Humanist Review* (New Politics, Vol. XVI No. 3, 2017) and *The Tendency for the Rate of Profit to Decline—And Why It Matters* (New Politics, Vol. XVIII No. 3, 2019).

Introduction

Pablo A. Baisotti

Setbacks

During the 19th century, Latin American countries were incorporated into the world trade system as exporters of primary products and recipients of capital, investment, and international migration, especially Argentina, Brazil, and Uruguay. At the top of the pre-war international economic system was Great Britain, which was a global financial power, a source of capital for the periphery, and a major importer of raw materials. This situation began to change after the end of World War I, as the United States became the most important market for most Latin American countries, with imports reaching 25% in South America and almost 80% in the Caribbean (including Mexico). Central America had an agrarian society with large coffee and banana plantations (mostly foreign-owned and linked to the US market) and small plots of land where some basic grains and other products were grown to meet domestic demand.

The consolidation of the dollar economy made Latin America feel the need to try to put a stop to the presumed escalation of US intervention in the region, as countries that wanted resources to develop were forced to accept US demands for free convertibility of currencies and open competition. Thanks to the opening of the Panama Canal in 1914, the United States penetrated South American markets with its exports (not so much in Argentina, which still depended heavily on Great Britain). The world conflict caused many difficulties to the Latin American republics highly dependent on the European market, but also to Great Britain, which depended on Latin American foods (e.g. meat, sugar) while making efforts to prevent Germany's access to raw materials on the continent (Bulmer-Thomas 1997, 4–6; Torres Rivas 2001, 14; Hey and Mora 2003; Kennedy 2017, 562, 563).

Subsequently, the gold standard was suspended, and Latin American economies lost momentum. Industrialization also advanced in the largest countries of the region, and Central Americans began to turn to the services of the US banks (which took over the public debt of Cuba,

DOI: 10.4324/9781003045632-1

Panama, Haiti, and the Dominican Republic by 1919). Only the banks in Mexico and Costa Rica continued to be run by European banks. US companies took control of most of the banana plantations in the isthmus countries, the sugar cane and cocoa of the large islands in the Antilles Sea, the gold mines of Nicaragua and Costa Rica, the silver mines of El Salvador, the oil fields of Guatemala, and the construction of railroads and the electrical installation of most cities. In the interwar years, about 75% of Central America's exports went to the United States. In some specific cases, such as in Honduras, dependence was almost total because large US companies, such as the Cuyamel Fruit Company (1911) and the United Fruit Company (1912), operated in the country. These companies dominated banana production and export, also meddling in the country's internal affairs for decades (Renouvin 1990, 906; Bulmer-Thomas 1997, 4–7, 10, 12, 29, 32, 34; Thorp 1997, 48, 50, 51–53, 57–59; Bulmer-Thomas 2001, 116–119, 121–123; Lemus 2001, 247; Halperin Donghi 2005). This last company also had a presence in Costa Rica during the 1920s and 1930s, although the country's production consisted of coffee, exported mainly to the United States and the United Kingdom (Cerdas Cruz 2001, 187, 200). In Haiti, coffee was the main commercial crop controlled by Washington, as efforts to stimulate large-scale production of other crops such as sugar, cotton, and sisal had limited success (Nicholls 1998, 270, 272, 274–276).

In the early 1920s, Ecuador went through a critical phase related to cocoa production and export, while US investment (especially in mining and oil) intensified over the next decade (Ayala Mora 2002, 259; Halperin Donghi 2005, 400; Acosta 2006, 82, 94, 97). In Cuba, sugar cultivation and US investment became massive. During the 1930s, thanks to the Jones-Costigan Act (1934), protectionist tariffs were lowered, and sugar export quotas were agreed upon. The renegotiation of the reciprocity treaty was accompanied by that of the Permanent Agreement, a legal form of the Platt Amendment, which opened the country to US imports in reciprocity for the purchase of sugar. The same happened with Nicaragua and Puerto Rico. In the latter country, the economy underwent a huge transformation, and sugar quickly replaced coffee and tobacco as the main export crop (Freeman Smith 1991; Cardoso 1992, 208; Anderson 1998, 296, 297, 303; Pérez Jr. 1998, 166–171, 174–176; Bulmer-Thomas 2001, 146, 148, 152, 157–161; Torres Rivas 2001, 20; Halperin Donghi 2005, 423, 424).

At that time, foreign companies dominated the economic life of Mexico and Venezuela, especially American companies in the oil sector. In Mexico, they also focused on mineral extraction and railroads, while in Venezuela, during the 1930s, the three big companies (Royal Dutch Shell, Gulf, and Standard Oil) controlled 98% of the oil, and in the following decade, the Creóle Petroleum Company, a subsidiary of Standard Oil, produced more than half of Venezuela's oil. President Isaías Medina

Angarita (1941–1945) enacted a new oil law (which remained in effect until the nationalization of the oil industry in 1976), repealing all previous legislation and stipulating that oil companies must share profits equally with the state (Ewell 2002, 301–303, 307, 311).

US loans were tied to foreign policy objectives, and several countries were forced to give up control of their customs or even their railroads in order to ensure rapid debt repayment. US banks and companies were set up in Brazil and Uruguay. In Argentina, during the decade of its dependence on exports to Britain, and even in the following decade, both countries negotiated a treaty, by which the British agreed that Argentine meat companies would supply 15% of their exports without imposing tariffs on Argentine grain imports. This was called the Roca-Runciman Treaty, which was signed in 1933 and extended in 1936. In return, Argentina agreed to reduce the duties on nearly 350 British imports to the level they had in 1930. Chile, on the other hand, during the 1920s, began a process that came close to the concept of the welfare state, but maintained profound inequalities. Between 1929 and 1932, saltpetre exports fell by nearly 90%, and agricultural exports by 86% (Renouvin 1990, 906; Rock 1992, 4, 5, 18–20, 37–39, 41–43, 46, 47, 113, 114; Bulmer-Thomas 1997; Thorp 1997, 48, 50, 51–53, 57–59; Lemus 2001, 247; Drake 2002, 219, 237, 243; Halperin Donghi 2005; Gazmuri 2012, 142–144, 194).

During World War II, Latin America lost most of its European markets, which represented 30% of its exports, causing prices to fall due to the accumulation of large export surpluses (wheat, corn, linseed oil, coffee, cocoa, sugar, and bananas). Nevertheless, sales to Great Britain increased in 1939 and 1940, although the payment, in most cases, was given through a sterling account that could be used to finance purchases in Great Britain, in their possessions, or to settle debts with British creditors. Likewise, US investments grew by 80% in Chile from 1940 to 1969, and the vast majority of this foreign capital was concentrated in mining. On the other hand, by 1945, Uruguay was highly industrialized, contributing 18% of the GDP thanks to the protectionist measures of the *Batllista* state that curbed foreign investment. The rural sector, on the other hand, continued to stagnate (Thorp 1997, 49–51; 1998, 199, 200; Drake 2002, 219, 237, 243; Halperin Donghi 2005, 237; Gazmuri 2012, 142–144, 194). During this period, Argentina had to face the trade barriers imposed by the United States as a result of its neutrality in World War II. When relations were normalized in 1947, US economic harassment continued in a covert manner through the Economic Cooperation Administration (ECA). Argentina's trade deficits of 1951 and 1952 marked a recessionary period, and since then the Argentine government has tried to contain the crisis while adjusting its industrialist strategy (Torre and de Riz 2002, 66; Sidicaro 2005). Unlike Argentina, Ecuador's trade relations with the United States were strengthened through the United Fruit Company, which became the largest producer of bananas and, together with the Standard Fruit, also American, and the Ecuadorian-owned *Exportadora Bananera Noboa* concentrated more than 50% of banana exports in the mid-1960s.

After the Cuban revolution of 1959, the direction of the economy was set by the state. It only respected the property of the peasant farmers, a very insignificant sector in Cuba, and even their production was incorporated into the distribution system in charge of the state. The rest, which included almost all the farms reorganized in the so-called people's farms, were modeled on the Soviet *sovjozes*. The government of Eduardo Frei in Chile (1964–1970) also tried to carry out an agrarian reform that was finally approved by Congress. The Frei years saw a high degree of economic concentration: 17% of all firms owned 78% of all assets, and 3% of firms controlled more than half of the industry's value added and almost 60% of the capital. By 1970, three US companies controlled the production of 60% of copper exports. With Salvador Allende (1970–1973), key areas of the economy such as mining were nationalized, and an agrarian reform was accelerated (Meller 1998, 60, 61, 111, 113, 196, 198, 233, 237, 267; Halperin Donghi 2005, 479, 515, 546, 606, 625, 626, 631–634; Gazmuri 2012, 328, 410, 473). Even without deep reforms, and thanks to the prosperity of the international economy, Mexico grew between 1963 and 1971 to 7% annually, and the GDP per capita increased by more than 3% annually. In the 1970s, the oil boom tried to be channeled into the basic problems of the socioeconomic structure, such as the low productivity of peasant agriculture. President José López Portillo (1976–1982) nationalized the bankrupt companies that were essentially private debts. His successor, Miguel de la Madrid (1982–1988), had to deal with a declining economy (barely a 0.1% annual increase). In 1987, that situation began to ease, and exports grew largely because of the expansion of transnational industries established on the US border. Venezuela also enjoyed a period of growth during the oil boom. The administration of Carlos Andrés Pérez (1974–1979) advanced on all economic fronts (from the nationalization of oil and petrochemical companies and iron mining to the construction of the giant steel center of Ciudad Guayana). In those years, oil represented about 90% of exports (Thorp 1998, 198, 199; Halperin Donghi 2005, 591, 592, 687, 674, 677, 678; Domínguez and Franceschi 2010, 280–282; Loaeza 2010, 584, 597; Rodríguez Kuri and González Mello 2010, 614). Despite all the problems that were recorded (disproportionate growth in debt payments, for example), between 1950 and 1973, Ecuador grew at an annual rate of 2.9%, higher than the average for a group of Latin American countries. It was also largely due to the oil boom and foreign debt that drove the industry's growth. In summary, in 1973–1974 and 1978–1979, rising oil prices, inflationary processes, and bipolar competition had negative effects on most Latin

American exports. Venezuela, Mexico, and Ecuador were able to benefit themselves as they were oil-producing countries (Acosta 2006, 100, 102, 118, 119, 121, 123, 124, 127); however, in general, the region began to adopt an approach based mainly on bilateral trade agreements of partial scope, and in the late 1980s, a new wave of regional integration occurred, which coincided with the transformation of industrialization and trade policies (Ffrench-Davis, Muñóz, and Palma 1997, 125–126; Pérez Herrero 2001).

Peru did not have this temporary prosperity, and during the early 1970s, the first symptoms of the crisis began to appear: balance of payments deficits, falling international reserves, rising foreign debt service, and cost of living. The military government controlled one-third of the national product, one-fifth of the productive sector's labor force, nine-tenths of exports, and half of the imports. During 1970 and 1975, the main source of credit was the international private banks that were terminated in 1976, so the government resorted to credits from the socialist countries (1976–1980). The recession manifested in the collapse of the GDP in 1985 to the levels of 1975 due to the adjustment policies and the US tariff policy limited Peruvian exports (Portocarrero Grados; Pease 1993).

After Pinochet's military coup in 1973, economic liberalization was promoted. The flow of credit, by maintaining a high parity for the Chilean currency, caused stagnation of exports and the negative balance of trade was alleviated in the payments by the avalanche of cheap credits. Pinochet limited himself to supporting key sectors and companies (mostly from the private sector). In 1975, gross product fell by 12.9%, while inflation remained at 340%. After an initial successful performance during the 1976–1981 period, known as the "Chilean miracle", the economy experienced an almost total collapse in 1982 to recover between 1983 and 1989 with an annual GDP growth of 6.9%. Chilean exports went from US$1.1 billion in 1970 to US$8.3 billion in 1990, and within these exports, copper drastically decreased from 80% to 45% in the period under consideration, demonstrating a diversification of exports (Meller 1998, 60, 196, 198, 233, 237, 267; Halperin Donghi 2005, 632–634; Gazmuri 2012, 410, 473).

The large external debt accumulated between 1973 and 1982, added to the recession, made the region more vulnerable, revealing its structural problems. In August 1982, Mexico declared the impossibility of servicing its foreign debt, followed by Argentina and Brazil. The origins of this crisis go back to the fall in commodity prices in 1976–1978, which had been balanced by increased credit. The average real interest rate on the debt of less developed countries rose from −6% in 1981 to 14.6% in 1982 (Ffrench-Davis, Muñóz, and Palma 1997, 84, 92; Thorp 1998, 232).

Latin American countries absorbed most of the private external debt and, in 1985, a structural adjustment led by the World Bank (Baker plan) was initiated. The inadequacy of this plan led in 1987 to a second Baker plan, which added debt buybacks, low-interest-rate exit bonds, and debt swaps. In 1989, the Brady Plan was launched, which included a modest reduction of debt balances and was followed by renewed access to private financing. Argentina, Brazil, and Mexico even began issuing their own bonds in the international market, but few countries managed to resume stable economic growth (Colombia, Chile, and Costa Rica) (Bértola and Ocampo 2010, 19, 20, 223).

In the 1980s, economic growth and the level of industrialization fell from 25.2% in 1980 to 23.7% in 1989; the share of exports in world trade fell from 7.7% in 1960 to 3.9% in 1988; high rates of inflation were generated in Bolivia (1985), Peru (1988–1990), Nicaragua (1988–1989), Argentina (1989–1990), and Brazil (1990). Other consequences were, for instance, the growth of the State's deficit, the imbalance in the trade and payment balances, the decrease in the per capita GDP, and the increase in unemployment.

During his second term, Hernán Siles Suazo (1982–1985) faced economic problems that Bolivia was suffering, exacerbated by the end of the bonanza as well as by the years of constant turbulence that had undermined military rule. Two years after taking power, with inflation already close to 1,000% and having abandoned foreign debt service altogether, the president was unable to control both the political and economic process (Pérez Herrero 2001; Halperin Donghi 2005, 707–709). The tin industry was depleted and decapitalized, and attempts to set the world price did not work. Natural gas had become Bolivia's main (legal) export. Between 1985 and 1988, during the government of Paz Estenssoro (1985–1989), the mines were evicted and privatized by a neoliberal state. Thousands of mineworkers were relocated and switched to coca leaf cultivation (Thorp 1998, 272; Whitehead 2002, 163, 166; Sanjinés 2004, 207, 211). In Argentina, the Alfonsín government (1983–1989) initially had to deal with an inflation rate of about 20% per month. Without deactivating any of the internal structural problems and seeing the failure of the renegotiation of the foreign debt, a new devaluation and tariff shock was produced, accompanied by a strong monetary restriction (*Plan Austral*, 1985). This allowed the government to maintain the political initiative until 1987. The last attempt at economic stabilization (*Plan Primavera*, 1988) was based on an agreement with the leading companies to decouple the interest rates applied to a credit or deposit operation from the remuneration of a financial instrument or a given index. Both the economy and social support began to decline, and negotiations with the corporate, economic, and union powers were commonplace for this government until the hyperinflation of 1989 that accelerated the departure of the radicals from the government (Damill 2005, 181, 191; Quiroga 2005, 96, 111). While in Venezuela, President Pérez promoted a broad program of reforms which was not approved, in its majority, by the Congress, added to a multitude of popular protests. The improvement in oil prices in 1990–1991 prevented the measures from leading to economic collapse. The government of Rafael Caldera reversed the reforms and re-imposed various types of controls, and the privatization program was suspended. When Caldera's controls were unsuccessful, a new plan suggested by the International Monetary Fund, the World Bank, and the Inter-American Development Bank was implemented (Thorp 1998, 280–282, Domínguez and Franceschi 2010).

The Latin American economic crisis temporarily coincided with the process of globalization, deepening its fragile situation. The concept of the "Washington Consensus" (neoliberal economic policy measures applied from the 1980s onwards) was revolted as the spearhead of market reforms. Governments in favor of this style carried out economic adjustment measures, suggested in many cases by international financial institutions such as the International Monetary Fund, as a previous step to renegotiating their foreign debts (Pleitez 2011, 108–110). For example, between 1989 and 1990, Mexico's foreign debt was renegotiated with a positive balance for the macroeconomic accounts, and yet in 1994, there was a sudden devaluation of the Mexican peso of almost 100%, bringing the economy down by more than 6% the following year.

At the same time, in January 1994, the North American Free Trade Agreement (NAFTA) was signed, committing the United States, Mexico, and Canada to reduce tariffs and quantitative controls in order to increase trade flows in the region. In addition to the reduction in trade barriers, NAFTA required its partners to reduce restrictions on foreign investment. The ban on foreign capital from participating in the financial sector, one of the last restrictions on foreign capital, was removed in 1998 (Márquez and Meyer 2010, 658, 661, 666). For Bértola and Ocampo (2010), for the first time in Latin American history, economic and political liberalism coincided since market reforms (aimed at reducing the scope of the public sector in the economy and liberalizing markets) had their correlation with macroeconomic stabilization policies (aimed at correcting external and fiscal deficits and controlling the inflationary explosion) (226, 227, 237). The euphoria and confidence in the new model cooled down with the Mexican (1994), Asian (1997), Russian (1998), and Brazilian (1999) crises. However, they did not succeed in breaking down its conceptual principles but rather helped to strengthen them, since many analysts defended that if it had failed in the short term, it was because it had not been applied with the necessary harshness (Pérez Herrero 2001, 341).

Before the socialist collapse, the Cuban economy had symptoms of stagnation due to structural problems such as low levels of productivity and competitiveness, limited capacity to generate internal savings, and international insertion based on exports of low added value, financial and commercial dependence on the Soviet Union and of only one product (sugar). With the disappearance of the Soviet Union, sugar left its privileged place to tourism and medical service exports, along with the opening of banks and foreign investment, redistribution of state agricultural property in favor of the cooperative sector, licensing of small private businesses in cities and dollarization, among other consequences. The period from 1990 to 1994 saw a free fall in the Cuban economy, which lost 36% of its GDP in three years, and more than 40% of the population's consumption. In 1993, the government initiated reforms, including legalizing self-employment, converting state farms into cooperatives, decentralizing economic decisions and allowing profit-oriented businesses to operate, reauthorizing the free market for agricultural (and then industrial) products, and eliminating a wide range of subsidies. The economy grew by 4% annually between 1995 and 2001, with relative modernization of certain sectors, improvement in food consumption, and the formation of a mixed-ownership economic sector. From 2001 to 2005, there was a recession, a fall in the prices of raw materials, an increase in the price of energy and food, and a contraction in tourist activities, etc. (Thorp 1998, 292; Valdéz Paz 2005, 91–93; Sánchez Egozcue 2011, 28).

After a start of macroeconomic reform, unleashed especially by the effects of the foreign debt crisis, in Ecuador, the government of Rodrigo Borja Cevallos (1988–1992) remained largely within the path of adjustment and promoted transformations that facilitated the deepening of the neoliberal scheme. Sixto Durán Ballén (1992–1996) and Abdalá Bucaram (1996–1997) deepened this tendency (Acosta 2006, 165). The law for the promotion of exports contributed to the diversification of exports. The share of oil in exports fell from 52% in 1990 to 36% in 1996, and non-traditional exports increased their share from 7% to 23%, thanks to the growing incorporation of modern technology in agricultural and fishing activities. For its part, the government of Alberto Fujimori in Peru implemented a set of neoliberal measures that included massive devaluation and adjustment of relative prices, coupled with a restrictive monetary and fiscal policy with a market-liberalization strategy that quickly attracted foreign financing. Fujimori dissolved Congress and discouraged any form of popular organization. The Peruvian economy grew, being supported by the inflow of foreign capital, overvaluation of the currency, and high interest rates (Thorp 1998, 270, 271, 283, 283).

In line with the Ecuadorian and Peruvian cases, in Argentina the government of Carlos Menem (1989–1999) made a transition to a "liberal" state by carrying out privatizations of state-owned companies, deregulations that sought the free functioning of the changed market, of labor, capital, prices, foreign trade, and an administrative reform to reduce public personnel and the decentralization of services. Between 1989 and 1995, the GDP grew by 32.3%, and between 1995 and 1999, by 8.8%. In December 2001, a period marked by institutional instability and the devaluation of the national currency began. In 2002, industry generated only 16% of the total product, while the participation of the service sectors reached 70% (Damill 2005, 160, 161; Quiroga 2005, 128, 129, 131, 144; Rofman 2005, 336).

In order to contain inflation and stabilize the economy, Brazil implemented some changes. President José Sarney (1985–1990) launched the *Cruzado* Plan in 1986 (Mota and López 2009, 638), and later the Collor Plan that froze prices and salaries, produced an administrative reform of the state and control of the public deficit. As in Argentina, state-owned companies were privatized and trade was opened up. This plan failed after a short period of apparent stability and inflation rose again. The government of Itamar Franco (1992–1995) continued with the reforms, especially those oriented in favor of opening the economy. In 1993, the Real Plan appeared: its architect was Fernando Henrique Cardoso, who later was elected president (1999–2003). He approved the project of State Reform, with the objective of carrying out privatizations and removing from the public administration the control of diverse sectors with the purpose of diminishing the role of the state acting as a regulator of the economy (Mota and López 2009, 647, 649, 650, 663).

In 1985, Julio María Sanguinetti became president of Uruguay in a situation of economic and social volatility. The maturities of the foreign debt, the relief of the internal debt, the problems linked to unemployment and the sharp drop in salaries, the overcoming of the consequences of the rupture of the exchange policy in 1982 were some of the issues he had to deal with. The surplus was reached between 1991 and 1993. Lacalle's government proposed a Law of Public Companies to alleviate the tax burden, open and deregulate service markets to competition. However, it was rejected through a popular consultation. Between 1995 and 2000, social security was reformed (1996), and in 2002 wages fell by 10%, manufacturing by 27%, commerce by 25%, and construction by 21% (Rilla 2008, 65, 67, 68, 75).

At the beginning of the 21st century, the region's total debt was about US$25 trillion, twice as much as in the early 1980s. The financial resources (net debt flows, foreign direct investment "FDI", bonds, and equity) that were present in Latin America between 1990 and 2001 reached US$1.0 trillion. The global economic and financial crisis ended a period of growth in Latin American countries between 2003 and 2008. After the fall experienced by regional product in 2009, in the context of the global economic crisis, activity expanded again between 2010 and 2011, supported by high Chinese economic growth and expansive monetary policies in some industrialized countries. This period of prosperity did not last long: from 2012 onward, there was a sharp economic slowdown, as evidenced in 2014 (1.1%) (Bértola and Ocampo 2010, 246; Cepal 2015, 16, 18; Webber 2019, 98, 106, 113). The Latin American economies, exporters of primary goods, were affected by the international context and by the exhaustion of the raw materials cycle. Between 2015 and 2016, primary products represented more than 70% of the value of the region's exports to China, while imports from China to Latin America represented 91% of low, medium, and high technology manufacturing. In other words, trade between Latin America, the Caribbean, and China basically translated into the exchange of raw materials for manufactures (OCDE/CEPAL/CAF 2015 17, 24; "Will China's…" 2017).[1]

In 2020, the unexpected Covid-19 pandemic took Latin America – like almost the rest of the world – away from any possibility of economic growth. In fact, 2020 was the year with one of the steepest drops in GDP in memory. Economic Commission for Latin America and the Caribbean's (ECLAC) preliminary conclusions point to a drop in economic growth from 1.3% to –1.8%, with possible unemployment climbing to 10% throughout the region. The blow may be greater if there is a strong export linkage with China: Argentina could fall 5%, Chile 3.8%, and Brazil 2.5%, while the collapse of tourism in the Caribbean would be around 25%. The addition of millions of people below the poverty and extreme poverty line stands out. Brazil's structural reforms, Argentina's adjustment plans, Mexico's prudent spending, and Chile's financial orthodoxy are no longer the government's priorities in favor of strengthening weak health systems and providing monetary relief to the hardest-hit sectors of societies. In October, a World Bank report highlighted that world trade is returning to pre-pandemic levels, which could benefit those countries that depend on exports of raw materials, whose price on international markets has been sustained, as well as the volume of remittances (Malamud and Núñez 2020, 19; Olmo 2020; Sánchez 2020).

Advances

By the end of the 1920s, the industrial sector had been developed in some of the largest republics (Argentina, Brazil, Chile, Colombia, Mexico, and Peru), and also in those prosperous enough with a large domestic market (such as Uruguay). The fall of the financial system in 1929 demonstrated the tenor of the debts and crises of the Latin American economies. Between 1928 and 1932, the unit value of Latin American exports fell by more than 50% in at least ten countries, due in part to the Hawley-Smoot (1930) and Revenue Act (1932), enacted during the Hoover presidency (1929–1933), which set the highest customs tariffs in its history. Great Britain, on the other hand, chose a system of imperial preference established at the Ottawa conference (1932), and Germany introduced the aski-mark, an inconvertible currency to pay for Latin American imports, only to buy items imported from Germany. Regulatory boards were created for each of the large primary production branches up to central banks (Renouvin 1990; Bulmer-Thomas 1997; Thorp 1997; Lemus 2001; Halperin Donghi 2005).

During the 1930s, several countries entered completely into the US trade orbit. Colombia and Peru were examples of this event. By 1932, the first country occupied second place in the order of importance of South America in its trade with the United States that at the same time invested in this country, especially in the sectors of oil, utilities and bananas. In this decade, and until the end of the 1950s, the coffee sector doubled the cultivated areas and represented 72% of the country's exports between 1945 and 1949 (Deas 1992, 280, 281; Abel and Palacios 2002, 176, 177, 181, 184, 185, 187; Murillo Posada 2007, 287). While Peru, during the dictatorship of Augusto Leguía (1919–1930), accelerated the expansion of the economy and public works through an avalanche of US investment and loans.

In general, Latin American exports fell steadily until 1934. Thereafter, a cycle of recovery began until 1937, followed by two years of declining international prices. Honduras, Argentina, and Mexico especially suffered a decline in exports until the beginning of World War II in part because of the preservation of their traditional export sector. Argentina was the country with the greatest difficulties since its exports were closely linked to the British market, and Cuba, whose tobacco exports were affected by the protectionist measures of the American market. Conversely, Colombia, Nicaragua, and Mexico benefited from gold and silver exports due to rising prices during the 1930s. Bolivia also benefited from rising tin prices, and the Dominican Republic increased its sugar exports, which also rose in value (Bulmer-Thomas 1997, 7, 10–12, 23, 30, 33; Torres Rivas 2001, 15, 17; Bertram 2002, 35; Halperin Donghi 2005, 339, 362). Rehabilitation through industrialization became evident from 1935 onwards, marginalizing smaller countries that did not have a domestic market of a certain size, such as Central America, or Ecuador where the level of consumption was very low. By the end of the 1930s, Argentina, Brazil, and Mexico were the only countries that had promoted industrialization and, to a lesser extent, Chile, Peru, Colombia, and Uruguay, which had made significant progress in diversifying their economic structure (Bulmer-Thomas 1997, 42, 45).

In Brazil, for example, Getulio Vargas (1930–1945) federalized the basic sectors of the economy, created the National Coffee Department becoming the largest agency of federal economic power and later the Institute of Cocoa, Sugar and Alcohol (1931–1932), and later the Institute of Mate (1938), Pine and Salt (1941). The Estado Novo de Vargas created the Technical Council of Economy and Finance and stimulated the agricultural production and industrialization that took place during World War II (Halperin Donghi 2005, 405; Mota and López 2009, 457, 464, 466, 479, 496, 497). Lazaro Cardenas in Mexico expropriated foreign oil companies in 1938. From this, the company Petróleos Mexicanos

(Pemex) was born. However, in the context of World War II, Mexico and the United States reached several agreements, at least in matters of debt, trade, braceros, water, technical assistance, and especially on the oil issue. The government's economic preference was oriented toward industry and cities; the idea of an agrarian country was relegated. The foundations were laid for a long period of economic growth that was sustained until the end of the 1960s (Freeman Smith 1991, 95; Thorp 1997, 52; Domínguez 2000; Lemus 2001, 250; Aboites Aguilar 2008, 481, 482, 484, 485, 491; Muñóz 2018).

In about the same period (1937) in Bolivia, Standard Oil was nationalized and *Yacimientos Petrolíferos Fiscales Bolivianos* was born. During most of the 1940s, Bolivia lived a temporary bonanza thanks to the boom of the mining companies, but then, with the post-war situation, the tin monopoly disappeared, affecting the economy and above all for the income of the State, which had to resort more than ever to the emission (Whitehead 2002, 115, 116; Halperin Donghi 2005, 488; Centellas Castro and Calderón Guzmán 2011, 102, 103).

The Bretton Woods agreement, celebrated in 1944, created the International Monetary Fund and the World Bank, restoring the gold standard, through which convertible currencies (in practice the dollar) were accepted as part of the currencies. With the Korean War (1950–1953), the United States began to invest significantly in strategic mineral resources in Latin America and the Caribbean, while European exports to countries such as Argentina, Brazil, Mexico, and Chile during and after the war fell by at least 20% between 1938 and 1950. This resulted in a benefit to the United States in terms of investment and exports to Latin America (Bulmer-Thomas 1997; Torres Rivas 2001; Halperin Donghi 2005). The ECLAC was established in 1948, and its objective was to explore and suggest policies for development, industrialization, and economic cooperation in the region. A series of integration measures were launched that included the liberalization of intraregional trade and the adoption of tariffs for external members. This position was seen as practicing "closed regionalism" based on dependency theory as a vehicle for accelerating economic development through import substitution with industrialization. It became evident in the 1980s that this approach had failed and that the more open regional approach in Asia seemed to be yielding better results. In 1959, the Inter-American Development Bank (IDB) was created as the hemispheric arm of the World Bank to provide financial assistance to Latin American nations. Its aid program clearly coincided with US efforts to rally political support against Cuban influence in the area. The OAS provided a space for some independent action by member countries, such as the creation of the Latin American Economic System (SELA) in 1975, a mechanism designed to promote cooperation in the areas of development and economic security among 25 Latin American countries (Knight, Castro-Rea, and Ghany 2016).

As the new industry became disinterested in consumer markets, the traditional industry became more dependent on this market. Brazil and Mexico advanced on the road to economic maturity, while Argentina had difficulty in maintaining its level of industrialization. In Brazil, Vargas started up the Volta Redonda plant, with equipment built by American steel mills. In 1954 he created Petrobras, a state-owned monopoly company for the import and exploitation of oil, as well as the state-owned electricity company, Eletrobras. From 1954 to 1964, the country was marked by developmentalist, reformist and populist policies. During the presidency of Juscelino Kubitschek, industrialization was promoted (especially in the automobile industry), trying to modernize the road and air infrastructure through the Metas plan, whose central point was the acceleration of the Brazilian industrial process. His successor, Goulart, tried to implement a plan of Base Reforms: agrarian reform against the latifundia; political reform allowing the illiterate to vote; military reform with the participation of non-commissioned officers in politics; educational reform in favor of public schools. With the 1964 coup, Brazil re-aligned itself with US policy by encouraging capitalism. At the same time, the military engaged in the process of modernizing the economy, creating the necessary infrastructure for industrial development. The "miracle" was due to excellent international market conditions that allowed the economy to expand at a rate of 8.8% in 1970, rising to 14% in 1973. In 1978 and 1979, the inflationary situation worsened, a symptom of the exhaustion of the economic model (Mota and López 2009, 461, 501, 514, 515, 517, 565, 570, 598).

Between 1945 and 1970, Argentina experienced a strong increase in industrial productivity. The rise in oil prices influenced the performance of the economy, in addition to the debt crisis. The lack of coherent policies affected development during the 1940s and 1950s. Initial plans to promote small and medium enterprises failed. In the two decades that followed, there was a return to industrial and trade policy, although in a lukewarm and erratic fashion (Thorp 1998, 197). During the government of Arturo Frondizi (1958–1962), attempts were made to attract multinational capital as a source of supply of technology and modern capital goods, trying to orient it toward branches that should complement the existing industrial fabric. On the other hand, during the Argentine Revolution (1966–1970), there was no attempt to orient foreign capital toward specific activities, but some sectors producing capital goods were encouraged. The relations between the state and the big businessmen came closer, benefiting some big national and foreign companies. Between the 1960s and 1970s, agriculture grew by 28%, while industry grew by 172%. Between 1956 and 1973, industrial productivity increased by 80%, while the total economy grew by 35% (Aronskind 2007, 72, 73, 113). The radical change in the functioning of the economy was carried out in the first four years of the military regime (1976–1983).

New groups of power benefited from a process of accumulation centered on a financial market that operated without restrictions and was open to the outside world. The opening of the economy, the exchange parity, and the tariff policy produced irreparable damage to the national industry and other productive sectors. The most tangible result was the bankruptcy of factories, the irruption of imported goods, and the invasion of new banks and financial institutions (Quiroga 2005, 53).

Between 1940 and 1946 in Paraguay, the value of exports tripled. In addition to traditional markets, Britain and the United States became important destinations for production. The main items continued to be preserved meat, quebracho extract, cotton fibers, wood, leather, tobacco, and yerba. The country registered in those years a high level of occupation and production, with a notable increase in the cost of living. On the other hand, the government adopted very significant provisions for the benefit of the workers: it established the minimum wage and mandatory social security. However, little progress was made during those years in the redistribution of rural property and in the access of farmers to the land they worked. Despite a policy of tax breaks to attract foreign investment and growing US aid under the Alliance for Progress program, economic growth from 1954 to 1973 barely exceeded population growth. During the 1973–1980 period, the annual economic growth rate was 9%, the highest in Latin America. In those years, there was no plan to use even the smallest portion of the enormous 50% of electricity generated by the Itaipu dam or to mount an industrialization program based on electricity-intensive activities. The expansion of soybean and cotton exports quickly replaced traditional export goods, such as tobacco and meat products, in the generation of foreign exchange and strengthened the agro-export bloc, whose interests were increasingly represented by the Stroessner regime (Thorp 1998, 204, 205; Nickson 2010; Scavone Yegros 2010).

Nevertheless, the Latin American economy expanded between 1950 and 1981, and the gross domestic product (GDP) grew at an average annual rate of 5.3%, although the average per capita income grew at an annual rate of 2.6%. The boom in international trade during the 1960s encouraged the diversification of Latin America's manufactured exports in those countries where import-substitution industrialization was most evident (Brazil, Mexico, and Argentina). Industrialization was established at a time when primary export interests remained strong and because of this continued to depend, to a large extent, on the foreign exchange generated by primary product exports. As a result, a "mixed model" combining import substitution with export promotion and regional integration emerged (Ffrench-Davis, Muñóz, and Palma 1997, 83, 84, 121; Bértola and Ocampo 2010, 168, 169, 183).

The growth strategy worked exceptionally well in Mexico until the 1960s, with an annual GDP growth rate of over 6% and per capita growth of 3.5% per year, one of the highest in the world. Export revenues did not decline, sustained by increased income from tourism and cotton sector activity. Transfers from agriculture to industry (through price controls) were an important part of the growing industrialization (Thorp 1998, 199; Halperin Donghi 2005, 674, 677, 678; Loaeza 2010, 584, 597; Rodríguez Kuri and González Mello 2010, 614). In the 1970s, Colombia was the fourth largest industrialized country in Latin America, and in the 1980s, the seventh-largest recipient of 90% investment in mining and oil. Resistance by urban entrepreneurs and workers to the abandonment of industrial protection measures helped slow the rate of growth of the industry, especially between 1975 and 1984 (Abel and Palacios 2002, 213).

In the 1950s, agrarian reform reappeared as an urgent issue on the Latin American agenda (the Guatemalan and Bolivian revolutions placed it at the center of their program of change). During this period, the agricultural sector's share of Central American production continued to decline, and by the mid-1970s, its share was just over 30%, but it absorbed 60% of the economically active population and contributed about 80% of extra-regional exports. Central America's economy in this period went through various stages of growth and contraction. El Salvador, which was the region's largest coffee producer, was the first to take advantage of new post-war opportunities and by 1949 was producing 73,000 metric tons of coffee, a figure that was not exceeded until 1957, when the figure was 83,200 tons. Guatemala began to increase its production in 1951 with 63,000 tons and maintained a constant growth throughout the period. Costa Rica slowly increased production levels from 1954 onwards. During this period, agricultural production was diversified (wood, cacao, hemp, sugar, meat, cotton). By the late 1950s, Central American cotton represented 6.6% of total world exports (Torres Rivas 2001, 31, 33, 34, 37, 40; Knight, Castro-Rea, and Ghany 2016).

In the 1960s, foreign investment in Bolivia focused on the mining and oil sectors. The Alliance for Progress financed much of the public sector activity and economic growth was high, reaching 6.6% from 1965 to 1969. During those decades, Peru's exports grew with a significant presence of foreign capital while import-substitution industrialization was carried out in response to unemployment and social unrest in the rural sectors (Thorp 1998, 202–204; Whitehead 2002, 142; Halperin Donghi 2005, 491, 579). In Chile, from 1940 to 1973, the economy was characterized by the growing role of the public sector and a strategy of ISI supported by high levels of tariffs and other non-tariff barriers. These characteristics were reinforced during the period 1970–1973, when the number and coverage of state interventions reached a high level (Drake 2002, 245, 250).

In the 1960s, an agrarian reform took place in Cuba, putting an end to foreign companies and the big landed bourgeoisie, dismantling the economic base of semi-colonial power. The first Agrarian Reform Law confiscated large properties (over 402 hectares) affecting US-owned sugar companies. Part of the land was given to tenants, sharecroppers, and landless peasants. Shortly thereafter, it signed a treaty with the Soviet Union to exchange sugar for oil, grain, and machinery. Later the refineries of Shell, Esso, and Texaco were nationalized for refusing to refine Soviet oil.

In the 1970s, however, the picture was much more difficult: a decline in export prices (except for a temporary increase in coffee in 1976 and 1977) and rising import prices, particularly for oil from 1973 onwards. In Central America, in the context of the Central American Common Market (CACM), the manufacturing and industrial industry grew, although in the 1970s, the situation became more unstable and moderate. The largest increases in the share of manufacturing in GDP between 1950 and 1974 were achieved in Argentina, Brazil, Colombia, and Mexico; in contrast, they were much lower in Peru and Venezuela (Bértola and Ocampo 2010, 168, 169, 183). Honduras had comparatively weaker growth, particularly between 1950 and 1959, while Nicaragua experienced a sharp drop in GDP between 1970 and 1979.

Industrialization without structural changes in agriculture and with limited internal and external markets was condemned in advance; this is precisely what happened in Guatemala, El Salvador, and Nicaragua. In Costa Rica, the expansion of the domestic market was guaranteed by the basic structure of the agro-export sector and the growth of the public sector (Pérez Brignoli 2017, 105, 107, 110, 111).

The Cuban economy grew again, dominated by sugar, whose production levels continued to exceed the pre-revolutionary figures thanks to the mechanization and technological improvement that had achieved an increase in productivity of both land and labor force (Halperin Donghi 2005, 681). Trade with the Soviet Union represented about 45% of Cuba's trade until 1975; by the early 1980s, it exceeded 60%. Cuba's trade with Eastern European countries also increased when they agreed to subsidize sugar prices (Domínguez 1998, 200, 201, 225).

In short, between 1945 and 1973, the manufacturing sector first became the engine of growth, with increases of more than 6% per year. Manufacturing exports increased from 3.5% per year in the 1950s to 11.3% per year in the period 1960–1973. In the latter period, imports remained at a high and increasing level, as agricultural production for the domestic market was not sufficient to meet the demand of the growing urban sectors (Thorp 1998, 169, 171, 173, 180). The 1970s saw the end of the upswing, marked by the overwhelming hegemony of the United States, the elimination of the fixed parity of the dollar and gold, and the first oil crisis. A period appeared marked by sudden changes, crises, and conflicts that intensified in Latin America (Halperin Donghi 2005, 442, 443, 445, 519, 585, 611; González Arana 2009).

The issues that dominated the agenda of many Latin American governments during the 1990s were trade, investment, democracy promotion, technology, innovation, environmental protection, international migration, and drug trafficking. The 1990s saw a period of flourishing multilateralism resulting from the end of the Cold War; the rapprochement of Latin American countries to international institutions to address financial problems and promote their development prospects; and the rise of democratic values that provided a justification for military, financial, trade, and political cooperation. However, there was also a growth in both poverty and political disaffection in a large number of countries in the region (Muñóz 2018; Domínguez 2000).

Between 2001 and 2008, Latin American economies recorded growth driven by a favorable external scenario of high commodity prices and strong improvements in terms of trade. This period coincided with China's entry into the World Trade Organization. High commodity prices have generally meant a higher percentage of export volumes – particularly in Bolivia (up 119% between 2002 and 2013), Colombia (98.5%), Ecuador (95.5%), Peru (73.4%), Uruguay (71%), Brazil (66%), and Chile (52%).

There was also a benefit from high levels of remittances from migrant workers. This set of favorable factors weakened from 2007 (remittances) and mid-2008 (end of the commodity price boom) into a strong negative external shock, as part of the international financial crisis that exploded in September 2008 and the major global recession that followed. The right-wing governments, like those of Colombia (under the regime of Alvaro Uribe and Juan Manuel Santos) and Peru (under the regime of Alejandro Toledo, Alan García, and Ollanta Humala), used the commodity boom even long after the recession (2003–2011) to consolidate the neoliberal pillars of their economies. While the center-left governments, like the ones of Luiz Inácio Lula da Silva and Dilma Rousseff in Brazil and Néstor Kirchner and Cristina Fernández de Kirchner in Argentina, entered into modest confrontation with some neoliberal precepts, leaving others intact. Finally, in more radical processes, such as those in Bolivia and Venezuela, under Hugo Chávez and Evo Morales, respectively, there were greater ruptures with the inherited order, but these were only partially and rarely carried out.

Regionalism and Open Regionalism

One of the factors that invigorated the regional economy in the 1960s was the CACM, which was signed in 1960 by Costa Rica, El Salvador, Guatemala, Honduras, and Nicaragua. Another factor was the creation of the Trade Partnership Program (LAFTA/LALC) by the Treaty of Montevideo also signed in 1960 by Argentina, Brazil, Chile, Paraguay, Peru, and Uruguay, and then Colombia, Ecuador, Venezuela, and

Bolivia. During this period, integration was characterized by extensive state intervention and deadlines for both the elimination of intra-regional trade barriers and the establishment of common external tariffs. Toward the end of the 1970s, there was a gradual gap between the initial high expectations and the actual achievements. In the Caribbean region, the Caribbean Free Trade Area (CARIFTA) was launched in 1968 and replaced in 1973 by the Caribbean Community and Common Market (CARICOM), reflecting more ambitious objectives such as common external tariffs, policy coordination in transport, financing, industrial development and the collection of statistics. The area was expanded to include the Bahamas in 1983, Suriname in 1995, and Haiti in 2002. Caricom was renamed the Caricom Single Market and Economy (CSME) in an attempt to provide the region's inhabitants with better opportunities to produce and sell their products and services and to attract investment. Caricom exported over $800 million in 1995, about 50% over its 1990 value. In December 1991, the Central American Integration System (SICA) was established with the signing of the Tegucigalpa Protocol, reforming the Odeca Charter. The participants were Belize, Costa Rica, El Salvador, Guatemala, Honduras, Nicaragua, Panama, and the Dominican Republic. Guatemala, El Salvador, Honduras, and Nicaragua also sought a political, cultural, and migratory integration called CA4. Costa Rica is part of the CA4, but only with regard to issues dealing with economic integration and regional solidarity. Despite these efforts, Central American integration was not successful. Its members have been negotiating together but signing and implementing separate agreements. Costa Rica has been especially active in reaching preferential agreements with Mexico, Venezuela, Chile, and the United States. Similarly, Panama concluded a separate Trade Promotion Agreement with the United States in July 2007 and in 2004 the Dominican Republic-Central America Free Trade Agreement with the United States (CAFTA-DR) was concluded, associating the United States, Costa Rica, El Salvador, Guatemala, Honduras, Nicaragua, and the Dominican Republic (Domínguez 2000; Knight, Castro-Rea, and Ghany 2016).

The Andean Pact (AP) was formed in 1969 by Bolivia, Colombia, Ecuador, Chile (the latter one withdrew in 1976), and Peru, later joined by Venezuela (1973), in an effort to accelerate the economic development of its members. All these nations were dissatisfied with the distribution of benefits within LAFTA and felt that their progress would be much greater in a group that excluded Brazil and Argentina. This pact sought the establishment of a common external tariff, joint industrial programming, rapid creation of a free trade zone, harmonization of economic and social policies, common treatment of foreign investment, plus other programs (Lincoln 2018). It established the Andean Development Corporation and an emergency financial common fund, the Andean Reserve Fund. This structure became a customs union before LAFTA became a free trade zone. However, the AP did little to liberalize trade among its members (Knight, Castro-Rea, and Ghany 2016). Based on the AP, the Andean Community of Nations (CAN) was formed in 1991 and was made up of Bolivia, Ecuador, Peru, and Colombia, and later Venezuela (which withdrew in 2006). The result was genuine investment and free trade liberalization in some sectors. In 2001, a common Andean passport was created, and since 2005, the movement of people between member countries has been facilitated. In 2003, CAN concluded a trade liberalization agreement with Mercosur. In 1998, intra-Andean Community exports exceeded US$5 billion, more than four times their value compared to 1990.

The Southern Common Market (Mercosur) came into force in October 1991, including Brazil, Argentina, Uruguay, and Paraguay (Bolivia is currently in the process of joining). Unlike previous Latin American regional agreements, the Mercosur countries drastically reduced intra-regional tariffs, lowered external barriers, and freed up investment. Intra-Mercosur exports grew by an average of 30% per year during its first five years of existence, amounting to more than US$21 billion, more than five times what they were in 1990.

In the late 1980s and the following decade, a series of new agreements were negotiated throughout the Americas through an approach called "open regionalism", focusing on industrialization on an intraregional rather than a national scale, attempting to liberalize and deregulate the continent's economies to attract them into the globalization process. The opening of the hemispheric economies was promoted and supervised by the International Monetary Fund (IMF), the World Bank (IBRD), the Inter-American Development Bank (IDB), and other international institutions. The loans granted to Latin American governments were conditioned on changes in their macroeconomic policies. The launch of the Caribbean Basin Initiative (CBI) in 1984 targeted 22 Caribbean countries, while the Initiative for the Americas (EAI) in 1990 was in principle open to all countries in the Americas, with the objective of forming a free trade zone system. In both cases, the main actors would be private companies that received tax or regulatory incentives to expand their business internationally with unprecedented economic openness.

Shortly before, in 1989, a Free Trade Agreement was signed between Canada and the United States (CUSFTA), which was the direct prede-cessor of the 1994 North American Free Trade Agreement (NAFTA). By 1998, the value of exports under NAFTA exceeded $500 billion, more than double their value in 1990. The open regionalism style of agree-ment was indirectly transferred to other Latin American countries such as the G-3 (Mexico, Colombia, and Venezuela), or bilaterally such as Mexico and Bolivia, and Mexico and Costa Rica. A US-Chile Free Trade Agreement was concluded in 2003, quickly followed by others that included Colombia, Panama, and Peru in 2006. Mexico also reached liberalization agreements with Uruguay (2003), El Salvador, Honduras, and Guatemala (2000), Nicaragua (1997), Bolivia (1994), and Costa Rica (1994). In addition, Mexico reached a framework agreement with Mercosur (2002) and preferential agreements with six South American countries plus Panama. Canada also reached agreements with the United States, Mexico, Chile and Costa Rica (2001), and Peru (2008). For its part, Cuba trades substantially with the Caribbean countries as well as with Mexico and Venezuela (Domínguez 2000; Knight, Castro-Rea, and Ghany 2016).

In the second decade of the 21st century, a wide range of intraregional and extraregional relations were formed in Latin America. Mexico, Argentina, and Brazil belong to the Group of 20 (G20); Peru, Colombia, Mexico, and Chile belong to the Association of Asia and the Pacific (APEC); Brazil belongs to the BRICS (Brazil, Russia, India, China, and South Africa) and the IBSA groups (India, Brazil, and South Africa); Chile, Peru, and Mexico belong to the Trans-Pacific Partnership (TPP). The Colombian government organized a Summit in the city of Santiago de Cali in January 2007, in line with the creation of the Latin American Pacific Basin Initiative or Pacific Arc (2006) and with a view to implementing open regionalism. In 2011, this initiative was transformed into the Pacific Alliance, a new regional bloc established by Colombia, Chile, Peru, and Mexico.

In the region, Venezuela and Cuba formed the Bolivarian Alternative for the Americas (ALBA); Brazil created the Union of South American Nations (UNASUR); Mexico and Brazil promoted the Community of Latin American and Caribbean Countries (CELAC). ALBA was born in 2001 as a unilateral proposal by Venezuela to confront the Free Trade Area of the Americas (FTAA), and in 2004 it became an integration scheme described as non-capitalist and not centered on trade and competition. It proposed a break with open regionalism and suggested a model of integration based on complementarity, cooperation, and solidarity. After the victories of Evo Morales in Bolivia, Daniel Ortega in Nicaragua, and Rafael Correa in Ecuador, the ALBA expanded and consolidated as a bloc in the Latin American regionalism scenario.

Starting in 2003, Venezuelan President Hugo Chávez began to consolidate his power and pushed for a new narrative on integration by rejecting neoliberalism and capitalism, at the same time as Luiz Inácio Lula da Silva and Néstor Kirchner won elections in Brazil and Argentina, respectively. These three leaders became the driving force behind the transformation of regionalism in South America that became a pole of power to balance the unilateralism of the United States. With the rise to power of Lula de Silva in Brazil and Néstor Kirchner in Argentina, a new economic model was sought for Mercosur that aimed to complement the original approach to trade with new social and productive dimensions (Briceño-Ruiz, 2017). The creation of the Structural Convergence Fund

(FOCEM) (2005), the approval of the Production Integration Program (2008), and the preparation of the Strategic Social Action Plan (2011) are examples of this new approach to regionalism in which free trade was only one of several objectives. This "turn to the left" also influenced the construction of a new regionalism currently represented by UNASUR. Originally in 1993, Brazilian President Itamar Franco (1992–1994) proposed the creation of a South American Free Zone (SAFTA) project and his successor, Fernando Henrique Cardoso (1995–2002), slightly modified the project at the first Summit of South American Presidents, held in Brasilia in 2000. On that occasion, Cardoso proposed a South American Community of Nations (SACN), whose focus remained the promotion of free trade, but with new objectives such as infrastructure development, energy cooperation, and political cooperation added. Chávez's alliance with Morales and, to a lesser extent, with Correa and Kirchner, added to Lula's pragmatism regarding free commerce and his interest in objectives such as the Initiative for the Integration of Infrastructure in South America (IIRSA) or the South American Defense Council resulted in a new political readjustment that led to the replacement of the SACN by UNASUR. In 2008, UNASUR helped alleviate the severe political crisis in Bolivia and during 2010, it served as a mediator between Colombia, Venezuela, and Ecuador. In April 2019, Argentina withdrew from UNASUR. Other countries have also temporarily left the organization such as Brazil, Chile, Peru, and Paraguay in 2018; Uruguay left in March 2020 and Bolivia is trying to leave UNASUR after the overthrow of Evo Morales. After this collective withdrawal, the South American organization has only four full members (Venezuela, Guyana, Suriname, and Bolivia) and four other members who have suspended their participation such as Brazil, Chile, Peru, and Paraguay, making a very complex political limbo. UNASUR has attempted to mediate regional conflicts, including the Triple Frontier, although its achievements have been rather limited, as border issues remain a central and contentious issue in South American relations, delaying the promotion of integration and the fight against organized crime in the region. For example, except for relations between Peru and Bolivia, already normalized by the CAN, relations between Peru and Chile remain outside the institutional agreements, and relations between Chile and Bolivia have not improved even though both are members of the same regional forum. It should be noted that multilateral forums have been just another conflict scenario for both countries. Other regimes such as ZICOSUR, the Pacific Alliance, ALBA, CELAC, and the OAS, among others, will not be useful in solving cross-border security problems if their rules, procedures, and institutions continue to overlap. These three regional schemes (ALBA, Mercosur, and UNASUR) are different from those of the 1990s (CAN, G3, and Mercosur of the Treaty of Asunción). In addition, the Community of Latin American and Caribbean States (CELAC) was created in December 2011 (Domínguez and Covarrubias 2015; Domínguez 2016; Briceño-Ruiz and Morales 2017).

Organization of the Book

The volume is divided into two large sections. The first one, called *Setbacks,* presents some negative characteristics for the development of the Latin American economy. The second section, called *Advances,* stands in stark contrast to the first one because it shows positive aspects of the economic situation in the continent. Of course, no article is completely negative or positive, but there is a mixture, a balance of both situations.

Setbacks

In Chapter 1, called *Why do Latin American countries suffer from long-term economic stagnation?* Pierre Salama studies the relationship between the global spread of the Covid-19 virus and the serious economic, social, and political crisis in Latin America, more serious than that of the 1930s. The pandemic, through containment measures and the shutdown of companies outside those essential to daily life and health, has highlighted the dysfunctions of hyperglobalization.

In Chapter 2, *Refeudalization in Latin America: On social polarization and the money aristocracy in the 21st century,* Olaf Kaltmeier discusses the social polarization in Latin America. While capitalism has promised, since the end of feudalism and the emergence of bourgeois society, the possibility of individual social upwards mobility based on meritocratic principles, a recently exponentially growing global social inequality has been observed that excludes de facto large population groups. It is probably only recently in periods of social crisis, like after World War II, or during political system-confrontation like in the Cold War, that political programs reducing social polarization emerged. Nevertheless, in capitalist semantics, key concepts like progress, development, liberty, democracy, etc., which emerged in the "Sattelzeit", a time of transformation from feudalism to bourgeois society in the context of the French Revolution, still predominate.

In Chapter 3, *New patterns of political and economic dependency: The relationship China-Latin America,* Juan Carlos Gachúz Maya and María Paula M. Aguilar Romero analyze the main characteristics of the transition process and the gradual increase of the Chinese presence in Latin America, particularly in some sectors such as the mining and energy industries. They also analyze the consequent displacement of United States Foreign Direct Investment (FDI) in the region and how this translates into political terms. The article highlights the precepts of the

Dependency Theory to explain the new scheme of external dependence center-periphery of Latin America with respect to China and underlines the main challenges for the region in this incipient scheme of economic and political dependency.

In Chapter 4, *The Argentine foreign debt, a recursive trap in two hundred years fighting for sovereignty,* Mario Rapoport and Noemí Brenta cover the different stages of Argentina's foreign debt. It reflects on the debt cycles reiteration, its link with the international context, and the country's ups and downs in the legal sovereignty defense, from the first large loan with the British bank to the present day, when the threat of a new default is looming after four years of accelerated indebtedness, with the same global and local logic. This financing, which was supposed to make up for the shortage of domestic capital and foreign currency for development, invariably became a significant obstacle.

In Chapter 5, called *End of the cycle: The International Court of Justice ruling in the case of Chile and Bolivia and its commercial implications,* Loreto Correa Vera researches the relationship between Chile and Bolivia and frames a sovereign exit's claim to the sea. In this context, Bolivia consistently argues that the absence of an autonomous and own exit to the Pacific hinders and diminishes its economic potential to the Asian continent and its closest partners, such as those of the Andean Community of Nations. This chapter demonstrates that Bolivia's trade problems are related to the production centers' distance from export ports and not to sovereignty and cargo manipulation lack, as suggested in recent studies.

In Chapter 6, *Economic History, Developmentalism and Neoliberalism in contemporary Brazil,* Gustavo Oliveira and Ivan Daniel Müller point out the differences between the old and the new Brazilian developmentalism. They locate and comment on the neoliberal period. Based on the differences between the old and the new developmentalism, the notion of neodevelopmentalism best allows analyzing developmentalism in a broader way in the context of neoliberal globalization. They conclude by suggesting that it can be fruitful to take advantage of the fading of recent Brazilian developmentalism to think about the idea of Latin American integration developmentalism.

In Chapter 7, *Capitalism and labor exploitation in Brazil: human trafficking and slave,* Élio Gasda introduces two forms of extreme labor exploitation in the history of Brazil: human trafficking and slave labor. The chapter goes through the history of Brazil in a chronological way. The first section demonstrates that human trafficking and slave labor aren't practices restricted to the origin of capitalism. The exploitation of human work fed by human trafficking has been one of capitalism pillars since its origin. The second section examines the Brazilian case of human trafficking and slave labor.

Advances

In Chapter 8, *The Latin American Economies since c. 1950: ideas, policy and structural change*, Colin Lewis explores the macroeconomy of Latin America since the mid-20th century. It takes a political economy perspective of the "state" and the "market", arguing that a modern economy is based on manufacturing: growth, industrialization, and development were viewed as one and the same. His approach is largely chronological, with the description of "cycles". The first one is the phase of the economically and socially active state (c. 1930–1970s) – a period of "growth from within", of interventionism, welfarism, and "forced" development. The second one is the phase of debt-led authoritarian development and "renewed" globalization beginning in the mid-1960s, which culminated in post-debt crisis democratization and later the Washington Consensus; then, post-Washington Consensus experiments of democratic, socially progressive market-led growth and contrasting late populist interventionism – in economy, polity, and society.

In Chapter 9, *The Dependency Hypothesis: A Theoretical Moment in Latin American Thought*, Felipe Lagos-Rojas and Edward L. Tapia offer a reconstruction of the dependency hypothesis outlining both the common threads and main differences among the authors encompassed under such an umbrella. They present a brief account of the two currents from which it borrowed the most, namely the *desarrollista* (developmentalist) or *estructuralista* (structuralist) school that emerged within the UN's ECLAC, on the one hand, and the different versions of imperialism argued through a Marxian prism, on the other. Next, they introduce the most important arrangements, general consensuses, central categories, and main debates and internal divisions of the dependency debate.

In Chapter 10, called *The transnational endeavor of ECLAC for the Latin American Development*, Veridiana Cordeiro analyzes the situation of the ECLAC against the traditional economic ideas of the 1950s by proposing strategies of development to the Latin American countries. Although it was placed in Santiago de Chile, ECLAC embraced many Latin American researchers (mostly Brazilian, Argentinian, and Mexican sociologists and economists) who focused on investigating the roots of the region's economic underdevelopment and its contemporary transformations. The author provides an overview of the creation of ECLAC and on the work of two Brazilian intellectuals, Fernando Henrique Cardoso and Celso Furtado, who enriched ECLAC's thinking with new interpretations on the development of Latin American development.

In Chapter 11, *The Evolution of Capital Markets in Latin America*, John Edmunds researches the turbulent financial system in Latin America, highlighting periods of euphoria, crises triggered by external shocks, and a litany of collapses brought on in large part by home-grown misdeeds. This unsettled underpinning has been a persistent obstacle to the development of capital markets throughout the region. This summary of this lurid and dramatic history will only touch on watershed events and reforms that are exemplars of the many waves of reform that have rolled through the region. These waves of financial reform and innovation are still coming. In each country, debate still simmers about what is the best way of organizing and regulating each national financial system.

In Chapter 12, *Workers' self-management in Latin America: from the first cooperatives to the workers' recuperated enterprises*, Andrés Ruggeri delves into the process of recuperation of enterprises by workers. This process began in Argentina in the 1990s and expanded during the great crisis of 2001–2002, and attracted worldwide attention for its massiveness and the radical nature of its practices in a context where it was growing the debate about globalization and its consequences. From Argentina, where the phenomenon was occurring, the vision was less idealized. Up close, the author observes that the workers occupied the factories that the bosses abandoned in the midst of the crisis to try to preserve the jobs and, in doing so, they unwittingly activated the resurrection of self-management, a concept that symbolized the "new left" of the sixties and seventies.

In Chapter 13, *Economic Policies and Development in Chile: From Dictatorship to Democracy, 1973–2013*, Ricardo Ffrench-Davis studies the economic policies, reforms, and development in Chile from 1973 to 2013. Chile has Latin America's highest per capita income (GDPpc), achieving this when democracy was restored in 1990 and during 1997. In 1989, at the end of the dictatorship, GDPpc was below the regional average. Among the ill-informed, there is a persistent belief that, since the 1973 coup, Chile has implemented a successful economic model. However, the fact is that the almost half-century since the overthrow of democracy is made up of sub-periods in which the emphasis, the external context, public policies, and the economic and social results have been quite different. Only in the first decade of democracy, growth was quite vigorous and somewhat inclusive, but since the end of that decade started to decline. When Chile suffered a "social explosion in late 2019, it surprised the believers.

Last but not least, in Chapter 14, *The economic development of Costa Rica based on public policies period 1920–2020: The model of social economy with a sustainable and cooperative approach*, Federico Li Bonilla and Monserrat Espinach Rueda present the characteristics of Costa Rica. He describes the country's politics, social, economic, and human rights that have generated leadership in the Latin American region, positioning itself in this region with the main indicators of global competitiveness. This compilation of political management actions to be taken constitutes an input of democratic strategic information of an economic, social, environmental, cooperative, and technological nature to be followed. It constitutes a guide of actions that promote current models of a sustainable economy and contributes to promoting the Social Progress Index and other indicators that measure the impact of political actions as a consequence of improving the quality of life of people.

Note

1. Most of the Chinese investments in Latin America were mainly in sectors related to natural resources such as iron, steel, and oil in Brazil; oil in Venezuela; copper in Chile; and oil and copper in Peru. In some countries there were also investments in the international marketing sector, as in the case of Chile. See Cepal (2017).

Bibliography

Abel, C. and Palacios, M. (2002). Colombia, 1930–1958. In *Historia de América Latina, vol. 16. Los países andinos desde 1930*, edited by L. Bethell. Crítica: Barcelona.
Aboites Aguilar, L. (2008). El último tramo, 1929–2000. In *Nueva historia mínima de México ilustrada*, México, D. F.: Secretaría de Educación del Gobierno del Distrito Federal/El Colegio de México.
Acosta, A. (2006). *Breve historia económica del Ecuador*. Corporación Editora Nacional: Quito.
Anderson, R. (1998). Puerto Rico, 1940-c. 1990. In *Historia de América Latina, vol. 13. México y el Caribe desde 1930*, edited by L. Bethell. Crítica: Barcelona.
Aronskind, R. (2007). El país del desarrollo posible. In *Nueva historia argentina, vol. 9. Violencia, proscripción y autoritarismo: 1955–1976*, edited by D. James. Buenos Aires: Sudamericana.
Ayala Mora, E. (2002). Ecuador desde 1930. In *Historia de América Latina, vol. 16. Los países andinos desde 1930*, edited by L. Bethell. Crítica: Barcelona.
Bértola, L. and Ocampo, J. A. (2010). *Una historia económica de América Latina desde la independencia. Desarrollo, vaivenes y desigualdad*. Secretaría general Iberoamericana (SEGIB). Retrieved from https://www.segib.org/?document= desarrollo-vaivenes-y-desigualdad-una-historia-economica-de-america-latina-desde-la-independencia
Bertram, G. (2002). Perú, 1930–1960. In *Historia de América Latina, vol. 16. Los países andinos desde 1930*, edited by L. Bethell. Crítica: Barcelona.
Briceño-Ruiz, J. and Morales, I. (eds.) (2017). *Post-Hegemonic Regionalism in the Americas. Toward a Pacific-Atlantic Divide?* New York and Abingdon: Routledge.
Bulmer-Thomas, V. (1997). Las economías latinoamericanas, 1929–1939. In *Historia de América Latina, vol. 11. Economía y sociedad desde 1930*, edited by L. Bethell. Crítica: Barcelona.
———(2001). Honduras desde 1930. In *Historia de América Latina, vol. 14. América Central desde 1930*, edited by L. Bethell. Crítica: Barcelona.
———(2001). Nicaragua desde 1930. In *Historia de América Latina, vol. 14. América Central desde 1930*, edited by L. Bethell. Crítica: Barcelona.
Cardoso, C. (1992). América Central: la era liberal, c. 1870–1930. In *Historia de América Latina, vol. 9. México, América Central y el Caribe, c. 1870–1930*, edited by L. Bethell. Crítica: Barcelona.

Centellas Castro, M. and Calderón Guzmán, E. (comp.). (2011). *Historia de Bolivia*. La Paz: Universidad mayor de San Andrés.

Cepal. (2017). *La Inversión extranjera directa en América Latina y el Caribe.* Santiago de Chile: Naciones Unidas.

_____(2015). *América Latina y el Caribe y China. Hacia una nueva era de cooperación económica.* Santiago de Chile: Naciones Unidas.

Cerdas Cruz, R. (2001). Costa Rica desde 1930. In *Historia de América Latina, vol. 14. América Central desde 1930*, edited by L. Bethell. Crítica: Barcelona.

Damill, M. (2005). La economía y la política económica: del viejo al nuevo endurecimiento. In *Nueva historia argentina. Dictadura y democracia: 1976–2001*, edited by J. Suriano. Buenos Aires: Sudamericana.

Deas, M. (1992). Colombia, c. 1880–1930. In *Historia de América Latina, vol. 10. América del Sur, c. 1870–1930*, edited by L. Bethell. Crítica: Barcelona.

Domínguez, J. (1998). Cuba, 1959-c. 1990. In *Historia de América Latina, vol. 13. México y el Caribe desde 1930*, edited by L. Bethell. Crítica: Barcelona.

_____(2000). The Future of Inter-American Relations: States, Challenges, and Likely Responses. In *The Future of Inter-American Relations*, edited by J. Domínguez. New York and Abingdon: Routledge.

_____(2016). The Changes in the International System since 2000. In *Contemporary U.S.–Latin American Relations*, edited by J. Domínguez and R. Fernández de Castro. New York and Abingdon: Routledge.

Domínguez, J. and Covarrubias, A. (eds.) (2015). *Routledge Handbook of Latin America in the World*. New York and Abingdon: Routledge.

Domínguez, F. and Franceschi, N. (2010). *Historia General de Venezuela*. Caracas. Retrieved from https://www.researchgate.net/publication/317886815_HISTORIA_GENERAL_DE_VENEZUELA

Drake, P. (2002). Chile, 1930–1958. In *Historia de América Latina, vol. 15. El Cono Sur desde 1930*, edited by L. Bethell. Crítica: Barcelona.

Ewell, J. (2002). Venezuela, 1930–c 1990. In *Historia de América Latina, vol. 16. Los países andinos desde 1930*, edited by L. Bethell. Crítica: Barcelona.

Ffrench Davis, R., Muñóz, O., and Palma, J. G. (1997). Las economías latinoamericanas, 1950–1990. In *Historia de América Latina, vol. 11. Economía y sociedad desde 1930*, edited by L. Bethell. Crítica: Barcelona.

Freeman Smith, R. (1991). América Latina, los Estados Unidos y las potencias europeas, 1830–1930. In *Historia de América Latina, vol. 7. América Latina: Economía y Sociedad, c. 1870–1930*, edited by L. Bethell. Crítica: Barcelona.

Gazmuri, C. (2012). *Historia de Chile 1891–1994. Política, economía, sociedad, vida privada*, episodios. Ril editores: Santiago.

González Arana, R. (2009). Nicaragua. Dictadura y revolución. *Memorias* 6(10).

Halperin Donghi, T. (2005). *Historia contemporánea de América Latina*. Madrid: Alianza.

Hey, J. A. K. and Mora, F. (2003). The Theoretical Challenge to Latin American and Caribbean Foreign Policy Studies. In *Latin American and Caribbean Foreign Policy*, edited by F. Mora and J. A. K. Hey. Lanham, MD: Rowman & Littlefield Publishers.

Kennedy, P. (2017). *Auge y caída de las grandes potencias*. Barcelona: DeBolsillo.

Knight, W. A., Castro-Rea, J., and Ghany, H. (eds.) (2016). *Re-mapping the Americas. Trends in Region-making*. New York and Abingdon: Routledge.

Lemus, E. (2001). Estados Unidos e Iberoamérica, 1918–1939: del intervencionismo a la cooperación. In *Historia de las relaciones internacionales contemporáneas*, edited by J. C. Pereira. Madrid: Ariel Historia.

Lincoln, J. K. (2018 [1981]). Introduction to Latin American Foreign Policy: Global and Regional Dimensions. In *Latin American Foreign Policies: Global and Regional Dimensions*, edited by E. Ferris and J. K. Lincoln. New York and Abingdon: Routledge.

Loaeza, S. (2010). Modernización autoritaria a la sombra de la superpotencia, 1944–1968. In *Nueva historia general de México*, edited by AA. VV. Colegio de México: Mexico D.F.

Malamud, C. and Núñez, R. (2020). La crisis del coronavirus en América Latina: un incremento del presidencialismo sin red de seguridad. *Real Instituto Elcano*. Retrieved from http://www.realinstitutoelcano.org/wps/portal/rielcano_es/contenido?WCM_GLOBAL_CONTEXT=/elcano/elcano_es/zonas_es/ari34-2020-malamud-nunez-crisis-del-coronavirus-america-latina-incremento-presidencialismo-sin-red-seguridad

Márquez, G. and Meyer, L. (2010). Del autoritarismo agotado a la democracia frágil, 1985–2010. In *Nueva historia general de México*, edited by AA. VV. México: Colegio de México.

Meller, P. (1998). *Un siglo de economía política chilena (1890–1990)*. Santiago de Chile: Editorial Andrés Bello.

Mota, C. G. and López, A. (2009). *Historia de Brasil: una interpretación*. Salamanca: Ediciones Universidad de Salamanca.

Muñóz, H. (2018 [1996]). The Dominant Themes in Latin American Foreign Relations: An Introduction. In *Latin American Nation in World Politics*, edited by H. Muñóz and J. Tulchin. New York and Abingdon: Routledge.

Murillo Posada, A. (2007). La modernización y las violencias. In *Historia de Colombia: Todo lo que hay que saber*, edited by L. E. Rodríguez Baquero. Taurus: Bogotá.

Nicholls, D. (1998). Haití, 1930-c. 1990. In *Historia de América Latina, vol. 13. México y el Caribe desde 1930*, edited by L. Bethell. Crítica: Barcelona.

Nickson, A. (2010). El régimen de Stroessner (1945–1989). In *Historia del Paraguay*, edited by I. Telesca. Himali: Himali Digital Editor. Retrieved from https://es.scribd.com/document/337622398/HISTORIA-DEL-PARAGUAY-IGNACIO-TELESCA-NUEVA-EDICION-LIBRO-DIGITAL-PORTALGUARANI

OCDE/CEPAL/CAF. (2015). *Perspectivas económicas de América Latina 2016: Hacia una nueva asociación con China*. Paris: OECD Publishing.

Olmo, G. (October 13, 2020). Coronavirus: los países de América Latina cuyas economías tardarán más en recuperarse de la pandemia de covid-19. *BBC News Mundo*. Retrieved from https://www.bbc.com/mundo/noticias-america-latina-54517758

Pease, F. (1993). *Perú Hombre e Historia. La República III*. Lima: Fundación del Banco Continental para el fomento de la educación y la cultura/Ediciones Edubanco.

Pérez Brignoli, H. (2017). *El laberinto centroamericano: los hilos de la historia*. San José, Costa Rica: Centro de Investigaciones Históricas de América Central.

Pérez Herrero, P. (2001). Estados Unidos y Latinoamérica en el nuevo sistema. In *Historia de las relaciones internacionales contemporáneas*, edited by J. C. Pereira. Madrid: Ariel Historia.

Pérez, Jr., L. (1998). Cuba, c. 1930–1959. In *Historia de América Latina, vol. 13. México y el Caribe desde 1930*, edited by L. Bethell. Crítica: Barcelona.

Pleitez, W. (2011). Las reformas neoliberales: un balance crítico In *El Salvador: Historia mínima*, edited by AA. VV. Secretaría de Cultura de la Presidencia de la República. Editorial Universitaria, Universidad de El Salvador, El Salvador.

Portocarrero Grados, R. *El Perú Contemporáneo*. Retrieved from https://es.scribd.com/doc/7031201/Historia-Del-Peru-El-Peru-Contemporaneo

Quiroga, H. (2005). La reconstrucción de la democracia argentina. In *Nueva historia argentina. Dictadura y democracia: 1976–2001*, edited by J. Suriano. Buenos Aires: Sudamericana.

Renouvin, P. (1990 [1955]). *Historia de las Relaciones Internacionales. Siglos XIX y XX*. Madrid: Akal.

Rilla, J. (August–December 2008). Uruguay 1985–2007: Restauración, reforma, crisis y cambio electoral. *Revista Nuestra América 6*.

Rock, D. (1992). Argentina, de la Primera guerra mundial a la Revolución de 1930. In *Historia de América Latina, vol. 10. América del Sur, c. 1870–1930*, edited by L. Bethell. Crítica: Barcelona.

Rodríguez Kuri, A. and González Mello, R. (2010). El fracaso del éxito, 1970–1985. In *Nueva historia general de México*, edited by AA. VV. Mexico D. F.: El Colegio de México.

Rofman, A. (2005). Las transformaciones regionales. In *Nueva historia argentina. Dictadura y democracia: 1976–2001*, edited by J. Suriano. Buenos Aires: Sudamericana.

Sánchez, F. (2020). América Latina en los tiempos del Covid-19. Retrieved from https://www.politicaexterior.com/america-latina-los-tiempos-del-covid-19/

Sánchez Egozcue, M. (2011). El cambio interno y la política norteamericana, en busca de la racionalidad perdida. In *Cuba, Estados Unidos y América Latina frente a los desafíos hemisféricos*, edited by L. F. Ayerbe. Barcelona: Icaria Editorial.

Sanjinés C. J. (January–April 2004). Movimientos sociales y cambio político en Bolivia. *Revista Venezolana de Economía y Ciencias Sociales* 10(1).

Scavone Yegros, R. (2010). Guerra internacional y confrontaciones políticas (1920–1954). In *Historia del Paraguay*, edited by I. Telesca. Himali: Himali Digital Editor.

Sidicaro, R. (2005). *Los tres peronismos. Estado y poder económico 1946–1955/1973–1976/1989–1999*. Buenos Aires: Siglo XXI.

Thorp, R. M. (1997). Las economías latinoamericanas, 1939–c. 1950. In *Historia de América Latina, vol. 11. Economía y sociedad desde 1930*, edited by L. Bethell. Crítica: Barcelona.

————(1998). *Progreso, pobreza y exclusión: una historia económica de América Latina en el siglo XX*. New York: Inter-American Development Bank, BID.

Torre, J. C. and de Riz, L. (2002). Argentina, 1946–c. 1990. In *Historia de América Latina, vol. 15. El Cono Sur desde 1930*, edited by L. Bethell. Crítica: Barcelona.

Torres Rivas, E. (2001). América Central desde 1930: perspectiva general. In *Historia de América Latina, vol. 14. América Central desde 1930*, edited by L. Bethell. Crítica: Barcelona.

Valdéz Paz, J. (2005). Cuba en el "Periodo Especial": de la igualdad a la equidad. In *Cambios en la sociedad cubana desde los noventa*, edited by J. Tulchin et al. Washington, DC: Woodrow Wilson International Center for Scholars.

30   *P.A. Baisotti*

Webber, J. (2019). Mercado mundial, desarrollo desigual y patrones de acumulación: la política económica de la izquierda latinoamericana. In *Los gobiernos progresistas latinoamericanos del siglo XXI. Ensayos de interpretación histórica*, edited by F. Gaudichaud, J. Webber, and M. Modonesi, Mexico: Universidad Nacional Autónoma de México.
Whitehead, L. (2002). Bolivia, 1930-c 1990. In *Historia de América Latina, vol. 16. Los países andinos desde 1930*, edited by L. Bethell. Crítica: Barcelona.
Will China's New Silk Road Reach Latin America? (2017). *Marketviews*. Retrieved from https://www.marketviews.com/latam/will-chinas-new-silk-road-reach-latin-america/

1 Why Do Latin American Countries Suffer from Long-Term Economic Stagnation?

Pierre Salama

Introduction

An Unfavorable Context to Resist the Effects of the Pandemic

The global spread of the SARS-CoV-2 virus has precipitated, not caused, a very serious economic, social and political crisis in Latin America, more serious than that of the 1930s. Indeed, in many countries the crisis existed before the pandemic hit: this is the case of Argentina, Venezuela, and Mexico, which entered into recession in 2019. In other countries, a slowdown in economic activity existed, and over a long period of time, all economies were suffering from a trend of stagnant per capita GDP growth. Considering that the pandemic has caused an economic crisis, one would think that once the contagion has disappeared, it would be possible to "start again as before", as the exogenous cause of the crisis has disappeared. This is not the thesis we develop in this article. The pandemic, through containment measures and the shutdown of companies outside those essential to daily life and health, has highlighted the dysfunctions of hyper-globalization. This pandemic is indicative of the failure of globalization as it has spread and imposed its rules of the game over the last 20 years. The irony of history is that the crisis of globalization has arrived when no economist, sociologist, or politician had foreseen it. None. Even if some people are now trying to make people believe that they had foreseen it.[1]

No one thought that the new forms taken by globalization, namely the international splintering of the value chain, could weaken the various economies to such an extent that they would be extremely vulnerable. Chaos theorists had shown that the flapping of a butterfly's wings could cause a collapse on the other side of the world and that the sword of Damocles could fall at any moment and lead to disasters. But this thesis, applied to finance, was not applied to globalization. It only took a pandemic to cause the current economic system to collapse by chain effects that feed off each other. The inability to supply segments of the international value chain here (China, the first to be affected by the pandemic,

DOI: 10.4324/9781003045632-2

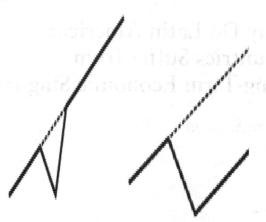

Figure 1.1 V-shaped and L-shaped recovery

the shutdown of most of its factories[2] and the consequences of confining the population to those working in the health, food, and transport sectors) is leading elsewhere to more or less significant production stoppages, increased unemployment and thus a drop in demand precipitating an economic depression in already weakened economies. This "flapping of the butterfly's wings" reveals above all that deindustrialization, the symmetrical feature of this globalization, is disastrous in terms of sovereignty – especially and above all in the pharmaceutical industry – and results in a heap of deaths.

The crisis has several dimensions. It does not arrive on a "healthy body" ready to bounce back once the pandemic is over. The social consequences, which are already significant, will be extremely severe, since a crisis mainly affects the most vulnerable, slightly less the middle classes, and much less the highest strata, in terms of income and assets, of the population. Like any crisis, this one will accentuate income inequalities: more poor people, more informality, and probably violence. The pandemic exacerbates all the ills that existed before it began. The unfavorable context and the exacerbation of the difficulties explain why the prospect of an L-shaped rather than V-shaped (see Figure 1.1) recovery tomorrow is the most credible, unless the crisis causes social and political upheavals that could profoundly alter these pessimistic prospects.

Latin American Countries Are Different and Similar

Some countries have a large population (Brazil with 207 million inhabitants, Mexico with 132 million), while others, such as Uruguay or the Central American countries, are relatively sparsely populated. GDP per capita is high in Brazil, Argentina, Mexico, etc. (between a quarter and a third of that of the United States), a little less in Colombia and Peru, and much less in others. Some countries are rich in natural resources, others much less so. Finally, the populations do not all have the same origin, more European in the southern cone of Latin America, more of Indian origin in the Andean countries, in Central America and Mexico, or more of African origin in other countries such as Brazil, in the Caribbean. Their histories are not exactly similar, even though throughout the 20th century, the most important among them may have had similar experiences both at the political level (Perón in Argentina, Vargas in Brazil, Cardenas in Mexico) and at the economic level (growth regime oriented toward the internal market known as import substitution).

From a structural point of view, most Latin American countries have a great deal in common, which in one way or another, constitute the eight wounds of Latin America[3]: (1) very high inequality of wealth and income; (2) a high level of job informality and poverty; (3) a reprimarization of the economy; (4) a significant deterioration of the environment; (5) a financial opening greater than the opening of trade; (6) early deindustrialization; (7) a tendency toward economic stagnation; and (8) an extremely high level of violence, especially in Mexico, Brazil, El Salvador, Honduras, and Guatemala. The lower the rate of GDP growth, the less social mobility there is, and all the more so if spending on education remains insufficient. The analysis of the causes that lead to economic stagnation is the subject of this chapter. With a weakened industrial fabric, will Latin American countries be able to show resilience in the face of the COVID-19 pandemic and its heavy economic and social effects, and under what conditions?

A Trend toward Economic Stagnation: The Facts

Average per capita growth rates over a long period of time in most Latin American countries have been between 0 and 2%. In particular, Mexico's per capita GDP growth rate between 1983 and 2017 was 0.8%. In the United States, over the same period, it was 1.7% according to World Bank data. Contrary to the doxa, if we focus on the per capita growth rate, Mexico is not an emerging economy; its GDP level is not close to that of the developed countries.[4] The same applies to Argentina. Its marginalization comes from afar. In 1913, Argentina's per capita income was equivalent to 65% of that of Great Britain. In 1945 it was 60% and in 2001 it was 39%. The comparison with the per capita income of the Spanish is even more eloquent. In 1913, it was almost five times (393%) higher than that of the Spanish, and in 2001, the year of the crisis, it was barely half (51%). Whether it is the differential in per capita income growth or productivity growth, the comparison with the United States is instructive.

Thus, over the last 40 years, their per capita GDP has tended to stagnate, particularly in Mexico, although most of them experienced a slight rebound in the first decade of the 2000s (Grupo Técnico de Expertos

Table 1.1 GDP and productivity growth differentials of the United States and Argentina

	1900– 1919	1920– 1930	1931– 1943	1944– 1972	1973– 1990	1991– 2007
GDP/tonne differential	−1	2.6	−6.6	2.2	−2.3	0.0
Labor productivity differential	0.4	1	−4.9	1.4	−1	−2.6

Source: Della Paoloera, Duran Amorocho, and Musacchio (2018) based on official data reconstructed by Bénétrix, H O'Rourke, and Williamson (2012).

2020; Ros, Moreno-Brid in Cordera (2015); Romero Tellaeche 2014). Contrary to a relatively shared idea, these economies have been little or no emerging. They have therefore not converged, or have converged very little, toward the per capita income level of the developed countries, unlike many Asian countries. Brazil, an emblematic country in terms of its economic weight, the influence of President Lula's policy (2003–2011) and the outcome of the last presidential elections that brought the extreme right to power in 2019, does not experience this convergence. Its GDP per capita, measured against that of the United States, is approximately the same as in 1960, although in the 1960s and 1970s and in the first decade of the 2000s it has come closer to it.

The trend toward stagnation over a long period of time does not manifest itself in the same way in all countries. A growth rate is only an average and the dispersion around it differs from country to country. Argentina, for example, is experiencing very high volatility in its growth, flirting with fairly high rates for several years and then plunging into the abyss of the crisis, which is less the case for Mexico or Brazil. All of them are now finding it difficult to bounce back after a crisis.

A Repartition of Economic Activities

In recent decades, most of the semi-industrialized economies that had previously managed to reduce the relative weight of their exports of raw materials in favor of exports of industrial goods have recovered. The example of Brazil, a country rich in raw materials, is representative: in 1997, exports of raw materials amounted to 21.2% of its total exports and those of products of the processing industry to 78.8%. In 2019, these values were 43.3% and 56.7%, respectively (IEDI n°974, 2020). Others, such as Peru, which were much less industrialized, have strongly developed their specialization in primary products. Those that were poorly or less endowed with natural resources (e.g. Central America, Mexico) "exported" part of their labor to the United States.

Table 1.2 Long-term growth of GDP/t from 1950 to 2017, (in 1950 GDP/t = 100)

	Argentina	Latin America	United States	Western Europe
1950	100	100	100	100
1960	111	125.14	118	141
1970	146	160.73	157	210
1980	165	211.35	194	274
1990	129	207.44	243	334
2000	169	263.03	300	415
2001	160	263.96	300	422
2002	141	266.85	303	426
2003	151	271.38	308	430
2004	160	283.35	316	441
2005	171	293.85	323	449
2006	183	307.17	328	462
2007	195	321.13	331	475
2008	200	330.51	327	473
2009	192	322.81	313	451
2010	206	339.55	319	457
2011	216	353.69	322	460
2012	212	365.27	326	459
2013	214	374.81	329	459
2014	207	378.76	334	466
2015	209	380.88	340	479
2016	202	380.30	343	485
2017	206	382.05	348	492

Source: OECD (2019), *Estudios económicos, Argentina*.

Notes: Western Europe includes here: Austria, Belgium, Denmark, Finland, France, Germany, Greece, Ireland, Italy, the Netherlands, Norway, Portugal, Spain, Sweden, Switzerland, and the United Kingdom; Latin America includes: Brazil, Chile, Colombia, Mexico, and Peru. From 1980 to 2016, average per capita GDP growth averaged 0.64%, lower than that observed for all other Latin American countries as a whole, 1.4% (Coatz et al. 2018).

The relationship between the reprimarization–deindustrialization couple and the tendency to stagnation is complex. Reprimarization–deindustrialization may lead to a slight increase in the GDP growth rate, even over a decade or so, but it may also be one of the factors that in the long term explains the low growth, firstly because it increases external vulnerability, and secondly because it undermines the profitability of companies in industry if no industrial policy is put in place, as we shall see. Reprimarization without significant deindustrialization, in the absence of a significant industrial fabric, can raise GDP growth, but it remains vulnerable because it is so dependent on the price of raw materials and the quantities sold over which the country has little control (Peru).

With reprimarization in most countries endowed with natural resources and exports of raw materials, the income transferred ("remesas") –

Table 1.3 Gross fixed capital formation as % of GDP, 2010 dollars, 2010–2018[a]

	2010	2011	2012	2013	2014	2015	2016	2017	2018[a]
Latin America	20.5	21.4	21.5	21.5	20.8	19.8	18.6	18.2	18.7
Argentina	16.6	18.4	17.3	17.3	16.5	16.7	16	17.5	16.9
Brazil	20.5	21.1	20.9	21.4	20.4	18.2	16.6	16	16.5
Colombia	21.1	23.4	23.3	23.6	25.2	24.2	23.7	22.6	22.8
Mexico	21.6	22.5	22.7	21.7	21.7	22.1	21.7	20.9	20.6

Source: CEPAL (2016).

[a] Provisional data. It should be noted that between 20% and 22% of GFCF is devoted to investment.

$30 billion for Mexico in 2019 – by immigrant workers in the United States to other countries and capital inflows net of repatriation of dividends and interest paid, external constraints declined sharply in the 2000s. This new situation, which many economists and governments thought to be sustainable, reinforced rentier behaviors that were latent in the countries. These behaviors are reflected in an insufficient investment rate to allow for high and sustainable growth likely to produce a significant and lasting improvement in social cohesion.

Stagnation Explained by the Latin American Structuralist Movement

First, Latin American countries have been deeply unequal, and those that were less so (Argentina, Chile, etc.) have become so over the last 34 years. Inequalities are numerous, and the main ones are the following: inequalities between the poor and the rich and between those who have no assets and those who have them from birth; inequalities in taxation; inequalities between immigrants, their children, and others; inequalities between those who go to good schools and those who have no choice but to go to poorer schools; inequalities between men and women; inequalities in dismissals; working conditions between those working in small and large enterprises; inequalities between those in informal employment and those in formal, protected employment; inequalities according to skin color; and, in general, inequalities in income. Most of these inequalities overlap. Income distribution is much more unequal than in developed countries. Worse, after direct taxes and social transfers, while the Gini – an indicator of inequality – falls by 10–15 points on a scale of 1–100 in the developed countries, its reduction in Latin America is only 2 points. None of the countries has implemented a tax reform that would allow a reduction in inequality. Income inequalities tended to fall in the 2000s until the advent of the crisis for 95% of the employed population.

The richest 5% and especially the richest 1% of the population[5] have experienced, including during the first decade of the 2000s, an increase in absolute and relative terms of their income – contrary to official discourse – mainly due to the growing weight of finance. With the crisis starting in the second half of 2010 – mainly affecting Brazil, Argentina, Venezuela – and the economic slowdown (Mexico, etc.), income inequalities are increasing, and poverty is growing again.

Evolution of Income Inequality in Brazil from 1981 to 2018

When the population is broken down into the poorest 30%, the next 40% considered to be middle classes and the richest 30%, a contrasting trend can be observed between family income (wages and social transfers) and income from capital (here referring to the income of self-employed workers, known as own-account workers). In 37 years, between 1981 and 2018, the family income of the poor increased by 42% and the income from capital (self-employment) by 106.8%, and that of the middle classes increased by 25.2% and 108.9%, respectively, and finally that of the richest 30% increased by 13.7% and 68.3%, respectively. These data can be explained for the poorest 30% on the one hand by the strong increase in the minimum wage (one-third of them have a formal job and benefit directly from this increase and the increase in social transfers), and on the other hand by a greater participation of women in the labor force, through an improvement in the education system and especially through the demographic transition. The families of the poorest 30% have seen their size dropped from 7 to 4.5 people living under the same roof, while the number of people living in the middle classes has dropped from 5.5 to 3.5, and from 3.8 to 3 for the richest 30%. This greater reduction in relative terms in the number of children per family for the poorest 30% of the population translates into a proportionally greater increase in their per capita income. Finally, from 1981 to 1994, hyperinflation affected more particularly the family income of the poorest (–30% for the poorest 30%, –15% for the richest 30%), so that when hyperinflation ended in 1994, a fraction of the poorest "mechanically" recovered purchasing power. Between 1993 and 2018, the increase in family incomes of the poorest 30% was 142% and that of the richest 30% was 72%; these increases are explained by the two above-mentioned factors and the end of hyperinflation for the former and low productivity growth for the latter.

Source: IBGE in O valor of 21 February 2020.

Second, in more than one respect, the structuralist current has been iconoclastic and innovative. As opposed to the theses developed by the IMF, this current, which was dominant in ECLAC[6] between the 1950s and 1970s, highlights the structures of inertia[7] to explain the obstacles to development. Contrary to the dominant ideas of the 1950s–1980s, ECLAC economists – so-called neo-Cambridgian, addictionist, and/

or Marxist economists – show that semi-industrialized economies do not suffer from a lack of capital and an abundance of labor. On the contrary, according to these currents, they suffer from idle production capacities, which are proportionally greater in number than in the developed countries, and from a lack of skilled labor. They are in fact forced to use production techniques more or less similar to those prevailing in the developed countries and therefore "waste" supposedly scarce capital. It is this paradox, in relation to the dominant teachings, that the Latin American structuralist movement seeks to explain. This is where its original and innovative aspect lies. It follows from these analyses that the way out of the crisis is not through demand restraint but through a policy that promotes industrial development oriented toward satisfying the domestic market. To be effective, this policy must be based on agrarian reform and a reduction in income inequality.

The theoretical explanations of the tendency to stagnation have been developed mainly by Furtado C. (1966) in two forms. The first has proved irrelevant. The second has regained some relevance. His first thesis put forward the impossibility of continuing the process of substitution of heavy imports (intermediate goods, capital goods) due to the increasing rigidity of the import structure. According to this reasoning, the external constraint, previously a source of dynamism ("growth driven by the internal market"), is gradually turning into its opposite. Indeed, the continuation of the process in its second phase, the so-called heavy phase, gradually generates imports of capital goods and intermediate products such that the value of the imported goods eventually exceeds that of the goods to be substituted by local production. As the countries of the semi-industrialized periphery are unable to accumulate sufficient debt, the relative lack of foreign exchange makes it impossible to fully convert money into capital in the industrial sector because of the impossibility of importing sufficient quantities of capital goods. The resulting increase in the relative prices of production goods also makes it more expensive to invest in the industry, and money is then channeled to other places of value-adding that require fewer imports, such as real estate or consumption of luxury goods, at the expense of industrial investment. The growth rate of gross fixed capital formation declines, unproductive consumption increases, and the rentier behavior of entrepreneurs increases.

The fragility of this demonstration comes from the fact that it presupposes the existence of major obstacles to external borrowing. However, this assessment has proved to be erroneous, since these countries have been engaged since the 1970s in a strong process of external indebtedness, particularly and above all under the dictatorship in Brazil between 1964 and 1979. The second explanation for the trend toward stagnation put forward by Furtado refers to the growing divorce between an income distribution that is not only particularly unequal but is becoming increasingly so, and the increasing minimum optimal dimensions of the supply of certain so-called "dynamic" products intended for a demand that is insufficient in absolute terms. More precisely, on the demand side, when production becomes more complex and requires not only higher capital intensity but also a more skilled and better-paid labor force than in the first phase of light goods import substitution, the distribution of income between employees becomes more unequal. On the supply side, minimum optimal production capacities become more important, especially for intermediate goods and consumer durables such as cars. The supply side of these goods corresponds lesser and lesser to the demand side, the demand side of the insufficiently numerous middle classes and the demand side of companies. Idle production capacity is increasing in these supply segments, raising unit costs.

Growing idle production capacity in the durable goods sector is affecting profitability. Despite the protectionism enjoyed by firms in this sector, they are partly subject to competitiveness constraints. Land reform and lower income inequality could provide a way out of this trap to escape economic stagnation. Instead, a coup d'état aimed at lowering the real wages of workers who do not consume these goods is "welcome" for the most conservative strata in that it lowers the cost of supply without affecting demand and makes it possible to revive a regime of inclusive growth, driven by the rise of both consumer durables and the middle classes that consume these goods. Over the past 30 years, the polarization of income in favor of the wealthiest 5% of the population has better explained the rentier trend of investors, the modest growth rate since the 1990s, and the high volatility of growth in Latin American economies. It is thus a combination of various factors – State withdrawal, the perverse effects of finance on productive investment and the polarization in favor of high incomes – that would rather explain the low average growth rate and its particularly volatile aspect since the 1990s.

Third, what updates? (1) It is common to consider that the greater the inequality, the lower the growth. In fact, this is not always true. Let us give a historical example: the advent of the dictatorship in Brazil at the end of the 1960s made it possible to greatly reduce the cost of labor for workers and to overcome the trend toward stagnation that was beginning to take shape. Given the degree of income inequality and the level of their incomes, workers did not have access to the most expensive consumer durables, such as automobiles. As they represented only a cost, the fall in their wages benefited the companies producing these goods, which found sufficient demand from the middle classes because of their level of income and their numbers (20% of 100 million inhabitants do not have the same economic significance as 20% of 10 million inhabitants). The improvement of their profitability (reduction in the cost of labor for workers, absence of demand effects on their part, importance of the demand of the middle classes directed mainly toward the consumption of durable goods) has made it possible to increase investment in this sector and thus to increase the hiring of executives likely to buy these durable goods, to increase growth and thus to increase the wages of workers in the long run. However, this growth is not sustainable. Ignoring a minimal ethic, growing inequalities undermine the sustainability of development, as we have seen with the exhaustion of dictatorship paving the way for a return to democracy. The demands for an indirect wage (greater social security), more education, etc., are becoming calls for renewed social cohesion. (2) Favoring the demand-driven approach is relevant in a closed economy; it is less so if we take into account the current trade globalization. Demand is more or less internal and more or less external, depending on the size of the country and its degree of openness. In the relatively closed Latin American economies, favoring internal demand is relevant if, however, increases in purchasing power are offset by an industrial policy aimed at increasing labor productivity growth and keeping the exchange rate depreciated in order to preserve a minimum of competitiveness.

Relatively Closed but Dependent and Increasingly Vulnerable Economies

In contrast to many Asian economies, Latin American economies are relatively closed to international trade and participate little in the international value chain – with the exception of Mexico and some Central American countries – but are generally very open to financial flows. From a trade point of view, they have opened up at the average rate of global openness. Tariffs are particularly high on capital goods and intermediate products and are falling relatively less than in Asia.

Generally speaking, in the first ten years of this new millennium, globalization in Latin America has had positive effects: less external debt, more growth, less inflation (except in Argentina), better-controlled budgets, higher real wages, and less poverty. However, they have entered a deep crisis from which they are struggling to emerge (Brazil then Argentina and to a lesser extent Mexico in 2019) or economic activity is slowing down. They are experiencing all the perverse effects of globalization, namely a fragmentation within each nation between the regions that "win" and those that lose with its manifestations in terms of increased unemployment, particularly among young people[8] and the inability to return to pre-crisis wage levels for Brazil and Argentina.

External constraint is one of the wounds of Latin American countries. Their high vulnerability is at the origin of strong devaluations of their currencies, devaluations followed by crises, and then economic recovery. Of course, it can be considered a priori that despite deindustrialization, to which we shall return later, the growing inability to export complex products – unlike many Asian countries – can be compensated for by a boom in raw material exports. It is true that, between 2000 and approximately 2014, the external constraint may have disappeared or eased due to both the rise in commodity prices and the volumes exported to fast-growing Asian countries that are partially devoid of these raw materials. But the mirage is short-lived and its effects are deleterious in several ways: it undermines corporate profitability and encourages deindustrialization via rising exchange rates. In contrast to the production of goods, where competitiveness depends on factors that can be controlled in the country, such as policies favoring innovation, social and training policies allowing mobility, or even labor flexibility, the abundance of foreign exchange from the export of raw materials delays the necessary structural reforms.

In the context of economies that are opening up to external trade, the production conditions for the internal market in terms of competitiveness must eventually approach and align with those prevailing on the external market (Salama 2012, 2019b; Brest López, García Díaz, and Rapetti 2019). In other words, not respecting these constraints means condemning oneself either to seeing entire segments of the industry disappear for lack of sufficient competitiveness or to practicing protectionism in whatever form, which is protective in the short and medium term for entrepreneurs, and protective in the short and medium term for employees. On the other hand, to align oneself in the long run with the conditions of production prevailing abroad is both to use aggressive protectionism and to demand that the State practice an industrial policy allowing the emergence of dynamic production sectors with increasing technological density and high elasticity of demand in relation to income, likely to acquire market shares abroad and to alleviate external constraints.

Can the "Para-Keynesian" Theses Be Applied to Semi-Industrialized Economies?

The trend toward stagnation in advanced economies has two main origins: excess savings, on the one hand, and the ineffectiveness of monetary policy on the other. Excess savings are mainly due to population ageing and growing inequality. The population is ageing and older people are saving more than working people. Inequalities in income and wealth are increasing significantly as a result of the growing weight of finance and technological change, and when tax measures are decided, the richest categories get most of the tax reduction. This development is somewhat offset by social transfers to the poorest, which are almost non-existent in Latin America.

Fiscal Regressivity Very Little Compensated by Social Transfers in Brazil

Recent studies confirm and clarify the relatively small positive effect of taxes net of transfers. Birdsall, Lustig, Meyer (2014),[9] thus distinguish four types of income: (1) primary income, i.e. all income received by individuals, whether active or inactive, (2) disposable income, i.e. primary income minus direct taxes and plus monetary transfers, (3) post-tax income, i.e. disposable income minus indirect taxes net of subsidies and finally (4) final income including a monetary estimate of public expenditure on health and education. In Brazil in 2009, as conditional cash transfers are more important for the poor (here less than 4 PPP dollars per day) and direct taxes are almost nil, their disposable income increases (+33%), that of vulnerable categories (between 4 and 10 PPP dollars per day) increases (+8.4%) while that of the richest (more than 50 PPP dollars per day) decreases (−6.2%) insofar as the latter pay direct taxes, and that of the middle classes (between 10 and 50 PPP dollars per day) remains relatively stable (+1.1%). The incidence of indirect taxes differs greatly according to income groups. The post-tax income of the poor rises by 15.1% relative to primary income, i.e. the difference between primary income and disposable income is halved because of the payment of direct taxes. The post-tax income of the middle classes is reduced by 14% and that of the richest by 20.7% in relation to their respective primary income. As a result, inequalities decrease slightly. It is only if one considers the final income that one observes a strong progressiveness from which the poor and the vulnerable benefit: this income is 125.8% higher than the primary income for the poor, 23.2% higher for the vulnerable categories but −6.6% for the middle classes and −19.7% for the rich.

According to this line of thought, increasing inequality increases the overall savings rate, with the better-off saving more than the poorer groups. In doing so, loanable funds grow, leading to a significant drop in interest rates. This fall in interest rates does not reduce savings and encourage consumption or investment, contrary to the teachings of the neoclassical trend. According to Summers, monetary policy is no longer effective today (Summers 2014; Summers and Lukasz 2019). Manipulating the interest rate consistent with full employment and low inflation (FERIR[10]) has lost its effectiveness. The interest rate has declined substantially in developed countries, but growth has not become sustainably higher. Lowering the basic interest rate to promote higher growth and escape the depressing effects of excess savings would lead to increased financial instability. Full employment, a higher growth rate, and financial stability cannot be achieved simultaneously through the interest rate alone. Fiscal policy therefore remains the preferred option, as effective demand becomes insufficient to generate investment that can fuel strong growth. From this point of view, it is a Keynesian thesis even if the analysis of the determination of interest rates departs from it. Fiscal policy could revive economic activity and help to escape the trend of stagnation.[11] This thesis therefore favors demand rather than supply to explain the tendency to stagnation. This thesis contrasts with the supply-side thesis, which considers that the decline in total factor productivity – produced by exogenous causes – would explain both the fall in potential growth, the reduction in actual growth, the decline in labor productivity leading to the reduction in real wages and, in turn, the fall in the growth rate. In the so-called demand hypothesis, the one we favor, the origin of the decline in growth is not exogenous. The liberalization of the labor market, the fourth technological revolution favoring a bipolarization of jobs and incomes, financialization, and the transformation of the age pyramid finally cause real wages to fall – or rise modestly – coupled with growing inequalities in labor incomes. The shortfall in effective demand leads to a relative decline in accumulation due to an attraction to financialization – financial "investment" is considered as savings –, a decline in potential growth and a decline in labor productivity growth, or even an increase in idle production capacity (Salama 2018b). The latter increases production costs and lowers margins unless it can be offset by a reduction, or small increase, in real wages.

Is Such an Analysis Relevant for Latin American Countries?

The "interest rate compatible with full employment and low inflation" (the RRIF) is not a relevant analytical tool for semi-industrialized countries and, in general, for developing countries. Full employment ignores the importance of informality in Latin American emerging countries. Informality is far from being marginal, as lower interest rates reduce the financial attractiveness of the country, which in turn leads to financial instability (internal and external) and deindustrialization. Their currency is not a key currency, and, as Haussmann pointed out, this is an original sin, and some of them, like Brazil, have practiced a policy of very high interest rates for several decades. It is only recently that this country has begun to align itself with the developed countries by sharply lowering its basic interest rate, without this having had a positive effect on growth, which remains very modest. The only positive effect has been a reduction in public debt charges, which is not negligible.

High Levels of Job Informality and Poverty

Informal employment is very important, as are absolute poverty rates. On the other hand, formal employment – including public employment – in 2015 was most often substantial. They varied from 30% of total employment in Bolivia to 37% in Peru, 42% in Colombia, 53% in Brazil, and 54% and 62%, respectively, in Mexico and Argentina.[12] Informality and absolute poverty declined in the 2000s, especially in countries led by progressive governments. But with the recent crisis, informality and poverty are increasing again, especially in Argentina and Brazil and Venezuela, deeply affected by an unprecedented economic crisis. Social spending (health, education, pensions) has increased more (Argentina, Brazil, Venezuela, etc.) or less (Colombia, Mexico, etc.) strongly, contributing to the structural decline in poverty and the virtual disappearance of youth illiteracy.

What about Informality?

Generally speaking, informality has two origins in Latin America: (1) The first is the result of specific production relationships: authoritarianism–paternalism has been predominant until recently in the countryside and in small towns. Employment then takes on aspects of favor, especially in small businesses, which make the person who finds a job feel obliged to his employer. The employer does not have to declare it, underpays it and imposes so-called non-decent working conditions in violation of the labor code. The counterpart of this authoritarianism is paternalism: The employer has a "moral" obligation to take care of his employee when he is sick. The fact is that with the generalization of goods and the rise of capitalism, this counterpart gradually disappears and then remains the informal, illegal aspect with regard to the labor code, social security, and taxation. (2) The insufficiently high investment rate, demographic growth, and migration from the countryside to the cities. Companies cannot then offer a sufficient number of formal jobs. The search for survival jobs, or even strict survival jobs, develops and informality with it. Thus, the informal sector in itself cannot be considered as an informal sector but rather as an interweaving of informal and formal activities (jobs), each relying on the other and vice versa.

More generally, with few exceptions, entrepreneurs are more rentier than Schumpeterian in America. This "cautious" behavior is reflected in a low investment rate. In Latin American history, at least in the 1950s–1970s, it was most often the state that replaced a failing social stratum and invested massively. When the state disengages, as has been the case for the last 30 years, the investment rate declines, public investment is reduced to purchases, is insufficient to remove the obstacles to sustainable growth and is not the necessary complement to stimulate private investment. The attraction of finance and investments abroad (Shorr and Wainer, 2018, etc.) remains. This rentier character, rooted in the history of Latin American countries, is changing. Less present when the state intervenes, more present when the state withdraws, and the country once again specializes in the production of income products. This is what we shall see.

Does Deindustrialization Explain the Low Growth Rate of GDP per Capita over the Long Term?

Should Priority Be Given to Research and Industry? An Overview of Where New Technologies Are Produced and Used

With the digital revolution, the unit price of computing power per second has fallen exponentially since 1950 and especially since the 2000s. Computer and digital technologies, integrated with other technologies, are improving performance. Finally, these technologies are paving the way for network effects[13] particularly powerful so that production is done at increasing yields. As noted by the Conseil d'orientation pour l'emploi:

> by encouraging the emergence of new models, digital technologies are no longer just a new brick enabling us to go further in terms of automating tasks and optimising production processes: they radically call into question the functioning and organisation of certain sectors and sectors, and enable the emergence of new ones, which raises regulatory issues. (2017, 15)

We Are Therefore in the Presence of a Profound Rupture

To a large extent, innovation performance reflects the effort made in new technologies. In a recent study, Scott Kennedy (2017) presents the set of composite indices constructed to measure innovation. These indices take into account the effort made in research and development as a percentage of GDP, the number of students enrolled in science, the number of scientific publications, exports of high-tech products, the number of patents, even the quality of institutions, etc. The sub-indices retained, their number and their weighting differ according to the composite indices calculated. The National Innovation Index constructed by the Chinese Ministry of Science and Technology includes 40 countries, with China ranking 18th, slightly up since 2011. The index compiled by Bloomberg is based on 69 countries. Between 2014 and 2016, China's ranking has dropped to 21st place. The index compiled by the World Economic Forum includes 135 countries. China ranked 29th in 2009 and 2016, with a dip between 2010 and 2015. The composite index of

Cornell University, INSEAD, considers 128 countries and is constructed from 103 indices. China ranks 25th in 2016, with a particularly high score for the sub-indices of technology production and knowledge (6th place) and a low score for the quality of institutions (79th place). Finally, it can be observed that in 2016, the highest score was obtained by the United States, followed by Germany and South Korea, then Japan, further by China, and much further by India and Brazil.

If we limit ourselves to the effort made in research and development, we see that China devoted a little less than 1% of its GDP in 2000 and a little more than 2.1% in 2016, far behind South Korea (4.3%), Japan (3.4%) and the developed countries (Germany and the United States: 2.9%) but much more than Brazil, 1.2% in 2014 or Argentina, 0.6%, according to the World Bank and UNESCO. When we measure this effort in absolute terms, the gap between China and Brazil is much greater. This gap is 12 to 1 since, with an equivalent GDP per capita (PPP), its population is seven times larger. It is understandable that "small" countries must devote more resources to research and development as a percentage of GDP than large countries (and have a more targeted policy) if they are not to miss out on the ongoing industrial revolution. This is what South Korea and Israel, for example, are doing, each spending 4.3% of their GDP on research and development. This is the case in the United States, which is spending 4.3% of its GDP on research and development.

The rise of digital technology and its applications is thus profoundly uneven from one country to another. A few developed countries are at the forefront of the production of new technologies, namely Japan, Germany, the United States, and Switzerland in particular, and some are highly specialized in a limited number of technologies: Israel. Some emerging countries are beginning to catch up with these developed countries: China and South Korea; other "emerging countries" – Brazil, Argentina, Mexico – are either being ousted or threatened with being ousted,[14] in spite of some flagships using imported new technologies such as Embraer in Brazil or Softtek in Mexico.

Table 1.4 Latin America, research and development as a percentage of GDP (2011)

Country	2004	2008	Pays	2004	2008
Paraguay	0.08	0.06	Chile	0.40	0.40
Colombia	0.16	0.15	Cuba	0.56	0.49
Panama	0.24	0.21	Argentina	0.44	0.52
Ecuador	0.07	0.25	Uruguay	0.26	0.64
Mexico	0.40	0.38	Brazil	0.90	1.09
Costa Rica	0.37	0.40	Latin America and the Caribbean	0.53	0.63
			OECD	2.17	2.33

Source: ECLAC, and OECD/CEPAL (2012).

It is important to distinguish between two cases: countries that produce new technologies and disseminate them in their industrial and service sectors and to consumers, and those that do not produce new technologies and only disseminate them in their industrial and service sectors and to consumers. The former, by producing these new technologies, enter the international division of labor in a positive way. Their exports acquire high income elasticity of demand and non-cost competitiveness. If they do not take advantage of this diffusion of new technologies to modernize their production apparatus and eventually participate in their production, their inclusion in the international division of labor becomes regressive because of their relative inability to export complex products (Ding and Hadzi-Vaskov 2017).[15]

Access to imported goods incorporating new technologies, especially capital goods, is increasingly dependent on the price of the raw materials they sell abroad. This risk of new dependence may limit their ability to invest when it becomes more expensive to import capital goods. This is not the only risk. It has often been written that industrial revolutions have not led in the medium term to increased unemployment precisely because many jobs have been created to manufacture new machinery. If these machines are not produced, then the risk of not being able to avoid an increase in unemployment is real.

Latin America is missing out on the ongoing industrial revolution. The spread of new technologies around the world is faster than in the past, but it is also more uneven between and within nations. It is less rapid in Latin America, including in the most powerful countries of the American subcontinent such as Brazil, Mexico, Argentina or Colombia, and Chile. From this point of view, Latin America is falling further behind the major Asian countries and the developed countries. It is uneven within nations, among companies and particularly in Latin America. Some firms are adopting new technologies quickly, while others are either slowing down their adoption or are unable to do so quickly enough. The already high dispersion of productivity levels in the industrial sector, broadly defined, is increasing. Barring institutional measures such as raising the minimum wage above productivity growth, there is a strong risk that inequalities in labor income, measured in terms of average wages, will increase between firms, those that adopt these technologies and those that do not do so to the extent necessary to remain competitive. In addition to these growing inequalities between companies, there are also inequalities generated by the use of these technologies. Routine jobs are being partly replaced by increased automation in certain sectors, leading to a bipolarization of jobs (highly skilled–low-skilled), which is likely to accentuate the bipolarization of labor income (Salama 2018b).

To the extent that Latin America has lagged behind, these effects have been slow to appear, although in some sectors, such as the automotive industry or finance, they are beginning to manifest themselves. But even if this diffusion is slower than elsewhere, it tends to accelerate, and these effects will appear more clearly. The job opportunities created by the production of these technologies are scarce, since they are almost non-existent; only those generated by their use remain. Also, it is possible that so-called informal activities may swell, this time as a result of the relative inability to create enough new jobs in sectors with increasing productivity.

Focus on Industry?

Some economists, particularly Brazilian ones such as Lisboa M., President of IBRE in Brazil, question the need to give priority to industry. Their arguments seem to make sense. Growth was a little more significant with the recovery of the economies in the 2000s – at least until around 2015 – than in the 1990s when industry was in decline. From this point of view, the reprimarization of the Latin American economies would not only be favorable to growth but would also lead to less external constraints (as long as sales of raw materials in value terms continue to grow at a sustained rate) and less inflation, thanks to the double effect (1) of the appreciation of the national currency causing a relative reduction in the price of imported products and (2) of their greater competitiveness resulting in lower prices. Thus, for these economists, it does not matter what the origin of growth is. It may come from services, the exploitation of raw materials, civil construction, or industry and it would be a mistake to consider that industry should be favored.

There is no consensus on this point of view. Kaldor and Vervoorn's work on the relationship between industrial growth rates and labor productivity, Hirschman's work on the upstream and downstream knock-on effects of industry and its most dynamic sectors and Thirwall's work on the limits to growth when the import capacities of other countries act as constraints on export growth, all show the strategic role of industry for growth and its capacity to generate jobs in other sectors. When the different sectors, ranked according to the relative importance of the formality of their jobs, are compared with the number of indirect jobs created, it can be seen that in Argentina in 2013, for example, for every direct job created in industry, 2.45 indirect jobs were created, far more than in trade, catering or civil construction, where informal jobs predominate, according to Coatz D. and Scheingart D. (2016, 37). Generally speaking, industry – understood in a broad sense, including telecommunications and certain sophisticated services – is a powerful multiplier of jobs in other sectors (services, construction, etc.), allowing a densification of the economic fabric, an opportunity to control the future.

There can be no doubt that in the past supporting industrialization may have led to a deterioration in the environment. Unfortunately, it is not the only one. The exploitation of raw materials, whether agricultural or mining, has a strong negative impact on the environment and the health of the people living in the areas close to these farms.

A Consequent Deterioration of the Environment

The exploitation of raw materials of agricultural and mining origin has been carried out both with contempt for the environment, with a questioning of the new rights obtained by the Indian populations increasingly returned to their status as sub-citizens of yesterday in the Andean countries, and a deterioration of the health of peasants and miners.[16] It is then "justified" by governments, including progressive ones, by the budgetary resources coming from the exploitation of these raw materials, which are used, in the best case, to finance an increase in social spending (schooling, health) so that the sacrifice of the present generation can be beneficial for future generations.

Conflict between the Present and the Future, Generations Sacrificed

A policy that takes into consideration all the pillars defining sustainable development (environmental, economic, social) is not easy to design without creating conflicts of interest. Indeed, sustainable development brings in its wake a number of essential questions concerning the "buen vivir": (1) Should the present be sacrificed in the name of future improvements, or more precisely, should we accept that the rights of the Indians, their living conditions, their health, their cultures and the symbolism in which they are exercised, be partially or totally cut back because the financial resources provided by the exploitation of mines, the construction of roads to transport raw materials, could finance expenditure on education, infrastructure, and health, which these populations, poor today, badly need in order to overcome their poverty in a sustainable manner? A conflict between present and future, which, in this case, takes on a particular value because of the past of exclusion that these populations have suffered and the more or less clear commitments of governments to break with this past. (2) Can sustainable development be conceived by respecting the capitalist logic taking into account the particularities of the situation of the Indians and the damage caused by the exploitation of megamines, damage that includes all the ecological, sanitary, social, and cultural dimensions? More precisely, we must be inspired by a statist approach, but what about pluri-nationality, or an approach that does not accept modernity in that it has enslavement and domination effects and insists on decentralization, local powers, a rejection of full and complete commodification, respect for ecology and an aspiration toward degrowth.[17] In reality, beyond the promises, it is the developmentalist position that has imposed itself to the detriment of the immediate interests of the Indian populations.

The conclusion that growth of the industry and preservation of the environment are always incompatible is not, however, demonstrated.

Industrialization can and must obey environmental constraints laid down by States. How? Within what limits? This is an essential discussion but one that goes beyond the scope of this paper. The growth of industry creates more jobs and productivity than any other sector, provided that companies are not allowed to seek maximum profit at the expense of the environment. For this reason, we attach particular importance to the negative consequences of deindustrialization on employment and growth.

Early Deindustrialization in Latin America Is Linked to the Low Rate of Investment and a Largely Insufficient Research Effort

Almost all developed countries are undergoing a process of relative deindustrialization of varying degrees. Industry is weighing down in relative terms to the benefit of increasingly sophisticated services. In contrast to these countries, Latin American countries are experiencing early deindustrialization. With the exception of Argentina, it occurs when per capita income at the start of this process is approximately half that of the developed countries at the time their deindustrialization begins. Deindustrialization is reflected in a relative and absolute decline in industrial employment, the destruction of part of the industrial fabric, and an inability to produce high- and medium-technology products on a sustainable basis. It is the hidden face of the rise of rentier economies, more precisely of rentier behavior with the rise of financialization and primary activities intended for export. Paradoxically, when the country opts for exports of manufactured products, as Mexico did in the 1980s, deindustrialization develops in industrial sectors oriented toward the domestic market because no industrial policy was implemented to locally integrate upstream or downstream activities.

Why Early Deindustrialization: What Are Its Effects on Growth?

Deindustrialization is not a linear process. It is irregular, differing among the major Latin American countries. In Mexico, deindustrialization concerns companies oriented toward satisfying domestic demand. Conversely, industrial goods are growing as demand from the United States and Canada intensifies. It is therefore a twofold process: deindustrialization and industrialization. There is a clear separation between the internal and external markets because there is no link between these two markets, except in part for the motor vehicle sector. In Argentina, the two processes of deindustrialization and industrialization are not concomitant. Deindustrialization is greater than in other countries, but a phase of deindustrialization is followed by a relatively brief phase of reindustrialization when the Convertibility Plan crisis was overcome

Table 1.5 Levels of GDP per capita (in 1990 PPP dollars) at the onset of deindustrialization in selected OECD and Latin American countries, 1950–2011

Country	Top share of manufacturing in GDP			Top share of manufacturing employees in GDP		
	Part (%)	Year	GDP per capita	Part (%)	Year	GDP per capita
Developed OECD countries						
Canada	23.29	1961	8833	22.73[a]	1970	12050
France	25.40[b]	1961	7718	27.89	1974	13113
Germany (Fed. Rep.)	40.65	1961	7952	39.39[a]	1970	10839
Japan	32.63	1970	9714	27.44	1973	11434
Spain	23.33	1972	7099	27.47	1971	6618
Sweden	26.94	1974	13885	28.29	1974	13885
Great Britain	36.90	1955	7868	41.83	1954	7619
United States	26.47	1953	10613	27.83	1953	10613
Latin American countries						
Argentina	34.85	1976	7965	24.69[c]	1984	7426
Brazil	32.47	1985	4914	17.08	1978	4678
Chile	19.57	1974	4992	16.80	1976	4347
Colombia	20.05	1976	3713	25.95[d]	1978	4042
Mexico	23.34	1988	5771	19.56	2000	7275
Peru	21.51	1988	3766	23.24[e]	1986	3946
Uruguay	23.42	1986	6015	30.57	1974	5123
Venezuela	30.85	1986	8725	17.18	1987	8805

Sources: Calculations by Victor Krasilshchikov (2020) from UNCTAD and ILO data (for 1970–2011); for the United Kingdom and the United States in the 1950s–1960s: UK Central Statistical Office (1961, 105–107, 130, 239, 243; 1965, 107; 1970, 118, 279, 285); US Bureau of the Census (1956, 296; 1959, 304, 307; 1961, 203, 207, 301, 304; 1965, 326); OECD (1979, 7–8, 103–104, 195–196); MoF (1998, table 1.6, 1); GGDC (2013).

Notes:
[a] Approved data before 1970 are not available.
[b] Data borrowed from the National Institute of Statistics and Economic Studies. Databases. Annual national accounts base 2010.
[c] Gran Buenos Aires.
[d] Seven main cities in the country.
[e] Lima and suburbans.

in the early 2000s, and then a phase of deindustrialization again.[18] In Brazil, deindustrialization is irregular: relatively pronounced from 1985 to 1996, slowed down afterward and then again, but then more subdued.

Why is there early deindustrialization in Latin America's semi-industrialized economies? Three variables have a direct impact on unit labor costs and thus on the competitiveness of industry[19]: the real exchange rate against the dollar, the wage rate, and labor productivity. The exchange rate tends to appreciate against the dollar over a fairly long period of time (Bresser Pereira 2019), interspersed, however, with sometimes severe exchange rate crises or, as at the end of 2010, currency depreciation. Labor productivity growth is very low, with the industrial wage rate growing in Brazil and Argentina – from 2000 to 2015 – beyond the low growth of labor productivity.[20] This is not the case in Mexico (Moreno-Brid et al. 2019). The appreciation of the currency against the dollar, wage increases and very low productivity growth are undermining the competitiveness of firms.[21] Their profitability is affected on average, hence the inadequacy of productive investment and the choices made toward finance, capital flight, and ostentatious consumption (Shorr, and Wainer 2018) result in the destruction of entire sections of the industrial fabric and the dismissal of employees (Salama 2012, 2018b, 2019a, 2019b). In addition to these direct factors, public investment in the infrastructure sector (railways, roads, and energy) has fallen drastically over the last quarter of a century, with public investment not seen as an inhibitor to private investment but as an obstacle to its development. Insufficient investment in infrastructure is today a serious obstacle to sustainable economic recovery, as the World Bank points out in its various reports.

Where the industrial fabric is not very dense and there is a wide variety of natural resources, as is the case in a few Latin American countries, such as Peru, higher raw material prices and increased export volumes have a positive effect on the growth rate. The massive imports allowed by sharply rising export earnings, facilitated by the appreciation of the national currency against the dollar, have little destructive effect on the industrial fabric, which is not very dense. All in all, the growth rate can be relatively high. The variety of natural resources mitigates the negative effects of a fall in the price of raw materials for a simple reason: prices do not all fall at the same time, and some may continue to grow while others decline. This is not quite the case as far as export volumes are concerned: these depend on international demand, which in turn depends on the situation in the importing country(ies). When the demand comes mainly from a single country, then the dependency translates into a high degree of vulnerability.

When the industrial fabric is relatively large, the effects of deindustrialization on the growth rate are different. Several factors explain this specificity. Reprimarization, through its effects on the decline in the competitiveness of industrial products, weakens the industrial fabric in a specific way. The appreciation of the national currency, the increase in real wages beyond a low growth of labor productivity in the industrial sector, affects especially the sectors producing medium-high goods (electrical machinery and equipment, motor vehicles, chemical products except pharmaceuticals, machinery and mechanical equipment, etc.) and high technology goods (aeronautics and space, pharmaceuticals, computer equipment, etc.). As a general rule, the trade balance of the processing industry rapidly turns negative, mainly due to the rise in net imports of medium (especially medium-high) and high-tech goods exports. This was the case as early as 2008 in Brazil (Carta IEDI 2020, n°974), Mexico, and Argentina (Shorr and Wainer, 2018; Lindenboim and Salvia 2015).

The analysis certainly needs to be refined: just because the net imports of medium-high and high-medium-high exports are increasingly negative it does not mean that the signal given is negative as well. On the contrary, negative net imports could signify an effort toward further modernization and the consequent expansion of branches with high growth potential. Unfortunately, this is more or less the case in Latin America. Net imports are more a sign of de-industrialization, especially in the high-potential sectors. They are made to the detriment of these sectors; they do not allow them to grow at the level of what would be necessary for the industrial fabric to be transformed toward greater complexity.[22] As we have seen, the complexity of exports is declining while that of Asian countries is increasing.[23]

Deindustrialization may therefore be accompanied for a time by an increase in the rate of GDP growth. This was the case under Lula's presidencies in Brazil (2003–2011). But this relative increase is moderate, of the order of one point on average compared to the 1990s. The relationship between reprimarization–deindustrialization and growth rates is in fact more complex. The deleterious effects of reprimarization on the profitability of industry, as well as the absence of a significant industrial policy but also fluctuating economic policies depending on conflicts of interest, result in an economic crisis. In the end, with reprimarization, without an industrial and foreign exchange policy to counteract its negative effects, and without fiscal reform, vulnerability increases, and the capacity to rebound weakens due to the weakening of the industrial fabric and the loss of weight of high-tech sectors, which explains the trend toward long-term economic stagnation (Salama 2016, 2019a, 2020a).

The Case of Mexico Is Particularly Emblematic

In order to overcome the crisis caused by an external debt that had become unsustainable, the Mexican government liberalized all its markets in the 1980s. External openness increased sharply at a time when Mexico's industrial fabric was particularly weakened by the debt crisis and the end of various forms of aid to industry. Mexico thus became the most open of the large Latin American countries to international trade. Contrary to the lessons of the doxa, the GDP growth rate did not increase, quite the contrary. From the 1950s to the 1970s, the rate of GDP growth was particularly high during the period when the country's economy was not very open. It was only afterward, with the opening up of its economy in the absence of an industrial policy, that the growth rate declined sharply (Calva 2019). The trend toward economic stagnation was therefore one of the most pronounced in Latin America. Mexico has specialized in the export of relatively sophisticated manufactured products, more so than those exported by other Latin American countries. Logically, these exports should have allowed a positive insertion into the international division of labor, which is a source of higher growth. This did not happen. In fact, the sophistication of the exported goods is only apparent. There is an optical illusion that fades away when we consider not the export of goods but the export of the value added produced in the country. Most exports of industrial goods – with the notable exception of the automotive sector, where integration is higher – are made up of assembled goods. There are therefore few spillover effects, as the degree of national integration is reduced to purchases. Exported goods are only apparently sophisticated, which is confirmed by the data on research and development efforts relative to Latin American GDP that we have seen. The liberalization of foreign trade, the choice to specialize in exports of assembled industrial goods and not to have chosen to increase their degree of integration as South Korea, Taiwan, and now China did, and the absence of industrial policy, explains the lethargy of GDP growth. It is therefore not a game for two (more openness, more growth), but for three (more openness, more State, and more growth) that must be considered.

By Favoring the Withdrawal of the State, Mexico is Missing out on Modernization

Rufino Matamoros-Romero (2018) recalls the arguments put forward in the early 1980s to justify the withdrawal of the state from Mexico under the presidency of Salinas de Gotari. According to Aspe, the president's programming secretary and theorist of state withdrawal, Mexico no longer needed state intervention to allow the upstream and downstream effects (the famous "puzzle" or Hirschman's puzzle, 1958) to be accomplished and economic development to take place. Mexico would have entered a second stage, making State intervention superfluous or even counterproductive.

> In Hirschman's example, once the 'puzzles', parts of the puzzle, have been solved, the remaining pieces begin to fall into place almost automatically. What this means for the role of the state in economic development is that after an initial period of state protection and intervention, growth no longer responds as strongly to increased interventionism as it did during the early stages of industrialization. Moreover, this analysis conveys the idea that, given the basic institutional framework, indirect support to economic activity through deregulation, privatization, trade liberalization and a competitive environment that.
> (Aspe and Gurría 1992, 9 quoted by Matamoros-Romero, 16)

The authors forget to point out that for Hirschman the "puzzles" mentioned can only be understood in terms of dynamics; in other words, that they are infinite. They are in fact reproduced each time an upstream or downstream effect has been achieved with the help of the State. Others appear to be generated by them. From then on, development can be identified with the density of these upstream and downstream effects. It is only in this way that the industrial fabric can acquire strength and allow for strong growth, generating employment and increasing labor income. As Rufino Matamoros-Romero shows, this has not been the case in Mexico since the withdrawal of the State. When comparing two periods, 1996 and 2011, there are relatively few changes toward both downstream and upstream. The "modernization" announced by the withdrawal of the State has not taken place. The upstream and downstream effects have not been realized or have been realized only to a limited extent, and it is the imports and exports of semi-finished products that have replaced a possible materialization of these effects, even if only partial, which have become very difficult in the absence of State intervention. The export industry, with the exception of the automotive sector, has functioned as an "enclave economy" (Calva 2019, 589), hence the few spillover effects (Ibarra 2008) and the ensuing weak growth (Romero 2020).

Specializing in the export of assembled industrial goods, Mexico has industrialized, yet it can also be considered to have deindustrialized. With the notable exception of its automotive sector, the domestic market is not connected to the external market and vice versa. The internal market is subject to external competition, many companies are closing due to lack of competitiveness, and entire sectors are disappearing, replaced by imports of final and intermediate goods. The causes are the same as those analyzed by more closed countries such as Argentina and Brazil or Colombia: insufficient productive investment, resulting in low labor productivity growth, and an appreciating exchange rate with the effect that wages in dollars appear too high even though they are low in local currency. The productivity–dollar wage pair therefore works in favor of deindustrialization on the domestic market. The external market,[24] cut off from the internal market, does not promote cluster effects; there is no dynamization of the internal market due to the lack of economic integration and thus no sustained and sustainable growth.

Does High Volatility Explain the Low Growth Rate of GDP per Capita Over the Long Term?

Volatility and GDP Growth in Latin America and Some Major Countries

There is a clear relationship between large fluctuations and an average growth rate of GDP per capita over a long period, as can be seen in Graph 1.1.

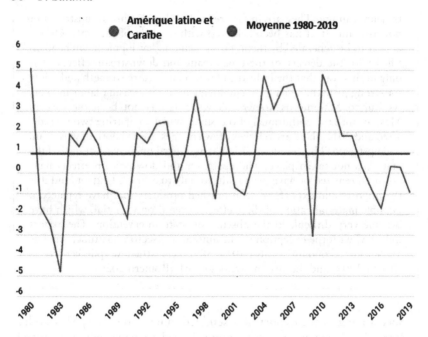

Graph 1.1 GDP per capita growth rates in Latin America and the Caribbean, 1980–2019, calculated in 2011 PPP dollars[25]

Conversely, Asian countries are experiencing low fluctuations and strong GDP growth over the long term. The standard deviation is often used as an indicator of volatility. Asian economies experience low volatility and high growth over long periods: China (1971–1979 and 1980–2004) and Taiwan (1976–2000), for example, and, over somewhat shorter periods, some Latin American countries (Argentina 1991–1998, Brazil 1966–1980, Mexico 1964–1981). According to Saludjian A., with the exception of Argentina, the combination of low volatility and high growth corresponds to a period prior to the debt crisis (1982) in Latin America. Finally, it can be observed that sometimes low volatility, over shorter periods, is accompanied by equally low growth, as in the case of Brazil (1998–2004) and Mexico (1999–2004). Zettelmeyer J. (2006) shows that periods when per capita growth exceeds 2% per year are less important in Latin America than in Asia and, above all, have been shorter since 1950. According to his work, since 1950, there have been 10 periods of growth of more than 2% per capita in Latin America against 11 in Asia, their average duration is 13.9 months in the first case while it reaches 26.1 months in the second, and finally in 30% of cases these boom phases exceed 15 years in Latin America against 73% in Asia. Solimano A. and Soto R. (2005)

likewise note that the percentage of crisis years (negative growth rate) over the period 1960–2002 is 42% in Argentina, 29% in Brazil but only 7% in South Korea and 5% in Thailand. Finally, the UN Economic Commission for Latin America shows in its 2008 report that the standard deviation of the growth rate between 1991 and 2006 is particularly high in Argentina (6.29) and lower in Brazil (2.02) and Mexico (3.05).

Growth Volatility Differs in Argentina, Brazil, and Mexico

In Argentina, phases of strong growth follow periods of deep crises, as can be seen in Graphs 1.2–1.4:

Growth volatility in Brazil is somewhat less pronounced than in Argentina.

The volatility of Mexico's GDP, although high, is relatively low compared to that of Argentina. However, the 1980s (debt crisis), 1993–1995 (tequila effect, the name given to the crisis caused by a very large double deficit in the current account balance and budget), and 2009 (international contagion of the so-called subprime crisis) were characterized by strongly negative growth rates.

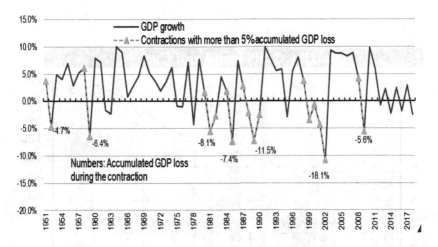

Graph 1.2 Cycles of GDP growth and GDP per capita growth in PPP (2011) in Argentina 1951–2017[26] (*Continued*)

Sources: (A) Kidyba, S y Suárez, L (2017) Aplicación de índices encadenados al empalme de series. Argentina 1950–2015. Programa de investigación en cuentas nacionales (PICNA) – FCE – UBA; OECD calculations. Cited by OECD Economic surveys: Argentina 2019. Laying the foundations for a stronger and more inclusive growth. © Organisation for Economic Co-operation and Development. Retrieved from http://www.oecd.org/economy/surveys/argentina-economic-snapshot/. (B) © Perspective monde – Université de Sherbrooke. Retrieved from https://perspective.usherbrooke. ca/bilan/servlet/BMTendanceStatPays?langue=fr&codePays=ARG&codeStat=NY.GDP.PCAP. PP.KD&codeStat2=x

58   *P. Salama*

Croissance annuelle de la population (en % de la population totale), Argentine

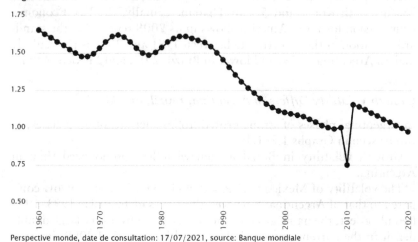

Perspective monde, date de consultation: 17/07/2021, source: Banque mondiale

Graph 1.2 (*Contiued*)

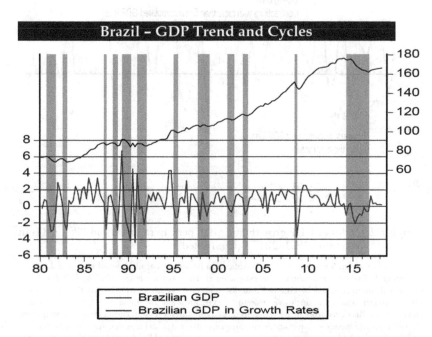

Graph 1.3 Growth rates (right intercept) and cycles (left intercept) in Brazil, 1980–2018.

Source: INEGI, Chauvet, M. (October 2019). Business Cycle Measurement and Dating. International Seminar on Business Cycle Dating. Mexico D.F., p. 10.

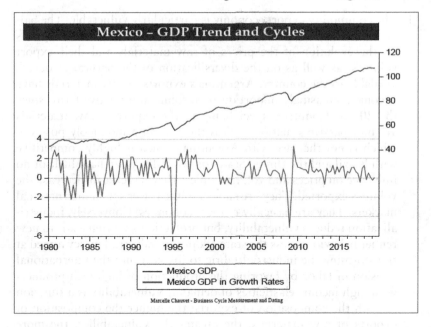

Graph 1.4 Growth rates (right intercept) and cycles (left intercept) in Mexico, 1980–2018.

Source: INEGI, Chauvet, M. (October 2019). Business Cycle Measurement and Dating. International Seminar on Business Cycle Dating. Mexico D.F., p. 12.

A Look Back at Argentina

Argentina's long-term average growth rate is below the average for Latin American countries, as we have seen. The volatility of its growth is particularly high. While in the case of Mexico, the combination of industrialization for export and deindustrialization at the level of the domestic market explains the low growth rate, in Argentina it seems that it is above all the multiplication of "stop and go" phases that underlies the low average growth rate. In Argentina there is a causal relationship between the very high volatility and the low growth rate. The problem then shifts to the analysis of the causes of the very high volatility. They are different according to periods and regimes of growth.

Table 1.6 Main characteristics of business cycles in Mexico, 1980–2009

	Number of Times	*Average Duration*	*Minimum*	*Maximum*
Recession	6	18	11	34
Expansion	5	44	12	71

Source: SICA de INGI, data of September 2019, in Technical Group of Experts for the design of a Committee for the Measurement of the Cycles of the Economy of Mexico (GTDCFC).

1 The commodity export economy is particularly vulnerable. The balance of trade, and most often the amount of tax revenues, depends on the evolution of the prices of raw materials and their export volumes, as well as on the diversification of the natural resources available to the country. Argentina's exports of raw materials have become increasingly important in absolute and relative terms since the 2000s. Countries specializing in the export of raw materials are in a passive situation, unless they are in a monopoly position, which is not the case with Argentina, which is highly competitive with Brazil and the United States on soya. They can have little or no influence on prices and volumes unless they increase or decrease the volumes exported. They are subject to the prices set on international markets. They are basically rentier economies. Conversely, industrialization reduces vulnerability, but protectionism often leads to new rentier behavior unless the state adopts an industrial policy aimed at transforming the industrial fabric to insert it into the international division of labor by favoring the production of high-tech products with high income elasticities of demand. Vulnerability is a function of both the composition of exports: the higher the composition of exports of raw materials, the greater the vulnerability; the more exports of industrial products increase, the lower the vulnerability, provided, however, that the structure of these exports evolves favorably (Fernández, and Curado 2019), which, as we have seen, has not been the case to any great extent.

2 The re-partitioning of economies in the 2000s increases vulnerability. For a long time, governments believed that the external constraint had disappeared because of both the sharp rise in the price of raw materials and the increase in export volumes due to the very strong growth demand from Asian economies.

The fluctuations – the "stop and go" – are mainly explained by the external constraint. The growing trade balance deficit and investors' fears that such a situation may last are causing devaluations of varying degrees of importance. In conditions close to full employment, devaluation is an important factor in price increases (what economists call the Anglo-Saxon expression of pass through[27]). Fearing that rising prices will erode and erase the price competitiveness regained by devaluation, the most frequently advocated economic policy response is to intervene in monetary and fiscal policy; higher interest rates should allow capital that had leaked out to return and restrictive fiscal policy should contain demand and thereby reduce inflation. These two policies in fact cause a recession, hence the term used by the structuralist current in ECLAC for recessive devaluation and their opposition, at least up to and including the 1980s, to such a policy (Keifman 2007).

After a while, the positive effects on the growth of a resumption of exports outweigh the negative effects of containment of domestic demand, especially with the resumption of growth, wages, and employment rise again, causing a further loss of competitiveness, a growing trade balance deficit, and devaluation. In fact, it is not the devaluation itself that is causing major fluctuations. The implosion of the convertibility plan at the beginning of the 2000s, together with the strong devaluation, did not lead either to a lasting price increase or to a recession, quite the contrary. Price increases were short-lived and growth was strong and relatively sustainable, and it was only in 2007–2008 that inflationary recovery became a problem. The competitiveness regained, thanks to the devaluation being only short-lived as long as it is not accompanied by a significant increase in industrial productivity. In other words, the regained competitiveness comes from the fall in wages expressed in dollars, added to which are the effects of the acceleration of price increases following the devaluation. But wages are only one of the variables that explain competitiveness. Two other variables contribute directly to an improvement in competitiveness: the increase in productivity and the maintenance of an undervalued exchange rate, added to which are other variables that indirectly play an important role: the level of education and physical infrastructure. The strong growth of the 2000s can be explained precisely by the maintenance of an undervalued exchange rate and by the use of high idle production capacities and the hiring of employees who were laid off at the end of the 1990s. The limits of growth are unable to improve productivity and to make a change in the industrial fabric toward dynamic sectors with a high research coefficient (Coatz et al. 2018; Lindenboim, and Salvia 2015, in particular the study by Grana).[28] On the other hand, if the elasticity of demand from abroad is low and if the elasticity of supply is insufficient because the industrial fabric has deeply deteriorated, then devaluation is slow to boost export growth. This is what happened during the exchange crisis of 2018; it was only in May 2019 that the trade balance became positive again, at the price, however, of a strong economic crisis coupled with very high inflation and significant drops in purchasing power (Salama 2019b).

Conclusion

The trend toward stagnation cannot be explained in the same way in all the large Latin American countries. Although it has common causes, the weight of each factor differs. Generally speaking, reprimarization has accentuated the rent-seeking behavior of pre-existing entrepreneurs. The rate of investment is low, leading to greater financialization and deindustrialization, which has long-term effects on growth. This concerns more particularly Argentina, Brazil and, to a lesser extent, Mexico, where "exported" labor is its raw material. The industrialization–deindustrialization couple in Mexico does not provide the effects that one would expect in terms of growth points. The reason is the withdrawal of the State and thus the small cluster effects, which are not achieved to

Table 1.7 Causes of the trend of stagnation in the GDP growth rate

	Argentina	Brazil	Mexico
Reprimarization	+	++	+
Industrialization-deindustrialization	+		++
Volatility	+++	+	+
Inequalities	+ then ++	+++	+++

Note: + denotes "more", ++ denotes "much more", and +++ denotes "extreme".

the benefit of imports. What remains is an industrialization by "assembly" unable to compensate for the deleterious effects of deindustrialization. The very high volatility has negative effects on growth. The "stop" leaves deep scars and the "go" does not allow to find the solution in the countries studied, but especially in Argentina. Last but not least, the most important factor is the very high inequality of both income and wealth. It is true that inequalities were not very high in southern cone countries like Argentina – compared to other Latin American countries – but they have become so since the 1990s, and these countries have become Latin American, so the tendency to stagnation until the 1990s was mainly due to external vulnerability and the frequency of "stop and go", since inequalities have played a major role on an equal footing with the northern cone countries in Latin America.

The crisis is structural in Latin America. Therefore, only responses at this level can overcome the obstacles to sustainable development, to the inclusion of those, the majority, who are rejected. Not deciding on them and proposing reforms is a bit like putting a band-aid on a wooden leg, which is most often the case, with the exception of interludes where progressive populist governments have been able to improve a lot of the poorest, without however undertaking radical reforms such as that of the tax system. There are seven of them:

1 The expansion of export agriculture has been to the detriment of peasants. The exploitation of mines has mostly been to the detriment of the Indian population. The reprimarization was carried out with disregard for the environment and the health of the farmers, miners, and the surrounding populations. It has resulted in a deterioration of their health and forced economic migration to the cities. Imposing environmental standards and respecting them is more and more a necessity for survival.

2 In the Latin American context, where the internal market plays an important role, it is necessary to increase the purchasing power from labor. This improvement in purchasing power can boost the internal market. Social justice paradoxically joins economic efficiency: more jobs, less informality.

3 This improvement mainly involves a reduction in social inequalities thanks to a tax reform that is no longer regressive and can promote solidarity. This is not only an ethical but also an economic necessity.

4 It is necessary to improve the capacity of the industrial fabric to respond to increased demand by increasing expenditure on research and development, substantially improving labor productivity and the rate of investment in the industrial sector and the high-tech services linked to it so that enterprises can produce complex high-tech goods on a par with what South Korea has done and is doing.

5 An aggressive industrial policy which places bets on the industries of the future, which will allow an increase in labor productivity and an increase in investments, conditions necessary to make compatible an increase in labor incomes and an improvement in competitiveness.

6 Developing a redistribution policy in favor of the most vulnerable categories.

7 Finally, the choice of an undervalued exchange rate is a sine qua non condition to avoid the perverse effects that an appreciated currency leads to on the industrial fabric. It is not, however, a miraculous measure in itself. In order to be effective and to enable re-industrialization to take place, it must be accompanied by a set of other measures, such as those we have just mentioned. Measures taken in isolation from each other are not effective. Brazil is proof of this: The drastic fall in interest rates and the depreciation of its currency have not been enough to revive the economy in the last two years. It is all of these measures that constitute a breakthrough. The crisis provoked by the pandemic can help foster this break, but it requires alternative projects to be supported by massive mobilization.

Final Conclusion

We are probably entering a new era of capitalism. Capitalism will probably find it very difficult to function in the same way as before. After neo-capitalism marked by increased state intervention after the Second World War and in some Latin American countries, after the withdrawal of the state from its productive capacity in the 1990s and the corresponding neo-liberal phase, we are probably entering a new phase, that of a return to neo-capitalism "without soviets, but with the digital revolution" or perhaps, with a great deal of optimism, that of the construction of socialism, combining soviets, digital and the programmed end of the state tout court rather than its consolidation via a predatory bureaucracy? The deleterious effects of globalization call for a return to protectionism, without it being clear whether this will be the total or partial abandonment of the international splintering of the value chain or whether it will be partial in the name of national sovereignty. The question from that moment on is to define the cursor, taking into account the sectors to be protected and the production to be relocated. We can see that behind this question is both the question of the limits of the merchant and his profit logic and the question of a new definition of the border between the merchant and the non-merchant.[29] "Let's be realistic, let's ask for the impossible" is the only way out of the well into which Latin American countries have been sinking for so many years.

Notes

1. It is true that there were many critics of globalization, whether from the right, often extreme or from the left. Some, emphasizing their conception of the Nation, advocated a return to protectionism, which sometimes could be likened to autarky; others, more left-wing and green, advocated alterglobalization, rejecting borders and seeking cooperation between States in order to impose much stricter ethical (decent work) and environmental standards.
2. With a few exceptions: The Wuhan memory factory continued to operate amid a period of containment and, more generally, the one producing integrated circuits, although Western demand weakened.
3. See Salama P, (2020b). Retrieved from http://ojs.sociologia-alas.org/index.php/CyC/article/view/155/180 and in a slightly different version accompanied by a text on pandemia in https://herramienta.com.ar/articulo.php?id=3177
4. Mexico is almost a textbook case. Despite its external openness, supposed to boost its growth according to experts from international institutions and many mainstream economists, Mexico's per capita GDP growth rate was much lower than that of the United States over the same period.
5. See Salama (2006a, 2006b, 2015 (English translation, 2016)). See also Medeiros et al. (2014), Afonso (2014), Morgan (2017), Iguales–Oxfam (2015) report.
6. United Nations Economic Commission for Latin America and the Caribbean (UN/ECLAC).
7. The main ones are income inequalities, the structuring of social groups and classes, the world economy thought of as structured and hierarchical, with the center on one side and the periphery on the other. See the analyses of Prébish, Pinto, Furtado, Sunkel, or Noyola from ECLAC. See Rodríguez (1988), Guillen Romo (1994), Weiler (1965), where the authors criticize the thesis of comparative advantages based on a static approach and favor the dynamic one, which consists in betting on new structures.
8. See OIT/ILO (2019). The youth unemployment rate is three times higher than the average adult population.
9. Birdsall, Lustig, and Meyer (2014).
10. FERIR, an acronym for "full employment real interest rate".
11. She's obviously not the only one. The increase in credit to people with modest incomes has a twofold effect in the short term: an increase in demand which is likely to increase the rate of growth despite the stagnation of real wages, or even their reduction, and the rise in income inequality, the possibility of building complex financial products, which are the object of strong speculation and gains. Increased financialization and high growth are compatible until the moment they are no longer compatible, as the so-called "subprime" crisis (2008) has shown.

12. Schteingart (2018). The literature on informal employment is abundant, including the following: Maurixio (2019).
13. A network effect for an activity is said to exist when the value of the use of the product or service increases with the number of users.
14. On the difficulties for Latin American countries not being overwhelmed by the digital revolution and the need for structural reforms, see Valladao (2017). If these countries do not succeed, then: "The alternative is bleak: a very long period of economic and social stagnation, and an ever more unbridgeable gap with the mature digital high-tech industrial societies of the Northern hemisphere" (18).
15. The complexity of a country's exports depends on the effort made in research and development, and the higher the research and development effort, the greater the likelihood that the economy can produce complex products. Exports have two characteristics: Their ubiquity and their diversification. Ubiquity depends on scarcity, which depends either on the natural resources that the country may or may not have or on the capacity to produce sophisticated goods that only a few countries can do. Only the latter is taken into account. In order to isolate the latter and construct an indicator of complexity, we seek to use the diversity of exports to measure the degree of ubiquity and, therefore, complexity. For the analysis of complexity, see the work of Hausmann et al. (2014).
16. There is an abundance of literature today on this subject; see in particular Svampa (2017), Buchardt et al. (2016).
17. Carbonnier, Campodónico, Tezanos Vásquez (2017). See also the Iguales–Oxfam (2015) report.
18. Specifically, between 1935 and 1974, Argentina's industrial production increased by 532%. This period is characterized by a very particular growth regime, known as import substitution. The development of import substitution was not continuous. It is interspersed with phases of stagnation (1948–1952, 1959, 1963, and 1966). In the period that followed (1975–1991) – with the advent of the military dictatorship – there was a decline in industrial production (–16%) and wide fluctuations. Conversely, the implosion of the convertibility plan at the beginning of the 2000s resulted in a sharp devaluation, with industry, once again protected by the devalued exchange rate, growing strongly. In total, between 1935 and 2012, industrial production grew by 945%. From 1974 onward, it lost jobs and its share in GDP fell. However, from 2002 onward, the situation changed. Argentina reindustrialized, but from the second decade of the millennium, the situation changed again (Grana 2015). According to UNIDO (2019), the processing industry index increased from 100 in 2010 to 97 in 2017, before the 2018 crisis. Between the same dates, this index in mainland China rose from 100 to 165. Like other Latin American countries, having opted for a reprimarization of its economy, Argentina is not following the path taken by Asian countries; it is (again) specializing in cash products to the detriment of its industrial fabric. This is an implacable fact. Argentina's economic path does not allow it to integrate positively into the international division of labor (Albrieu et al. 2015).
19. According to the calculations made by Frenkel and Rapetti (2011), the appreciation of the real exchange rate is a major cause of the rise in unit labor costs between 2002 and 2010, followed by the productivity differential. Indeed, labor productivity growth is lower in Brazil, Chile, Argentina, and Colombia than in developed countries or China, followed by higher wage growth than productivity growth in some countries such as Brazil and Argentina. Recall that both the average level and the growth of labor

productivity are very low in Argentina, as well as in other Latin American countries. According to Coatz and Scheingart (2016), at the 2005 peso–dollar exchange rate, if labor productivity growth in the industrial sector is 3% per year in the United States and 4% in Argentina, it would take 101 years to cancel out the productivity differential between these two countries, and if it were 10% per year in Argentina, it would take 15 years. The problem is that we are far from the 3% per year (43).

20. Average data are not always relevant. Dispersion around the average is particularly high in semi-industrialized economies, more so than in advanced economies. Productivity levels differ widely across and within sectors, as do wages for equivalent qualifications, depending on firm size and nationality (OECD/CEPAL 2012). The exchange rate mainly affects the exposed sectors, but differently depending on whether the share of imports in the production of a good is higher or lower.

21. It is, therefore, not the increase in wages alone that affects competitiveness, but the relationship between these three variables. A higher increase in productivity and the maintenance of a depreciated exchange rate can lead to improvements in competitiveness even if wages increase within certain limits.

22. The processing industry grew from 2004 to 2008 in Brazil, then fell, recovered slightly and collapsed in 2015 and 2016, with very little recovery thereafter. These movements are amplified both upward and downward for the high-tech and medium-high tech industries. This is not the case for the other industries, those of medium-low (construction, ship repair, rubber and plastics, metal products, etc.) and low technology (food, drink, textiles, wood, etc.), the latter resisting the crisis slightly better in recent years insofar as it does not collapse. It is falling less than the average for the processing industry. All in all, it can be observed that high-tech and especially medium-high-tech industries experienced a very significant increase in their production until the eve of the 2008 crisis. However, this growth is below that of imports and therefore of domestic demand. For these products, deindustrialization is, therefore, relative at least until that date.

23. For more details, see IEDI (2020).

24. The only major difference from the 1990s is that Mexico is no longer the exclusive assembly plant of the United States. A third player has entered the picture: China. China exports both for the domestic market consumer goods, intermediate goods that participate in the deindustrialization of its domestic market, but also more and more intermediate products that are assembled with goods exported from the United States to Mexico and then re-exported to the United States. This explains both the country's large surplus vis-à-vis the United States and its huge deficit vis-à-vis China (for every dollar exported to China, Mexico imports $9 worth of goods) and the Trump administration's demand for a renegotiation of the agreement between Mexico, Canada and the United States (Ramírez Bonilla 2017).

25. Amérique latine et Caraïbe: Latin America and the Caribbean Moyenne: Average.

26. Croissance annuelle de la population (en % de la population totale), Argentina: Annual population growth (% of total population), Argentina. This translation was not created by the OECD and should not be considered an official OECD translation. The OECD shall not be liable for any content or error in this translation Perspective monde, date de consultation 17/07/2021, source: Banque mondiale: World Perspective, date of consultation 17/07/2021, source: World Bank.

27. See Destaque Depec-Bradesco, March 27, 2019: Argentina: aversao a volatilidade cambial deve continuar a politica economica [Argentina: aversion to exchange rate volatility should continue economic policy].

28. It should be noted that very often, economists who calculate supply elasticities over long periods of time do so on the assumption that the perimeter of the industry remains unchanged, which is far from being the case when deindustrialization is advancing.
29. Knowing the costs of the non-market without making it an absolute constraint is what is at stake, and behind it are not only the relations between the market and the State but also the State's capacity to impose more coercive rules, from which the market had exempted itself by internationalizing itself. It is also that of state control through popular participation, accompanying that of parliament since the state is neither ex machina nor neutral and too often capable of defining its interventions according to a logic of preserving and strengthening its own bureaucracy.

Bibliography

Afonso, J. R. (2014). Imposto de renda e distribuição de renda e riqueza: as estatísticas fiscais e um debate premente no Brasil [Income tax and wealth distribution: tax statistics and a pressing debate in Brazil]. *Revista de Estudos Tributários e Aduaneiros* [Journal of Tax and Customs Studies] I(1).

Albrieu, R., Carciofi, R., Katz, S., Machinea, J. L., Martinez Nogueira, R., Pineiro, M., Rozemberg, R., and Rozenwurcel, G. (2015). *Argentina: una estrategia de desarrollo para el siglo XXI* [Argentina: A Development Strategy for the 21st Century]. Buenos Aires: Turmalina.

Aspe, P., Gurría, J. A. (1992). Keynote Address: The State and Economic Development: A Mexican Perspective. *The World Bank Economic Review* 6, https://doi.org/10.1093/wber/6.suppl_1.9

Bénétrix, A. S., H O'Rourke, K., and Williamson, J. G. (2012). The Spread of Manufacturing to the Poor Periphery 1870–2007. National Bureau of Economic Research.

Birdsall, N., Lustig, N., and Meyer, C. (2014). The Strugglers: The New Poor in Latin America? *World Development* 60.

Bresser Pereira, L. C. (2019). Secular Stagnation, Low Growth and Financial Instability. *International Journal of Political Economy* 48(1).

Brest López, C., García Díaz, F., and Rapetti, M. (2019). El desafío exportador de la Argentina [Argentina's export challenge]. Working Document n°110. CIPPEC.

Buchardt, H-J., Domínguez, R., Larrea, C., and Peters, St. (eds.) (2016). *Nada dura par siempre, neo-extrativismo tras el boom de las materas primas* [Nothing Lasts Forever, Neo-Extrativism after the Raw Materials Boom]. Kassel, Germany: ICDD; Quito, Ecuador: Andean University Simón Bolivar.

CEPAL. (2016). *Latin American Economic Outlook (2016). Towards a New Partnership with China*. Santiago de Chile: CEPAL.

Calva, J. L. (2019). La economía mexicana en su laberinto neo-liberal [The Mexican economy in its neo-liberal labyrinth]. *El Trimestre económico* 343.

Carbonnier, G., Campodónico, H., and Tezanos Vásquez, S. (eds.) (2017). *Alternative Pathways to Sustainable Development: Lessons from Latin America*. Leiden: Brill/Nijhoff.

Cassini, L., García Zanotti, G., and Schorr, M. (2019). Estrategias de financiación en las producciones primarias de la Argentina durante los gobiernos del kirchnerismo (2003–2015) [Strategies for financing primary production in Argentina during the Kirchnerist governments]. *Cyclos* 53.

Chauvet, M. (2019). Business cycle measurement and dating. (Seminar). https://www.inegi.org.mx/contenidos/eventos/2019/cide/P_Marcelle_Chauvet.pdf

Coatz, D., García Díaz, F., Porta, F., and Schteingart, D. (2018). Incentivos y trayectorias de cambio estructural [Incentives and Trajectories of Structural Change]. In *Ensayos sobre desarrollo sostenible, la dimensión económica de la agenda 2030 en Argentina* [Essays on Sustainable Development, the Economic Dimension of the 2030 Agenda in Argentina], edited by R. Mercado. Buenos Aires: PNUD.

Coatz, D., Scheingart, D. (2016). La industria argentina en el siglo XXI: entre los avatares de la coyuntura y los desafíos estructurales [Argentine industry in the 21st century: Between the vicissitudes of the economic situation and the structural challenges]. *Boletín informativo Techint* [Techint Newsletter] 353.

COE. Conseil d'orientation pour l'emploi [Employment guidance council]. (2017). Automatisation, numérisation et emploi, Vol. 1 [Automation, digitization and employment]: Les impacts sur le volume, les structures et la localisation de l'emploi [Impacts on the volume, structure and location of employment]. Retrieved from http://www.coe.gouv.fr/

Cordera, R. (ed.) (2015). *Más allá de la crisis, el reclamo del desarrollo* [Beyond the Crisis, the Call for Development]. Mexico: Fondo de Cultura Económica, and UNAM. More specifically see: Grupo Nuevo curso de desarrollo, El cambio reciente de Mexico [Group New Course of Development, Mexico's Recent Change] (15–76); Ros, J. La trampa del lento crecimiento y tres reformas recientes [The slow growth trap and three recent reforms] (159–182); Moreno-Brid, J.C. Cambio estructural para el crecimiento económico: grandes pendientes de la economía mexicana [Structural change for economic growth: The Mexican economy's great slopes] (183–214).

Della Paoloera, G., Duran Amorocho, X. D., and Musacchio, A. (2018). The Industrialization of South America revisited. Evidences from Argentina, Brazil, Chile and Colombia 1890–2010. Working paper n°243450, NBER.

Ding, X., Hadzi-Vaskov, M. (2017). Composition of Trade in Latin America and the Caribbean. Working paper 17/42, IMF.

Fernández, D. L. and Curado, M. L. (2019). La matriz de competitividad argentina: evolución de la inserción internacional del país ante la controversia de los recursos naturales [The Argentine competitiveness matrix: Evolution of the country's international insertion in the face of the natural resources controversy]. *Revista de la Cepal* 127.

Flexor, G. and da Silva, D. (2019). *La désindustrialisation, les ressources naturelles et Nouveau – Développementisme: le cas du Brésil* [Deindustrialization, Natural Resources and New Developmentalism: The Case of Brazil]. Mimeo.

Frenkel, R. and Rapetti, M. (2011). Fragilidad externa o desindustrialzacion: ¿cuál es la principal amenaza para América Latina en la próxima década? [External fragility or deindustrialization: What is the main threat to Latin America in the next decade?]. *CEPAL, Macroeconomia del desarrollo* [Macroeconomy of development] n°6.

Furtado, C. (1966). *Développement et sous-développement* [Development and underdevelopment]. France: PUF.

GGDC (Groningen Growth and Development Centre) (2013). Maddison Historical Statistics. Maddison Project Database. Retrieved from https://www.rug.nl/ggdc/historicaldevelopment/maddison/data/mpd_2013-01.xlsx

Grana, J. M. (2015). Evolución comparada del sector industrial argentino y estadounidense, entre el rezago productivo y el deterioro salarial [Comparative evolution of the Argentine and U.S. industrial sectors, between production lag and wage deterioration]. *H-Industria* 17.

Grupo Técnico de expertos para el diseño de un Comité para el fechado de los Ciclos de la Economía de México [Technical Group of Experts for the Design of a Committee for the Dating of the Cycles of the Economy of Mexico] (GTDCFC) (2020).

Guillen Romo, H. (1994). De la pensée de la Cepal au néolibéralisme, du néolibéralisme au néo-structuralisme, une revue de la littérature latino-américaine [From Cepal's thought to neoliberalism, from neoliberalism to neo-structuralism, a review of Latin American literature]. *Revue Tiers Monde* [Third World Review] 140.

———(2018). *Los caminos del desarrollo del tercer mundo al mundo emergente* [Third World Development Pathways to the Emerging World]. Buenos Aires: Siglo veintiuno.

Hausmann, R., Hidalgo, C. A., Bustos, S., Coscia, M., Simoes, A., and Yldirim, M. A. (2014). *The Atlas of Economic Complexity, Mapping Paths to Perspectives.* Cambridge, MA: Center for International Development, Harvard University.

Hirschman, A. (1958). *The Strategy of Economic Development.* New Haven: Yale University Press.

Ibarra, C. (2008). La paradoja del crecimiento lento de México [The paradox of Mexico's slow growth]. *Revista de la Cepal* 95.

IEDI. (Instituto de Estudos para o Desenvolvimento Industrial [Institute of Studies for Industrial Development]) (2020). A Complexidade das exportações brasileiras e a concorrência da China [The Complexity of Brazilian Exports and China's Competition] 973. https://iedi.org.br/cartas/carta_iedi_n_972.html

——— (2020). *O retrocesso exportador da industria* [The industry's export setback] 974.

Iguales–Oxfam. (2015). Privilegios que niegan derechos, desigualdad extrema y secuestro de la democracia en América Latina y el Caribe [Privileges that deny rights, extreme inequality and the hijacking of democracy in Latin America and the Caribbean]. https://oxfamilibrary.openrepository.com/bitstream/10546/578871/3/cr-privileges-deny-rights-inequality-lac-300915-summ-es.pdf

Keifman, S. (2007). Le rapport entre taux de change et niveau d'emploi en Argentine. Une révision de l'explication structuraliste [The relationship between the exchange rate and the level of employment in Argentina. A revision of the structuralist explanation]. *Revue Tiers Monde* 189.

Kennedy, S. (2017). *The Fat Tech Dragon, Benchmarking China's Innovation Drive.* Washington, DC: Center for Stratégic and International Studies.

Krasilshchikov, V. (2020). *Brazil as the Case Study of the Middle-Level Development Trap.* New York: Palgrave.

Lindenboim, J. and Salvia, A. (eds.) (2015). *Hora de balance: proceso de acumulación. Mercado de trabajo y bienestar, Argentina, 2002-2014* [Balance sheet time: Accumulation process. Labour market and welfare, Argentina, 2002-2014]. Buenos Aires: Eudeba.

Lo Vuolo, R. M. (2016). Argentina, ¿nos conviene esta receta económica? [Argentina, does this economic recipe suit us?]. Retrieved from https://www.sinpermiso.info/textos/argentina-nos-conviene-esta-receta-economica

Maurixio, R. (2019). *Formal Salaried Employment Generation and Transition to Formality in Developing Countries: The Case of Latin America.* Geneva: ILO.

Medeiros, M., Fereira de Souza, P., and Avila de Castro, F. (2014). O Topo da Distribuição de Renda no Brasil: Primeiras Estimativas com Dados Tributários e Comparação com Pesquisas Domiciliares (2006–2012) [The Upper Tip of Income Distribution in Brazil: First Estimates with Income Data and a Comparison with Household Surveys (2006–2012)]. Retrieved from https://www.scielo.br/j/dados/a/DFDmPCrcnfCnrn7rkTWX63f/abstract/?lang=pt

MoF. (Ministry of Finance of Malaysia). (1998). *Economic Report 1998/1999.* Kuala Lumpur: MoF.

Moreno-Brid, J. C., Monroye-Gomez-Franco, L. A., Salat, I., and Sánchez-Gómez, J. (2019). La evolución de los salarios, causa y reflejo de la desigualdad en México [Wage trends, cause and reflection of inequality in Mexico] (47-67). In *América Latina frente a la hora de la igualdad: avances, retrocesos y desafíos* [Latin America and Equality: Advances, Setbacks and Challenges], edited by A. Barcera Ibarra, R. Cordera Campos. Santiago de Chile and Mexico City: CEPAL – UNAM.

Morgan, M. (2017). Falling Inequality Beneath Extreme and Persistent Concentration: New Evidence for Brazil. Combining National Account, Survey and Fiscal Data. Working paper n°12, WID.

OECD. (1979). *National Accounts of OECD Countries 1960-1977.* Vol. II. Paris: OECD.

OECD. (2018a). *Estudios económicos* [Economic Studies]. Mexico: OECD.

_____(2018b). *Economic Survey.* Brazil: OECD.

_____(2019). *Estudios económicos.* Argentina: OECD.

OECD/CEPAL. (2012). *Perspectives économiques de l'Amérique latine, transformation de l'Etat et développement* [Latin American Economic Outlook, State Transformation and Development]. https://repositorio.cepal.org/bitstream/handle/11362/1450/S2012600_fr.pdf?sequence=1&isAllowed=y

OIT/ILO (2019). *Panorama laboral, América Latina y el Caribe* [Labour Overview, Latin America and the Caribbean]. https://www.ilo.org/americas/publicaciones/WCMS_732198/lang--es/index.htm

Ramírez Bonilla, J. J. (2017). Mexique – États-Unis, d'une relation bilatérale asymétrique à une triangulation productive avec l'Asie pacifique [Mexico - United States, from an asymmetrical bilateral relationship to a productive triangulation with Asia Pacific]. *Revue Recherches Internationales* [International Research Review] 110.

Rifkin, J. (2016). *La nouvelle société du coût marginal zéro, L'internet des objets, l'émergence des communaux collaboratifs et l'éclipse du capitalisme* [The New Society of Zero Marginal Cost, the Internet of Things, the Emergence of Collaborative Communities and the Eclipse of Capitalism]. Paris: LLL.

Rodríguez, O. (1988). *La teoría del subsesarrollo de la Cepal* [ECLAC's Theory of Underdevelopment]. Buenos Aires: Siglo XXI.

Romero, J. (2020). La herencia del experimento neo-liberal [The legacy of the neo-liberal experiment]. *El trimestre económico* 345.

Romero Tellaeche, J. A. (2014). *Los límites al crecimiento de México [The Limits to Mexico's Growth].* Mexico: El Colegio de México, and UNAM.

Rufino Matamoros-Romero, G. (2018). El camino mexicano del lento crecimiento económico: una interpretación espuria de la metáfora del desarrollo como un rompecabezas de Albert O. Hirschman [The Mexican path of slow economic growth: A spurious interpretation of the development metaphor as a puzzle by Albert O. Hirschman]. *Ensayo de Economía* 29(54).

Salama, P. (2006a). *Le défi des inégalités, Amérique latine/Asie: une comparaison économique* [The Challenge of Inequality, Latin America/Asia: An Economic Comparison]. La Découverte. In Spanish: *El desafío de las desigualdades. América Latina/Asia: una comparación económica* [The challenge of inequalities. Latin America/Asia: An economic comparison] (2008). Buenos Aires: Siglo XXI.

_____(2006b). ¿Por qué esa incapacidad para alcanzar un crecimiento elevado y regular en América Latina? [Why this inability to achieve high and regular growth in Latin America?]. *Foro Internacional* XLVI(4).

_____(2012). Les économies émergentes latino-américaines, entre cigales et fourmis [Emerging Latin American economies, between cicadas and ants]. A. Colin. In Spanish with postface (2016). América Latina en la tormenta [Latin America in the Storm]. Colegio de la Frontera Norte and University of Guadalajara.

_____(2015). ¿Se redujo la desigualdad en América Latina? Notas sobre una ilusión [Has inequality been reduced in Latin America? Notes on an illusion]. *Nueva sociedad* 258. Subsequently published in *Problemes économiques*, la documentation française [Economic problems, French documentation] (2016).

_____(2016). Reprimarización sin industrialización, una crisis estructural en Brasil [Reprimarization without industrialization, a structural crisis in Brazil]. *Herramienta*.

_____(2018a). Is Change in Globalization's Rythm an Opportunity of Latin American Emerging Countries? In *The Political Economy of Lula's Brazil*, edited by P. Chadaravian. New York: Routledge.

_____(2018b). Nuevas tecnologías: ¿bipolarización de empleos e ingresos del trabajo? [New technologies: bipolarization of jobs and income from work?]. *Problemas de desarrollo* [Development Issues] 195.

_____(2018c). Argentine, Brésil, Venezuela, Populisme progressiste des années 2000, l'heure des bilans [Argentina, Brazil, Venezuela, Progressive Populism in the 2000s, time to take stock]. Revue Contretemps [Setbacks Journal] 38.

_____(2019a). Le Brésil à reculons? [Brazil going backwards?]. *Revue Les Possibles* [The Possibles Journal]. https://france.attac.org/nos-publications/les-possibles/numero-20-printemps-2019/dossier-lien-entre-l-evolution-des-rapports-internationaux-et-la-democratie/article/le-bresil-a-reculons

_____(2019b). Argentina, para avanzar sin retroceder [Argentina, to move forward without retreating]. *Herramienta* 62.

_____(2019c). Los dos "pecados originales" de los gobiernos progresistas de Argentina y Brasil. Revista de Economía Institucional 21(40).

_____(2020a). América Latina: adiós industria, hola estancamento [Latin America: Goodbye industry, hello stagnation]. *Realidad Económica* [Economic Reality] 329(49).

_____(2020b). Notas sobre las ochos plagas latino-americanas [Notes on the eight Latin American pests]. *Revista ALAS*. Retrieved from http://ojs.sociolo-gia-alas.org/index.php/CyC/article/view/155/180

Saludjian, A. (2003). *De la volatilité macro-économique à la vulnérabilité sociale: le cas du Mercosur, une critique du Régionalisme Ouvert* [From macroeconomic volatility to social vulnerability: The case of Mercosur, a critique of Open Regionalism]. Thesis Paris XIII. (L'Harmattan 2006).

Schteingart, D. (2018). El rompecabezas del mercado laboral latino-americano [The puzzle of the Latin American labour market]. *Nueva sociedad* 275.

Serrano, F. and Summa, R. (2012). A desaleracao rudimentar da economia brasileira desde 2011 [The rudimentary slowdown of the Brazilian economy since 2011]. *OIKOS* 11(2).

_____(2015). *Aggregate Demand and the Slowdown of Brazilian Economic Growth in 2011-2014*. Washington, DC: CEPR.

Shorr, M. and Wainer, A. (eds.) (2018). *La financiarización del capital, estrategias de acumulación de las grandes empresas en Argentina, Brasil, Francia y Estados Unidos* [The Financialization of Capital, Accumulation Strategies of Large Companies in Argentina, Brazil, France and the United States]. Buenos Aires: Futuro Anterior.

Solimano, A., Soto, R. (2005). *Economic Growth in Latin America in the Late of 20th Century: Evidence and Interpretation*. Santiago de Chile: CEPAL. Serie macroeconomía del desarrollo [Development Macroeconomics Series] 33.

Storm, S. (2020). *Demand-Side, Secular Stagnation of Productivity Growth.* Institute for New Economic Thinking. https://www.ineteconomics.org/perspectives/blog/demand-side-secular-stagnation-of-productivity-growth

Summers, L. H. (2014). Reflections on the "New Secular Stagnation Hypothesis" (27-41). In *Secular Stagnation: Facts, Causes and Cures*, edited by C. Teuling, R. Baldwin. CEPR. https://voxeu.org/article/larry-summers-secular-stagnation

Summers, L. H. and Lukasz, R. (2019). On falling neutral rates, fiscal policy and the risk of secular stagnation. *Brooking papers on economic activity.*

Svampa, M. (2017). *Del cambio de época al fin de ciclo, gobiernos progresistas, extractivismo y movimientos sociales en América Latina* [From the Change of Era to the End of the Cycle, Progressive Governments, Extractivism and Social Movements in Latin America]. Buenos Aires: Edhasa.

UK Central Statistical Office. (1961). Annual Abstract of Statistics, 1961. L.: Her Majesty's Stationary Office. – XI.

_____(1965). Annual Abstract of Statistics. (1965). L.: Her Majesty's Stationary Office. – XIII.

UNCTAD (United Nations Conference on Trade and Development). (2019). UNCTADstat. Gross domestic product: GDP by type of expenditure, kind of economic activity, total and shares, annual. Retrieved from http://unctadstat.unctad.org/wds/TableViewer/ tableView.aspx

US Bureau of the Census. (1956). *Statistical Abstract of the United States: 1956.* Washington, DC: US Bureau of the Census. – XVI.

_____(1959). *Statistical Abstract of the United States: 1959.* Washington, DC: US Bureau of the Census. – XII.

_____(1961). *Statistical Abstract of the United States: 1961.* Washington, DC: US Bureau of the Census. – XII.

_____(1965). *Statistical Abstract of the United States: 1965.* Washington, DC: US Bureau of the Census. – XII.

Valladao, A. (2017). Climbing the Global Digital Ladder: Latin America's Inescapable Trial. Working Paper, OCP Policy Center.

Weiler, J. (1965). *L'économie internationale depuis 1950* [The International Economy since 1950]. Paris: PUF.

Zettelmeyer, J. (2006). Growth and Reforms in Latin America: A Survey of Facts and Arguments. Working paper 06/210, IMF.

2 Refeudalization in Latin America

On Social Polarization and the Money Aristocracy in the 21st Century

Olaf Kaltmeier

One of the basic contradictions inherent to capitalism is the question of social polarization. While capitalism has promised since the end of feudalism and the emergence of bourgeois society the possibility of individual social upwards mobility based on meritocratic principles, a recently exponentially growing global social inequality has been observed that excludes de facto large population groups. It is probably only recently in periods of social crisis, like after World War II, or during political system-confrontation like in the Cold War, that political programs reducing social polarization emerged. Nevertheless, in capitalist semantics, key concepts like progress, development, liberty, democracy, etc., which emerged in the "Sattelzeit", a time of transformation from feudalism to bourgeois society in the context of the French Revolution, still predominate. Even in postmodern theory, deconstructivism predominates a track of this future-optimistic thinking, if we speak of post-development, post-democracy and, of course, post-modernity. The prefix "post" indicates that our thinking is still directed toward an uncertain beyond.

Refeudalization is the guiding concept of this essay. Against the boom of sociological and philosophical concepts with the "post"-prefix, the prefix "re" is applied here to eliminate implicit, or even explicit, progress-optimistic concepts. Instead, historical cycles are highlighted that may in form and content refer to the past. This historical perspectivation is – in some elements – similar to Aymara-thinking arguing that it is important to look back into the past to see the future (Sanjinés 2013). In his dialectical approach, Karl Marx also argued, "Hegel remarks somewhere that all great, world-historical facts and personages occur, as it were, twice. He has forgotten to add: the first time as tragedy, the second as farce" (1978, 115).

My central hypothesis is that we are witnessing a global historical conjuncture of refeudalization in the early 21st century that is based on extreme social polarization worldwide and in a self-repeating manner on all other spatial levels passing from world-regions to nation-states and urban agglomerations. Obviously, the repetition of historical events

DOI: 10.4324/9781003045632-3

as farce is not a unique characteristic of the contemporary process of refeudalization. In the so-called-Gilded Age in the economic and social history of the United States, we can identify a similar conjuncture of refeudalization (Kaltmeier 2019). But the contemporary process is a global one that affects the entire capitalist world-system.

The anti-capitalist movement "Occupy Wall Street" has the distinction of directing the public's attention toward the top 1% of the richest people in the world. The non-governmental organization Oxfam took up these global social inequalities in its report "An Economy for the 99%" in January 2017 and brought them into the broader political debate (Oxfam 2017). Twenty years ago, the United Nations Development Programme (UNDP) had warned in their World Development Report 1996 that the socio-economic cleavages had grown significantly, so that the net to-wealth of the 358 richest people of the world corresponded to 45% of the wealth of the world population, or 2.3 billion people in absolute numbers (UNDP 1996, 15, 16). Nowadays, the situation is even worse. Since 2015, the richest 1% of the world's population has accumulated more wealth than the entire rest of the world's population. And to translate these naked figures to real flesh and blood: the richest eight men (the gender classification is also meaningful) have as much wealth as 3.6 billion people – or half the world's population. Especially in the last two decades, the number of billionaires has increased significantly. In 2015, the number of billionaires was 2,473 (Wealth-X 2016, 2). The average billionaire in 2014 has a net wealth of USD 3.1 billion (Wealth-X 2016, 16). These numbers indicate a dramatic deepening of worldwide social inequality.

The emergence of hyper-wealth is a worldwide phenomenon that is by no means limited to the geographic north – formed by North America and Western Europe (Krysmanski 2015). The number of billionaires has also increased rapidly in the geographical south. In recent decades, this has been particularly true of Central and South America and the Caribbean. According to Wealth-X, Latin America will have the world's largest growth rate of billionaires in 2014.

Moreover, hyper-richness is even more pronounced in Latin America than in the rest of the world. In contrast to their peers in other world regions, Latin American billionaires are disproportionately rich. Mexico has the world's highest average wealth for billionaires at USD 6.2 billion, although this is mainly due to the hyper-richness of Carlos Slim. In second place among the countries of the world's richest billionaires is Brazil, with an average wealth of USD 5.2 billion.

This historically unprecedented extreme gap between many poor and "average earners" on the one hand and a handful of hyper-rich on the other raises the question of whether the conventional sociological models of social inequality and stratification are still meaningful here. With sober statistical figures, it can be argued that the concentration of wealth has increased rapidly after the crisis of Fordism with its welfare state regulations, the collapse of the Soviet Union and the worldwide rise of neoliberalism. With regard to the United States, economist Thomas Piketty has shown that in the last 30 years, the income of the bottom 50% has not increased, while the income of the 1% of top earners has increased 300 times (2014). A similar situation can be observed in Latin America. In the region of the world where the social gap is widest, the wealth of multimillionaires has increased by 21% per year in the last five years alone. Thus, the morphology of the social structure in many countries in terms of social inequality is again approaching the historical period of the *Ancién Regime* in Western Europe. On the eve of the French Revolution, France's corporative society consisted of 1% to 2% of the nobility, 1% of the clergy, and approximately 97% of the Third Estate. This top 1% of the *Ancién Regime* concentrated 50% to 60% of its income on itself (Piketty 2014, 313, 330) – this is strikingly similar to the figures of today's unequal distribution in world society. Only with regard to this extremely polarized form of social structure, in which the democratic and bourgeois promise of equality has been abandoned, can one speak of a striking tendency toward refeudalization.

But refeudalization not only describes transformations in the social structure, it can also be used as an analytical and articulating concept to understand social transformation in turbo-capitalism, driven by the financial markets (Kaltmeier 2018). As German sociologist Sighard Neckel puts it, "I understand 'refeudalization' in this context as an example of social change involving a paradoxical form of modernization at the heart of modern capitalism. It does not simply lead back to the past. Instead, it refers to a social dynamic of the present in which modernization takes the form of a rejection of the maxims of a bourgeois social order" (Neckel 2010, 5). In this sense, refeudalization is a complex, multifaceted concept that allows for articulating different social dynamics that are usually analyzed in separate ways. Beyond the crucial question of social polarization and its consolidation in estates – an aspect that we discuss in this chapter – we have to take into account the transformation of the value-systems and social norms, the shift in the process of accumulation toward accumulation by dispossession, and in spatial terms the return of multiple walls – from North-South borders to the multi-fragmented urban environments, a shift from neoliberal governmentality toward a renewal of sovereign power and state of exception, and finally, we see a feudal duplication of economic and political power, best expressed with billionaires as presidents – from Donald Trump in the north to Mauricio Macri, Sebastián Piñera and Guillermo Lasso in the south.

Refeudalization: Instructions for Use

Feudalism is a shimmering and controversial term in Latin American social history. As Steve Stern makes clear in his classic overview of the feudalism debate in Latin America, "the feudal 'diagnosis' of the colonial inheritance" (1988, 832) dates back to the 19th century. This feudal persistence is primarily attached to the agrarian regime and the persistence of forms of debt bondage until the 1960s and 1970s. José Carlos Mariátegui already judged accordingly in 1928 in his "Seven Interpretive Essays on Peruvian Reality": "The estate owning *aristocracy* of the colony, holder of power, maintained intact its *feudal rights* over the land and, therefore, over the Indian" (2007, 35).

An almost classic strand of debate on the relationship between feudalism and capitalism from the 1970s onward can especially be found in the Latin American socio-historical and sociological debate in connection with the theory of dependence. The conceptualization of feudalism here is dominated by Marxist theoretical approaches that focus on the exploitation of labor. The debate was given a new twist by the world system approach, which Immanuel Wallerstein presented in the mid-1970s and is still relevant in Latin America today. Wallerstein argued that Europe solved the crisis of feudalism by expanding into the Americas and subsequently building a capitalist world system. On the basis of a broad concept of capitalism – the exploitation of labor for the capitalist world market – the representatives of the world-system approach then argued that in Latin America in the 19th and 20th centuries, feudalism could no longer be spoken of, since these economies were already largely integrated into the international division of labor of the capitalist world market.

Ernesto Laclau, on the other hand, argued that although there was integration into the world market, this would not change the fact that in Latin America, there were several different modes of production at the same time, including a feudal one, which finds its highest expression in the hacienda regime. This is not the place to resolve this debate completely. However, following on from Laclau, it is important to note that within the framework of a world capitalist system, there may well be several interdependent modes of production. This simultaneity of the non-simultaneous is not a relic but is – as the representatives of the Bielefeld approach of articulation using the example of the articulation of subsistence production and capitalist production of commodities – essential for the functioning of the capitalist world system (Evers 1987).

In today's use of terms from the semantic field of feudalism that describes contemporary society, however, it is striking that the question of the exploitation of labor and the status of wage labor in the economic field, a central point of discussion in the socio-historical feudalism-capitalism debate, is hardly ever addressed. Although the question of new slavery does arise in some regions, including Latin America, the exploitation of labor has generally lost its central position as a focus of analysis in times of a globalized post-industrial, financial market-driven economy. In fact, worldwide, there is more likely to be an oversupply, especially of unclassified labor. This finds expression in a growing informal sector and the emergence of "superfluous" (Bauman 2005), which goes far beyond the debate about the "industrial reserve army". In this context, it becomes almost a privilege to be exploited through wage labor. In this respect, the conceptualization of refeudalization processes chosen here hardly ties in with the Latin American feudalism-capitalism debate of the 1970s.

A completely different approach to thinking about refeudalization can be found in the early works of the social philosopher Jürgen Habermas on the transformation of public space in Europe. In his work on the structural transformation of the public sphere, he introduced the concept of refeudalization into critical theory. Habermas explores the relationship between the public and the common on the one hand and the private on the other. For Habermas, the concept of the public sphere is defined by the principle of universal access, in Habermas' words, "A public sphere from which specific groups would be ipso excluded was less than merely incomplete; it was not a public sphere at all" (Habermas 1962, 85). In post-industrial societies, Habermas identifies a dynamic of weakening the public sphere due to the pressure of commercial interests and its penetration by strategies for attaining political legitimacy (Habermas 1962). With this approach, it is precisely the changes in everyday culture, social dynamics, and political representation already hinted at that can be examined.

However, unlike Habermas, who ultimately focused on bourgeois, nation-state public spheres in the western centers, the concept of refeudalization proposed here is to be understood as a business cycle within the capitalist world system. The starting point is the extreme enrichment of the few and the impoverishment of the majority of the population in global financial market-driven capitalism. Seen from this perspective, even in regions of the world – such as Latin America – where historically there has been no feudalism in the Marxist sense, and where feudal elements had been introduced through the process of colonization – there can also emerge a historical conjuncture of refeudalization. In contrast to what Ramón Grosfoguel has coined *feudalmanía* (Grosfoguel 2008, 307) – the imagination of a universal stage of development where feudalism served as an instrument to produce temporal distance denying coevality between Latin America and the so-called advanced European countries, refeudalization presumes coevality and similar processes in different world-regions of the capitalist world-system.

The Tendency toward the Refeudalization of the Social Structure in Latin America

In Latin America, this tendency toward the refeudalization of the social structure has deep roots in the colonial legacy and has also been deepened by various historical cycles, such as the neoliberal turn of the 1980s and 1990s. In the 1990s, the Gini coefficient of income distribution in

Latin America was 0.522, while it was 0.342 in Western Europe and 0.412 in Asia. This means that the inequality of income distribution is highest in Latin America compared with other regions of the world. The richest tenth of households earned 48% of total income, while the lowest tenth earned just 1.6% (de Ferranti et al. 2004).

Although social inequality is a cross-country constant in Latin America, regional differences can be observed. Whereas in the 1990s, countries such as Brazil, Chile, and Colombia were characterized by the greatest social inequality, Uruguay, Costa Rica, and Venezuela were among those Latin American countries where the income distribution of households was more balanced. The social scientists Alejandro Portes and Kelly Hoffman have made one of the few attempts to analyze the class composition of selected Latin American societies more closely. For them, the ruling class consists of the segments of capitalists, executives, and senior managers. For 2000, they conclude that the ruling class represents 5.2% (in Brazil) and 13.9% (in Venezuela) of the total population. The uppermost segment of the ruling class, the capitalists, comprises between 0.85% (in Panama) and 2.2% (in Colombia) of the total population. This uppermost segment of the Latin American ruling class thus corresponds to the group we have called the 1% here, following the global debate on social inequality.

In sociological terms, the emergence of a global elite of hyper-rich people can be understood as an integral aspect of an ongoing process of refeudalization (Neckel 2010, 2013, 2020; Kaltmeier 2018). In general terms, it seems that contemporary social structures are more similar to those of pre-revolutionary France than those of Fordist modern societies. In a similar vein, it seems that class analysis also has a problem in understanding the tendency toward incrustation and encapsulation. New terms, such as cosmocracy, a neologism of cosmopolitism and aristocracy, seem to be more adequate to conceptualize the new process of refeudalization (Kaltmeier 2019, 29, 30).

Social Inequality in the 20th Century

In Latin America, in the course of the policy of import-substituting industrialization and the expansion of state bureaucracy in the 1940s, there was a growth in the middle class in which civil servants, the self-employed, and formal workers found themselves. The national projects of Juan Perón in Argentina, Víctor Raúl Haya de la Torre in Peru, Getúlio Vargas in Brazil and Lázaro Cárdenas in Mexico are worthy of mention. This model of social development continued throughout Latin America until the 1970s, with regional variations (Kaltmeier and Breuer 2020; see also Thorp 1998; Boris et al. 2008; Kaltmeier 2013).

This industrialization policy allowed for the expansion of an urban working class. Already in the 1960s, the majority of the economically active population in Latin America were no longer employed in agriculture. Instead, between 1960 and 1980, the industrial proletariat grew to its demographic and political zenith. Politically, this was expressed in an increasing degree of organization, especially in unions. Nevertheless, it must be noted that the industrial proletariat remained relatively small – especially in comparison to the industrial development processes in the United States. Instead, the composition of the working class has been historically characterized by a high proportion of informal urban proletariat, which lives primarily from non-formal industrial relations (Portes 1985). In the rural regions, the quasi-feudal relations of dependence determined by hacienda and other forms of large-scale land ownership were dissolved in the course of the agricultural reforms of the 1960s and 1970s. However, these agricultural reforms only led to an extremely limited redistribution of land and thus had hardly any socio-structural effects. Instead, in most cases, the structures of ownership and exploitation in the countryside were modernized, resulting in an increasing semi-proletarianization of the peasants, which is accompanied by rural-urban (commuter) migration. The consequence is that Latin America has been considered the region with the highest social inequality in the world since the 1960s (Deininger and Squire 1996, Table 5).

Neoliberal Polarizations

The first attempts to form a middle class started in the 1940s but were then destroyed by the neoliberal structural adjustments of the 1980s. This included the true pulverization of the middle class as well as the formally employed working class (Boris 2008). At the end of the 1990s, according to the International Labor Organization (ILO), half of the economically active population in Latin America was already working in the informal sector. This is due to the neoliberal policy of privatization and the promotion of micro-entrepreneurship (Portes and Hoffman 2003, 50). In the 1990s, the proportion of state employees declined in line with the growth of the informal proletariat, as did the proportion of formally employed workers. By the end of the 1990s, the social structure had become so polarized that it resembled the divided society of the colonial era.

A particularly striking example of the rapid social decline of the middle class is the change in the social structure in Argentina as a result of the 2001 crisis. With the end of the convertibility of the dollar and peso, there was galloping inflation and devaluation of savings and a decline in the economic power of about 20%. Small- and medium-sized enterprises were plunged into a deep crisis so that many of them had to be closed down (Svampa 2008, 53). At that moment, large sections of the middle class plunged socio-economically into the precariat, even though they still possessed a high level of cultural capital. This descent of the middle class into the lower class was described in social science literature as the "new poverty" (del Cueto and Luzzi 2010, 36).

But there were not only victims of the crisis. The oligopolies in the service and financial sectors were able to benefit. While the share of traditional shops fell from 57% to 17% between 1984 and 2001, supermarkets increased their share from 27% to 53% (Svampa 2008, 55).

The Pink Elevator: Social Structure in the "Pink Tide"

Significant changes in the social structure did not occur until the millennium change. At the beginning of the 21st century, almost all of Latin America and the Caribbean experienced an astonishing boom of left-wing governments proclaiming a turning away from neoliberal economic policies. The peak of this "pink tide" economy was in the mid-2000s with the governments of Hugo Chávez in Venezuela, Ignacio Lula da Silva in Brazil, Rafael Correa in Ecuador, Néstor Kirchner in Argentina, and Evo Morales in Bolivia. With these governments, a more active social policy was introduced, which was particularly successful in combating poverty. In the context of a favorable economic situation with high economic growth rates, the left-wing governments were able to increase social spending and push through higher minimum wages.

This led to an enormous upward mobility into the middle class, while the poorer population groups benefited from special support measures. The Gini-coefficient regarding income inequality in Latin America fell from 0.53 in 1995 to 0.48 in 2015 (Messina and Silva 2018, 12) Even in Chile, which due to the continuity of neo-liberal economic policies tends to be regarded as a moderate representative of the "pink-tide", social policy programs took hold, especially during the reign of Michelle Bachelet. While social inequality continued to rise in the 1990s, and a hardcore of poverty formed around 20% of the population, the Chilean state succeeded in significantly reducing poverty rates in the 2000s. From 2003 to 2006, the poverty rate fell by 5% from 18.7% to 13.7%. In 2013, the poverty rate was then only 7.8% (Larrañaga and Rodríguez 2015, 17), which can be attributed to an increasingly active social policy geared toward redistribution.

In a study on the effectiveness of the heterodox economic policies of left-wing governments, the social scientists Francesco Bogliacino and Daniel Rojas Lozano speak of a "Chavez effect", which made redistribution measures feasible again (2017, 31). While the global financial crisis of 2007–2009 shook the (post-)industrial nations of the West, Latin America experienced an economic miracle. Benefitted by high world market prices of primary resources and backed-up by progressive social politics, democratic neo-extractivism was established as the new socio-economic paradigm. Although the development path was not quite new, economic development based on the extraction of natural resources had been determining Latin-American economies since the beginning of colonialism – possibly only interrupted by import-substitution industrialization from the 1940s to the 1960s.

Despite all the successes, the sustainability of the social policy support programs of the left-wing governments has been surprisingly limited. The reduction of social inequality was mostly based on the reduction of poverty figures. However, the left-wing governments were only able to achieve this largely because of state support programs whose financing was based on favorable economic situations. During this time, there were hardly any significant measures for the social redistribution of wealth. The state programs in the course of so-called neo-extractivism were financed by revenues from the increased export of raw materials – from crude oil to soy and palm oil. With the collapse in commodity prices that has set in since the 2010s and the economic crisis that has accompanied it, entire segments that have risen in recent decades now appear to be falling back into the lower classes.

Conversely, the top 10% have been hardly affected by the social decline. Even during the period of left-wing governments, which led the conservative press to paint a picture of the horrors of egalitarian communism, which was often attempted during the Cold War, posed no threat to the money aristocracy. Paradoxically, according to a survey by the financial services company Capgemini, which certainly cannot be suspected of left-wing activities, the number of billionaires rose massively, especially during the term of office of left-wing governments. From 2008 to 2016, for example, the number of the super-rich (or technocratically: high-net-worth individuals, HNWI) in Latin America rose from just under 420 to almost 560 (Capgemini 2017). Of course, it does not limit the concentration of wealth to the billionaires alone. More than 500,000 millionaires live in the seven Latin American countries alone. This ranking of millionaires is led by Brazil, with almost 200,000 millionaires, and Mexico (164,000), followed by Chile with almost 45,000 millionaires.

Wealth-X explains this increase in the number of billionaires in the region by demographic upheavals, especially by inheritance. Latin America is the region where the average age of billionaires is the highest, so that wealth transfers to the next generation have already taken place here in recent years. In this way, the number of billionaires has increased, but without an increase in total wealth (2014, 8, 9). This transfer of wealth to the next generation points to a basic problem of many Latin American societies that has not been effectively addressed even during the phase of left-wing government: The insufficient or even non-existent inheritance tax. Burchardt argues,

> The regional taxation rate is only half as high as in Europe, most taxes are heavily dependent on the economy or, like value-added tax,

are regressive – in other words they are a particular burden on the low-income population. For the economic elite, on the other hand, Latin America remains a tax haven: wealth taxation has been further reduced and contributed just 3.5 percent to total tax revenues in 2013. Overall, the tax-related redistribution effects are less than ten percent in the region (Germany: around 40 percent). Individual tax reforms, such as those in Argentina or Ecuador, have either dried up or failed. (2016, 7)

But the explanatory model of increasing the number of billionaires through inheritance is not sufficient to explain contemporary developments in this segment of society. For Latin America, for example, from 2000 to 2008, not only have the number of billionaires increased – which supports the inheritance division theory – but also the available assets. While HNWIs in Latin America still had private assets of USD 3.2 trillion in 2000, this figure had already risen to USD 5.8 trillion by 2008. Worldwide, Latin America has by far the highest rate of growth in billionaire assets over this period, at 81% (followed by the Middle East with 40%) (Beaverstock 2012, 382).

However, there are significant differences in the national distribution of billionaires in Latin America. Let's take 2014 as a reference point: Brazil is the country with the most billionaires with 61 billionaires, followed by Mexico with 27 and Chile with 21. A similar regional distribution can also be seen with regard to millionaires in Latin America. By far, the most millionaires in Latin America are found in Brazil and Mexico, followed by Chile, Colombia, Argentina, and Peru. Fewer millionaires are found in the central Andean countries such as Ecuador and Bolivia, the French Guiana, and Uruguay, which is known for its social system.

While the former countries have deep historical roots in the formation of a money aristocracy, individual countries in the region were also subject to rapid historical cycles. In Bermuda, for example, the number of billionaires increased from 4 to 7 between 2013 and 2014, giving this island – after Liechtenstein – the highest spatial concentration of billionaires in the world. However, none of these billionaires were born in Bermuda. Here the extreme concentration of wealth is based less on endogenous dynamics than on immigration. Bermuda, as well as Antigua, Barbados, Grenada, St. Kitts, Nevis, and Dominica, offers low-tax citizenship for sale.

Further Dimensions of Refeudalization

For the critical and solidary coming to terms with the "pink tide" and the shortcomings made by the left-wing governments, the lack of redistribution programs for social wealth is the first priority from the perspective of the theory of refusal. This is an aspect that should not be neglected by the left-wing governments still in office – Mexico under the López Obrador government (2018-) and Peru with Pedro Castillo (2021-) are worthy of consideration – or back in the office – as it is the case of Alberto Fernández in Argentina and Luis Arce in Boliva (2000-). Nevertheless, the historical context has changed. With the chronically low commodity prices, a neo-extractivist policy of redistribution seems not to be realizable, not to mention the disastrous ecological costs of this model (Svampa 2018). But also, the political conjuncture has changed and has been characterized since the midst of the 2010s by a dramatic shift to the right and toward refeudalization. This shift partly occurred through "cold coup d'état" as in Honduras, Paraguay, Brazil, and Bolivia. With the governments of Mauricio Macri in Argentina (2015–2019), Sebastián Piñera in Chile (2010–2014, 2018–) and Guillermo Lasso in Ecuador (2021-) – all billionaires by the way – as well as Jair Bolsonaro (2019–) in Brazil and Iván Duque in Colombia (2018–), the money aristocracy itself or its political representatives are in political power. Here, initiatives toward social justice are hardly to be expected; instead, a further tendency toward redistribution from the bottom up is foreseeable, using the tax reform of Donald Trump as an example. And so far in Latin America, it is not foreseeable that the billionaires themselves recognize the systemic problems of extreme inequality. In the United States, 400 billionaires had spoken out against the abolition of inheritance tax in 2017 and warned, "It is neither wise nor fair to grant further tax rebates to the rich at the expense of working families" (quoted after TAZ 2017). This may have been a PR chess move, but it shows that the debate about the new money aristocracy has arrived in the United States. In Latin America, such a debate cannot be expected. Change can only be expected through popular power from below, as it has been exerted in Chile since the end of 2019.

But the unwillingness of the elite to reduce social inequality – a historical question since Latin-American independence – is obvious. And this is all the more worrying because we are also dealing with a doubling of economic power within political power that is capable of calling democratic principles into question. The money aristocracy not only influences politics through foundations and think tanks but also provides the president of the republic itself. In addition, the lifeworlds of the "1 percent" are increasingly decoupling from those of the majority population. The cosmopolitan super-rich are concentrated in the chic quarters of Latin American metropolises, with socio-spatial polarization increasingly turning into self-segregation, not unlike the fortified castles of the European feudal regime. In this sense, it is an ironic move of history that Latin America, which has never been feudal, now, in the 21st century, is increasingly characterized by its insertion into the capitalist world-system of elements that we might call feudal.

Bibliography

Bauman, Z. (2005). *Vidas desperdiciadas. La modernidad y sus parias*. Buenos Aires: Paidós.

Beaverstock, J. (2012). The Privileged World City: Private Banking, Wealth Management and the Bespoke Servicing of the Global Super-rich. In *International Handbook of Globalization and World Cities*, edited by B. Derudder, M. Hoyler, P. J. Taylor, and F. Witlox. Northampton: Edward Elgar Publishing Ltd.

Bogliacino, F. and Rojas Lozano, D. (2017). The Evolution of Inequality in Latin America in the 21st Century: What Are the Patterns, Drivers and Causes? In *GLO*. Discussion Paper 57. Retrieved from http://hdl.handle.net/10419/156723

Boris, D. et al. (2008). *Sozialstrukturen in Lateinamerika: Ein Überblick*. Wiesbaden: Springer.

Burchardt, H.-J. (2016). Zeitenwende? Lateinamerikas neue Krisen und Chancen. *Aus Politik und Zeitgeschichte 39*.

Capgemini (2017). *World Wealth Report*. Latin America. Retrieved from http://www.worldwealthreport.com/reports/population/latin_america

De Ferranti, D. et al. (2004). *Inequality in Latin America. Breaking with History?* Washington, DC: The World Bank.

Deininger, K. and Squire, L. (1996). A New Data Set Measuring Income Inequality. *The World Bank Economic Review 10(3)*.

Del Cueto, C. and Luzzi, M. (2010). Betrachtungen über eine fragmentierte Gesellschaft. Veränderungen der argentinischen Sozialstruktur (1983–2008). In *Argentinien heute: Politik, Wirtschaft, Kultur. Frankfurt am Main*, edited by P. Birle, K. Bodemer, and A. Pagni. Frankfurt am Main: Vervuert Verlag.

Evers, H.-D. (1987). Subsistenzproduktion, Markt und Staat. Der sog. Bielefelder Verflechtungsansatz. *Geographische Rundschau 39*.

FAO (2017). América Latina y el Caribe es la región con la mayor desigualdad en la distribución de la tierra. Retrieved from http://www.fao.org/americas/noticias/ver/es/c/879000/.

Grosfoguel, R. (2008). Developmentalism, Modernity, and Dependency Theory in Latin America. In *Coloniality at large*, edited by M. Moraña, E. Dussel, and C. Jáuregui. Durham: Duke University Press.

Habermas, J. (1962). *Strukturwandel der Öffentlichkeit: Untersuchungen zu einer Kategorie der bürgerlichen Gesellschaft*. Frankfurt am Main: Suhrkamp.

Kaltmeier, O. (2013). Soziale Ungleichheiten in Lateinamerika: Historische Kontinuitäten im sozialen Wandel. In *Soziale Ungleichheit in den Amerikas: Historische Kontinuitäten und sozialer Wandel von der Mitte des 19 Jahrhunderts bis heute.*, edited by O. Kaltmeier. KLA Working Paper Series 9.

———(2018). *Refeudalización. Desigualdad, economía y cultura política en América Latina en el temprano siglo XXI*. Guadalajara, Bielefeld, San José, Quito, Buenos Aires: Calas.

———(June 2019). Invidious Comparison and the New Global Leisure Class: On the Refeudalization of Consumption in the Old and New Gilded Age. *Forum for Inter-American Research (FIAR) 12(1)*.

Kaltmeier, O. and Breuer, M. (2020). Social Inequality. In *The Routledge Handbook to the Political Economy and Governance of the Americas*, edited by O. Kaltmeier, A. Tittor, D. Hawkins, and E. Rohland. London/New York: Routledge.

Krysmanski, H.-J. (2015). *0,1 Prozent – Das Imperium der Milliardäre*. Frankfurt am Main: Westend Verlag GmbH.

Laclau, E. (1971). Feudalism and Capitalism in Latin America. *New Left Review* 67.

Larrañaga, O. and Rodríguez, M. E. (2015). Desigualdad de ingresos y pobreza en Chile 1990 a 2013. In *Las Nuevas políticas de protección social en Chile*, edited by O. Larrañaga and D. Contreras. Santiago de Chile.

Mariátegui, J. C. (2007). *7 Ensayos de interpretación de la realidad peruana*. Retrieved from http://resistir.info/livros/mariategui_7_ensayos.pdf

Marx, K. (1978 [1852]). Der achtzehnte Brumaire des Louis Bonarparte. In *Karl Marx/Friedrich Engels – Werke*, Vol. 8. Berlin: Dietz Verlag.

Messina, J. and Silva, J. (2018). *Wage Inequality in Latin America. Understanding the Past to Prepare the Future*. Washington, DC: World Bank Group.

Neckel, S. (2010). Refeudalisierung der Ökonomie: Zum Strukturwandel kapitalistischer Wirtschaft. *MPIfG* Working Paper 10(6). Cologne: Max Planck Institute for the Study of Societies.

_____(2013) "Refeudalisierung" – Systematik und Aktualität eines Begriffs der Habermas'schen Gesellschaftsanalyse. *Leviathan* 41(1).

_____(2020): The refeudalization of modern capitalism. *Journal of Sociology*. 56(3).

Oxfam (2017). An Economy for the 99%. Oxfam Briefing Paper. Retrieved from https://www.oxfam.org/sites/www.oxfam.org/files/file_attachments/bp-economy-for-99-percent-160117-en.pdf

Piketty, T. (2014). *Capital in the Twenty-First Century*. Cambridge, MA: Harvard University Press.

Portes, A. (1985). Latin American Class Structures: Their Composition and Change during the last Decades. *Latin American Research Review* 20(3).

Portes, A. and Hoffman, K. (2003). Latin American Class Structures: Their Composition and Change during the Neoliberal Era. *Latin American Research Review* 38(1).

Sanjinés, J. (2013). *Embers of the Past: Essays in Times of Decolonization*. Durham and London: Duke University Press.

Stern, S. J. (1988). Feudalism, Capitalism, and the World-System in the Perspective of Latin America and the Caribbean. *The American Historical Review* 93(4).

Svampa, M. (2008). Kontinuitäten und Brüche in den herrschenden Sektoren. In *Sozialstrukturen in Lateinamerika: Ein Überblick*, edited by D. Boris. Wiesbaden: Springer.

_____(2018). *Las fronteras del neoextractivismo en América Latina Conflictos socioambientales, giro ecoterritorial y nuevas dependencias*. Guadalajara, Bielefeld, San José, Quito, Buenos Aires: Calas.

Taz (November 13, 2017). US-Milliardäre gegen Steuernachlässe. Retrieved from https://taz.de/Trumps-geplante-Steuerreform/!5462257/

Thorp, R. (1998). *Progress, Poverty and Exclusion. An Economic History of Latin America in the 20th Century*. New York: Inter-American Development Bank.

UNDP (1996). *Bericht über die menschliche Entwicklung*. Bonn: UNDP.

Wealth-X (2013). World Ultra Wealth Report. Retrieved from http://wuwr. wealthx.com/Wealth-X%20and%20UBS%20World%20Ultra%20 Wealth%20Report%202013.pdf

———(2014). The Wealth-X and UBS Billionaire Census. Retrieved from http://inequalities.ch/wp-content/uploads/2014/10/BCensus-2014_latest.pdf

———(2016). Billionaire Census Highlights 2015–2016. Retrieved from http://www.agefi.fr/sites/agefi.fr/files/fichiers/2016/08/billionaire_census_ 2015-2016_highlights.pdf

3 New Patterns of Political and Economic Dependency

The China-Latin America Relationship

Juan Carlos Gachúz Maya and
María Paula M. Aguilar Romero

Introduction

Historically, the Latin American countries have experienced various degrees of external dependence, from colonial times to the present day. The region has been conditioned by a series of political, economic, and social factors. The colonial period was characterized by marked exploitation of natural resources, indigenous labor, and the appropriation of the wealth generated by the countries colonized by the European powers. After the independence process, and with the emergence of new emerging powers, the dependency relationship of Latin America moved gradually toward the United States of America.

This dependency pattern was especially accentuated at the end of the Second World War and rethought the peripheral role of Latin America with respect to the new hegemonic power. Latin America's new role was to consolidate its position as a producer and supplier of raw materials for domestic, regional, and export trade, especially to the United States. In this context, the Latin American countries also served as markets for the commercialization of products and services from multinational companies from central countries, North American, European and Japanese companies, commercialized value-added products in the region and reinforced the role of Latin American countries as producers of raw materials although there was already incipient manufacturing development in some Latin American countries with a greater degree of domestic industrial development.

At the end of the 1990s, however, a structural change was observed in the new dependency pattern in the region; China, as an emerging power, began to increase trade ties with the region and exponentially increased Foreign Direct Investment (FDI) in Latin America. The region began to strengthen closer ties with the Asian giant and this has been gradually displacing (especially in commercial terms) the enormous historical dependence of Latin America with respect to the United States.

In this context, the chapter's main objective is to analyze the main characteristics of the transition process and the gradual increase of the

DOI: 10.4324/9781003045632-4

Chinese presence in Latin America, particularly in some sectors such as the mining and energy industries. The consequent displacement of the US FDI in the region and how this translates into political terms. The analysis highlights the precepts of the Dependency Theory to explain the new scheme of external dependence center-periphery of Latin America with respect to China and underlines the main challenges for the region in this incipient scheme of economic and political dependency.

Dependency Theory Revisited: The New China-Latin America Dependency Scheme

The analysis of the structures of power and domination at the domestic and international level and the concept of the relative autonomy of the State continue to be relevant elements for analyzing contemporary international dynamics. Even in a different international context in which the theory was developed (especially in the 1970s), there are theoretical and methodological elements based on this approach that are useful today to elucidate some relevant processes of contemporary international complexity. The inequitable exchange between multinational companies and peripheral countries are central aspects to analyze contemporary economic scenarios. This theory offers relevant arguments for the explanation of these phenomena (Gachúz 2012).

A key feature of this approach is that it takes into consideration structural problems rooted in the economic and political system of the less developed countries; in this context, the theory evaluates the economies of peripheric countries toward the economies of the center or hegemonic ones. Raul Prebisch, General Manager of the *Banco Central de la República de Argentina* [Argentine Central Bank] in 1943, introduced a critical analysis of a contemporary crisis embodied in the Great Depression. That event allowed for the incorporation of a critical Marxist analysis of the effects it had on peripheric and developed economies. Given this static international structure of dependence, Theotonio Dos Santos states that there is a relation of dependency between those countries in the periphery and those developed. He explains that the economy of certain countries directly relies on the development and expansion and political agenda of other countries, which creates a submissive relation of the first toward the late ones. However, the key is to uncover a dynamic where the dependent countries are under a global scheme that keeps them behindhand and exploited by their dominant counterparts (Dos Santos 1978).

Center-developed countries are predominant in technology, trade, capital factors against the less developed countries. Dos Santos explains that this is characterized by the capitalist economic system allowing some countries to have advanced industrial development while limiting the frame and conditions for others to achieve a structural change. This is perceived as the center dominating the periphery. Prebisch explores the conceptualization of peripheric and center countries, where the industrialized economies have advanced industrial sectors while the periphery countries are mainly suppliers and producers of raw materials and providers of low-cost labor (Prebisch 1983).

André Gunder Frank sets forth that the colonial character of the peripheric countries is linked to the historical domain of the region, which has determined the dependency structures between north and south. Gunder Frank describes that this tendency goes further as the periphery countries even accept this situation as a natural condition or a static unrevoked structure (Marini 1977).

Samir Amin provided a broader understanding by introducing the concepts of power monopolies and dependency in the international economic structure, media, and power groups which strongly contribute to the continuation of the dependency dynamics. More accurately, he defines five monopolies: (1) new technologies; (2) control of financial flows on a global scale; (3) control of access to natural resources; (4) control of media; and finally, (5) control of mass destruction weapons (Amin 2001). As we will see later, this input is a key issue to understand the historical dependence of Latin America, first with the United States and later with China, particularly in some industries producing raw material industries.

Fernando Henrique Cardozo and Enzo Faletto highlight the importance of cultural and historical ties that exist between Latin American countries and the ways and strategies they could work upon against the obstacles that do not allow the region to develop. Additionally, they explain a relevant component that has to do with the differences between the political and economic realms of the peripheric and center countries and how these represent a contradiction between development and autonomy (Cardozo and Faletto 1977, 35).

Immanuel Wallerstein suggests that modern capitalism can be characterized as a neocolonial system that provides the center economies a hegemonic role in the organization of the capitalist apparatus, a monopoly in the production of capital goods, leaving the peripheric countries with little or no participation in this system. Another relevant contribution is that Wallerstein goes beyond the "nation-state" concept to introduce the "system-world" approach. The system is made of many institutions – States, production companies, brands, classes, groups, determinants – that make up a matrix that allows the system to work but also creates conflict (Wallerstein 2005, 21). There is also a semi-periphery, where some medium-size economies participate in the production of some manufactured goods but keeping dependency patterns toward multinational companies. Those determinants are somehow related to the construction of the *Washington Consensus* and *Beijing Consensus*, two central concepts to understand the evolution of the dependency pattern in Latin America and its relationship to the United States and China, respectively, which will be later addressed in the upcoming sections.

In the 60s and 70s, most emerging and middle-income economies in Latin America, such as Mexico, Brazil, and Argentina were facing huge debts from international creditors. The high interest rates of these borrowings led these countries to accept and follow the recommendations of the International Financial Institutions (IMF and World Bank) to create domestic structural reforms programs that included fiscal discipline, reorganization of public expenditure characteristics, tax reform, liberation of interest rates, competitive exchange rates, free foreign trade, liberalization of inward Foreign Direct Investment (FDI), privatization, deregulation and the development of property rights.

In general terms, Latin American countries experienced stronger debt while narrowing their public resources. The post-Washington consensus brought about (in peripheral countries) inequality, mass unemployment, inability, exclusion, and marginalization. On the other hand, the center countries acquired privatized companies from the periphery, enjoyed the openness of the less developed economies, and they also gained the monopoly of scientific and technological development (Dos Santos 2010). The Washington Consensus proved to be a model that favored center countries at the expense of the peripheral ones. The existence of a structural model based on dependence relations is taken as the main obstacle of the peripheric countries to develop; Thomas Lum states that it is a model that incorporates soft and hard power, aid budget, trade, and investment but also that "is able to capture the attitudes and actions (hearts and minds) of people, states, and nonstate actors in the world" (Lum 2010, 8).

The widespread failure of the policies proposed by the Washington Consensus in the late 1990s coincided with the implementation of new Beijing policies based on the precepts of China's *Peaceful Rise*. Even though the relation between America and China began in the 1970s as president of the United States Richard Nixon, is not until the end of the 1990s that the links between both regions started to improve and consolidate in economic and political terms (Santoro 2019).

At the beginning of the 21st century, the government of Hu Jintao knew beforehand the geopolitics of the Unites States Foreign policy and its influence on the International Monetary Fund and World Bank. The discontent of the Washington Consensus as a policy prescription for development was filled by a new Beijing strategy to expand its power globally and reinforce alliances in different regions, including Latin America.

The concept of *Pacific Rise* was present for the first time in an official speech of the Chinese government in autumn 2003; nevertheless, a theoretical basis had been developed previously by Zheng Bijian, vice-president of the Central Committee of the Communist Party's

School. Taking advantage of the global context and presenting China as a new emerging hegemonic power, the basis of the *Pacific Rise*, according to Zheng, is based upon three fundamental principles:

a "Continuing with political and economic reform through the promotion of a socialist market economy,
b Seeking international support to legitimize the Pacific Rise of China, and
c Balancing the interests of different sectors, internally and in an international level. [...] Making an emphasis on Confucianism, soft power, and cooperation above traditional war and military alliance mechanisms" (Cheung 2008, 5).

In the new *Pacific Rise* precepts, Chinese Foreign policy was focused for the first time on achieving global presence and to compete in a straightforward strategy versus the United States in terms of soft and hard power. The terms of the *Pacific Rise* were the cornerstone of a new foreign policy based on western concepts such as interdependence and international cooperation but emphasizing the power of the communist party and showing no intention of political reform at the domestic level. Andrew Scobell considers that emphasizing the concept of *Pacific Rise* is deeply related to the obsession of elites in Beijing for promoting a peaceful and prosperous image that would not hinder the country's development by other States, or which could halt possible contention policies of other countries against China. The possibility of shaping new alliances was also enhanced with the new approach. Scober considers that

> this new concept of security is an effort to defend the reputation of this Asian country and promoting a 'desirable' image overseas. Leaders are quite sensible to the external image of their country, and they want it to be positive and consistent. Beijing does see reputation as a vital dimension of a country's power in the world. Status is critically important [...]. The overseas perception of a powerful and benevolent State is of deep importance for Chinese elites (Scobell 2012, 21).

Hence the aforementioned, the dissatisfaction of many developing nations with the Washington Consensus made the Beijing Consensus an alternative to a new world order. The Beijing Consensus contends that

> nations can fit into the global system without abandoning their way of life or compromising their independence. Countries can choose the most useful aspects of the Western model and avail themselves of foreign investments and technology without themselves becoming 'Western' (Lum 2010, 8).

According to this statement, there are three declared principles on the matter:

- Use of innovation and cutting-edge technology to create change that moves faster than the problems that change creates;
- Management of chaos caused by change; and
- Self-determination or using leverage to hold away larger powers that may be tempted to tread on your toes. (Lum 2010, 8).

Additionally, when it comes to soft power, there are three categories: (1) the arc of instability which goes from North Africa through the Middle East and into South Asia, (2) other countries in play where Latin America is categorized alongside Southeast Asia, Sub-Saharan Africa, and Central Asia, and finally, (3) new and re-emerging centers of power as BRICs (Brazil, India, Russia) (Lum 2010, 13). As for Latin American countries, at the beginning of the 2000s, there were two main objectives for the Chinese Foreign Policy: "(1) win the race against Taiwan for diplomatic recognition, specifically in Central America and the Caribbean and (2) strengthen relations with those countries that could potentially fed PRC's resources needs" (Lum 2010, 127).

Chinese Policy toward Latin America: Expansion, Influence, and Dependence

In 1999, for the first time, a Chinese president paid a visit to the region, Jian Zemming signed more than 20 agreements with six Latin American countries, the Chinese government also started to implement new policies to reinforce Beijing's influence over more than 10 countries mainly in Central America and the Caribbean, which still had diplomatic relations with Taiwan. This first Latin American tour became a precedent for the presentation of the guiding principles for the relationship that were introduced in 2004 by Premier Wen Jiabo. Those bilateral principles were "mutual respect, equal treatment, promotion of economics via politics, integration of politics and economics, mutual benefit and treatment, co-development, diversified forms, and emphasis on actual effect" (Dussel Peters 2007).

Beijing published in 2008 the Document on China's Policy toward Latin America and the Caribbean, in which the Chinese government emphasized four main objectives in the region "joint growth, transformation and updating, interconnection and strategic cooperation". This document represented a cornerstone of bilateral relations in subsequent years and it enhanced economic, political, and military exchanges between the two regions (Document on China's Policy towards Latin America and the Caribbean 2008).

From 2004 to 2014, trade between China and Latin America grew ten times, China became

> the biggest economic partner of Brazil and Chile and the second or third of Argentina, Colombia, Mexico, Perú, and Venezuela, with an exchange of US$300 billion per year. China imports from the region about 10% of its oil consumption, 1/3 of its iron ore and 60% of its soy.
>
> (Gallagher 2016)

The CELAC-China Cooperation Plan 2015–2019 (China-CELAC Forum 2015) represented a renewed effort to promote cooperation between the regions in various areas, likewise the scheme identifies the needs not only of China but also of Latin America to continue on the path of economic growth and obtaining advantages of the bilateral relationship, commercial diversification and increase in FDI in different areas. In 2016, China published its second policy white paper on Latin America, which reinforces the objectives of increasing the economic and trade relations and enhance financial and investment cooperation.

In 2017, the estimated amount of Chinese FDI in the region was $105 billion, the investment was focused mainly on some sectors: agriculture, energy, and mining. Additionally, China has invited most of the Latin American countries to participate in the Belt and Road Initiative, 19 nations have joined, some others have signed memorandums of understanding although the majority comes from small states in the Caribbean. Meanwhile, the United States government has been more focused on contending the Chinese advance in some specific sectors, such as telecommunications and the construction sector, while ignoring the need for incentives of North American companies to have a presence in Latin America (Santoro 2019).

In terms of loans and financial cooperation, Beijing has also consolidated as the main player in the region, "China Development Bank and China Export Bank have become the largest lenders in Latin America" with loans that accumulate $140 billion from 2005 to 2010. Of these, the top receivers are Venezuela, Brazil, Ecuador, and Argentina, as shown in Table 3.1.

In a recent report by *The Economist*, it is pointed out that Latin America has become a strategic region for China and an increased interest of Beijing in terms of trade, investment, and political cooperation demonstrate this, particularly in the last decade, the report states that "China has approached the region, calling Latin America a "natural extension" and an "indispensable participant" in the Belt and Road Initiatives" (The Economist 2018).

In this context, relations between China and Latin America have been strengthened, particularly in the last decade, Beijing has signed free trade

Table 3.1 China's FDI in Latin America (2005–2018) (US billions)

Country	Amount
Venezuela	$67.2
Brazil	$28.9
Ecuador	$18.4
Argentina	$16.9
Trinidad and Tobago	$2.6
Bolivia	$2.5
Jamaica	$2.1
Mexico	$1.0
Other countries	$1.3
Total	$141.3

Source: Congressional Research Service, *China's Engagement with Latin America and the Caribbean*, 2019.

agreements with Chile, Peru, and Costa Rica and has signed trade agreements with most of the countries in the region. According to data from the Economic Commission for Latin America and the Caribbean (ECLAC), "in 2017 the value of trade in goods between the region and China grew by 16%, approaching 266,000 million dollars (…)" (CEPAL 2018).

Trade between the region and China multiplied by 22 times between 2000 and 2013. Although Chinese investments in the region are present in different sectors and industries, the energy and mining sector stands out. In Graph 3.1, we can see the participation of some Latin American countries in mining exports to China. The production of raw materials is still the most important export sector to China, and that is a common dependence pattern in the trade relationship between both regions.

Chinese multinational companies are central actors in the process of China's economic expansion in Latin America. State owned and private companies have arrived in Latin America to invest heavily in different industrial sectors but mainly in raw materials production. Sometimes

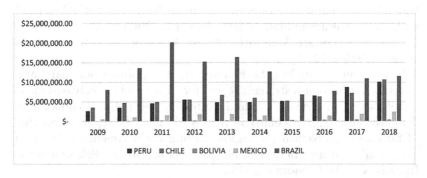

Graph 3.1 Mining exports of selected Latin American countries to China (2009–2018)

these Chinese companies have signed Joint Ventures with local domestic companies or with multinational companies from other countries. In Table 3.2, we can see the most important Chinese companies in the mining sector in some Latin American countries.

The current predominant pattern in the trade relationship China-Latin America shows the conceptualization of peripheric and center relations, where the hegemonic economies have advanced industrial sectors and participate actively as financial investors while the periphery countries are mainly suppliers and producers of raw materials and providers of low-cost labor. The growing Chinese investment in the mining sector and the massive exports of minerals from Latin America to China are a clear example of this new pattern. In 2018, China-Latin America total trade was \$306 billion; China's imports from Latin America and the Caribbean amounted approximately \$158 billion, accounting

Table 3.2 Chinese mining companies in selected Latin American countries

Peru

1	Chinalco	6	Junefield Group
2	Shougan Hierro	7	Zijin Mining Group
3	Shouxin	8	Chinalco
4	Nanjinzhao Group Co	9	MMG
5	Jianxi Copper		

Chile
1 Tianqui
2 Jianixi Copper
3 Jiaouzu Creation
4 Shenyang YYD
5 Codelco

Bolivia
1 Jungie Mining Industry
2 China natural Resources
3 Feishang hesheng INV
4 Yunnan Chihong
5 Double Grow International

Mexico

1	AA Mine Holding	6	Jinchuan Group LTD
2	Eurofro Mineral Group	7	Ningbo Mining Investment
3	Gan-Bo Investment	8	Shaanxi Dong Ling Group
4	Harbor Mining	9	Tianjin Binhai Harbor
5	JC Mining	10	Tianjin North China

Brasil
1 Hebei Jingye Group
2 Honbridge Holdings
3 Euroasian resources Group
4 Sul America
5 Bamin

Source: AsiaLink (2019).

for almost 7.5% of China's overall imports. In terms of exports, they amounted $148 billion, accounting for 5.9% of China's total exports (Congressional Research Service 2019, 1). In the following section, we will see with more detail some specific cases of the bilateral relationship of China and Latin American countries that show not only an increased presence of Beijing in the area but also a stronger dependence of the region toward China.

Brazil

China is Brazil's largest trading partner, with Beijing reliant on the Latin American country for the imports of agricultural goods, iron ore, and crude oil to fuel its economy. In 2018, the China-Brazil bilateral totaled an estimated and record high trade of more than $100 billion. Brazil's balance of payments shows that 25% of Brazilian exports are sent to China, while the most important export products are iron ore, oil, and soy. The participation of China in Brazil is focused on energy, agriculture, and mining and is made up around $70 billion (*Ministério da Economia* [Economy Ministry] 2019). Brazil is the only Latin American country belonging to the BRICS bloc and was the first country to establish a strategic partnership with China in 1993. Throughout 1996 to 2010, Brazilian trade with China has grown rapidly, China's investment and trade have replaced the United States as the top investor and trade partner with the South American country and this is not a new pattern, China has been the largest trade partner and export market of Brazil for a decade.

Chinese investment in Brazil is experiencing a process of diversification, it is now different in many areas ranging from agriculture and mining to energy, electricity, manufacturing, and technological innovation; more than 300 Chinese enterprises are established in Brazil, which has a direct impact on the creation of new smaller domestic companies (Zhou and Wenzheng 2019).

In a context of political crisis, in 2018, Jair Bolsonaro, then-candidate to the Brazilian presidency, claimed that China was "buying Brazil" and built a discourse toward the control of its key natural resources, he even visited Taiwan, something any other leader ever did (Zhou and Wenzheng 2019). Currently, with Jair Bolsonaro as president (not a candidate anymore), the situation has changed and there have been vows to deepen the strategic partnership and to analyze ways to integrate China's Belt and Road Initiative with Brazil's Partnership and Investment Program (Zhou and Wenzheng 2019).

Nicaragua

Nicaragua is another relevant case in Central America. In 1949, the Central American country officially recognized the government of Taiwan. After the success of the Sandinista Revolution, in 1985, Nicaragua became the first country in the region to recognize the People's Republic of China. In 2007, after the political success of *Unión Nacional Opositora* [National Opposition Union], Nicaragua recognized Taiwan once again. Currently, Taiwan holds an Embassy in Nicaragua and the late country has a truce with both Taiwan and PRC (Grau Vila 2016, 207).

In 2006, both countries signed a trade agreement to boost bilateral investment and cooperation. In 2015, the Nicaraguan exports to China totaled $2.240 billion and Chinese imports to Nicaragua grew to $5.412 billion. The relationship China-Nicaragua is not only economic, Beijing is also involved in the country promoting military exchanges and technical cooperation in several sectors. Chinese influence, however, is perceived as a threat by the United States, "Chinese facilities there could be used in time of conflict to collect intelligence data or as a launching point for operations against the US" (Wu and Kassab 2015).

Venezuela

The bilateral relationship of Venezuela-China has been strongly reinforced in the last ten years; China has granted several billionaire concessional loans to Venezuela to fund infrastructure, energy, and social projects. China's contribution to Venezuela has paid back with oil and other petroleum resources (Lum 2010, 57).

The death of President Hugo Chavez did not change the dynamics of the bilateral relationship.

Chinese FDI and trade finance continued with news of a successful transition. However, public bankers have been more skeptical of Maduro's ability to manage the economy and repay Venezuela's debts, particularly as Venezuela's cash crunch stymied repayments on both its "loan-for-oil" deals, and the financing of its $7.5 billion high-speed railway project.

The above mentioned made that in 2015, any central government fund was stopped to switch to a funding through joint ventures. In this sense, for the period 2014–2017, Venezuela made up 18% of China's total lines of credit to Latin America (Kaplan and Penfold 2019, 13).

Chile

The Chilean case is relevant as it was one of the first Latin American countries to establish diplomatic relation under Salvador Allende's regime in 1970 and thereafter, the first country to sign a Free Trade Agreement (FTA). Even after Chile's *coup d'etat*, China maintained its diplomatic relation with Augusto Pinochet's regime (Gachúz 2012).

In 2002, China proposed to Chile to start the negotiations of a bilateral Free Trade Agreement, the negotiations began in Beijing in January 2005. As of the entry into force of the FTA, on October 1, 2006, China expanded its presence in national trade until it became Chile's first trading partner during 2010 and recipient of 20% of Chile's total exports to the world. With the signing of the FTA, trade between both countries has increased; however, it is not a balanced bilateral trade. Chile still faces several risks due to the nature of its exports. While China's exports of manufactured and value-added products to Chile are increasing, Chilean exports rely highly on mineral products and agricultural products. As we analyzed earlier, this situation represents a common pattern of dependence in the relationship China-Latin America and in the case of Chile, it is a structural obstacle to advance in the development of other industrial sectors. This is a lesson that other Latin American countries should learn from the Chilean case (Gachúz 2012). China's FDI in Chile is also limited, in a likely manner, and due to good governance, Chile "hasn't felt compelled to adapts its laws and regulations, such as those governing public procurement, to attract Chinese loans or investors" (Ellis 2017). Currently, imports to Chile are of $16.55 billion while exports are of $7.822 billion (Trading Economics 2020). Recently, Chilean government efforts have been reoriented toward lithium, a strategic metal used in modern batteries. In the telecommunications sector, Huawei has won a contract for one of three tranches of a project to build a submarine fiber-optic cable connecting the south of Chile from Puerto Montt to Puerto Williams (Ellis 2017). Moreover, it is acknowledged the relevance of Chile as a shaper of the relationship between China and Latin America.

Mexico

Importing raw materials, especially mineral products, is one of the main priorities for the Chinese government, and Mexico is one of the main countries that exports minerals to China. According to data from the Mexican Embassy in China, Mexico is one of the world's top 10 producers of 17 different minerals in recent years and it has positioned itself as the 6th destination for investment in mining exploration in the world. This is mainly due to the relative macroeconomic stability of the country, strategic geographic location, skilled labor, legal certainty, world-class deposits, and mining vocation. The country's mining legislation grants relevant concessions such as long-term concessions (some for 50 years) and with the possibility of being renewed for another 50 years, there are also few restrictions for the companies to operate in the country 100% Foreign capital.

China has remained the second most important market for Mexican mining exports, which reached $1.5 billion in 2015. At present, Mexico has various investment promotion projects and activities supported by the Mexican Embassy in China and the Secretary of Economy within the framework of the "High Level Dialogue on Mexico-China Mining" (Gobierno de México [Mexican Government] 2018).

The number of Chinese multinational companies (private and state) established in the country has been increasing, data from the *Sistema Integral sobre Economía Minera* (Integral System on Mining Economy [SINEM]) currently indicate 12 Chinese companies participating in highly relevant projects in the country (Gobierno de México [Mexican Government] 2018):

- AA Mine Holding
- China Minerals Resources Group
- Eurofro Mineral Group
- Gan-Bo Investment
- Harbor Mining
- Jdc Minerals
- Jinchuan Group Co Ltd (Jinchuan Resources Ltd)
- Ningbo Yinyi Group Co Ltd
- Shaanxi Dong Ling Group
- Tianjin Binhai Harbor Port Int Trade
- Tianjin North China Geological Exploration Bureau
- Zhong Ning Mining Investment Co

It is important to underline the fact that the export of raw materials and "flexible" legislation in the mining sector has brought a series of negative repercussions. There are several criticisms regarding the performance of some Chinese companies in Mexico that imply various violations in environmental and working conditions legislation. Jesús Lemus, an independent Journalist, in an Indigo Report argues that

Some of the Asian companies registered with mining activity in the Ministry of Economy did not limit themselves to the exploration, or development of the mineral settlements to which they have permission; they went beyond this, trading minerals that they are not allowed to access. They also promoted immoderate logging and traded precious woods (Lemus 2015).

Conclusions

Foreign Direct Investment and the expansion of Chinese companies in Latin America imply a series of structural problems related to dependency and unequal center-periphery relations. Despite the fact that Chinese FDI has brought tangible benefits in the region in terms of job creation and infrastructure and has also contributed to the diversification of trade relations, there are some challenges that need to be reevaluated for the Latin American countries in its relationship with China.

Dependence on the export of raw materials and the exponential increase in value-added goods from China have also brought the loss of competitiveness of domestic companies in the region and enhanced the lack of participation of Latin American companies in global industrial chains. This problem is a common pattern in the center-periphery dependency relations and is present nowadays in most Latin American economies that produce raw materials. It is important to highlight the fact that it is the responsibility of peripheral states, however, to work on domestic policies to enhance local participation of small and medium companies in the development of new value-added products and services that have the potential to export.

Additionally, it is also needed to establish more efficient regulatory frameworks to clarify contracts with Chinese companies on issues of environmental legislation and working conditions.

Dependency theory is a reference to address the nature of the relations between China and Latin American countries and offers relevant insights to understand the new patterns of dependency in the relationship China-Latin America. Beijing Consensus provided an alternative to several Latin American countries that were discontent with the leadership of the United States in the region in terms of FDI and trade relations. China has succeeded in achieving central political and economic goals: the recognition of diplomatic relations with China by most of the countries in the area and the signing of free trade agreements and strategic alliances with some of the most important economies and those potential natural resources' suppliers. It is a challenge for Latin American countries to take advantage of trade exchange with China, the countries in the region need to diversify exports and develop new value-added products, while current international exchange structures represent an obstacle, its political willingness and assertive economic policies at domestic level that could bring initially, a change in dependency patterns with center hegemonic countries.

Bibliography

Amin, S. (2001). Capitalismo, imperialismo, mundialización [Capitalism, imperialism, globalization]. In *Resistencias mundiales* [Global Resistance] *(De Seattle a Porto Alegre)*, edited by J. Seoane and E. Taddei. Buenos Aires: CLACSO.

AsiaLink. (2019). China llega con 100 expositores a feria minera chilena [China brings 100 mining companies to mining fair at Chile]. Retrieved from https://asialink.americaeconomia.com/economia-y-negocios-mineria/china-llega-con-100-expositores-feria-minera-chilena

Bartesaghi, I. (2015). La política exterior de China desde la perspectiva e intereses de América Latina [Chinese foreign policy from Latin America interests and perspectives]. In *Política Exterior China: relaciones regionales y cooperación* [Chinese Foreign Policy: cooperation and regional relations], edited by J. C. Gachúz and R. I. León, 245–278. México: Benemérita Universidad Autónoma de Puebla.

Cardozo, F. and Faletto, E. (1977). *Dependencia y Desarrollo en América Latina* [Development and Dependency in Latin America]. Buenos Aires: Siglo XXI.

CEPAL (2018). Explorando nuevos espacios de cooperación entre América Latina y el Caribe y China [Exploring new cooperation scenarios between Latin America and the Caribbean and China]. Santiago de Chile:. Retrieved from https://repositorio.cepal.org/bitstream/handle/11362/43213/1/S1701250_es.pdf

Cheung, G. (2008). International Relations Theory in Flux in View of China's "Peaceful Rise". *The Copenhagen Journal of Asian Studies.*

China: ¿cuánto creció el comercio con Latinoamérica desde el año 2000? [China: How much has trade with Latin America grown since 2000?] (2018). *La Prensa* (Perú). Retrieved from https://laprensa.peru.com/actualidad/noticia-china-economia-latinoamerica-77219

China-CELAC Forum. (2015). Cooperation Plan (2015–2019). Retrieved from http://www.chinacelacforum.org/eng/zywj_3/t1230944.htm

Choo, J. (2009). China's Relations with Latin America: Issue, Policy, Strategies and Implications. *Journal of International and Area Studies* 16(2).

Congressional Research Service. (2019). *China's Engagement with Latin America and the Caribbean.* Retrieved from https://fas.org/sgp/crs/row/IF10982.pdf

de México, Gobierno. (2018). *Sistema Integral sobre economía minera* [Integral System on Mining Economy *(SINEM)].* Retrieved from https://www.sgm.gob.mx/Web/SINEM/mineria/empresas_mineras.html

Documento sobre la Política de China Hacia América Latina y el Caribe [Document on China's Policy towards Latin America and the Caribbean] (2008). Retrieved from http://confucio.uc.cl/es/noticias-sobre-china/273-documento-sobre-la-politica-de-china-hacia-america-latina-y-el-caribe-prologo

Dos Santos, T. (2010). Development and Civilisation. *Social Change* 40(2).

———(1978). *Imperialismo y Dependencia* [Imperialism and Dependence]. México: Era.

Dussel Peters, E. (2007). China's Challenge to Latin America. *Project Syndicate.* Retrieved from https://bit.ly/2vXEO7S

Ellis, E. (2017). China's Relationship with Chile: The Struggle for the Future Regime of the Pacific. *The Jamestown Foundation Global Research and Analysis: China Brief* 17(15). Retrieved from https://jamestown.org/program/chinas-relationship-chile-struggle-future-regime-pacific/

Ferchen, M. (February 28, 2020). Why did China stand by Maduro in Venezuela?. *Carnegie-Tsinghua Center for Global Policy.* Retrieved from https://bit.ly/3aO4a6Y

Gachúz, J. C. (2012). Chile's Economic and Political Relationship with China. *Journal of Current Chinese Affairs* 41(1). Retrieved from https://journals.sagepub.com/doi/pdf/10.1177/186810261204100105

———(2014). La teoría de la dependencia y los nuevos esquemas de dependencia económica [Dependency theory and the new economic dependency schemes]. In *Teorías de las Relaciones Internacionales en el Siglo XXI: Interpretaciones críticas desde México* [International Relations Theories in the 21st Century: Critical Review from Mexico], edited by J. Schiavon, A. Sletza et al., 343–366. México: Benemérita Universidad Autónoma de Puebla.

Gao, T. and Gurd, B. (2019). Organizational Issues for the Lean Success in China: Exploring a Change Strategy for Lean Success. *BMC Health Services Research* 19(1). Retrieved from https://doi-org.udlap.idm.oclc.org/10.1186/s12913-019-3907-6.

Grau Vila, C. (2016). Between China and Taiwan: The Case of Nicaragua and the Grand Interoceanic Canal. *Revista CIDOB d'Afers Internacionals* 114.

Kaplan, S. and Penfold, M. (2019). *China-Venezuela Economic Relations: Hedging Venezuelan Bets with Chinese Characteristics.* Wilson Center Kissinger Institute. Retrieved from https://www.wilsoncenter.org/publication/china-venezuela-economic-relations-hedging-venezuelan-bets-chinese-characteristics

Lemus, J. (2015). *Saqueos Chinos.* [Chinese Looting]. Retrieved from: https://www.reporteindigo.com/reporte/saqueo-chino/

Lum, T. (2010). *China and the U.S.: Comparing Global Influence* (China in the 21st Century Series). New York: Nova Science Publishers. Retrieved from https://udlap.idm.oclc.org/login?url=https://search-ebscohost-com.udlap.idm.oclc.org/login.aspx?direct=true&db=nlebk&AN=340260&lang=es&site=eds-live

Marini, R. M. (1977). *Subdesarrollo y Revolución* [Underdevelopment and Revolution]. México: Siglo XXI.

Ministério da Economia [Economy Ministry], *Indústria, Comércio Exterios e Servicos* [Industry, Foreign Trade and Services]. Retrieved from https://bit.ly/39GEt82

Prebisch, R. (1983). Cinco etapas de mi pensamiento sobre el Desarrollo [Five stages of my thinking about development]. Retrieved from http://aleph.org.mx/jspui/bitstream/56789/1/DOCT2065096_ARTICULO_10.PDF

The Economist (2018). China moves into Latin America. Retrieved from https://www.economist.com/the-americas/2018/02/03/china-moves-into-latin-america

Trading Economics (2020). Chile imports and exports. Retrieved from https://tradingeconomics.com/chile/exports

Santoro, M. (2019). Latin America and China: Reflections on the 70th Anniversary of the PRC. Retrieved from https://bit.ly/2vSvUbK

Saray, M. O. (2019). Washington Consensus, Neo-Liberalism and Beyond: Does Beijing Consensus Break the Routine? *Journal of Yasar University* 14(55).

Scobell, A. (2012). Learning to Rise Peacefully? China and the Security Dilemma. *Journal of Contemporary China* 21(76).

Surowiecki, J. (2007). Sovereign Wealth World. *The New Yorker.* Retrieved from https://bit.ly/2TCHPTY

Wallerstein, I. (2005). *Análisis de sistemas-mundo, una introducción* [World-systems analysis, an introduction]. México: Siglo XXI.

Wu, W. and Kassab, H. S. (2015). Boiling in Battlefield or Reaching for Sunrise? Perspectives and Trends in Contemporary Sino-Central American Relationship. In *China-Latinoamérica: Resultados de una Relación Económica en Transición* [China-Latin America: Results of a Transitional Economic Relation], edited by J. C. Gachúz and R. I. León, 149–184. México: Benemérita Universidad Autónoma de Puebla.

Zhou, M. and Wenzheng, K. (2019). China's Relations with Brazil Have Grown for 45 Years. *China Daily.* Retrieved from https://bit.ly/38Kqtc8

4 The Argentine Foreign Debt

A Recursive Trap in Two Hundred Years Fighting for Sovereignty

Mario Rapoport and Noemí Brenta

Introduction

The foreign debt runs through a good part of Argentina's economic history. Since the first years of independent life, foreign loans accumulated, and their inability to pay them. The international economic cycles had the primary transmission mechanism in Argentina's external debt, which was influenced negatively by the internal situation, which gave the political debt nuances. The rules imposed by creditors conditioned local economic policies. This financing, which was supposed to make up for the shortage of domestic capital and foreign currency for development, invariably became a significant obstacle.

Most of these loans were contracted at very high rates and with conditions detrimental to national sovereignty. Moreover, they did not add resources to production, and a substantial part was diverted to speculation and luxury consumption. Since the foreign debts were not used to strengthen the productive apparatus, at the end of each cycle of indebtedness, there were deep monetary, fiscal, and balance of payments crises, with their correlation of depression, unemployment, and misery.

This chapter covers the different stages of Argentina's foreign debt. It reflects on the debt cycles reiteration, its link with the international context, and the country's ups and downs in the legal sovereignty defense, from the first large loan with the British bank to the present day, when the threat of a new default is looming after four years of accelerated indebtedness, with the same global and local logic.

The Beginnings: The Baring Loan

The first milestone in the history of Argentine debt was the Baring loan. It foreshadowed all the vices that would characterize future indebtedness processes: surcharges, corruption, external conditioning on internal politics, deviation of funds, opacity in the use of resources, etc. It occurred in the context of the disputes between England, France, and the rising United States, for affirming their influence in the River Plate,

DOI: 10.4324/9781003045632-5

and was not unconnected with the British recognition of Argentina's independence.

As part of an ambitious program of political and economic restructuring of a unitary nature, whose mentor was Bernardino Rivadavia, the Buenos Aires government contracted a loan of £1,000,000 with the Baring Brothers bank in London 1824. Its purpose was to provide funds to build a direct docking port in the city of Buenos Aires, to install a running water network, and to found three cities in the province defending its border, works of vital importance for the program development; it was also hoped to obtain cash strengthening the working capital and the Banco de Descuentos coffers (or Banco de Buenos Aires). The operation contemplated an annual interest rate of 6%, plus a 0.5% disbursement as an amortization fund; this added up to approximately 13% of the province's income, an excessive burden that anticipated difficulties. The province granted as a guarantee public assets, rents and land, and prohibited sale. The British house took the loan at 70% of its nominal value. It deducted in advance two years of interest and amortization (£120,000 and £10,000). In short, the Government of Buenos Aires received only £570,000. Moreover, Baring sent almost no gold, but instead, bills of exchange against British merchants based in Buenos Aires to pay the amounts indicated to the provincial government. The funds were not applied to works; they were applied to the war with the Brazilian Empire and loans to landowners, merchants, and financiers who employed them in business and speculative activities (See Ferns 1974, chap. 5; Burgin 1975, 87, 88; Scalabrini Ortiz 2001). It was not until 1856 that new external loans were contracted. However, in 1857, intense indebtedness began again. In that year, when the debt amounted to £2,500,000, the provincial government made the final payment arrangement, recognizing interest arrears of £1,641,000. At the beginning of the 20th century, the loan was finally canceled. Agote calculated that Argentina ended up paying £4 for each one received.

From the New Capital Flows to the Crises of 1890 and 1913

The first significant flow of foreign capital, almost exclusively British, to Argentina, began under the presidency of Bartolomé Mitre and lasted until the world and the domestic crisis of 1873/75. Most of the funds, 56.2% in 1875, went to government borrowing. Initially, they aimed to cover budgetary needs, especially military expenditures, for the war with Paraguay. Later they were also applied to infrastructure and railroads and were accompanied by direct investments from private companies, especially in railways, public services, banks, and industries. The halt in the influx of capital since the world crisis of 1873 reversed that movement. It reduced reserves so abruptly that the government decreed inconvertibility.

Once the existence of a national state and the capitalization of Buenos Aires were resolved, the Roca government sought to create a national monetary system with a single currency in circulation throughout the country in 1881. At the end of 1883, the gold standard was established. The replacement of banknotes in circulation by others, on a par with gold, was ensured. However, this fragile system did not have accumulated metal reserves, but the gold was expected to be obtained through new loans (see Prebisch 1991, 134–138). From the early 1880s, capital resumed flow, consisting of direct investment and, above all, large loans. Thus, the total external debt of 33 million gold pesos in 1880 had increased almost tenfold by the end of the decade and reached 300 million. Already in 1885, a crisis forced the abandonment of the gold standard and convertibility.

Simultaneously, a speculative cycle began that would culminate in the crisis of 1890, fueled by liquidity from foreign loans and the weakness of the banking system. The Law of National Guaranteed Banks, promoted by President Juarez Celman, allowed the creation of some twenty banks of issue in the country. However, as these could only function with public debt titles guarantee, depositing in the National Bank the sealed gold destined to purchase these funds, the banks took on external loans, increasing their indebtedness and speculative maneuvers, disregarding production and trade. The national government also placed new securities to cancel loan maturities or cover guarantees by constructing the railways and public works (Vázquez Presedo 1971, 31).

The cocktail of indebtedness, trade deficit, speculation, shady deals, and exaggerated expectations of a rapid economic expansion turned the euphoria into a crisis when the inability to pay the debts appeared. There was a banking and exchange run, the government's financial strangulation, banks and companies' bankruptcy, inflation, fiscal adjustments, deterioration of the employees' purchasing power, and, finally, cessation of payments. The shock showed that the production structure had significant vulnerabilities, especially in its external accounts (Prebisch 1991). From that moment on, in periods of international illiquidity, shocks would be commonplace. Moreover, economic tensions were exacerbating political conflicts; the crisis of 1890 was combined with a revolution and palace intrigues that ended Juarez Celman's mandate.

The Baring House, the emblem of Argentina's financial business abroad, almost paid for its bad deals with its bankruptcy. It was rescued mainly by the Argentine government (see Ferns 1992). The feverish negotiations led to an agreement with the creditors in January 1891, negotiated with a committee appointed by the Bank of England, and headed by Baron Rothschild. For three years, Argentina was exempted from Europe's payments and prohibited from applying for new foreign loans. The consolidation loan was guaranteed by customs revenues, a highly questioned guarantee because it risked the State's only secure income.

The agreement did not decompress the tensions. Lasting stability depended, among other things, on cleaning up the banking system, a task that Carlos Pellegrini undertook during his presidency, which completed Juarez Celman's term. In this way, the Argentine government understood in November 1891 that foreign banks were accumulating gold to speculate on possible price increases while distributing large dividends amid the crisis. For that reason, various measures were applied directly or indirectly targeted that group of banks. Thus, the sale of gold on the stock exchange and the circulation of foreign gold coins were prohibited. A 2% tax was implemented on all deposits in foreign banks (Ferns 1974, 460).

Between 1890 and 1892, the debt grew due to the moratorium loan (£15 million), discounting cancellations, and amortizations. In mid-1893, the Romero Arrangement, the name of the then Minister of Finance, extended the deadlines for payment of interest and repayments of the debt and established fixed annual amounts. The full services were typically paid again from 1897 (see Table 4.1).

The agro-export stage weakness was the meager tax revenues,[1] insufficient to cover an expanding State's expenses, which resorted to indebtedness to finance fiscal deficits. Nevertheless, the central axis revolved around the external value of the currency and the possibility of carrying out a monetary policy through an alternation of fixed exchange rates and convertibility, on the one hand, and inconvertible currency on the other hand. José Antonio Terry, Minister of Finance in several governments, argued that the monetary disorder, financial crises, and inflationary processes of the time were closely related to external indebtedness. In the expansion, Terry said

> Governments and individuals carry out new credit operations. The money that enters the country through loans is a new activity and speculation element [...] the excess of imports over exports and the service of foreign capital forces the extraction of cash [...] and [ends up] producing scarcity or poverty in the environment of circulation.
> (Terry 1893, 8, 9)

In the open agro-exporting economy, the money emission depended on the payments' balance fluctuations, and, according to the free trade ideas of British hegemony, in order to achieve stability, a regime tied to the automatism of the gold standard and the functioning of a currency board, with its inherent costs on production and growth, had to be established. This claim always led to severe economic crises, as in 1873,

Table 4.1 Argentina external public debt by government, 1824–1900

		External debt (in £)	
Year	President	Amount	% Increase between governments
1824	Rivadavia	765,100 (only Buenos Aires province)	***
1862	Mitre	2,434,740	96.2
1868		4,777,660	
1874	Sarmiento Avellaneda	14,479,408	203.0
1886	Roca	38,000,000	162.4
1890	Juárez Celman	71,000,000	86.8
1900	Roca	78,064,000	9.9

Source: Own elaboration based on Galasso (2002).

Note: *** is equal to unknown.

1885, 1890, and 1913 (on the characteristics of the economic crises of the agro-export era, see Gerchunoff, Rocchi, and Rossi 2008; Rapoport 2012).

However, an economy so closely linked to foreign trade fluctuations and not producing gold could only have a stable exchange rate and convertible currency with a permanently favorable trade balance, which did not happen in the 1880s. Moreover, landowners and exporters' interests prevailed. They preferred a devalued currency because it increased their income, as the domestic prices of the products they sold to the world increased. In contrast, wages and other costs in national currency rose in a smaller proportion.[2] The situation changed in the 1890s end when the income of gold from the agro-export boom began to appreciate the currency. To stop this revaluation, exporters and agricultural producers demanded a return to the fixed exchange rate and convertibility.

Silvio Gesell was the theorist of this return to the gold standard. His book, the monetary question, of 1898, justified this idea to avoid the currency's valuation, which caused all the evils for him. "To achieve it", he said, "there must be a project to return to the metallic money system" through a fixed exchange rate and the operation of the Currency Board (quoted in Fernández López 2000, 22).[3] This was the case in Great Britain, which was guided like Argentina by free trade demands.

For Raúl Prebisch, the conversion only worked with favorable balances of payments that guaranteed the debt's payment. Otherwise, the result was "greenhouse plants fed with the fickle sap of foreign gold", as happened in the centenary's lavish year when almost all the liabilities were covered by new debt.

José María Rosa, the finance minister who implemented the 1899 Conversion Law, publicly acknowledged another reason for maintaining a fixed exchange rate and the gold standard: "Foreign capital flees from any country where the currency is unstable. The English Commission (which studied the issue for India) considered a lot Alfred Rothschild's testimony who said that English capital would flow (there) if there were a fixed exchange rate between the two countries" (quoted in Fernández López 2000, 36). This was not entirely true and depended on the plethora of capitals in the metropolises; for example, after the gold standard's departure in 1885, English capitals continued to flow to Argentina until a new crisis occurred in 1890. The search for greater profitability, the uncontrolled loans, and the Baring Brothers' responsibility in this situation responded to the debtors' needs and the creditors' greed.

Prebisch Maintained That

The causes of the extraordinary flows of loans [...] coming to Argentina will have to be sought, to a large extent, in the capital-exporting countries [...] When there are confidence and prosperity in the European money markets, the deficits in our balance of payments [...] are [...] compensated by new loans. The export of gold does not become necessary. However, when [these] money markets are stressed, and the discount rate rises, the export of capital comes to a standstill, and our balance of payments becomes unbalanced (Prebisch 1991, 125–126. Similar opinion is held by Aldcrof 1999).

This is how economic crises were generated in an analysis that foresees the germ of his center-periphery theory 30 years earlier.

On the one hand, this process involved international capital movements, many of a speculative nature, and on the other hand, confidence in the evolution of domestic economic and monetary variables. It also included the time needed for investments to bear fruit, which did not coincide with the repayment of loans.

The 1890 crisis exit combined the expansion of exports that denoted the agro-export model's maturation and the fall in imports due to the recession and the peso devaluation.[4] External capital entered from the first five years of the 20th century. However, it was mostly concentrated in direct investment in diversified productive sectors. External debt fell to less than a third of the capital inflow. Other competitors, especially the United States, were already questioning British dominance.

Debt continued to grow until the outbreak of World War I. In 1913, the external imbalance unleashed a new crisis, producing chain crashes and forcing the government in 1914 to suspend convertibility.

The debt services show the increase of indebtedness and its importance in the balance of payments simultaneously. After the post-crisis moratorium of 1890, the interest paid grew continuously. The three years before the war outbreak, it tripled in value before the crisis (Table 4.2).

Table 4.2 Argentina borrowing and foreign investment, foreign debt service and trade balance, 1881–1914 (in millions of gold pesos)

Period	New borrowings and investments	Debt service	Trade balance	Exports	Debt service as % of exports	Average annual interest charge
1881–83	87	47	–19	179	26.2	15.7
1884–86	146	77	–60	222	34.7	25.7
1887–89	555	147	–136	275	53.5	49.0
1890–92	54	92	17	317	29.0	30.7
1893–95	17	38	32	316	12.0	12.7
1896–98	122	134	34	352	38.1	44.7
1899–01	173	178	163	507	35.1	59.3
1902–04	360	237	243	665	35.6	79.0
1905–07	360	300	150	911	32.9	100.0
1908–10	490	371	209	1,136	32.7	123.7
1911–13	750	419	116	1,289	32.5	139.7

Sources: J. H. Williams, *Argentine International Trade under Inconvertible Paper Money, 1880–1900*, Cambridge, Massachusetts, Harvard University Press, 1920. *Tercer Censo Nacional, 1914*, Tomo VIII. Walter Beveraggi Allende, *El servicio del capital extranjero y el control de cambios*. México, 1954.

Note: Payment of the foreign debt was suspended in 1891 and resumed in 1894. Own elaboration.

The Volatility of the Interwar Period, the Crisis of 1929, and the Scenario of World War II

The first post-war period, and in particular the 1920s, was a period of extreme volatility. Argentina was highly dependent on the fluctuations of the world economy. It received strong capital inflows, especially from the United States, for investment and to finance imports. Convertibility returned in 1927, but the New York Stock Exchange boom a year later produced a great flight of capital, which, together with the fall in Argentine export products' prices, frustrated that policy. The world crisis unleashed in 1929 created great difficulties for the agro-export model. The prices and volume of exports fell drastically, while the leading powers tended to repatriate their capital. In addition, agricultural production showed signs of stagnation, while competition from other producing countries intensified.

Unlike most indebted countries, Argentina continued to service its debt and introduced measures to adjust its trade balances and control the exchange market. With the Central Bank creation in 1935 and the payment of debts to the United States with reserves in the second half of the 1930s, external debt was partially reduced (see Table 4.3).

The successive trade surpluses obtained during World War II ended up freeing Argentina temporarily from its foreign debt (Beveraggi Allende 1954, 67). At the war's end, the country was a creditor of its former

Table 4.3 Argentina external public debt by government, 1916–1938

Año	President	External debt (in £)	
		Amount	% increase between governments
1916	End of conservative governments	121,240,000	* * *
1928	Radical governments	143,000,000	17.9%
1931	Military government	147,800,000	3.3%
1935	Justo	148,000,000	1.3%
1938	Ortiz	106,100,000	–3.9%

Source: Own elaboration based on Galasso (2002).
Note: * * * means unknown.

metropolis because many of its trade surpluses were made up of pounds blocked with gold guarantees at the Bank of England (Fodor 1986; Skupch 2009). This allowed the country to ultimately pay off its foreign debt and nationalize the public service companies in the Peronist government's early days. However, toward the end of the decade, various problems were added to the Argentine economy. Industrialization required dollars to buy in the United States, the only available supplier of the products needed. However, the export difficulties imposed by the pound inconvertibility, the Marshall Plan implementation (which preserved European markets for the United States), and the trade terms deterioration led to a crisis in the external sector. Although in 1950, the Argentine government guaranteed a US$125 million loan from Eximbank, this was granted to a consortium of private and official banks (Rapoport, and Spiguel, 2005, 322) and was mainly used to pay commercial debts to US companies based in the country. However, trade surpluses in 1953 and 1954 made it possible to reduce the new public foreign debt in 1955 to an amount equivalent to only 6% of annual exports (see Table 4.4).

Table 4.4 Argentina external public debt by government, 1943–1955

Year	President	Amount external debt (in millions of dollars)
1943	Castillo	325
1945	Farrell	265
1948	Perón	0
1955	Perón	57

Source: Own elaboration based on Galasso (2002).

From the Post-War Period to the Dollar and Oil Crisis

After the overthrow of Peronism, a process of financial liberalization was consolidated when the country joined the international financial institutions, the IMF and the World Bank. Shortly before that, Argentina signed the Paris Club countries' financial agreements to consolidate Argentina's short and medium-term official and commercial debts over ten years as part of the new foreign policy orientation. The Paris Club negotiations turned commercial debt into financial debt since Argentina had to denounce the bilateral agreements it had with other countries to adhere to multilateralism principles (Vicente 2004, 175–186). It was also seeking to obtain foreign exchange earnings instead of a somewhat compromised relationship between short-term debt and reserves. This trend was consolidated in 1957 by signing an agreement on the first tranche of IMF credit (see Table 4.5).

The balance of payments reveals Argentina's heavy indebtedness between 1957 and 1962. The Capitals account includes loan inflows from the IBRD (World Bank), the Inter-American Development Bank (IDB, created in 1959), the Eximbank, and the US Treasury. It also includes advances and short-term trade credits, direct investments, and various short- and long-term movements, particularly during the Frondizi government between 1958 and 1962 (see Table 4.6).

The Illia government (1964–1966) reduced the foreign debt, supported by trade surpluses and a more independent economic policy concerning foreign capital. However, during the military governments of 1966–1973, the debt increased again. Adalbert Krieger Vasena, Economy Minister from 1967 to 1969, imposed a fixed exchange rate policy, reduced tariffs, and advanced the capital flows liberalization, anticipating following neoliberal policies. Private external debt tripled.

Increased indebtedness increased financial services, which, since the early 1960s, increasingly affected the balance of payments and public spending. The gap between the debt interest deficit and the trade balance intensified in the 1970s when the international crisis increased oil import prices and reduced Argentine exports.

Table 4.5 Argentina external public debt by government, 1956–1962

Year	President	Amount external debt (in millions of dollars)
1956 (December)	Aramburu	500 (estimated)
1958 (April)	Aramburu	1,051
1962 (March)	Frondizi	1,868

Source: R. Prebisch, *Informe preliminar acerca de la situación económica*, Secretaría de Prensa de la Presidencia de la Nación, 1955, and FMI.

Table 4.6 Argentina balance of payments: main items and exports/GDP, 1957–1962 (in millions of dollars)

Year	Trade balance	Net services	Current account balance	Short-term and long-term[a] equity net balance	Expo/PBI %
1957	−335.6	34.3	−301.3	62.9	10.0
1958	−238.7	−19.1	−257.8	43.5	9.7
1959	16.0	−1.8	14.2	113.4	10.9
1960	−177.1	−20.2	−197.3	357.2	10.1
1961	−496.3	−75.8	−572.1	425.2	8.7
1962	−140.5	−127.6	−268.1	−47.3	12.0

Source: Own elaboration based on Mallon and Sourrouille (1976), and BCRA.

[a] No compensatories.

Although the debt was not yet massive, the external growth constraint in the Argentine economy was presented cyclically as a balance-of-payments crisis (stop-and-go cycles), as theorized by various economists of the time.[5] The exchange-rate arrears and trade deficits caused by the boom in imports and the inelasticity of exports were followed by devaluations, severe adjustment plans, and more outstanding indebtedness in foreign currency favored by international financial bodies (see Brenta 2019, chaps. 6–12).

In turn, throughout Argentina's history, access to credit depended on developed countries' economic cycles. Except in the Great Depression, in the upward phases of the cycle, the investment process's strength in developed countries left little capital to lend to peripheral countries like Argentina. On the contrary, the country "benefited" in lean times. Falling returns in the core countries in the downswing encouraged riskier but much more profitable operations in the periphery. The period between the end of World War II and the end of the "golden years" of capitalism seems to be no exception. In general, there was a demand from most Argentine governments to take funds and a shortage in the supply of credit, associated with the high growth and investment rates of the potential lending countries. This moderated indebtedness, rather than a deliberate policy. Except for Perón and Llia governments, where domestic policies and the domestic and international situation made it possible, in specific years, to dispense with new loans and also to pay them back in full or in part.

In any case, the recurrent problems in the balance of payments periodically led to complicated negotiation processes with creditors, more frequent after the first turbulences in the international economy. At the time of the overthrow of the constitutional government in 1976, the external problem was one of the main ones, and negotiations with creditor banks and the IMF to obtain fresh funds came to the fore (see Table 4.7).

Table 4.7 Argentina public and private external debt, 1963–1975 (in millions of dollars)

Year	Public	Private	Total	Financial services	Trade balance
1963	2,327	503	2,830	162	384
1964	2,043	882	2,916	263	333
1965	1,956	684	2,650	111	294
1966	1,959	704	2,663	151	469
1967	1,999	645	2,644	120	370
1968	1,754	1,051	2,805	205	199
1969	1,996	1,234	3,230	219	36
1970	2,143	1,732	3,875	223	79
1971	2,527	1,998	4,525	256	−128
1972	3,046	2,046	5,092	334	36
1973	3,316	1,670	4,986	394	2,037
1974	3,878	1,636	5,514	333	296
1975	4,941	3,144	8,085	430	−986

Source: Own elaboration base don BCRA data.

The Expansion of Foreign Debt under the Dictatorship and the Return to Democracy (1976–1989)

In the early 1970s, the dollar and oil crises generated a plethora of capital in the major countries that began to be recycled through bank loans to peripheral countries. This provided the dictatorship of the so-called Process National Reorganization Process (1976–1983) with the necessary financing to impose its economic policy – a precursor of neoliberalism in the world – based on State terrorism, with severe repression of popular forces, a drop in the standard of living of most of the population and deep deindustrialization.

These policies received international financial organizations' support for whom dictatorships such as Pinochet in Chile and Videla in Argentina fully represented developing countries' insertion into international capital's financial circuits. A decisive contribution to consolidating this strategy was the 1977 Argentine financial reform designed by the military dictatorship's finance minister, José Alfredo Martínez de Hoz (Jr.).

This reform placed the financial sector in a hegemonic position. It was in charge of absorbing and allocating resources in the economy, liberalized interest rates. It tied the local and international financial markets' links. Workers' incomes were reduced by 40%, and a process of deindustrialization began that would be accentuated in the following governments.

One of the operations that contributed to the private sector's foreign debt, later nationalized, consisted of borrowing in dollars and changing them into pesos to take advantage of the high local interest rates, and then convert them back into dollars to escape abroad. The government facilitated this process with an "exchange table", an advance schedule of small devaluations, which was in place from December 1978 to early 1981. Speculative capital benefited from the high differential between the dollar and peso interest rates in a three-digit inflationary context throughout the period 1976–83.[6] This created an explosive system. Indebtedness increased the need for future foreign currency income to service loans, while capital flight accelerated.

While harming society as a whole, this system benefited certain groups, such as officials who transferred resources to external bank accounts or bought assets abroad, financiers and business people who took advantage of speculation, and the armed forces, who bought arms worth more than $10 billion. Through capital flight, companies that had contracted debts abroad canceled their liabilities without declaring them, which allowed them to benefit from the subsequent official strategy of nationalizing the private sector's debt (Ferrer 1983; Calcagno 1985; Minsburg 1991; Olmos 1995, Schvarzer 1998).

Since 1979, however, the United States' growing fiscal deficits and the change in its monetary policy led the Federal Reserve to raise interest rates sharply to curb inflation. International financing became expensive and scarce, making it difficult to obtain fresh funds and meet interest payments.

After the collapse of the initial scheme, from June 1981 onward, new mechanisms allowed to keep the businesses linked to the debt. The Central Bank offered exchange rate insurance, with a premium of 2% per month, and an indexation formula to remove credit operations risk. Under these conditions, several business groups secured foreign currency at the moment's price canceling their liabilities; inflation did the rest, liquefying private debts while the State borrowed in dollars to maintain the operation. The first step in the nationalization of the private foreign debt was completed. It was a costly fraud that paid off the bulk of society (see Calcagno 1985, 59, 60). In 1982, the State took on most private external debt, transforming it into internal debt for the entrepreneurs at a fixed exchange rate. To this were added compensatory subsidies for the devaluation at the crisis' beginning and swap and pass operations.

The foreign currency's massive outflow was financed by new debt, this time from state enterprises such as YPF (which contracted more than $5 billion without explanation in its productive operations), which turned the currencies over to the BCRA to hand them over to the fleeing speculators.

The indebtedness left behind by the dictatorship, five times greater than annual exports and increased by the rise in interest rates, required high commercial and fiscal surpluses to service it. The foreign debt multiplied by five, reaching $45 billion toward the end of the dictatorship.

Alejandro Olmos and others denounced the illegitimacy of much of this debt, which is the product of terrorism, corruption, and speculative

Table 4.8 Argentina public and private external debt, 1975–1983 (in millions of dollars at the end of the year)

Year	Public sector	Private sector	Total	Reserve variation
1975	4,941	3,144	8,085	−791.1
1976	6,648	3,091	9,738	1,192.4
1977	8,127	3,635	11,762	2,226.5
1978	9,453	4,210	13,663	1,998.4
1979	9,960	9,074	19,034	4,442.4
1980	14,450	12,703	27,162	−2,796.1
1981	20,024	15,647	35,671	−3,433.1
1982	28,798	14,836	43,634	−5,080.5
1983	31,561	13,526	45,087	−4,204.3

Source: BCRA Memories.

movements. A ruling by Judge Ballesteros convicted those responsible in 2000, although the penalties were already prescribed (see Table 4.8).

When President Raúl Alfonsín took office, arrears amounted to $3.2 billion. The new administration tried to renegotiate the debt firmly and tried unsuccessfully to create a Latin American debtor club. However, the creditor banks and international financial organizations' intransigence, the effort's magnitude to achieve macroeconomic equilibrium, and the government's weak political support deteriorated the original strategy.

Unfavorable international market conditions forced a severe internal adjustment to obtain the necessary trade balance to cover services. The Plan Austral did little to foster sustained growth, as the economic structure lacked a strong export or import substitution base. The adjustment allowed for a reasonable trade surplus but within a recessionary framework that deteriorated public accounts. Thus, the internal debt also grew, giving rise to a "bond festival" that once again fed the speculative wheel (Rozenwurcel and Sánchez 1994). The external debt grew by some $15 billion until 1989, causing the failure of economic policies and deriving in a run on the exchange rate that led to a hyperinflationary process in which local interests participated.

The crisis and hyperinflation crowned a government's decline beset by its weaknesses, the interest groups created under the dictatorship's wing, political rivalries, and the growing harshness of the creditors and multilateral financial organizations.

A New Phase of Massive Indebtedness (1990–2001)

After the early delivery of the presidential mandate, a consolidated model had been strengthening since 1976, commanded by the enormous economic groups linked to transnational capital. The performance of the Argentine economy in the 1990s was linked to the inflow of foreign capital and the newly favorable conditions in international financial markets. The situation differed from that of the late 1970s. What mattered now was the excess of global liquidity and the balance of what had happened – despite the crisis, the indebted countries had made substantial payments – the development of new financial products and the substantial interest rate differential concerning the United States (Salama 1999, 14). This opened the way for Carlos Menem's government's neoliberal policies, with absolute acceptance of the Washington Consensus and its rules promoted by the IMF and the international and local financial establishment.

At the 1989 end, already during Menem's government, a new hyperinflationary wave was unleashed due to a drastic devaluation and economic uncontrol, which surpassed 2000% in 1990. This led to the Bonex Plan implementation in January, which froze the time deposits of savers. After a small cash refund, those deposits and the State's internal debt securities were converted into dollar-denominated bonds redeemed in ten years. The "currency puncture" led to losses for depositors, reduced liquidity, and deepened the recession. However, hyperinflation cut the public debt in pesos sharply.

Other successive measures sought to clean up public finances in preparation for the subsequent stage that would come with the assumption of Domingo Cavallo as Minister of Economy in January 1991. The figs were ripe for an economic plan tailored to neoliberal orthodoxy. Its apparent objective was to curb inflation within the framework of firm external commitments from the indebtedness inaugurated by the dictatorship and implement the Washington Consensus's structural reforms.

The convertibility regime, in fact, a fixed exchange rate between the peso and the dollar of 1 to 1 that did not respond to the purchasing power parity between both countries and allowed the pesos' immediate conversion to dollars, gave at first specific stability of prices and imposed a monetary corset, because the increase in the base was subject to the income of foreign currency. However, as the international context worsened, investors became suspicious of Argentina's ability to overcome the recession; in turn, the country lacked the monetary and fiscal policy instruments to deal with it. A vicious circle formed that led to a deep depression. The outflow of capital further increased interest rates and indebtedness, the perverse dynamics of which would eventually lead to default in December 2001.

On April 7, 1992, Argentina joined the Brady Plan, an IMF-led debt restructuring that consisted of exchanging illiquid bank public debt, which weakened the creditor institutions' assets, for bonds guaranteed by the US Treasury. A portion of the Argentine Brady bonds was applied to pay interest, in addition to a cash payment, settling arrears incurred since 1988. Also, this conversion of debts made it challenging to identify their illegitimacy since then. The bonds could be used as part of the privatization payment, generating an excellent private business at the cost of diminishing the social patrimony.

With the Brady Plan, the privatization of the leading state assets, and then the pension system, the then Minister Cavallo predicted "that the gross public debt would stabilize in nominal values at around $46 billion, to begin to reduce by 1997. By the year 2000, it is possible to project a gross public debt/GDP ratio in the order of 15.4%". True to the precept that no one is a prophet in his land, he argued that "net of reserves and guarantees bought under the Brady Plan, public debt will be negligible by the end of the century" (Cavallo 1994, 37).

Under these conditions, a new flow of debt, public and private, was again triggered, whose impact on expanding production was as scarce as in the second half of the 1970s. On the contrary, it fueled a prolonged speculative bubble, financed large trade and current account deficits, and another strong capital flight (see Table 4.9).

Instead of starting a downward curve, a public external debt almost doubled, and private debt increased 14-fold between 1991 and 1999. Total external debt grew by 127% to 10.8% per year cumulatively between 1993 and 2001 (Kulfas and Schorr 2003, 25).

Interest was increasingly weighing on public and external sector accounts. The remittance of profits by foreign companies generated a growing drain on foreign exchange. At the convertibility beginning, the problem was not appreciated in its magnitude, as privatizations generated income in the capital account and strengthened reserves. However, once the public companies were liquidated and, after the Mexican crisis in 1994, indebtedness began to show its most negative side.

Table 4.9 Argentina gross foreign debt, interest paid and capital flight, 1991–1999 (in millions of dollars)

Year	Non-financial public sector BCRA	Non-financial private sector	Financial sector without BCRA	Total	Paid interests	Debt/ export	Debt/ GDP %	Argentine capitals abroad
1991	52,739	3,521	5,074	61,334	4,815	5.1	33.1	60,416
1992	50,678	5,568	6,520	62,766	3,479	5.1	27.7	53,430
1993	53,620	9,708	8,881	72,209	3,591	5.4	30.5	56,846
1994	61,268	15,457	10,800	87,524	4,756	5.5	33.3	62,710
1995	67,192	20,519	13,752	101,462	6,337	4.8	38.2	74,705
1996	74,113	24,650	15,660	114,423	7,300	4.8	40.3	83,828
1997	74,912	34,464	20,589	129,964	8,750	4.9	42.5	96,490
1998	83,111	42,217	22,306	147,634	10,188	5.6	46.6	101,876
1999	84,750	44,185	23,628	152,563	11,122	6.5	51.2	106,966

Source: Own elaboration with data from the Ministry of Economy.

Note: Data as of December 31 of each year.

The peso's overvaluation added a problem, making imports cheaper and damaging Argentina's foreign sales and industrial production competitiveness. As a result, foreign exchange income from exports declined, the output from imports grew, and dependence on international loans increased.

Since 1994, capital market conditions have worsened. The Mexican crisis ("the tequila effect") had a substantial impact on Argentina. Rising interest rates in the United States reversed money flows, the banking system lost deposits rapidly, the stock market collapsed, and reserves fell, in an attempt to save several financial institutions from bankruptcy. The result was a restructuring of the financial system, with a more concentrated and foreign bank, which played a significant role in the growth of foreign debt, as agents of public debt placement.

Since 1994, economic growth was erratic, and from 1998 a persistent recession began, which lasted for the next four years. Foreign exchange income from privatizations and foreign direct investment was minimized, and indebtedness was the almost exclusive source of dollars. This dynamic brought the public debt in that year to $90 billion. In the year 2000, the gross external debt, public and private, exceeded $150 billion, while capital flight, which accumulated to $115 billion, was accentuated (see Basualdo 2000, 34). The international context of the Asian, Russian, and other countries' crises was not favorable either.

It was clear that the deterioration of public accounts, despite the permanent adjustment, and the new indebtedness arose from the inability to service the debt. The crisis almost totally interrupted the flow of new funds to the peripheral countries.

The year 2000, already with the De la Rua government, emerged from the alliance between radicalism and other political forces, closed with a gross public debt of 128,018 million pesos, almost entirely in foreign currency. The State was burdened by a massive foreign debt that, at the end of 2001, exceeded $160 billion, including bonds and letters of public debt in dollars in the hands of financial entities that the government converted into loans guaranteed by collecting certain taxes. The public debt's interest had doubled in five years; 22% of public expenditure was allocated to this item.

De la Rúa maintained convertibility. He deepened fiscal adjustment by increasing taxes on the middle sectors, lowering salaries and pensions, the labor flexibility law, and other measures, which reduced domestic demand and aggravated the situation. It also decided to relieve the private sector of the burden of a hypothetical devaluation and default. Thus, as of 2000, the cancellation of tax liabilities with public debt securities, quoted below their nominal value and recognized by the State at full value, was allowed. Mistrust of the misaligned exchange rate and the ability to repay commitments ended up taking the country out of the capital market, where it was offered only double-digit interest rates. Faced with the looming crisis, with an accelerated outflow of deposits and currency flight, in December of that year, the government organized, together with the IMF, the financial engineering known as "armor" while organizing a bond swap with longer terms. The multilateral agency, together with other governments and some banks, made available lines of credit for US$40 billion in exchange for following the orthodox economic adjustment program. However, the operation increased mistrust, and the measures deepened the recession.

Cavallo, who had returned to the Ministry of Economy, set the deficit at zero, which further contracted economic activity and tax revenues, and carried out a ruinous mega-sovereign securities exchange. This operation did not seek to end the debt problem but rather to lengthen maturities to grant securities with better conditions. The implied interest rates were very high, even leading to legal disputes due to accusations of illegality (Cafiero 2002).

The deterioration of national finances was another problem: disputes with the provinces, which increased financing difficulties. Simultaneously, the central government demanded that they eliminate their deficits and cut back on co-participation transfers. The conflict was partially alleviated through the issuance of quasi-cashes, which increased liquidity despite the scarcity of dollars, the primary money-issuing base. This contradicted the dollarization attempts proposed by the Argentine and US establishment sectors since quasi-currencies implied convertibility's de facto demise.

The regime reached its end in 2001, with the permanent fall of the country's international reserves, which were supposed to support the monetary base. The capital flight from the non-financial private sector in that year was $30 billion.

In this context, the government decided on a series of measures that came into effect on Monday, December 3. The main provisions of the "corralito" limited withdrawals from bank accounts to 1,000 pesos or dollars in cash per month, at a rate of 250 per week; restricted foreign currency purchase for travel outside the country and prohibited foreign currency transfers abroad, with some exceptions. Economic policy based on external debt and the liberalization of all but two variables, the exchange rate, and the monetary base, was cornered, with the idea of buying time to complete the debt swap. A few days later, the IMF announced that it would not release the expected disbursement of US$1.264 billion, thus paving the way for the cessation of payments. The convertibility scheme turned out to be a simple mirage based on false premises: Argentina is not the United States and does not issue dollars. It ended up with a formidable crisis.

The IMF's responsibility in the Argentine crisis is one of the central themes of discussing the foreign debt problem. For years the organization has praised the policies of the country, whose economy was under

Table 4.10 Argentina total external debt (public + private + financial sector) by government, 1976–2001

Period	President and type of government	External debt in millions of dollars	% Increase in debt compared to previous period
1976–1983	Military dictatorship	Went from 8,700 a 45,100	+418%
1983–1989	Alfonsín Democracy	65,300	+45%
1989–2000	Menem Democracy	152,563	+134%
2000–2001	De la Rúa Democracy	166,272	+10.8%

Source: Prepared with data from the Ministry of Economy.

continuous audit by the Fund's technicians (Mussa 2002). The terms of the relationship are also significant: the public sector debt with international organizations (IMF, World Bank, IDB, and others) amounted to $31,849 million as of March 31, 2002. This situation has led to a discussion on the need to have a neutral mediator. The usual interlocutor, the IMF, was also the main party as a creditor in the negotiations (Raffer 2002) (see Table 4.10).

Argentina's most dramatic economic crisis was accompanied by a political crisis and a social explosion on December 19 and 20, 2001, which forced President De la Rúa to resign. On December 21, the day's deadlines were not met. On December 23, the first day of his concise term in office, Rodríguez Saa announced the suspension of foreign debt payments. Convertibility also collapsed, and on January 10, 2002, the "corralón" was established, rescheduling the dates for the return of fixed-term deposits.

It was necessary to de-dollarize, a very complex and conflictive process. In early February 2002, the government slightly relaxed the corralito and decided on some central features of pesification. Large and small-dollar debts would be pesified at a 1:1 exchange rate; deposits were pesified at 1:1.4; a dollar bond option was implemented for deposits of less than US$30,000, an indexation guideline for pesified deposits and credits. Banks would be compensated by the asymmetric pesification of debits and credits to socialize losses. Pesification benefited some economic sectors and hurt others, especially those with fixed incomes. The currency was strongly devalued, and in mid-2002, the exchange rate stabilized at 3.5 pesos. Therefore, the GDP calculated in nominal dollars was reduced by one-third, from $270 billion to $90 billion. Due to this phenomenon and the compensation, restructuring, and rescue programs to the private sector, in 2002, the public debt reached a historical record of 140% of the GDP. More than half the population was submerged in poverty and a quarter in extreme poverty.

The 2003–2015 Debt Relief and Debt Swaps

In 2003, with Néstor Kirchner's arrival as President, the external position gradually improved, with a managed floating exchange rate regime, accompanied by an increase in the price of exportable products and a new process of industrialization and growth. The government initiated a complex negotiation with creditors, which led to the restructuring of the external debt in 2005, reducing the total nominal public debt by 43%, with 76% of the creditors accepting.

International organizations received preferential treatment of their claims, with no write-offs or grace periods. However, their intransigence in the face of the most basic social and budgetary measures resulted in increasingly frequent frictions with the government. Finally, in September 2004, the government suspended the program with the IMF, which intended to conduct the foreign debt's renegotiation in unstable conditions in favor of the creditors. In January 2006, Argentina canceled in advance the debt with this institution for $9.8 billion. This measure's main objective was to dismantle dependence on the international organization to obtain greater economic policy sovereignty.

The debt reduction with the private sector initiated during the government of Néstor Kirchner and continued by Cristina Fernández significantly reduced the amount of foreign debt with those creditors. The cancellation of capital and interest since 2003 was covered with the foreign exchange obtained from the trade surplus achieved in the first years and, as of 2010, added the use of a debt relief fund created with the surplus reserves of the Central Bank. During this period, Argentina took minimal external financing and only issued under national legislation. Public debt in domestic currency with the private sector was reduced for various reasons, such as the elimination of the AFJPs and the repurchase of debt by various government agencies, taking advantage of the fall in public securities, "making the State itself the main creditor of public debt in domestic currency" (De Lucchi 2014, 51–64).

In May 2010, the swap was reopened, and the accumulated acceptance increased to 92.4% of the creditors, with a new reduction of the external debt of US$4,379 million. The remaining 7.6% represented a total of $26.5 billion, a part of these holders initiated a lawsuit in New York, which resulted in the ruling of Judge Griesa that we will discuss in the next section.

This policy and the high rates of economic growth allowed Argentina to pay from 2003 about US$190,000 million, of which US$100,000 were in foreign currency. For that reason, the total debt over GDP, which was 166% in 2002, was reduced to 53% by the end of 2015, and the

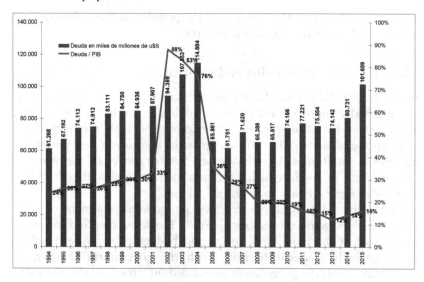

Graph 4.1 Argentina's public external debt and its relationship with the GDP, 1994–2015. Thick lines: Debt in USD billions. Thin line: Debt/GDP.

public external debt fell to 16%. According to data from the Ministry of Finance, the external debt ratio to international reserves fell from 8.4 times in 2002 to 2.5 times in 2015.

Other debts were regularized in 2013 and 2014. On the one hand, US$677 million were paid in bonds for the ICSID arbitration awards in favor of the shareholder companies; and US$5 billion in compensation for the expropriation of 51% of the hydrocarbon company YPF, within the scope of the CNMUDI. Also, in 2014, a settlement was reached with the 16 creditor countries of the Paris Club, for US$9.7 billion; all the quotas were paid until the next administration only paid the minimum in 2018 and 2019, leaving US$1.9 billion plus punitive interest, which in 2020 rose from 3% to 9% per year for this delay and must be renegotiated. In 2015, the external debt was no longer a central problem in the Argentine economy. Since the last dictatorship, only the vulture fund issue remained to be resolved (see Graph 4.1).

The Action of the Vulture Funds

Since 2002, lawsuits by bondholders in the United States, England, Germany, and Italy have become more frequent. The courts rejected most of the group claims. However, they accepted individual bondholders, among them the vulture funds commanded by NML Capital, domiciled in the Cayman Islands, and controlled by Elliot Management belonging to the American tycoon Paul Singer, intimately linked to the Republican

Party as a lobbyist and campaign financier. The $48.7 million that the bonds cost NML gave it a 1600% profit, thanks to a legal action that violated legal principles. Section 489 of the New York Judiciary Act, based on the Champerty Doctrine, considers "the purchase of debt or expired loan documents with the intent to bring an action against it to be unlawful" (Kupelian and Rivas 2013, 92). However, setting a disastrous precedent, Elliott's lawsuit against Peru achieved a favorable ruling in the second instance, bringing into play all his influences, which validated his claims and filled the sovereign debt restructurings with uncertainty.

New York District Judge Griesa ruled in favor of the vulture funds with a twisted interpretation of the pari passu clause (equal treatment of all creditors), and in 2012 ordered Argentina to serve the restructured bonds and pay the vultures the full value of their claims. This ruling was upheld by New York's highest courts and became final in 2014. However, if the country obeyed, the restructuring would have collapsed because of the RUFO clause in the swapped bonds, which required equal treatment of all creditors. So Argentina deposited the payment to the swapped bondholders on time, frozen at the depositary bank, despite claims by those receiving the funds.

In September 2014, Argentina managed to get the United Nations General Assembly to approve en masse (124 votes in favor, 41 abstentions, and only 11 against) a resolution containing its proposal for an international framework for sovereign debt restructuring that would prevent its blockage by minority groups of creditors. However, this victory did not alter the vultures' positions, who played without dissimulation in the general elections of October 2015 in favor of the candidates most favorable to their interests, which proved to be victorious.

A New Cycle of Over-Indebtedness: 2015–2019

The public external debt increased by an unusual magnitude, 83%, in the four years of Cambiemos' government and returned to the forefront of Argentina's problems. As GDP fell by 4% in that period, the country's ability to pay deteriorated seriously. Already in early 2018, access to capital markets was lost. However, the IMF came to the rescue with the largest stand-by in its history, at $56.7 billion, 11 times Argentina's quota, further increasing the debt. Even though in July 2018, the agency's technicians considered "the debt as sustainable but not with high probability", the IMF still disbursed $44.5 billion until July 2019, very close to the primary elections held in August. This raised suspicions about interested support from the US government through the agency.

In September 2019, the country fell into a technical default of the short-term debt when the Economic Ministry started to re-profile it to extend its payment terms. By December, the national government's debt represented 89.4% of GDP, well above the critical threshold for emerging countries and 52.3% at the end of 2015, when its term began. Public debt in foreign currency was already 77.8% of the total. As usual, the debt did not strengthen the country's productive or payment capacity but, as in previous cycles, provided dollars for speculative purposes, to service the growing debt itself, and to sustain the trade deficit caused by the overvaluation of the peso that made imports cheaper and only gave way to devaluations and a sharp drop in demand.

This increase in public external debt went through three stages. From December 2015 to April 2016, the debt was used to open the capital account, remove restrictions on foreign currency purchases, and pay vulture funds. The Public Debt Normalization and Credit Recovery Act (27.249) approved the issuance of US$16.5 billion under foreign jurisdiction, the most massive operation of the year in emerging markets. They opened the second stage, of disproportionate amounts. Public external debt increased by US$87 billion between 2015 and 2019. Among the instruments issued, foreign currency bonds stand out, nearly $40 billion in 2016, $18 billion in 2017, including a 100-year bond at a very high rate of 7.125%, whose conditions and opacity triggered multiple legal complaints and 11 billion in early 2018. Indebtedness allowed the reimplantation of a model based on the financial valuation and income of natural resources. It facilitated the regressive redistribution of income by lowering taxes on rental sectors and reducing real wages and pensions. The third stage began in March 2018, following a failed bond placement and a persistent capital outflow. The government requested a stand-by from the IMF, which was approved in June, with a large initial disbursement, extended in October, and disbursed at 80% by July 2019 to reach the August 2019 primary elections without significant disruptions. However, this was impossible, identical policies led to identical results, and renewed liberalism ravaged Argentina once again. The fiscal adjustment in all the Macrist management – except in 2017, a year of legislative elections – reinforced by the conditions of the IMF program, together with the stratospheric interest rates, the exceptionally high energy rates, the wage arrears, and unemployment, plummeted investment, consumption and production, especially the industrial one, which fell 14% in those years, also affected by imports. In the same period, contrary to orthodox theory, with ultra-conservative monetary policy, inflation averaged high double digits (40%), and in 2019, it reached 53%.

The debt became unpayable; interest already represented a fifth of public expenditure, as in 2001. In July 2019, the IMF sustainability analysis of Argentina's public debt painted 12 of its 13 variables in red. The debt was very high, it said, with a considerable percentage in foreign currency and short-term maturities; a significant devaluation, a fall in GDP, an increase in interest rates could cause serious solvency problems. All this

Table 4.11 Argentina External Debt, 2015–2019 (in millions of dollars)

As of December 31	Total external debt	General government	Central Bank	Deposit-taking companies, except BCRA	Other financial companies	Non-financial companies
2015	167,412	87,701	13,958	3,930	1,363	60,461
2016	181,432	108,957	13,066	3,848	1,491	54,072
2017	234,549	142,829	18,461	5,794	3,065	64,401
2018	277,932	173,584	23,746	5,650	3,983	70,970
2019	277,648	172,819	24,503	4,761	4,042	71,523

Source: Prepared with data from the National Directorate of International Accounts, INDEC.

happened in 2019: the exchange rate went from 38 to 63 pesos per dollar between January and October; the GDP fell continuously (–2.2% in the year), and the reference interest rate reached 83% in September when the government started to re-profile the letters after its defeat in the PASO. Despite its free-market ideology, the rapid fall in reserves forced the government to limit foreign currency purchases. The sizeable foreign debt would have justified deepening the model of savage capitalism if it had won the elections. However, it would also condition the next government if it lost them, as indeed it did. The opposition characterized as "scorched earth" the economic and social situation it encountered upon taking power on December 10 (see Table 4.11).

The 2020 Renegotiations

Upon taking office, the new President Alberto Fernández, of the Frente de Todos, announced that he would seek a sustainable renegotiation of the debt. However, first, it was necessary to "get Argentina back on its feet" through economic growth; this would require extending debt payments for a few years and reaching a more reasonable maturity profile than the one inherited, which concentrated payments of $200 billion between 2020 and 2023, equivalent to more than half the gross domestic product. Martín Guzman, an economist, specializing in sovereign debt restructuring and a close collaborator of Joseph Stiglitz, was appointed as finance minister. Congress soon passed the law to restore the foreign public debt's sustainability. Guzmán began detailed work to convene creditors and prepare a swap offer. The President obtained the political support of European governments, such as Germany, Spain, France, and Italy, from Pope Francis, and somewhat more lukewarmly from US President Donald Trump. The IMF also made a favorable statement to the country on February 19, after the visit to Buenos Aires of a mission of the organization: "the Argentine debt is not sustainable (...) Consequently, a definitive debt operation is required, which would generate an appreciable contribution from private creditors".

Simultaneously with the preparations to renegotiate the debt, the coronavirus pandemic was spreading worldwide in the first months of 2020. In March, it reached Argentina. To limit its progress, as in most countries, the government imposed mandatory social isolation, except for essential activities, and a series of measures to alleviate the economic slump, following the recommendations to spend, issue, and subsidize made by international organizations. Thus, the capacity to service the debt deteriorated sharply. On the one hand, State resources decreased because tax and social security collection depend on activity and employment level, which were significantly affected. On the other hand, public spending is growing to sustain the economy and the health emergency. The margin for servicing the debt contracted further.

Minister Guzmán presented Argentina's offer on April 17, 2020, consisting of different menus of bonds, which include a reduced average capital withdrawal of 5.4%, a three-year grace period, interest of around 2% in the first years, in line with the low rates in force in the world, even negative ones, and then increasing to 5%, and lengthening of terms, which vary according to the bonds in question. Creditors, led by the world's largest investment funds,[7] rejected the proposal, claiming, among other criticisms, that it was unilateral and that they had not been heard. However, this is false, as witnessed by the communications exchanged between the minister and the creditors' representatives, including an aggressive proposal by Black Rock, the largest bondholder, to collect in cash and in-kind, rejected by Argentina.

The collecting in-kind idea is too similar to the state assets dispossession that the country already suffered in the 1980s and 1990s. Cholvis points out that the clause extending jurisdiction in favor of foreign courts authorized in the vulture payment law omitted assets from Section 236 of the Argentine Civil and Commercial Code from the list of assets for which Argentina would not cede immunity. These assets

> are gold, silver, copper, and other mineral and fossil substances that make up the mining code. Here are included lithium, oil, Vaca Muerta, and the various mineral resources that Argentina has. In addition to these goods in the last paragraph of this article 236, there are the national provincial and municipal State's public goods. Such as the State companies, for example, Aerolíneas and YPF. By this article 236, the natural resources and the State goods are in a guarantee of this indebtedness

said the President of the Sampay Institute, who denounced in court the decision to guarantee the public debt with the mentioned goods.

In these rising sovereign debt times due to the coronavirus, the Argentine case is of strategic importance to guide future renegotiations. This was stated on May 6 in a text signed by 135 academics of international prestige, including Nobel Prize winners, among them Joseph Stiglitz, Edmund Phelps, Carmen Reinhart, Jeffrey Sachs, Thomas Piketty, Kenneth Rogoff, Carlos Ominami, and many others, entitled "The restructuring of Argentina's private debt is essential". They state that "only an economy that grows sustainably can meet its financial commitments".

The agreement with the private creditors allows gaining time and resources to finance the recovery. It was made possible by the government's decision to articulate a supportive national and international front and the IMF's support, with which talks will now begin. In this context, taking on debt to buy back debt appears as a possible alternative.

The Debt Restructuring Agreement of August 4, 2020

After a day of rumors and jumps in the financial markets, the government finally issued a statement announcing the debt creditors' agreement. However, it has yet to be formalized, and the legal details are known (see Brenta August 4, 2020; Zaiat August 4, 2020).

The restructuring covers $66 billion (63% corresponds to Macri's government and the rest is bonds issued in the governments of both Kirchners in exchange for debt defaulted in 2001). In high finance's slippery slope, nothing can be considered finished until it is because of that custom of "running the bow" to achieve some advantage from haste or necessity or simply win through fatigue. Whatever the restructuring closings exact number, between the $53.5 net present value per 100 that Argentina offered in the SEC (the equivalent of the US Securities and Exchange Commission) last July 21, and the $56.5 claimed by the cartelized creditors, the settlement for just over 54 represents significant savings in outgoing dollars and fiscal resources to be paid over the next few years, estimated at just over $40 billion.

It is undeniable that the Argentine side negotiation showed political leadership and strategy, with defined objectives: sustainability of the debt and a grace period reactivating the economy; growth before starting to pay lower interest and longer-term amortizations, and to alleviate the fiscal effort on a population already severely punished by the recession, the fall in employment and income in the Macrist years. These objectives were sustained with tenacity and Buddhist patience throughout the process, despite the pressures received from various sides, where sometimes they operate loose and sometimes in collusion with challenging opponents, business groups, the media, high-profile creditors and their representatives, through disqualifications, false information, attempts to eject officials to impose other interests, and other unsanctified tricks.

The government sought to align support from within and without the governors, the unions, the business people, the political parties, some European governments (Germany, Spain, France, and Italy), a lukewarm Trump, Pope Francis, foreign economists of the first line and varied plumage, and economists from within who wanted to support. He also got the IMF to certify the country's limited payment capacity and urge creditors to relax their positions in a "collaborative process of engagement [...] to maximize their participation in the debt operation". Here again, President Fernandez's political crochet was combined with close contacts with Nobel laureate and former World Banker Joseph Stiglitz, mentor of Minister Guzman but also a frequent visitor to Argentina in the time of Cristina Fernandez de Kirchner, and the wind in Kristalina Georgieva's favor, also a former World Banker.

It should be remembered that as the new managing director of the IMF, Georgieva received the hot potato from an exorbitant and unpayable stand by, granted under pure pressure from the United States favoring Macri's election, as revealed a few days ago by Mauricio Claver Carone, Trump's advisor, in a video conference with the Chilean Council for International Relations. Given that the State has a single pocket, and that the IMF does not remove or forgive debts to middle-income countries like Argentina, its possibility of resolving this new irregularity of the organization without a tremendous reputational cost is to seek a solution in which they and the country are not left too severely off, something complicated in the classic terms of the Fund's programs. Also, the debtor countries' plethora on the default verge put the Argentine case in the spotlight, and even more so amid a pandemic. This opens up the possibility that the country will – once again – be a global test laboratory for sovereign debt through a debt buyback program.

When a state has a budget surplus, it can apply it to buy back its debt securities at market prices. These are well-known operations, widely used in large companies. As fiscal deficits are more frequent than surpluses, they are rarely applied in countries. For example, Argentina implemented debt buyback programs since 2004 for relatively small amounts to anticipate the cancellation of services that should be faced in the future.

Debt buybacks can also be financed with borrowed funds. For example, suppose a country's bonds in crisis have fallen to 30 or 40 cents of their nominal value. In that case, it can take them out of the markets at that value, pay them back with a loan, and thus reduce its indebtedness.

Alarmed by the enormous amount that more than one hundred low- and middle-income countries must pay this year, in the middle of the coronavirus crisis, to service their debt, on Friday, July 31, Stiglitz published an article with Bengali economist Hamid Rashid where he suggests that the IMF should implement a voluntary sovereign debt buyback program to alleviate the debt burden and the exposure of countries to dangerous private creditors, such as vulture funds or very aggressive funds. This would also avoid, they add, "the harsh terms that usually come with debt swaps".

This article mentions the case of Argentina:

> History shows that for many countries, a debt restructuring that is too small, too late, sets the stage for a new crisis. Moreover, Argentina's long struggle to restructure its debt in the recalcitrant's face, short-sighted, stubborn and hard-hearted private creditors shows that collective action clauses designed to facilitate restructuring are not as effective as believed.
>
> (Stiglitz and Rachid July 31, 2020)

"At this exceptional time", the article continues,

> Argentina's proposal also presents an opportunity for the international financial community to demonstrate that it can resolve a sovereign debt crisis in an orderly, efficient and sustainable manner. The absence of an international legal framework for sovereign debt restructuring should not deprive indebted countries of the possibility of protecting their people and providing economic recovery during the greatest global crisis in our memory.
>
> (Stiglitz and Rachid July 31, 2020)

History regularities, such as those of Argentina's foreign debt, are sometimes broken by totalizing events, such as a war or a pandemic, in Ramonet's words, which reshape the board of power relations and renew the cycles of accumulation. The negotiations have just begun, Argentina has demonstrated its willingness to pay the debt, but it needs time to recover its capacity to pay it. Creditors are playing the same game as always, but times have changed.

Results of the agreement:

1 Payment relief for the next five years totals $42.5 billion.
2 The interest rate of the new bonds will be, on average, 3.07% annual, while the previous one was 7%.
3 In the next five years, the debt payments will be $4.5 billion when the original amount was $30.2 billion.
4 In this restructuring process, the lowest commissions in history were paid. Debt issue: Macri paid from 0.14% to 0.18 5%, and in this agreement, it will be 10%.

The agreement with the private funds does not imply that the foreign debt problem has been resolved because there remains to be negotiated the considerable debt with the IMF.

The Jurisdiction of Debt Repayment and Legal Sovereignty

In addition to jurisdiction over sovereign debt, what is at stake is debtors' right to restructure their debts sustainably – impossible when the creditor sets the conditions and changes them to its advantage – and the nature of the macroeconomic policies that accompany debt relief.

Thus, an Argentine doctrine on debt enunciated at the end of the 19th century and the beginning of the 20th century by the jurists Carlos Calvo and Luis María Drago is updated. Calvo, in his work Derecho Teórico y Práctico, 1868, establishes two basic principles: sovereign States enjoy the right to be free from any form of interference by other States, and foreigners have the same rights as nationals and, in the event of lawsuits or claims, they will be obliged to use all legal remedies before local courts without seeking the protection and diplomatic intervention of their country of origin. Consequently, disputes with foreign nationals must necessarily be dealt with in local courts. Many Latin American countries included this doctrine in their constitutions or laws. However, the United States rejected it because it threatened their property abroad (see Tamburini 2002).

The Drago Doctrine, which rejects the use of force to resolve these issues, emerged in 1902 due to the blockade of Venezuelan ports by Germany, Italy, and England. They did so, requesting their companies and investors for debts that the Venezuelan government considered an internal matter and, as such, within the local courts' jurisdiction. On that European military intervention, the Argentine Minister of Foreign Affairs, Luis María Drago, sent a note on December 29 of that year to his ambassador in Washington, Martín García Mérou, declaring that a State's debt cannot be an argument to justify military aggression or the occupation of its territory. This is the Drago Doctrine, which was based on the support that the United States was supposed to provide with the Monroe Doctrine's application, directed against foreign powers' interference throughout the Americas. However, Drago did not consider that the new and powerful enemy in the compulsive collection of debts was the same northern power, as successive interventions by Washington with that purpose in different countries of the region soon showed (See Zalduendo 1985, 7–13).[8]

The dictatorship broke this doctrine, allowing foreign jurisdiction to contract foreign debt. Likewise, as part of the structural transformations, in 1991, Argentina joined the International Centre for Settlement of Investment Disputes (ICSID), an agency of the World Bank, to which it ceded the jurisdictional sovereignty of the country in order to attract foreign investment, in opposition to the Calvo and Drago doctrines.

Financial globalization puts the legal sovereignty of States at stake, imposing creditors' will, forcing debtor countries to renounce their sovereign status in the issuance of their debts, and submitting to other countries' private law rules. It thus allows the legal action of vulture funds, which replace the old European gunboats or the American invasion troops. This creates a privileged situation for the creditors who intend to ensure the repayment of their loans or seek extraordinary profits through a justice that is permeable to their influences.

Final Reflections

The foreign debt issue constitutes one of the knots in Argentina's economic, political, and social history. The country's perennial demand for funds arose from an initial difficulty in accumulating capital and the scarcity of international means of payment, which prompted its governments to supply them with debt, even when this was the long run enormously burdensome. However, the debt did not respond mainly to the needs of development, but the existence of liquid funds in the capitalist powers, modeling the process of Argentine indebtedness and its sharp oscillations.

Those powers' capital goes to the periphery looking for differential profitability, helped by policies of openness, deregulation, and exchange stability promoted by them to ensure its placement, mobility, and repayment. If they contributed to growth at times, they were generally a route of easy profits for creditors, and speculative movements, corruption, and escape of domestic savings, through capital flight, of the local elite. Since the last half of the 20th century, they have also been a tool for economic discipline by international financial institutions, forcing debtors to apply harsh adjustment policies to guarantee the commitments made, and also a way of unloading systemic crises in peripheral countries. In this context, indebtedness processes are characterized by marked instability and caused more damage than benefits to the country. The flows that enter the country leave multiplied back to their places of origin. Instead, they resemble a black hole in space that swallows, along with our wealth, the hopes of a better future. With the predominance of finance in the world economy over productive activity has come what Marichal calls "the dilemma [...] between national sovereignty and financial globalization" (Marichal, July 2014). External indebtedness has increasingly sacrificed the legal sovereignty of debtor countries to the interests of creditors. This has benefited a new type of financial piracy of apparently legal forms promoted by vulture funds. Because of the disruptions, they induce restructuring sovereign debts; the solution lies in eliminating them from the global economic scene and fully recovering our legal sovereignty.

A profound change is needed in the international monetary and financial system to limit those sectors' attempts to influence the great powers, condition the economic policies of other countries, or even try to boycott or overturn governments, this time employing economic coups or through lawfare.

The essential point is to address proposals for medium or long-term development and eliminate once, and all the perished policies' residues. To this end, lines must be drawn that make it possible to sustain over time, without the foreign debt's oppressive weight, new infrastructure pillars, efficient, high technology and environmentally sustainable industry, and a progressive redistribution of income.

Real democracy must be not only political and truly representative but also social and economic. A country that gives everyone opportunities equally, providing them with the same initial instruments to develop their potential: education, health, technical knowledge, moral principles, notions about the national and the world. To this end, our economic policies must stimulate the generation of the necessary internal capital or obtain financing that guarantees the growth of productive activities and not speculation or capital flight.

At the bottom of the bidding with the minority sectors that put Argentina in the straitjacket of debt, a constant in national history, there is a cultural battle for most of the population to become aware of this fact. This means creating a kind of link with the world based on that majority's interests, which means strengthening national identity, which will make it possible to negotiate what is needed from the outside with a sovereign perspective, very different from that of the past.

Notes

1. The tax incidence in Argentina was much lower than in comparable countries such as Australia, hence the difficulties in financing public expenditure. Argentina's tax collection was heavily dependent on customs taxes and it was not until 1931 that an income tax was established (Levy and Ross 2008, 170).
2. *The Financial Times* (June 7, 1886) accuses the *estancieros* of being the greatest enemy of Argentine politics because they pay their expenses in paper money and obtain high prices in gold for the sale of their products.
3. Of German origin, Gesell lived several years in Argentina and was praised by Keynes in his General Theory.
4. Exports rose from an average of £16 million in 1881–1890 to £24 million in 1891–1900; and imports, which peaked at £33 million in 1889, fell to £13.4 million in 1891 and averaged £22 million in 1891–1900 (Vázquez Presedo 1971).
5. Among the cyclical explanations of this process, typical of Argentine industrialization, the model formulated by Oscar Braun and Leonard Joy and the so-called Diamond Pendulum stand out.
6. Inflation during the dictatorship ranged from a high of 343% in 1983 to a low of 100.8% in 1980. See also Musacchio (2002).
7. There are three ad-hoc groups of self-called creditors that bring together about 40% of the debt holders: the Bondholder Group, the Argentine Creditors Committee, and the Swap Holders Group, as well as other

creditors that did not join these groups. The main creditors are BlackRock, Greylock, Pimco, Templeton, Ashmore, Fidelity, Monarch, HBK Capital Management, Cyrus Capital Partners LP, VR Capital Group, and others.

8. The Drago-Porter Convention foresees the activation of a political arbitration mechanism between its signatory states that would precede the eventual use of force by one of them or by a coalition. See Ventura (April 1912).

Bibliography

Aldcrof, D. (1999). El problema de la deuda externa desde una perspectiva histórica. *Ciclos en la historia, la economía y la sociedad* 17.

Basualdo, E. (2000). *Acerca de la naturaleza de la Deuda Externa y la definición de una estrategia política.* Buenos Aires: FLACSO.

_____(2017). *Endeudar y fugar. Un análisis de la historia económica argentina.* Buenos Aires: Siglo XIX.

Beveraggi Allende, W. (1954). *El servicio del capital extranjero y el control de cambios.* Buenos Aires: FCE.

Brenta, N. (2019). *Historia de la deuda externa argentina. De Martínez de Hoz a Macri.* Buenos Aires: Capital Intelectual.

_____(2013). *Historia de las relaciones entre Argentina y el FMI.* Buenos Aires: Eudeba.

_____(August 4, 2020). "30 mil millones menos". *Le Monde Diplomatique.* https://www.eldiplo.org/notas-web/30-mil-millones-menos/

Burgin, M. (1975). *Aspectos económicos del federalismo argentino.* Buenos Aires: Solar-Hachette.

Cafiero, M. (2002). *Deuda externa Argentina: evolución y determinantes.* Buenos Aires.

Calcagno, A. E. (1985). *La perversa deuda externa.* Buenos Aires: Legasa.

Calcagno, A. E. and Calcagno, E. (1999). *La deuda externa explicada a todos (los que deben pagarla).* Buenos Aires: Catálogos.

Cavallo, D. (1994). La reforma económica: volver a crecer. *Informaciones del exterior*, Buenos Aires: Konrad-Adenauer-Stiftung (KAS).

De Lucchi, J. M. (2014). Macroeconomía de la deuda pública. El desendeudamiento argentino (2003–2012). Centro de Economía y Finanzas para el Desarrollo de la Argentina. Documento de Trabajo 53.

Fernández López, M. (2000). *Cuestiones económicas argentinas.* Buenos Aires: A-Z Editora.

Ferns, H. S. (1974). *Gran Bretaña y Argentina en el siglo XIX.* Buenos Aires: Solar-Hachette.

_____(May 1992). The Baring Crisis Revisited. *Journal of Latin American Studies* 24(2).

Ferrer, A. (1983). Como se fabricó la deuda externa argentina. In *Transnacionalización y periferia semiindustrializada*, edited by I. Minian. Mexico: CIDE.

Fodor, J. (1986). The Origin of Argentina's Sterling Balances, 1939–1943. In *The Political Economy of Argentina 1880–1946*, edited by G. Di Tella and D. C. M. Platt. New York: Palgrave Macmillan.

Galasso, N. (2002). *Historia de la deuda externa argentina.* Buenos Aires: Colihue.

Gerchunoff, P., Rocchi, F., and Rossi, G. (2008). *Desorden y progreso, Las crisis económicas argentinas, 1870–1905*. Buenos Aires: Edhasa.

Greenspan, A. (2008). *La era de las turbulencias. Aventuras en un nuevo mundo*. Buenos Aires: Ediciones B.

Kulfas, M. and Schorr, M. (2003). *La deuda externa argentina. Diagnóstico y lineamientos para su reestructuración*. CIEPP-OSDE.

Kupelian, R. and Rivas, M. S. (2013). Fondos buitre. El juicio contra Argentina y la dificultad que representa en la economía mundial. Cefidar. Documento de Trabajo 49.

Levy, J. and Ross, P. (2008). Sin impuestos no hay política social. *Ciclos en la historia, la economía y la sociedad* 33/34.

Mallon, R. and Sourrouille, J. (1976). *La política económica en una sociedad conflictiva. El caso argentine*. Buenos Aires: Amorrortu.

Marichal, C. (July 8, 2014). Argentina y el juicio del siglo en los Estados Unidos. El regreso de las deudas externas. *Página Popular*. http://www.obela.org/book/export/html/1705

Minsburg, N. (1991). La deuda externa, factor fundamental en la reestructuración de la economía argentina. In *Respuesta a Martinez de Hoz*, edited by O. Barsky and A. Bocco. Buenos Aires: Ediciones Imago Mundi.

Musacchio, A. (December 2002). El endeudamiento externo de Argentina: algunas regularidades históricas. *Indicadores Económicos FEE 3*.

Mussa, M. (2002). *La Argentina y el Fondo: del triunfo a la tragedia*. Buenos Aires: Planeta.

Olmos, A. (1995). *Todo lo que usted quiso saber sobre la deuda externa y siempre le ocultaron*. Buenos Aires: Editorial de los argCentinos.

Prebisch, R. (1991). Anotaciones sobre nuestro medio circulante. In *Obras, 1919–1948*, edited by R. Fundación and T. Prebisch. Buenos Aires: Fundación Prebisch.

Raffer, K. (2002). *The final demise of unfair debtor discrimination? Comments on Ms. Krueger's Speeches*. Vienna.

Ramonet, I. (2020). La pandemia y el sistema-mundo. *Nodal*. Retrieved from https://www.nodal.am/2020/04/la-pandemia-y-el-sistema-mundo-por-ignacio-ramonet/?

Rapoport, M. (2012). *Historia económica, política y social de la argentina, 1880–2003*. Buenos Aires: Emecé.

———(2013). *En el ojo de la tormenta. La economía política argentina y mundial frente a la crisis*. Buenos Aires: Fondo de Cultura Económica.

———(January–June 2014). La deuda externa argentina y la soberanía jurídica: sus razones históricas. *Ciclos en la historia, la economía y la sociedad 42*.

Rapoport, M. and Spiguel, C. (2005). *Política exterior argentina*. Buenos Aires: Capital Intelectual.

Rozenwurcel, G. and Sánchez, M. (1994). El sector externo argentino desde la crisis de la deuda. *Ciclos en la historia, la economía y la sociedad 6*.

Salama, P. (1999). *Riqueza y pobreza en América Latina. La fragilidad de las nuevas políticas económicas*. México: Fondo de Cultura Económica.

Scalabrini Ortiz, R. (2001). *Política británica en el Río de la Plata*. Buenos Aires: Plus Ultra.

Schvarzer, J. (1998). *Implantación de un modelo económico*. Buenos Aires: A-Z Editora.

Skupch, P. (2009). Las relaciones económicas anglo-argentinas en la post-guerra: entre la convertibilidad y el bilateralismo. *Ciclos en la historia, la economía y la sociedad* 35/36.

Stiglitz, J. and Rachid, H. (July 31, 2020). Como evitar la inminente crisis de deuda soberana. *Portal de Proyect Sindicat.* https://www.project-syndicate.org/commentary/how-to-prevent-looming-debt-crisis-developing-countries-by-joseph-e-stiglitz-and-hamid-rashid-2020-07/spanish

Tamburini, F. (2002). Historia y destino de la 'doctrina Calvo': ¿actualidad u obsolescencia del pensamiento de Carlos Calvo?. *Revista de Estudios Histórico-Jurídicos* 24.

Terry, J. A. (1893). *La crisis 1885–1892. El sistema Bancario.* Buenos Aires: El Ateneo.

Vázquez Presedo, V. (1971). *El caso Argentino. Migración de factores, comercio exterior y desarrollo: 1875–1914.* Buenos Aires: Eudeba.

Ventura, C. (April 1912). Dettes souveraines, mécanisme européen de stabilité, pacte budgétaire. *Mémoire des luttes.* París.

Vicente, R. (2004). El gobierno de la Revolución Libertadora y un nuevo relacionamiento económico internacional argentino. *Ciclos en la historia, la economía y la sociedad* 28.

Williams, J. H. (1920). *Argentine International Trade under Inconvertible Paper Money, 1880–1900.* Cambridge: Harvard University Press.

Zaiat, A. (August 4, 2020). Acuerdo de la deuda: las claves de la negociación. *Página 12.* https://www.pagina12.com.ar/282760-acuerdo-de-la-deuda-las-claves-de-la-negociacion

Zalduendo, E. (1985). *La deuda externa.* Buenos Aires: Ediciones Depalma.

5 End of the Cycle

The International Court of Justice Ruling in the Case of Chile and Bolivia and Its Commercial Implications

Loreto Correa Vera

Restoring Trust: Chile and Bolivia toward the Third Decade of the 21st Century

For years, the Chile and Bolivia relationship crunches and frames a sovereign exit's claim to the sea. In this context, Bolivia consistently argues that the absence of an autonomous and own exit to the Pacific hinders and diminishes its economic potential to the Asian continent and its closest partners, such as those of the Andean Community of Nations.

From Bolivia's figures, this chapter demonstrates that Bolivia's trade problems are related to the production centers' distance from export ports and not to sovereignty and cargo manipulation lack, as suggested in recent studies.

Therefore, the text explains the Hague lawsuit's effects around maritime claim – concluded in 2018 – then discusses the effective problems that the Bolivian cargo has to leave for the Pacific, issues related to distance, and lack of significant investment in other routes.

The Maritime Claim and the Effects of the End of the Hague Lawsuit

The formation of national states in South America was completed with severe stumbles in the 19th century. These difficulties occurred due to definitions of boundaries between the developing countries but due to the absence of mechanisms to resolve international problems within frameworks that would undermine the war. In Chile's case, and particularly with its two northern neighbors, Peru and Bolivia, the conflicts' trajectory led to two wars during the 19th century. The first one was for the Peruvian-Bolivian government's insistence regarding a Confederate project's reticulation from the old Tahuantinsuyo spaces (1836–1839). The second, the saltpeters' control dispute between the parallels 24 and 25 south latitude, led to a second war to the states between 1879 and 1883, which left a new territorial configuration in the Pacific coast area. Thus, this Second Pacific War opened an extensive series of studies on

DOI: 10.4324/9781003045632-6

Chilean-Bolivian relations throughout the 19th and 20th centuries with an extensive list of works of all levels (Rodríguez 2018), in which we notice some constants that lasted for decades:

1 The modification of territorial boundaries concerning the colonial period in the area.
2 The absence of fluid contacts between Chile, Peru, and Bolivia, to which we should add to Argentina, which, although on the other side of the continent, was strategically affected.
3 The impossibility of achieving common goals or objectives in national development, contacts, national interests, or collective projections.

These facts, coupled with the individual strategy of incorporating the world economy into the area, led to these countries' rapprochements being sporadic, uncertain, and full of mistrust until almost the second half of the 20th century in the context of collective participation in hemispheric bodies. Indeed, it is noticeable that only the Organisation of American States (OAS) configuration first and other international bodies allowed some fluidity in interstate contact, but not the desired integration joint.

However, one aspect in Chile and Bolivia has overshadowed the entire bi-national relationship: the Pacific Ocean sovereign access' loss due to two reasons. First, the territories in the north of Antofagasta were occupied by Chile and then final agreements to resolve the war of 1879. It should be remembered that Chile never crossed the Andes Mountain Range on the western side toward Bolivia's territories. Nor did it occupy territories widely populated by Bolivia. On the contrary, Bolivia had virtually a nominal occupation on the Pacific coasts, which covered administratively with great difficulties since its foundation (Cajías de la Vega 1977).

It is striking that, during both wars, Bolivia could never restore institutionality nor adequately populate the area. That is why both Chilean and operational Peruvian forces could enter a relatively fragile political space without difficulty.

Once the wars were resolved, one of the key points in understanding the 1904 Treaty, an instrument that ends the conflict, could be called the sale of the salt one-way to the coast by Bolivia. We call it a sale because the 1904 treaty clauses are typologically identical to Bolivia's clauses with Brazil a year earlier in the Acre Treaty signed with the latter country.

Indeed, in this first international treaty, it is the railways and the compensation and other amounts for the cancellation of Bolivia's debts, which operate as conditions for the surrender of territories. In the 1904 Treaty, which has the same conditions (Correa et al. 2007; Correa and Salas 2018), the coast delivery had detractors in the Bolivian Congress, censors who failed to impose themselves, it must be said in a majority of Congress when in February 1905, the document was ratified.

For Bolivia, the coastline's loss has long been expressed as a substantial decline in the territory. However, Bolivia often omits that it reported 300,000 pounds of the time, the Chile absorption of a railway line's construction cost built from Chile between La Paz and Arica, the additional payment of other debts incurred by the Bolivian state, and the specificity of granting the widest and free transit to Bolivia's import or export goods. In exchange for this, in perpetuity, Bolivia gave way to the sovereign exit to the sea.

Given this background, for this agreement, and to the fact that Bolivia lost from 1825 to 1904 almost 1 million square km with all its neighbors, it was this space, the Pacific, that gave it the actual loss of a strategic impairment that the country did not size. Moreover, it did not, because Bolivia's concern at the 20th-century beginning was not to have coasts access but to take out somewhere its riches, which at that time went out on the back of a mule through the Andes mountain range because there was no railway. Thus, Bolivia managed to get out to the shore, but since 1913, through a railway without sovereignty. However, the international geopolitical outcome for the signing of the 1904 Treaty was early and failed challenged in 1920 before the League of Nations, questioned during different governments throughout the 20th century and in an unprecedented national effort, failed in a dispute raised again before the International Court of Justice between 2013 and 2018.

Lon Bolivian demand of 2013 aroused a thought homogeneity in Bolivia never seen and isolated. Undoubtedly, complementary topics between the two countries were a secondary attention source during the administration of Evo Morales. The most important of these is Bolivia's trade scopes relating to free transit and foreign trade, which are topics that motivate this research.

It should be emphasized that the recent dispute aimed at establishing Chile's obligation to negotiate in good faith and virtually an agreement granting Bolivia fully sovereign access to the Pacific Ocean. This demand was justified based on moral aspects, an irreparable historical loss to the Bolivian soul. The International Justice Court ruled that there were no valid legal arguments and, by 12 votes to 3, ruled that Chile is not required to negotiate an exit to the sea for Bolivia (Aparicio et al. 2019). However, Bolivia's indictment highlighted an alleged impairment of the country's trade. For this reason, and under the numerous backgrounds seen between the two states in more than a century of conflicting relations, Bolivia legally sued Chile in 2013 by attributing that these backgrounds shaped:

a   The existence of an obligation to negotiate a sovereign exit to the sea,
b   Chile's failure to comply with this obligation, and
c   Chile's duty to comply with that obligation.

Bolivia claimed that both countries maintained "agreements, diplomatic practice and a series of statements attributable to [Chile's] highest representatives" that "forced" Chile to respond for its sayings, practices or alleged negotiations toward Bolivia; events that, according to Bolivia, would have taken place between the Peace Treaty's conclusion of 1904 and 2012. In that sense, these actions' ultimate goal was to gain sovereign access to the Pacific Ocean.

The trial's extraordinary, a scarcely highlighted subject by Bolivia itself in this concept, is that the country accepted when filing the lawsuit, its membership of the 1948 Bogota Pact in 2012. In this context, Bolivia consents to the legality and validity of the Treaty of Peace and Friendship of 1904, which allows us to speak in the third decade of the 21st century, of an "end of the cycle" between the two nations. This, because, hereafter, however deplorable the conditions under which Bolivia signed the 1904 treaty, are the truth that they are legal, legitimate in law, and enforceable at all levels of jurisdiction to Chile. In this respect, trade takes on extraordinary importance because almost 80% of Bolivia's cargo, which is not gas, goes through Chilean ports.

In a political context animated by state propaganda, during the government of Evo Morales, the Bolivian stance insisted that, if there were an obligation on Chile's part, Chile would have to make the commitments that it had failed to make (Guzmán 2017).[1] On the contrary, if the International Court ruled that Chile had not legally committed itself, Bolivia should dismiss Chile's ongoing charge of non-compliance and misconduct toward Bolivia.

Moreover, this was precisely what resoundingly happened on October 1, 2018, when the judges ruled that the eight points presented by Bolivia in its lawsuit did not create any legal-international obligations over time. Therefore, Chile had not failed to comply with any obligation to negotiate and had no obligation to go down with Bolivia.

Given the magnitude of the ruling, it should be remembered all Bolivia's argumentative lines areas because of the dispute with Chile:

1 Bilateral Agreements. Bolivia represented before the International Court that virtually all bilateral dialogs throughout the 20th century constituted international negotiations. These would have happened in 1920, in 1950 with the exchange of bilateral notes, Charaña's 1975 declaration, the 1986 communiqués calling for the "fresh approach" of relations, the Algarve declaration of 2000 on the idea of dialog without exclusions, and the one which in our view was the most controversial and which affected many dimensions of the bilateral relationship, the agenda of the 13 points of 2006.
2 Chile's declarations and other unilateral acts, through which Chile would have been forced to give a sovereign exit.

3 The consent by which Chile would have agreed to a sovereign exit.

4 The estoppel, referring to a series of acts in which Chile would have been obliged to provide that exit.

5 Legitimate expectations, an area that had Bolivia expected to meet expectations for a sovereign exit.

6 Article 2.3 of the UN Charter and Article 3 of the OAS Charter, which required Chile, renouncing the conflict with Bolivia, to surrender a sovereign space so that the maritime claim would end.

7 The Resolutions of the OAS General Assembly, a request for Chile to verify the state of relations with Bolivia and to give it a sovereign exit.

8 The legal scope of the instruments, minutes, and elements of conduct was considered cumulative. Chile had an obligation to allow sovereign access to the coasts for Bolivia.

The fact that the International Court of Justice has dismissed all how Chile may have incurred obligations to providing sovereign access to costs defines the issue's closure. Indeed, the South American country will not discuss the item with Bolivia again. This has been pointed out by its authorities and various experts on the subject in the last year and a half following the Court's opinion.

Beyond this opinion, and given the economic dimensions it represents for the Bolivian economy, we propose this text to review Bolivia's future trade implications. Therefore, the aim is to answer two questions regarding the relationship between Chile and Bolivia. First, if the ruling could or may lead to significant deterioration or trade improvements about its exports and imports. Secondly, if this judgment adversely affects Bolivia's trade situation. Moreover, in the face of both questions, we have as a hypothesis that Chile is not interested in harming Bolivian trade and that if anything has been done in all these years is to make the trade through its ports feasibility in the best way that it has been able to do it, and indeed, with the limitations that a South American country has.

To do this, two exercises will be carried out. Concerning the post-Hague foreign policy projections between October 2018 and March 2020 between the two countries and a second financial year, it aimed at an economic valuation of Bolivia's foreign trade performance. However, it is to be emphasized that, within the context and global meaning of the affecting countries, this study leaves this factor out of the analysis in the projection, focusing on the structural elements of international relations and the economic conditions that are projected for Bolivia in trade matters and that with or without pandemic, are configured in the practical framework of this nation's trade.

Structural Elements of Bolivia's International Economic Relations at the Time of the International Court of Justice Ruling

The economic performance for Bolivia during the management of Evo Morales is discouraging toward 2018. Several authors agree that the country's macroeconomic structures wasted an extensive cycle of favorable commodity prices and squandered revenue from the star product of the decade: gas.

Milenio's (2019) *Informe*, published by the *Millennium Foundation of Bolivia*, shows the variations between 2018 and 2019, showing a systemic fall in GDP between 2015 and 2019 of two points and a considerable indebtedness resulting from public spending. Less investment and growth in the fiscal deficit found Bolivia mired in a phase of export decline and a negative balance in terms of goods and services in the trade balance. This negative global trend of the Permanent Bolivian economy since 2016 in the context of imFOB carriers and exports undoubtedly causes a progressive deterioration of certain export areas directly involved in Chile's relationship because these are the goods that enter and leave the country.

In this context, the national economic report portrayed that external debt rose to 40% of GDP, Net International Reserves (RNOs) going down (from $15 billion in 2014 to $8.5 billion in 2018) and artificial control of the type of change or, a "bubble" artificially maintained by the government.

In this context of global figures, how is it possible that some sectors and analysts estimate Bolivia's economic miracle? There are two elements to this: Firstly, the accounting of Bolivia's economy has been carried out from official data in which the drug economy is not accounted for. In other words, there is a formal reporting economy and an informal economy that is unknown in both macro and microeconomic effects. In this sense, Velasco (2015) submits that the operation's value of this "part of the economy" would correspond to almost half of the formal movement. In a table, Velasco draws it openly and concludes that by 2014, the informal economy is equivalent to one-third of the country's total economy. Velasco's chart outlines it in Table 5.1.

Secondly, because in the last years of the administration of Evo Morales (2006–2019), the reading on the realization of the economic conduct of the country considered as positive practices the following:

1 Sustained public indebtedness.
2 Maintaining the fixed exchange rate as a government policy.
3 Nationalization of natural resources, even if business balance sheets were negative.
4 Public investment in deficit companies for the country.

Table 5.1 Estimation of the size of the informal economy

Period	Rate of informality	Formal GDP	Informal GDP
2000	0.60882	22,061,380	13,431,441
2001	0.59686	22,729,984	13,566,525
2002	0.59944	22,901,200	13,727,935
2003	0.58759	23,350,520	13,720,513
2004	0.59006	24,238,325	14,302,116
2005	0.57832	25,300,073	14,631,600
2006	0.58068	26,429,314	15,347,036
2007	0.56906	27,397,407	15,590,652
2008	0.57130	28,365,500	16,205,286
2009	0.55979	29,333,593	16,420,623
2010	0.56192	30,301,686	17,027,214
2011	0.55052	31,269,779	17,214,710
2012	0.55254	32,237,872	17,812,820
2013	0.54126	33,205,965	17,972,913
2014	0.54316	34,174,059	18,562,105

Source: Own elaboration based on Velasco (2015). Courtesy of Danilo Velasco Valdez.

5 Low unemployment rates, which, according to preliminary figures as of July 2018, would be around 4.1%, even if there were mostly informal employment.
6 Growth in remuneration, at the cost of compulsory bond payments – two a year – and delivery of state subsidies.
7 Control of the country's strategic industries such as Bolivian Fiscal Oil Fields and other energy, railway, communications, and other companies (Arévalo, 2016).

From a foreign trade perspective, the situation is limited. The study of Chumacero (2019) is categorical in these topics:

"Bolivia's recent economic bonanza is mainly due to the extremely favorable external conditions it faced, and which, in any case, domestic factors prevented Bolivia from enjoying greater benefits". Moreover, Chumacero is conclusive in quoting that the "Heritage Foundation classifies Bolivia in 173rd place of 180 in terms of general freedom, characterizing it as "repressed". Other countries in this category are Cuba (178), Venezuela (179), and North Korea (180)".

Landing the issue with foreign trade or a historical picture of imports shows a sustained increase, with an interruption in 2016 alone. Thus, between 2011 and 2019, the value of these went from US$1.747 million to US$2.620 million (see Graphs 5.1, 5.2, 5.3, and 5.4).

For its part, in the case of exports, they showed a decrease in the same period.

However, concerning the composition of exports, gas is seen as the most relevant product, with almost 43% in early 2010.[2] Moreover, for

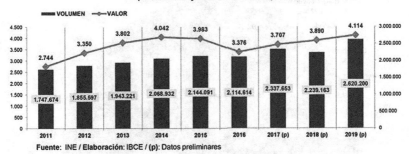

Graph 5.1 Bolivia: imports. Comparison: January–May 2011–2019 (in tons and millions of dollars; by volume [volumen] and value [valor]).

Source: INE/Elaboration: IBCE/(p) Preliminary data.

those who are not in the southern hemisphere, it will be remembered that no pipeline leaves for the Pacific, but only to Brazil and Argentina. Consequently, there is no relationship between the origin of Bolivia's higher income and Chile. As is well seen in the export composition figures:

According to the information available by the international consultancy South *American Connections* for the beginning of the second decade of this century, Bolivia ranks ninth among South America's economies. Its composition remained composed mostly by the hydrocarbons sector, mining, and trade in other raw materials. This fact, coupled with

Graph 5.2 Bolivia: exports. Comparison: January–May 2011–2019 (in tons and millions of dollars; by volume [volumen] and value [valor]).

Source: INE/Elaboration: IBCE/(p) Preliminary data. Note: It does not include re-exports.

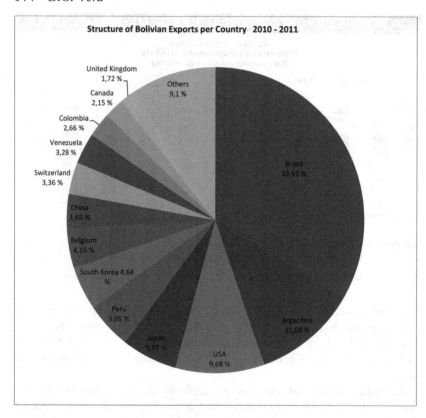

Graph 5.3 Structure of Bolivian exports per country 2010–2011.

Source: Own elaboration based on bulletin N° 199 from IBCE. https://ibce.org.bo/images/publica-ciones/ce_199_cifras-comercio-exterior-boliviano-gestion-2011.pdf

the fact that underrate the government of Evo Morales, Bolivia's extreme dependence on natural resources reached an average of almost 70% of total GDP, determines a real physical dependence and a need for effective connectivity neighboring countries. In terms of imports, Bolivian demand is focused on capital and consumer goods and fuels that mostly enter through Chilean routes.

Bolivia Imports 2010

Although the Bolivian economy showed a significant economic growth structure maintained over the decade and based in the traditional sectors, increasing income was achieved from a fiscally fixed redistributive policy (Arévalo 2016; Chumacero 2019).

Thus, a stable economic model's rationality of economic management from the "redistribute the surpluses of transnational corporations

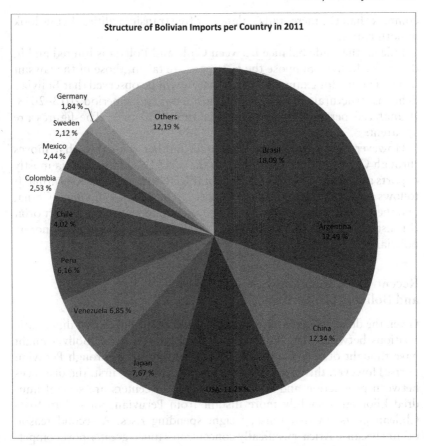

Structure of Bolivian Imports per Country in 2011

Germany 1,84 %
Sweden 2,12 %
Mexico 2,44 %
Colombia 2,53 %
Chile 4,02 %
Peru 6,16 %
Venezuela 6,85 %
Japan 7,67 %
USA 11,28 %
Others 12,19 %
Brasil 18,09 %
Argentina 12,49 %
China 12,34 %

Graph 5.4 Structure of Bolivian imports per country in 2011.

Source: Own elaboration based on bulletin N° 199 from IBCE. https://ibce.org.bo/images/publicaciones/ce_199_cifras-comercio-exterior-boliviano-gestion-2011.pdf

and the State itself to the middle and indigenous sectors". The thesis of Andean-Amazonian capitalism, therefore, updates that ancient bourgeois narrative that promoted the transformation of the small producer into capitalist and the transformation of a society of small producers into a capitalist society, ideas indeed legitimized by a strong indigenist discourse of cultural identity, which has become the hallmark of "national" and "popular" in Bolivia over the last few years. In short, the MAS's political program aims at industrialization through the transformation of natural resources, the development of the domestic market, and the export of raw materials and industrial products (Mogrovejo 2010, 4, 5).

Therefore, assessing the role of Bolivian foreign trade ports through Chile is an important issue, not to mention capital. When binational trade is relatively scarce in the formal, the situation is somewhat more complex than the mere trade balance or free transit facilities. Let us look at both issues.

Indeed, the trade balance between Chile and Bolivia is limited and in deficit for Bolivia. Suppose the last years are taken, those of the lawsuit in The Hague, for example. In that case, it will be observed that Bolivia's deficit is structural with Chile, at almost 6 to 1 in the period 2013–2018. If analyzed per year, the situation is almost 10 to 1. The figures are apparent:

However, one issue is the trade and another the cargo that moves through Chilean ports. According to the 2017 INE data, Bolivia mostly exports gas totaling almost 35% of total GDP to Brazil and Argentina. It follows South Korea, the United States, Japan, India, Colombia, China, and the United Arab Emirates. Chile does not appear in the export orbit (Ministerio de Economía y Finanzas Publicas. Memoria de la economía boliviana 2017, 102).

Recent Trade Relations between Chile and Bolivia: The Peru Factor

Given the deficit trade situation with Chile and the absence of diplomatic relations between the two countries, it makes sense that Bolivia might have thought of diverting some or most of the cargo through Peruvian ports. However, this never happened for two reasons: first, the distances between production and export consolidation centers are several hundred kilometers slightly more distant from Peruvian ports than from Chilean ports. In that sense, freight spending rises. A second reason occurs because Arica specifically concentrates much greater port competitiveness than the rest of the Peruvian and even Chilean ports in the area.

In the case of economic relations with Chile, several contact aspects should be distinguished at the foreign trade level.

1 The trade balance has shown no significant variations in structural terms for three decades. Bolivia and Chile are mining countries, and agricultural markets either compete or are not attractive to Chile, which prefers tropical fruit consumption from Ecuador or Peru.
2 Bolivia takes hold of a historical deficit trade balance with Chile as appreciated in Table 5.2. As far as this century, $3.938 million is counted. Therefore, the bilateral trade relationship can be described as moderate and asymmetrical.
3 From Chile's commercial perspective, the figures are much more discrete. This can be seen in Table 5.3, concerning Chilean exports and in Table 5.4, on imports from Chile. Bolivia is not a relevant trading partner, as Peru and Argentina, including Paraguay.
4 Given the above, Chile is not a relevant market for Bolivia but a transit country for its departure.

Table 5.2 Trade Exchange of Chile–Bolivia (in US$ FOB) 2013–2018

Year	Exports	Imports	Trade balance
2013	1,785,678,631	127,858,255	1,657,820,375
2014	1,702,463,405	144,211,256	1,558,252,149
2015	1,285,999,655	95,304,281	1,190,695,374
2016	1,207,832,719	102,214,497	1,105,618,222
2017	1,201,616,423	106,411,157	1,095,205,266
2018	1,158,164,671	114,477,810	1,043,686,861
General Totals	8,341,755,504	690,477,256	7,651,278,247

Source: Own elaboration based on official data. Directorate of Studies, DIRECON, with data from the Central Bank of Chile. Figures are subject to revision of value variation.

Note: FOB is Free on board.

According to data from The Under secretariat for Chile's International Economic Relations, trade reached US$1,248 million in 2018, of which US$1,120 corresponds to Chilean exports to Bolivia (mainly vehicles and fuel), and that said in passing have fallen steadily since 2013, leaving the only US$128 million of exports from that country to Chile. For its part, Bolivia peaked in exports to Chile in 2012 with US$226 million and 2013 in imports with US$574 million. That is about trade.

What Happens between Peru and Bolivia?

According to data from the Bolivian Institute of Foreign Trade (IBCE) in 2018, 72% of Bolivia's cargo was mobilized by Chilean ports. This is 3.8 of the 4.2 million metric tons of cargo that came out or entered from the Pacific. In this scheme, only 1.1 million tons went out of the Paraná Paraguay Waterway toward the Atlantic. As a result, Bolivia's most massive production does not depend on the Pacific so far, but on the efficiency, price, and markets of neighboring Atlantic-side countries relative to their star production: gas. That is in values, but not in load volumes, the most significant incidence of which is related to Chile for several reasons:

a Bolivia's lack of interest is in adapting its road infrastructure to the freight exit markets in Peru and through the Paraná-Paraguay Waterway. Since the 1990s, Peru has offered a port for Bolivia in Ilo. This port has been underutilized until the ruling of the International Court.
b The absence of commercial services, but above all, of Bolivia's port logistics in Ilo, has caused Bolivian cargo to transit more through Chilean ports than Peruvian ports systematically.
c Following the CIJ's ruling, President Evo Morales traveled to Ilo in a symbolic sign of not maintaining Chilean dependence on the

Table 5.3 Chilean exports according to market of destination – 1st trimester
of each year (amounts in US$ millions)

Countries	1T 2017	1T 2018	1T 2019	1T 2020	Var. % '20/'19	US$ Dif. '20/'19	% Part. 2020
TOTAL	15,676	19,385	18,252	17,529	–4%	–722	100%
China	3,832	5,882	5,624	6,017	7%	393	34.30%
United States	2,636	3,216	2,674	2,539	–5%	–135	14.50%
European Union	1,969	2,234	2,000	1,612	–19%	–388	9.20%
Japan	1,530	1,879	1,946	1,588	–18%	–358	9.10%
South Korea	922	1,184	1,246	1,285	3%	40	7.30%
Common Markets of the South (MERCOSUR)	1,205	1,152	1,069	1,044	–2%	–25	6.00%
Canada	389	312	276	335	21%	59	1.90%
Pacific Alliance	868	880	937	879	–6%	–58	5.00%
Bolivia	280	289	243	224	–8%	–20	1.30%
India	451	446	335	183	–45%	–152	1.00%
Russia	146	273	187	173	–7%	–14	1.00%
Ecuador	114	102	115	125	9%	11	0.70%
Thailand	87	120	106	109	3%	3	0.60%
Middle East	100	130	122	104	–14%	–18	0.60%
Africa	33	101	148	72	–52%	–77	0.40%
Australia	57	53	54	64	18%	10	0.40%
Vietnam	65	78	70	59	–15%	–10	0.30%
Turkey	55	60	43	56	29%	13	0.30%
Philippines	70	11	38	31	–19%	–7	0.20%
Indonesia	14	17	27	20	–24%	–7	0.10%
Malaysia	17	37	68	19	–72%	–49	0.10%
Singapore	16	15	28	15	–47%	–13	0.10%
New Zealand	19	18	22	12	–44%	–9	0.10%
Norway	10	8	9	10	13%	1	0.10%
Venezuela	14	28	29	6	–79%	–23	0.00%
Others	384	410	342	568	66%	226	3.20%

Source: Department of Trade Information. Department of Studies, SUBREI, with amounts
from the Central Bank of Chile.

Bolivian cargo. On his journey, he oversaw the arrival of 13,000
tons of Bolivian cargo and thus also learned about the capacity
of the port of Matarani, located a little further north of Ilo. This
excited many discouraged by the outcome of the Court and caused
the managers in charge of managing the port of Matarani to pay
more attention to business with Bolivia. However, Matarani is also
managed by a private company, Tisur, which efficiently as early as
2017, moved 6.9 million tons of cargo.

d Matarani's advantages are spatial. Matarani has 40 hectares with an
expansion potential of 100 hectares, while Ilo has only 8 hectares.

Table 5.4 Chilean imports according to market of origin – 1st Trimester of each year (amounts in US$ millions)

Countries	1T 2017	1T 2018	1T 2019	1T 2020	Var. % '20/'19	US$ Dif. '20/'19	% Part. 2020
TOTAL	14,632	16,428	16,449	14,245	–13%	–2,203	100%
China	3,340	4,095	4,150	3,431	–17%	–719	24.1%
United States	2,664	2,986	2,914	2,994	3%	80	21.0%
Brazil	1,241	1,475	1,311	1,061	–19%	–250	7.4%
Argentina	657	715	805	816	1%	11	5.7%
Germany	599	653	650	533	–18%	–117	3.7%
Mexico	477	540	547	377	–31%	–171	2.6%
Japan	529	509	593	342	–42%	–251	2.4%
Peru	236	281	225	306	36%	81	2.2%
Spain	311	351	362	303	–16%	–59	2.1%
Colombia	245	277	272	281	3%	9	2.0%
Ecuador	348	331	401	276	–31%	–124	1.9%
Italy	252	269	303	253	–17%	–50	1.8%
South Korea	519	405	369	243	–34%	–126	1.7%
Vietnam	195	199	164	225	37%	61	1.6%
France	284	342	323	200	–38%	–123	1.4%
India	170	200	236	198	–16%	–38	1.4%
Paraguay	132	134	161	159	–1%	–2	1.1%
Thailand	187	260	169	132	–22%	–37	0.9%
Canada	159	186	183	129	–29%	–54	0.9%
United Kingdom	122	142	144	119	–18%	–25	0.8%
Others	1,966	2,076	2,166	1,868	–14%	–298	13.1%

Source: Department of Trade Information, Department of Studies, SUBREI, with amounts from Central Bank of Chile.

Additionally, three of the four docks managed by Tisur operate 24/7/365. The ileño pier has no continuous operation. However, Matarani is the furthest port in Bolivia compared to its competitors. It is an additional 90 kilometers to Arica's port and 80 kilometers more than Ilo's port from La Paz. Moreover, that is not the most complicated thing for cargo issues: the frequency of container ships' arrival is every fortnight. Arica, the arrival of ships, is daily, so it mobilizes almost 79% of Bolivian cargo.

Bolivia's Exporters Chamber Commercial Manager (CADEX), Martín Salces, interviewed for this research, summarizes the problem as follows:

South Peruvian Ports are at a disadvantage compared to the Chileans because of the irregular round-trip freight of the trucks. There is no burden to bring to Bolivia. This is because, unlike Arica, the ports of southern Peru do not receive sufficient import cargo. Thus Bolivian trucks would return empty to the country.

(Interview with Martin Salces, September 23, 2019)

It should be noted that, until the 2018 International Court of Justice ruling, Bolivia made no major initiative to shift Chile's cargo to other ports. Moreover, exportations, Bolivia's transfers used as the main port of entry and exit of non-traditional exports, the port of Arica by 57% (ALADI 2017, 23).

IBCE's 2019 report, according to the mode of transport, showed a volume of 78.36% of pipeline exports, 12.50% by road, 3.92% by rail, and 5.04% by waterway. Air transport reached 0.18% of the total exported as imports are mostly defined through Chilean ports in a hegemonic volume. However, Arica is not the only port. From north to south, it is followed by the port of Iquique, whose Franca area is the gateway to goods and goods from Asia. This is a space with a contact potential from extra to least in the last decade due to the increase in smuggling and Bolivian importers' reluctance to articulate their imports through the free zone's tax exemptions.

The motive is not unique. On the one hand, the rules for the entry of goods do not accommodate the Bolivian importer, rules that have to do with the total declaration of the goods, and their actual valuation in dollars. The chief lawyer of the Free Trade Zone of Iquique, Johanna Díaz,[3] argues that the exit checks of the goods entering from Iquique usually bring goods smuggled or entry specifications not under the control rules by Bolivian authority. This occurs when there are inconsistencies between the cargo manifests, a document indicating the shipment contents, and when the shipment contents are not responsible for what is stated in the document.

This has led to the progressive Bolivian importer's refusal to pass through ZOFRI, avoid explanations, checks, and carry out the procedures, directly in port. Thus, it is directly transported from the berthing vessel or FAS of Iquique to Bolivia.

In this regard, and under the provisions of the 1904 Treaty, which defines the free transit of goods to and from Bolivia, the Chilean authorities cannot interfere in Bolivian trade. Therefore, to blame Chile for the increase in smuggling in the border area, based on the above dynamics, is not to understand how international trade works, the real weight of trade practices, and the ways its agents use to reduce the costs of taxes, manipulation, and other collections. In this context, the ports of Arica, Iquique, and Antofagasta/Mejillones are a set of critical ports of contact of goods to and from the Pacific to Bolivia and operate as a system. Peru has no articulation, nor default, any real incentive to achieve deflection of the Bolivian cargo or, overlapping Ilo or Matarani, above the comparative advantages that the port of Arica represents, an aspect that highlights the 2017 ALADI report. In the context outlined, the critical aspects of the trade are given by two elements: a) the port efficiency, measured when the cargo is in port or on the vessel's side; and b) the distance from the goods' dispatch centers or destination.

This is not a stowing issue of the merchant ship, but precisely the organization on the ground, which deals with the de-stressing cargo, and its subsequent transfer to the trucks that come to the side of the ships to look for the cargo or to the storage areas arranged in the port of Arica, fundamentally. It is also the distance between the port of shipment of goods and the distance with the border. In this sense, the situation of Arica is key to the bulk cargo that leaves or can enter Bolivia, whereas that in the case of Antofagasta/Mejillones has a mostly mining cargo destination that has a different but equally functional operation, since most Bolivian export minerals are in Oruro and Potosí. These places historically put the port of Antofagasta/Mejillones as the main port for mining. In this scheme, port efficiency and the places of destination/origin of the cargo are fundamental to Bolivian trade in all cases.

International Court Post-Judgment Controversies

Agramont and Peres Cajías (2016, 19–24) provide an analysis on how to assess a possible increase in costs for Bolivian trade through Chilean ports. The analysis concentrates on this sphere given its importance in explaining the negative effects of mediterraneity. On the other hand, ALADI's report (2017) researches the decline when strikes occur in Chilean ports. In order not to be biased, let us put the assumptions of this previous study:

> Considering the value of exports (non-hydrocarbon and not exported by air) that are out of Chilean customs, the result shows that the impact of a day of unemployment in Chile amounts to US$7.9 million in Bolivian exports by 2016. In particular, the most export-relevant customs offices are Arica and Antofagasta. It should be noted that the affectation does not imply a cost or a direct assessment of the effect of Chile's unemployment on Bolivian foreign trade. The exercise simply involves calculating the average daily amount of trade flows that pass-through customs to account for the order of magnitude affected by a day of unemployment. A day of unemployment in Peru, meanwhile, has a daily affectation of US$1.4 million of Bolivian non-hydrocarbon exports, followed by Brazil (US$1.2 million) and Argentina (US$270 thousand).
>
> (ALADI 2017)

Thus, the most significant impacts of transit countries' stoppages for Bolivia's non-hydrocarbon external sales occur at Pacific customs, particularly in Chile, and to a lesser extent, Peru, because these are the largest steps burden of minerals and non-traditional exports emerge. Frozen meats, lemons, sugar, quinoa, and perishable products are generally the most affected products (ALADI 2017, 23, 24).

The Chilean port situation corresponds to the definition of private services established decades ago in the country. A character that curiously was only called into question during the recent Hague trial. As we have seen in a recently published text, Bolivia has exported everything it has put into port since 1904. However, Bolivia's deteriorating relationship with Chile during Morales' judicial dispute did indeed directly damage relations between the port authorities of Arica and the Bolivian authorities and did so at various levels:

1   About the interlocutors in the face of everyday situations.
2   Concerning the payments to be made by the Port Services Administration – Bolivia (ASP-B) regarding the Terminal of the Port of Arica according to payments for port services and their fees.
3   Depending on the conditions of stay and transit of Bolivian truckers in Arica.

Still, assuming difficulties, port strikes in Chile relate to central Chile situations and not port workers' conditions in northern Chile. In this perspective, what defines affordability and good port performance have been the subject of the study of Salgado and Cea (2012) and which is summarized in Figure 5.1:

Neither the study of Cajías and Agramont nor that of LAIA refers to the conditions represented by Salgado and Cea, nor to the conditions or importance of maintaining a fluid dialogue when, of course, in commercial activities, there are inconveniences between the actors. Nor do Bolivian studies refer to port exemptions, port entrepreneurs' efforts with the authorities of the ASPB, Bolivian Customs, or the various transport chambers, exporters, or other entities. In this regard, it is interesting to note that costs must be measured in transport time and based on the immovable variable of distance in the equation: that is between the place of origin and the national customs; between the national customs office and the customs office of the transit country; between the customs office of the transit country and the port of transit; between the port of transit and the destination of the product, which is why, if trade agents are not understood, there will always be an additional cost in case of fortuitous situations and no case driven by the State of Chile.

Considering these variables, the conditions of trade are given by two aspects:

1   Bolivia's production facilities manage to get their goods out at a high cost because the distance is more significant than a Bolivian coastal territory. False. This is because the production centers are located at long distances. In that context, customs management is undoubtedly vital. However, at almost 4,000 meters high, and after

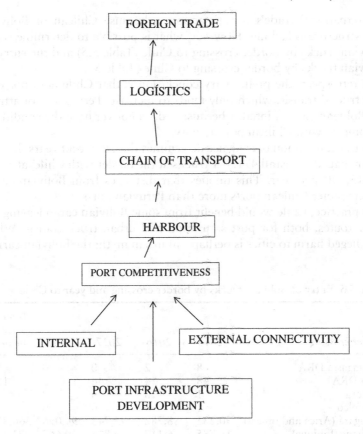

Figure 5.1 Foreign trade.

Source: Salgado Oportus, O. and Cea Echeverría, P. (2012). Análisis de la conectividad externa de los puertos de Chile como un factor de competitividad. Ingeniare. Revista chilena de ingeniería 20 (1). https://www.scielo.cl/scielo.php?script=sci_abstract&pid=S0718-33052012000100004&lng=en. License: CC BY 4.0.

two mountain ranges, the problem is the same: distance if the load comes from Santa Cruz.

2 The second element, is there any merchandise that cannot be effectively removed by Chilean ports? The answer is clear: no.

What has been said about ports is further complex and landed if the port variable is added to the accumulation of evidence in border transport. Between 2015 and 2018, Bolivia has managed to install 471,401 trucks on the border with Chile, at a rate of 115,000 per year. This implies that distances from Bolivian cargo centers prefer Chilean ports to Peruvians. Again, the problem is not the infrastructure but the distance. The survey cited by Agramont and Peres Cajías (2016) does not discriminate if international trade's dissatisfaction is because Chilean or Bolivian infrastructure is lacking. However, what is possible to determine is the Bolivian trucks by border crossing to Chile (Table 5.5) and the entry of Bolivian trucks by border crossing to Chile (Table 5.6).

In retrospect, the preliminary conclusion is that Chile does not prevent trucks' transit, which only tends to increase. Peru does not attract the Bolivian cargo's interest because it does not yet have the conditions to compete with Chilean port activity.

The accumulation of evidence determines that, in recent years, Bolivia has managed to install 471,401 trucks at the border with Chile, at a rate of 115,000 per year. This implies that distances from Bolivian cargo centers prefer Chilean ports more than Peruvian ports.

In practice, Chile would benefit from some Bolivian cargo leaving for other routes, both for port saturation and urban truck transit. While the alleged harm to cities is perhaps an urban myth: the Bolivian carrier

Table 5.5 Entry of Bolivian trucks by border crossing and year to Chile

Border crossing	2015	2016	2017	2018	Total by place of income
Antofagasta DRA	8	2	0	0	10
Arica DRA	48	14	46	8	116
Cancosa	1	0	0	0	1
Chincolco	1	0	0	0	1
Chungará (Arica and others)	90,232	88,782	93,743	94,096	366,853
Colchane (Iquique)	16,785	16,112	19,813	19,667	72,377
Concordia Chacalluta	1,099	870	543	270	2,782
Christ the Redeemer The Liberators	1,636	1,723	1,820	2,017	7,196
The Transit	0	0	1	0	1
Huemules	0	1	0	0	1
Southern Integration Monte Aymond	4	9	3	0	16
Iquique DRA	13	2	10	4	29
Iquique Patio Autos	0	1	0	0	1
Iquique Patio Sellaje	1	1	0	0	2
Jama	47	6	3	1	57
Ollahue (Antofagasta)	2,997	3,144	5,280	8,190	19,611
Puerto Angamos	0	1	0	0	1
San Pedro de Atacama	49	37	195	148	429
Visviri	103	479	1,276	59	1,917
Total	113,024	111,184	122,733	124,460	471,401

Source: Own elaboration based on National Customs Service Records (2019). Reserved report requested by the transparency law regarding the free transit of Bolivian trucks in Chile.

Note: The total number of Argentine and Peruvian trucks that transited through Chile in the same period is 329,562 and the number of trucks with Peruvian patents is 43,309.

Table 5.6 Bolivian trucking income by year and destination in Chile

	2015	2016	2017	2018
Arica	41,407	43,282	40,111	41,987
Iquique	2,750	4,782	7,199	9,269
Antofagasta	388	874	2,054	4,170
Chungará	48,592	45,235	52,568	51,122
Colchane	13,580	11,332	12,910	10,540
Christ the Redeemer	822	411	375	825
The Andes	808	1,308	1,443	1,189
Ollague	2,414	1,985	2,287	2,875
Concordia	1,137	1,985	2,287	2,875
Iquique Autos	274	129	222	219
Visviri	102	436	1,203	60
Chincolco	12	43	63	47
Puerto Angamos	6	49	63	37
No Information	-	49	63	37
Total	112,292	111,900	122,848	125,252

Source: Own elaboration based on National Customs Service Records (2019).

hardly spends almost no time in Chile because truck drivers sleep in their trucks and bring what they eat. Taking this evidence as the basis for generating a public policy, Chilean free-transit cooperation must reassess Bolivian transport costs on national routes. Port saturation is not paid by Arica, Iquique, and Antofagasta's concession ports, but by the Arica's people, *iquiqueños* and *antofagastinos* themselves.

It is enlightening to understand that the idea of harming northern Chilean ports, diverting the cargo, was a maneuver by Morales' government to maintain an antagonistic discourse with Chile. In practice, and after his resignation, it is tough for the mining cargo of the West (Oruro-Potosí) that leaves for Antofagasta, to be diverted to the East; it is more challenging to think that the miners of Oruro or Potosí, decide to take their ore out of Peruvian ports that are much more left to the north.

Indeed, it is difficult to think that Bolivian entrepreneurs decide to spend more money to move the burden toward Ilo. What is frankly a fantasy is that all Bolivian cargo can be diverted to East ports by the Paraná Paraguay Hydrovia. For the cost and the shallow draft, Hydrovia is a usable space. However, it requires costly conditioning and implies values that Bolivia's entrepreneurship cannot cover. Also, in the case of Bolivian Eastern exports, these are mostly agricultural.

On the other hand, the absence of port infrastructure, warehouse, and climate humidity make the export of soybeans impractical and other products by Puerto Suárez, Puerto Aguirre, and nearby docks, whose temperatures and humidity are incompatible with the bulk sale of both agricultural products, soybean oil or manufactured wood. To this, it should be added that the railway to the East is old and almost maintenance-free.

Thus, Bolivia's distance and port infrastructure are factoring that Bolivian trade must continue to weigh among its variables to consider. Let us look at some examples. Between Santa Cruz and Puerto Suarez (east of the country), there are 638 km., which increases to almost 900 km between Cochabamba to Puerto Suarez and reaches 1705 km between La Paz and Puerto Suarez. The road that will run from Patacamaya to Ilo is under construction. Meanwhile, the distance between Arica and Ilo is 178 km and two more customs, Santa Rosa on the Peruvian side and Chacalluta, on the Chilean side. On the opposite side, geographically, the most relevant is that trade to Chile only represents significant spending on permanent routes and constant urban pressure for Arica, while the Port of Arica has been making all kinds of investments to accommodate the exit of the growing Bolivian cargo.

Bolivia receives from Chungará between 115 and 250 trucks a day on the A11 route. The distance from La Paz to Arica is 510 km, from Cochabamba reaches 671 km, while Santa Cruz reaches 1,171 km to Arica in Chile. Further south, in the case of Route A15 – from Colchane – Pisiga to Iquique –, truck traffic with Bolivian patent is close to 19,000 per year, at the rate of 25 trucks per day approximately on the descent to the port of Iquique.

According to the destination, the entry chart of Bolivian trucks is key to determining the frequency of roads' frequency, which routes to Iquique and Antofagasta have only tended to its growth. In these terms, cargo diversion is a discourse but not a possible reality. These are consolidated routes, armed businesses, and known logistics. The consolidation of the Bolivian Port System, consisting of the ports Aguirre, Gravetal, and Jennefer, and soon Puerto Busch, are in the planning phase and estimate a saving of between 13% and 14%, compared to the use for example of Arica.[4] It will undoubtedly be an excellent exit when operational for the East of the country's cargo.

However, interconnection on the Western side meets the country's export demand. However, it must be admitted, these are two-way routes, with little signage and control, in a very complex geographical environment, both for the Andean piedmont and for the vast infrastructure expenditure that represents its continuous deterioration each summer season and the rains that are observed there. For this reason, a good relationship between countries cooperates with trade and does not determine or condition it.

Conclusions

There is no evidence based on Bolivian trade data that Chile instructed, encouraged, or conditioned obstructions of Bolivian trade by Chilean ports. Indeed, there were drawbacks during the Hague lawsuit, which could undoubtedly be improved by a considerable effort by the actors involved, rather than thanks to the state management level led by Evo Morales.

For Chile, for its part, it is not a profitable business, and it is a waste of free trade and the economic model to argue that the condition of the Mediterranean is what harms Bolivia's trade abroad. Economic evidence indicates that Bolivia has not seen in depth the benefits of a trade articulation under the port competitiveness prism.

From a legal perspective, respecting the conditions of the 1904 Treaty is verified by conditions of cargo traffic, movement of persons, and trade under standard conditions in the country. Moreover, the trend of a progressive increase in cargo and people by port and commercial destination in Chile counteract accusations, and Bolivian political propaganda can reverse the market developed by Chilean ports, especially by ZOFRI.

However, there is one issue that Chile must pay attention to: it is the estimated cost of interruptions to the Arica-Tambo Quemado section. In short, in 2013, 6 days of interruption cost US\$30 million; in 2014, 14 days cost \$70 million; in 2015, 12 days cost \$60 million; in 2016, 20 days cost \$110 million and in 2017, 9 days meant US\$55 million losses.[5]

Indeed, the International Court's ruling of October 1, 2018, marked a turning point in bilateral diplomatic history, as it is an international and binding body that rejected the existence of Bolivia's sovereignty right to access the Pacific Ocean. Commercially, however, changes have occurred regarding greater freedom of the Port of Arica by optimizing the Bolivian cargo flow and movement, freeing it from storage that, strategically, was not profitable. Iquique and Antofagasta have gone along the same optimization line, not without additional costs, either in the accumulation of Bolivian cargo trucks on the slopes of Iquique and Alto Hospicio; either by promoting a diversion of Bolivian cargo to the Port of Mejillones due to urban saturation problems in the city of Antofagasta.

To be sure, the ruling represented a bitter defeat that attempted to dilute with alternative transit proposals for foreign trade and public calls for dialogue with Chile, called in a sui géneris interpretation of the ICJ's judgment. However, the diplomatic rapprochement with Chile[6] is advisable and necessary. It has been seen with the end of the government of Evo Morales and the new relationship established by Jeanine Añez. In this context and to establish a stable, collaborative, and forward-looking relationship, the trade issue, from all sides: trade, exports, free transit, business opportunities, corridors, and a long etcetera, should be a priority for Bolivia.

In a comparative look and considering the effects of the pandemic, a final observation is essential to size the weight of transport in Bolivia's foreign trade: during the rigid quarantine established by Bolivia, this is from March 22, 2020, to May 31, 2020, Bolivia moved a total load of 122,402 tons from ports in Chile and 11,799 tons from Peru (Página Siete, June 8, 2020). This implies that the chances of expansion of

Bolivian exports through Peru or eventually through the Paraná River Waterway are slim. Consequently, Bolivia's commercial dependence through Chilean ports will continue over time. In this sense, the abuses of the Bolivian Port Services Administration regarding Bolivian importers are an issue to be resolved by Bolivia. This, in order not to endorse the Chilean Port of Arica responsibilities regarding charges on Bolivian imports.

Finally, even though Bolivia left a 14-year government, it is essential to mention that it has failed to overcome coastal loss's prolonged trauma. Moreover, if not, reaffirming maritime aspiration as an irreducible objective, economic growth possibilities will remain on a projective level. Therefore, and in this new post-Hague era and unless the Mediterranean country seriously revises its claim paradigm and replaces it with a collaborative one, Bolivia's economic delay is expected to remain throughout the 21st century.

Notes

1. Interestingly, in an interview given by economist Andrés Guzmán, he pointed out the following: "In that time, I did not know that these promises were legally enforceable. I was interested to know why they had failed, because while there were many approaches in history, the problem could never be solved. My intention was to identify the factors by which the negotiations had failed. In the process, the lawsuit came and I gave it that legal approach that it then acquired and has now also become a support for the thesis that Bolivia is presenting to the International Court of Justice, supporting the arguments we have".
2. A study from early June 2020 notes that in the coming years, the refining of liquid hydrocarbons will decrease by almost 50%, and that Bolivia will therefore have to import most of the oil and diesel it consumes. See https://www.lostiempos.com/actualidad/economia/20200607/preven-caida-del-40-produccion-hidrocarburos-liquidos-5-anos
3. Interview conducted on June 21, 2019.
4. Logistics chain cost matrix. CEBEC 2018.
5. The cost is calculated by a CEBEC – CAINCO study, based on the product input methodology. *Company and Development Journal*, No. 159, Santa Cruz, Bolivia, p. 20. One issue that Chile could assess is compensation in this area. It would be a valuable gesture, and perhaps a deterrent to Bolivian arguments.
6. This study should highlight the recent rapprochement between the chancellors of Chile and Bolivia in the framework of the pandemic, a rapprochement that extends to a real improvement in contacts between port authorities and Bolivians engaged in trade. In this regard, Chancellor Karen Longaric stressed and thanked the Chancellor, and the people of Chile, for "the close, supportive and fruitful cooperation in the repatriation of Bolivian citizens". See, Duty, 07.06.2020. Retrieved from https://eldeber.com.bo/182740_karen-longaric-la-orden-de-designacion-del-consul-en-barcelona-llego-directo-de-palacio; while the Bolivian authorities recognize much better functioning after the departure of Evo Morales.

Bibliography

Agramont, D. and Pérez Cajías, J. (coord.) (2016). *Bolivia un país privado de litoral. Apuntes para un debate pendiente*. La Paz, Bolivia: Oxfam/Plural editores.

ALADI. Estudio sobre impactos y costos al comercio exterior boliviano relacionados a la conflictividad interna en países de tránsito. DAPMDER/N° 01/17. Retrieved from http://www2.aladi.org/nsfaladi/estudios.nsf/204F8AB8AC7A5 E870325814E0069126A/$FILE/DAPMDER_01_17_BO.pdf

Aparicio, J. et al. (2019). *Bolivia en La Haya. Lecciones de la demanda contra Chile*. La Paz: Plural.

Arévalo, G. (2016). Economía y política del modelo boliviano 2006–2014: Evaluación preliminar. *CENES* 35(61).

Arrarás, A. and Deheza, G. (2005). Referéndum Del Gas En Bolivia 2004: Mucho Más Que Un Referéndum. *Revista Ciencia Política* 25(2).

Burgoa Terceros, R. (2017). Efecto de la demanda marítima en La Haya sobre el flujo comercial bilateral Bolivia-Chile. *Revista Latinoamericana de Desarrollo Económico* 28. Retrieved from http://www.scielo.org.bo/scielo. php?script=sci_arttext&pid=S2074-47062017000200002&lng=es&tlng=es

Cajías de la Vega, F. (1977). *La provincia de Atacama. 1825–1842*. La Paz: Instituto Boliviano de Cultura.

CEPAL. (2018). *Balance Preliminar de las Economías de América Latina y el Caribe*. Estado Plurinacional de Bolivia. Retrieved from https://repositorio. cepal.org/bitstream/handle/11362/44326/130/BPE2018_Bolivia_es.pdf

Chumacero, R. A. (2019). Habilidades versus Suerte: Bolivia y su reciente Bonanza. *Latin American Economic Review* 28(7).

Correa, L. (2019). El libre tránsito de Bolivia a través de Chile: controversias y gasto económico chileno. 2005–2011. *Si Somos Americanos*. Retrieved from https://scielo.conicyt.cl/scielo.php?script=sci_arttext&pid=S0719-09482019000100111&lng=es&nrm=iso

Correa, L. and Salas, A. (2018). Bolivia en 1904. ¿Por qué firma el Tratado con Chile? *Revista Política y Estrategia* 130. Retrieved from http://www.politic-ayestrategia.cl/index.php/rpye/article/view/128/241

Correa, L., Garay Vera, C., Vaca-Díez, A., and Solíz Landívar, A. (2007). Bolivia en dos frentes: las negociaciones de los tratados de Acre y de límites con Chile. *Universum* 22(1). Retrieved from http://www.scielo.cl/scielo. php?pid=S0718-23762007000100017&script=sci_arttext

Donoso, R. C. and Serrano, P. G. (eds.) (2011). *Chile y la Guerra del Pacífico*. Santiago de Chile: Centro de Estudios Bicentenario – Universidad Andrés Bello.

El canciller David Choquehuanca será el encargado de informar a la 42° Asamblea de la OEA el estado de las relaciones entre Bolivia y Chile. Su homólogo chileno espera que el foro no intervenga (June 5, 2012). *América Economía*. Retrieved from https://www.americaeconomia.com/politica-sociedad/politica/ bolivia-acusara-chile-por-la-violacion-de-once-resoluciones-favor-de-la-d

Milenio, F. (2019). Informe de Milenio sobre la Economía de Bolivia 2019. La Paz, Retrieved from https://fundacion-milenio.org/informe-de-milenio-sobre-la-economia-de-bolivia-2019-no-41/

Guzmán, A. (2017). *Un mar de promesas incumplidas*. La Paz: Plural.

Ministerio de Economía y Finanzas Publicas. Memoria de la economía boliviana (2017). Retrieved from https://medios.economiayfinanzas.gob.bo/MH/docu-mentos/Memorias_Fiscales/Memorias/Memoria_EB_2017.pdf

Mogrovejo Monasterios, R. J. (2010). Modelo político y económico de evo morales y la nueva constitución política del estado plurinacional de Bolivia. *Revista Estudios Jurídicos* 10. Retrieved from https://revistaselectronicas. ujaen.es/index.php/rej/article/view/541

National Customs Service Records (2019). Reserved report requested by the transparency law regarding the free transit of Bolivian trucks in Chile.

Orías, R. (2004). Bolivia-Chile: La cuestión de la mediterraneidad. Algunas consideraciones desde el Derecho Internacional. *Revista Fuerzas Armadas y Sociedad* 18.

Siete, P. (2020). Durante la cuarentena rígida Bolivia importó un 57% menos de carga con respecto a 2019. Retrieved from https://www.paginasiete.bo/econo-mia/2020/6/8/durante-la-cuarentena-rigida-bolivia-importo-un-57-menos-de-carga-con-respecto-2019-257797.html

Restrepo Botero, D. I. (2016). Bolivia: de la crisis económica al ciclo rebelde, 2000-2005. *Anuario Colombiano de Historia Social y de la Cultura* 43(1).

Rodríguez, N. (2018). Crónica de la demanda marítima de Bolivia ante la Corte Internacional de Justicia. *Revista Análisis Político de Investigación* 21.

Salgado Oportus, O. and Cea Echeverría, P. (2012). Análisis de la conectividad externa de los puertos de Chile como un factor de competitividad. *Ingeniare. Revista chilena de ingeniería* 20(1). https://www.scielo.cl/scielo.php?script=sci_abstract&pid=S0718-33052012000100004&lng=en. License: CC BY 4.0.

Salces, M. (2019). Entrevista realizada en la Cámara de Exportadores de Bolivia. 23 de septiembre de 2019.

Velasco Valdez, D. (2015). Economía informal en Bolivia: análisis, evaluación y cuantificación en base al enfoque monetario de la demanda de efectivo (periodo 1994–2014). *Revista Investigación & Desarrollo* 2(15). Retrieved from http://www.scielo.org.bo/scielo.php?script=sci_arttext&pid=S2518-44312015000200006

6 Economic History, Developmentalism, and Neoliberalism in Contemporary Brazil[1]

Gustavo Oliveira and Ivan Daniel Müller

Introduction

In Economics, Brazil became worldwide known in what the specialized literature and political discourses agreed to call as *a developmentalist country*. This was due to the public policies that the country experienced throughout the 20th century. Such economic characteristic is not exclusive to Brazil, being also noticed in other Latin American countries. The period that began to characterize the country's economic policy abroad began in the so-called 1930 Coup or Revolution, which brought the former president Getúlio Vargas to the front of the national scene. That cycle lasted until the end of the military dictatorship in the 1980s. It was a period marked by highs and lows in democracy, since the economic policies that sustained and characterized that period were implemented both in authoritarian and democratic contexts.

With possible approximations to *Keynesianism*, a concept formulated in Europe to explain especially the European and the United States' experiences, developmentalism is a concept and an economic policy practice particular to the countries of the geopolitical South, with emphasis, to a certain extent, in some Latin American countries. In an effort to combine both concept and practice, Fonseca (2015, 20) evidences that it suggests "a convergence of a possible 'common main core' or conceptual core".[2] For him, classical developmentalism means the combination of, at least, three core attributes: (i) a national project, (ii) industrialization, and (iii) State intervention in the economy. Therefore, for a governmental project to be characterized as developmentalist, it requires owning a project of future aimed at the nation, emphasizing the fact that economic policies guide both development and power of a country; it needs to take specific actions toward developing the national industry; and, lastly, it is the State that orchestrates and induces the internal economy.

Although the focus of this text is to think about Brazil, it is important to say that national Latin-American economies present similarities to a certain extent and combine historical periods. After the end of the period that characterized much of the region as developmentalist – with

DOI: 10.4324/9781003045632-7

emphasis on Brazil, Argentina, and Mexico – and the shift to neoliberal orthodoxy, in the 1980s and 1990s; the first years of the 21st century marked a period known as *post-neoliberal* (Gaudichaud 2016), or as *the pink wave* (Menezes and Vieira 2012; Silva 2014; Arantes 2016; Ianoni 2017). The pink wave is the period in which several countries in Latin America – Brazil, Argentina, Uruguay, Paraguay, Bolivia, Venezuela, and Ecuador – were governed by political parties with popular projects, in the Brazilian case, the Workers' Party (Partido dos Trabalhadores – PT); self-defined as left or center-left and that, with the novelty of the effort to materialize policies of income redistribution, notably presented inspirations in classical developmentalism.

The recent economic policies in Brazil, specifically those of the PT governments – from 2003 until the coup in 2016 (Freixo and Rodrigues 2016; Monteiro 2018) – produced an invigorated effort for the researchers on the subject, forcing them to think about developmentalism in a different context from that in which both concept and practice originally manifested. Updates to the classical concept of developmentalism emerged. On the one hand, there are those who argue in favor of *new developmentalism* (Bresser-Pereira 2009); on the other hand, those who consider it to be *social-developmentalism* (Carneiro 2012) and, yet, those who think of it as *neo-developmentalism* (Boito Jr. 2017; Boito Jr. and Berringer 2013).

In the context presented above, our objectives are: (i) to revisit the concept of developmentalism; (ii) to organize a historical analysis of the economic models adopted by the country, with special attention to the different developmentalist experiences and the neoliberal orthodoxy; (iii) to break down the differences between classical developmentalism (1946–1979) and "developmentalist trials" (1930–1945/2003–2016), pointing out the need to reconceptualize the economic policy that has recently reappeared in the country.[3] Without the intention of discussing which variant is the most appropriate to plan the future of Brazilian economic policies, these texts aims, quite in the opposite direction, to reach a diagnosis by focusing on the economic policies of contemporary Brazil.

We ask, what were the internal characteristics of the different forms of developmentalism in the three periods that Brazil experienced it? Which are the main characteristics of the conceptual updates to contemporary developmentalism? In what context does neoliberalism gain space? What type of economic policy characterized the PT government periods? Is it possible to think about neoliberal developmentalism? To reach these objectives and point out the differences between classical developmentalism, and the two other periods of developmentalist approach; we try to answer the questions above cited with a text of qualitative grasp based on bibliographical research. That way, we shed light on the suggested questions and argue in favor of our approximation to the concept of neo-developmentalism (Boito Jr. 2017; Boito Jr. and Berringer 2013), thinking on the recent economic policies of the PT governments.

Beyond this introductory section, the text is organized in the following manner: first, we present the classical concept of developmentalism and its political-economic characteristics. Next, we follow a historical path beginning on the period from 1930 to 1945; then we analyze the period from 1946 to 1979 and we continue with the decades of the 1980s (so-called "the lost decade") and the 1990s (neoliberal orthodoxy); at last, we end with a section about the PT's experience from 2003 until 2016. Finally, we present some reflections on the diagnosis that the text comprises, as well as some projections about the current Brazilian context.

Classical Developmentalism: The Conceptual Dimension

We believe it to be important, before starting the historical contextualization, to present some reflections over the concept of developmentalism and the context of its arising, which was followed by other key concepts for the economic understanding of Latin America and, specifically, of Brazil. So, what is developmentalism? It is a category that is part of the many that we evaluate as being in constant dispute for practical and political sense. The use of this category, as part of political discourse, makes it deeply diffuse and polysemic. There are many others that share the same characteristics, such as autonomy, neoliberalism, orthodoxy, citizenship, self-management, co-optation, etc. Besides polysemy, the category of developmentalism is a two-dimensional one, since it appears both in the Latin-American political discourse – the empirical dimension – and as a theoretical-analytical tool for specialized analyses – the theoretical dimension.

In a thoughtful work of literature revision and analysis of Latin-American political discourses, Fonseca (2015) proposes a formulation of the concept of developmentalism based on the theoretical reflections of authors who had approached that term and the concrete actions upon the policy implementation that they determined to be developmentalist policies. From that theoretical and practical analysis, Fonseca (2015, 40) defines developmentalism as an Economic policy formulated and/or executed, deliberately, by (national or subnational) governments, in order to, through the growth of production and productivity, under the leadership of the industrial sector, transform society with the aim of achieving desirable ends, especially the overcoming of the country's economic and social issues, within the institutional framework of the capitalist system.[4]

It is important to provide some relevant remarks about the author's formulation. (i) It is intentional, that is, thinking on the empirical dimension, the concept was forged from the intention present in the political discourses and not from the check-up of whether these discourses became economic policies or not. (ii) The set of reflections present in the author's full text makes explicit what is implicit in the application that we reproduce here: that development means the sum of (a) a national project, (b) a strong State intervention in the economy, and (c) industrialization. (iii) Developmentalism, more than a theoretical proposition for political action, is a concrete/practical response to the socioeconomic issues it aims to overcome. (iv) It is highly important that developmentalism is not confused with economic development; still, the practice of developmentalism may lead to economic development, that is the actual possible relation between both categories. Finally, (v) developmentalism was thought as a form of economic management within capitalism, not as means of overcoming that system.

In empirical terms, currently, there is agreement that developmentalism rose as a Latin American response to the problems caused by the Great Depression of 1929. In theoretical-analytical terms, there were variations in the comprehension of the concept. The Economic Commission for Latin America and the Caribbean (ECLAC) was the main organism within the United Nations (UN) to produce knowledge about the economic formation of the Latin American countries in the 20th century and, consequently, about the conceptual discussions on developmentalism. At ECLAC, authors such as Raúl Prebisch, José Echavarría, Osvaldo Sunkel, Maria da Conceição Tavares, Celso Furtado, Fernando Henrique Cardoso (FHC), José Serra, Enzo Faletto, Aníbal Pinto, among others, gained salience as researchers of this specialized literature. The main distinctive mark of ECLAC researchers and, in turn, of ECLAC itself, was the theoretical-normative assumption that the State is supposed to be the organizer of economic development; in other words, that the most appropriate political-economic model for Latin America was developmentalism (Bielschowsky 2000).

In addition to developmentalism itself, other concepts were developed at ECLAC, such as *underdevelopment, core-periphery, imports substitution, dependency,* and *associate dependency,* among others. The method they used for the scope of their reflections about those concepts was historical-structuralism, which resembled a Marxian inspiration. From the 1950s on, ECLAC focused on thinking about solutions to Latin-American economic issues. In the 1950s, how to achieve industrialization; in the 1960s, the necessary reforms to unblock industrialization; in the 1970s, the reorientation of development "styles" toward social homogenization and pro-exports industrialization; 1980s, overcoming of the issue of foreign debt through "adjustments with growth"; and in the 1990s, the productive transformation with equality (Bielschowsky 2000).

The idea that underdevelopment was not a temporal condition that referred to a delay in the stages of development in the comparison between rich and poor countries, but a structural condition of global capitalism

(Furtado 1965) was a widely discussed idea in the ambit of ECLAC. As for the concept of underdevelopment, those countries located at the geopolitical periphery would never achieve the condition of fully developed countries, as were those at the core. Core developed countries, in turn, are only so in the function of the periphery-core relation engendered by the socioeconomic structure of global capitalism. Fonseca (2015) points out that developmentalism was assessed as an attempt to overcome that structural condition of underdevelopment.

The concept of dependency (Cardoso and Faletto 1977) helps to understand that there is a socioeconomic structure directed by those countries at the core, which conditions the economic policies of the peripheral countries by keeping them in such conditions of underdevelopment. For Marini (1973), the relations between the underdeveloped – especially those in Latin America – and developed countries carry along with forms of overexploitation and labor intensification. Hence, as some countries emerge economically, others are aggrieved. This happens due to the integration of dependent countries into the world market, where the increase of labor intensity appears with the increase of surplus obtained through the greater exploitation of workers. With the return of liberalism on a global level, now with innovations that transformed it into neoliberalism, the attributes of these concepts (underdevelopment and dependency) became ever more evident, as well as the conditions of the relation between core and periphery. Next, we move to analyze the historical path.

Historical Analysis of the Economic Policies Adopted in Contemporary Brazil

The First Developmentalist Trial: 1930–1945

Brazilian economic formation is marked, in temporal terms, by a profound shift perceived at the turn of the 1920s into the 1930s. The First Republic, a period that lasted from 1889 until 1930 and which preceded the period that we call as the first developmentalist trial, was signed by economic liberalism (*laissez-faire*). It was a period in which capitalism worked without much State intervention in the economic realm; that is, the dynamics of that socioeconomic system had its dynamic core and power core in the free market. It consisted of a Brazilian version of the economic liberalism that emerged in Europe. Until 1930, Brazil was a country of rural economic predominance, deeply distinctive by monoculture; it was the Brazil of coffee, of the agrarian economy: Agro-exporter Brazil. The capital flux until this period had an external origin and the consumption of industrial products was an elite's privilege, achieved through imports. There was no configuration of a dynamic national industry until that historic moment.

To understand some developments of the domestic economy of any given country, it is important to think about how the structure of world capitalism influences its singular economic formation. Hence, in the Brazilian case, it is important to realize the character of the country's development in regards to that structure. The arrival of Getúlio Vargas to power, in 1930, represented a true paradigmatic shift for the Brazilian economy. There, the processes of industrialization and urbanization in Brazil deepened. What hasty readings could consider an economic development plan for the country was, in fact, the way Vargas found to protect the agrarian elite in the process that became known as *import substitution* (Tavares 2010).

The world context was that of the Great Depression, marked by the 1929 crisis, which made it impossible to continue exporting coffee as the dynamic activity for the Brazilian economy. Vargas, in addition to determining the purchase of most of the coffee stocks available on the market, initiated a customs policy that prevented and hindered the import of industrialized products. The agrarian elite, with no prospect of maintaining profits through the coffee sector, was the first to develop a national industry, producing and offering the demanded products no longer imported.

In the quest to maintain monetary income in the country in conditions of a declining import capacity, the policy of favoring the coffee sector became, in the last analysis, one of industrialization. With the rapid devaluation of the currency, the relative prices of imported goods increased, thus creating extremely favorable conditions for domestic production. From the perspective of profits for cropping, coffee was now in decline because the favored treatment presented by the government to the producers only compensated in part for the decline in the real value of the exports, and the production of consumer goods for the domestic market became the field of most attractive investment in the Brazilian economy. In this way, investment was diverted from the traditional export sector, mainly from the production and commercialization of coffee, and channeled to the manufacturing industries. During the period 1929–1937, total imports decreased by 23% and industrial production increased by 50% (Furtado 1965, 253–254).[5]

Celso Furtado (1965) shows that the first steps of Brazilian industrialization were not taken as to construct a project of national development, on the one hand, nor by a spontaneous process of the market, on the other. Such an absence of market spontaneity marked the end of economic liberalism in Brazil. For the author, what happened was a deliberate action from Vargas government to meet the wishes of the agrarian sector, that is, of the national economic elite from that period. In other words, the State fulfilled a blank space left by the market and acted toward protecting the agrarian elite that would soon transform into an agro-industrial elite. Industrial development, along with the urbanization process that enabled that development, was not done, nonetheless, in a planned manner. World economy induced domestic economy to look inwards into its internal possibilities.

With Getúlio Vargas already in power and starting a process of State intervention in the economy, to a large extent feasible by an increase in State bureaucracy, the autonomous labor unions proceeded to march in the struggle for their rights (Araújo 2002). Therefore, even at the stake of damaging the organization of the working class due to the division created between the autonomous unions and those that would soon become corporatized, it was that increase in the size of the State that, first, regulated those unions and, subsequently, met the demand for labor rights partially. For better or worse, it was the upscale of the State that carried along with the regulation of the now corporatist unions, as Araújo (2002) argues. This created the conditions of the economic development of the country with a certain social order.

In less than ten years after ascending to the presidency of Brazil, Getúlio Vargas would face the political-economic world context of the Second Great War, which also contributed to the development of a domestic-based economy in the function of the world instability caused by the war. In that context, there was the idea that industrialization could lead the countries at the world's geopolitical periphery to the same condition of development of the countries at the core. This was the classical 20th-century thought of progress and modernization.

The First Developmentalist Trial: 1930–1945

The period described above was marked, as we could see, not by the spontaneity of the market, but by an already present intervention of the State on the market. However, they were reactive, with no or little planning. It was only a few years later, especially from the beginning of Juscelino Kubitschek's (JK) government in 1956, and his Target Plan (*Plano de Metas*, in Portuguese), that Brazil would experience a development plan for the country (Lafer 2002). If the Brazilian developmentalist experience was insufficient in relation to the "national project" attribute during its first period, even with a striking industrial growth and the relocation of the population from the countryside to the cities, it was JK who remedied that deficit with the formulation and implementation of the Target Plan; which left explicit and organized both the industrialization and economic modernization of the country. It was at the turn of the 1940s to 1950s, especially in the decade of the 1950s, that we are able to perceive the three central attributes of classical developmentalism – (i) a national project, (ii) industrialization, and (iii) State intervention in economic affairs – operating in Brazil.

JK's Target Plan represented a leap in quality for the history of Brazilian development since its organized State intervention by prioritizing sectors of the economy, defining ways and degrees of State induction on the market. The State had a central role in the financing of the industrialization process of that period on the one hand, and a leading role in the sectors of heavy industry and the implementation of the required infrastructure for industry to bloom, on the other. It was during this period that expressions such as "to grow 50 years in 5" and "to make the cake grow to divide it later" became known, according to the expectations set around JK's national developmental project. The plan advanced, the national industry strengthened, yet, the divide of the "cake" did not happen. Wealth continued to accumulate among the same elites, as it always did – then agrarian, now agro-industrial.

From the mid-1950s to the early 1960s, Brazilian industrialization underwent decisive structural transformations. Such advancement was made under the impulse of the Kubitschek government's (1956–1960) Target Plan and was characterized by an intense industrial differentiation in a relatively short period of time, directly articulated by the State. In that period, automobile, shipbuilding, heavy electric material, and other machinery and equipment industries were installed in the country, allowing a significant expansion of the capital goods sector. At the same time, basic industries such as steel, non-ferrous metals, heavy chemicals, oil, paper, and cellulose expanded considerably. For the aforementioned advancements, apart from the State investments in infrastructure and in the direct production of supplies, the following were decisive as instruments of economic policy: (i) Instruction 70 and the increase in the tax burden and the fiscal deficit, as sources of financing; (ii) Instruction 113, as a means of attracting foreign direct investments in the short term; (iii) subsidized official credit to stimulate the accumulation of the private sector in sectors considered to be priorities; and (iv) the creation of executive groups with representatives of SUMOC, CACEX, BNDE, and entrepreneurs, to organize, encourage (for example, through industrial land concessions, import exemptions and special lines of credit) and monitor the implementation of the different sector goals (Serra 1982a, 23).[6]

The rhetoric around the Target Plan indicated that the industrial elite would be served by the State's induction to the economy, which granted heavy investments in the national industry, on the one hand; while also promised to the working class they would be served in terms of the jobs generated with the investments in the industry. If we take into consideration once again the contributions made by Fonseca (2015, 42–43), we could realize that this was a period of

> national-developmentalism, of a more nationalist ideology, [which] proposed a greater role for the State to leverage resources and make investments considered as priorities. Production was centred on popular consumer goods, led by the national private sector. As a project,

it proposed to advance industrialisation for capital and intermediate goods; and politically, it expressed an alliance between that entrepreneurial class, some segments of the 'middle classes' (including the bureaucracy) and urban workers, proposing the 'incorporation of the masses', which political expression would be 'populism'.[7]

The world political-economic context was of resuming by the core countries. With the end of the Second Great War, the Cold War initiated, and the dispute between the two socioeconomic blocs (communism[8] and capitalism) was about measuring their power in relation to progress and development. The world macroeconomic structure began to express harder and the United States and allied countries started to expand loans to transnational corporations in peripheral economies. Latin America was a focal point for those expansions. So much so that in Brazil, in the post-war period, transnational companies dominated the sector of durable and capital goods (Serra 1982a). Much of the wealth produced by the country's industrialization flowed abroad: directly through the profits of the private initiative or through loan payments by the State.

The context of the Cold War divided the world, once and for all, into two blocs: communists and capitalists. The capitalist bloc experienced a period of lesser perversity from capitalism, which was the experience of Social Welfare State in Europe. Economic liberalism lost power in the post-war, allowing a political-economic model in which States strengthened by, supposedly, overcoming the idea that the market and its "invisible hand" would be able to accommodate social demands and solve them. The period signed by the experiences of Social Welfare State adjourned, to a certain extent, the process of market internationalization; yet, the dispute between capitalism and communism continued to produce consequences.

The decade of the 1960s began and, along it, the national economy slowed down. The downturn, more evident since 1962, was due to different motives, such as: the cyclical nature of the world capitalist system; bad economic policies since 1963; high inflation during the period (resulting from the very downturn and other foreign/external factors); and, finally, the drought of 1963 (Serra 1982a). The increase in unemployment, poverty, and socioeconomic inequality in the early years of the decade, and the social agitation there engendered, were the necessary fuel for the Military Coup in 1964. There was an explicit support of the capitalist bloc, especially from the United States, for the coups in Brazil and Latin America to be possible. If, politically, the 1964's coup marked a period of political and civilian rights deprivation, specifically in the closure of democracy, economically, it presented periods of highs and lows.

The military government took a while until it finally achieved to reroute the country's economic growth. Only in 1968, four years after the coup, indexes began to register high levels. From 1968 to 1973, Brazil registered a developmentalist period with the highest growth, it was the so-called "Economic Miracle". The main characteristics of that period were: high-peak indexes in the industries of capital goods and durable consumer goods. Unlike the previous period of growth, there was an industrial growth without a decrease in imports; exports increased drastically and rapidly. The agricultural sector took its exports profile again to a higher level, and the State directed once more public resources toward industrialization (Serra 1982a).

The economic growth registered during that period was only possible, nonetheless, in function of the conditions that the military government found in the country: idle installed capacity, which means that there was installed capacity with no need for further infrastructure investments; a high rate of foreign currency from exports; and the possibility of taking foreign credits, as well as high internal liquidity from internal credit.

Some imbalances were perceived during this "miracle" and, even in 1973, a strong retraction emerged. The five years that the "economic miracle" lasted also registered: a wide inequality in the development of the different industrial sectors; in the agricultural sector, when the production could be oriented for internal consumption, the levels of exports grew; inflation increased, pushed by the international market inflation; in addition, the capital goods imports increased. Everything contributed to a sharp drop in the GDP from 1973 on. That drop was due to the little demand for durable and non-durable goods. The drop in non-durable goods was strongly related to the wage loss caused by the high inflation; but the durable goods' one may also be related to that motive, given that the years before the drop were marked by an increased acquisition of those products, which provoked the demand goes down and, when wages came down it was replaced by the preference of demand for non-durable goods (Serra 1982b).

In 1974, the Second National Development Plan (II PND; *II Plano Nacional de Desenvolvimento*, in Portuguese) was launched in an attempt to restart an era of high economic indexes. Nevertheless, the plan could only succeed in the imports substitution, which resulted in the development of the capital goods area of the domestic economy. To that end, there was the direct support of the BNDE (National Development Bank)[9] and the CDI (Industrial Development Council). What kept the economy in development, even though a downturn, were the civil construction and the durable goods sectors, although the latter was the one that had the strongest downturn. The lower investment after 1975 is another important explanation factor for the perceived downturn in the economy during that period. Another causal explanation is the international context of the economic crisis (the oil world crisis). Finally, a third explaining factor was high inflation (Serra 1982b).

The "Lost Decade" (1980s) and the
Neoliberal Orthodoxy (1990s)

Unlike the long period of expansion of the Brazilian economy that began in 1930 and was potentialized during the 1950s, the 1980s presented very short periods of retraction and expansion. However, the decade was marked more by the retractions, becoming known as the "lost decade" (Maricato 2002). The 1980s was a decade qualified by the absence of foreign investments in the Latin-American countries. The oil world crisis (1979) made that the core economies brake the investments in the peripheral countries, with exceptions on few Asian countries. Such action had a devastating effect on Brazil, since the country was already deeply indebted – most of the second half of the 1970s showed high indebtedness, which was the solution found by the military government to avoid the complete stagnation of the economy. There were exports in that period; anyhow, the resources that came into the country through those exports were drained outback abroad for the payment of the foreign debt. In other words, the domestic economy was constantly threatened by the lack of investments and the rising inflation (Carneiro 2002).

The international political context of that period presented the first steps toward the strengthening of neoliberalism – which was first experienced in the region under Pinochet's dictatorship in Chile. Margaret Thatcher in England and Ronald Reagan in the United States set the tone for the new political-economic model that would take over the world. With the end of the Cold War, the actions of these two politicians in their respective countries would fade the Social Welfare State model, resulting in the expansion of that orthodox model with the neoliberal creed that became widely known after the Washington Consensus (1989). It contained: tax reforms (a tributes reduction for the large companies to allow them to increase profits), commercial opening (easing both imports and exports through the reduction of customs and tariffs), privatization policies (ending the leading role of State in economic affairs), and the State's fiscal downsizing (which was the literal reduction of the State) (Carneiro 2002). In that context, as we can clearly see, any chance of developmentalist resume was out of chance.

In Brazil, the 1990s were marked by the creation of the Real Plan (*O Plano Real*), by FHC, inaugurating a contradiction regarding the Brazilian economy within the world structure of capitalism: on the one hand, the neoliberal creed suggested a floating exchange rate to attract foreign financial capitals; meanwhile, on the other hand, the Real Plan introduced a fixed rate and the wide appreciation of the national currency. Notwithstanding, it was only so. All other policies of FHC's governmental plan indicated an alignment with the countries that led global neoliberalism. FHC's governments also represented a great antagonism with developmentalist projects. There was no national project since the broad orientation was "the more transnational corporations, the better"; there was no public investment nor State intervention in strategic sectors of the national economy; thus, there were no efforts toward industrialization and strengthening the national industry.

By following the neoliberal creed, FHC's economic policies were known to be orthodox policies; that is, of a radical pro-market and non-State orientation. In that context, the main mark of FHC's government was the privatization of State-owned companies – remarkably, Vale do Rio Doce. The former president even hesitated in relation to the investments in infrastructure, which hindered industrial development. There were no actions dedicated to guaranteeing access to quality public health and education, nor to solving the problem of socioeconomic inequity, poverty, and unemployment. Brazil, nonetheless, was not an isolated case in Latin America; other countries followed the same orthodox orientation. Argentina implemented even more orthodox policies than the Brazilian ones; Chile, Colombia, Peru, and Mexico could also be pointed out as countries that bought such "fashionable" idea. In the same way that the country was not an isolated case of neoliberal orthodoxy, the wave that was yet to come also reached other countries in the region.

The Second Developmentalist Trial: 2003–2016

With a very similar discourse, in comparison to that of the politicians during the populist period,[10] Luiz Inácio Lula da Silva (Lula) arrived to the federal executive power in 2003 – after winning the presidential elections in 2002. He had promised to meet the demands and interests of Brazilian society as a whole, satisfying all classes and strata of it. Lula was elected in 2002 with an economic development plan of developmentalist inspiration for the country. Resuming State intervention in the economy and an alleged industrialization would confirm the PT national project, which guaranteed controlled inflation, employment, and income generation and the combating poverty. These promises were kept and achieved; first, by the very election, which was only possible by depending on a social pact assured by Lula, which conformed to a "front" (Boito Jr. and Berringer 2013, 31):

Such front reunites the greater internal bourgeoisie, which is its directing force, the lower middle class, the urban working class, and peasantry. The front also incorporates that wide and heterogeneous social sector, composed of unemployed and underemployed people, autonomous workers, peasants in need, and other sectors of that which Latin American critical sociology of the past century calls "marginal mass".[11]

Second, when already in power, Lula maintained the macroeconomic policies of the last FHC's term, which guaranteed economic stability for his first governmental steps. What were such policies? Floating exchange rate, the primary surplus, and controlled inflation. As the different social sectors were "accommodated", ordered, the PT government dedicated itself to one of the attributes not considered at the core of the concept of classic developmentalism, but that started to gain more and more followers in relation to developmentalism in the post-orthodox experience: income redistribution. That way, Lula's developmentalism exhibited (i) a national project, (ii) industrialization – a low-intensity industrialization that has opened important debates in specialized literature; most analysts disagree about industrialization being present in the PT governments, hence it was rather a *deindustrialization* or *reprimarization* process (Fonseca, and Salomão 2017) –, (iii) State intervention, and (iv) income redistribution. Distribution occurred through a nationwide minimum wages real valorization and redistribution through *Bolsa Familia* program (conditional cash-transfer program, PBF), Continuous Cash Benefits (*Benefício de Prestação Continuada,* BPC) and, even indirectly, education, healthcare, infrastructure, and housing policies. Redistribution was already a subject of study at ECLAC in the 1990s when a way out for productive transformation with equity was sought.

These policies, known as social policies, went along with economic policies during the PT governments, and also yielded plenty of research and discussions (Arretche 2010; Fleury 2011), emphasizing the role of PBF. Governmental attention given to social policies yielded as well a first subtype for the concept of classical developmentalism from the outset of PT's experience, social-developmentalism (Bielschowsky 2000; Carneiro 2012). It became known as social-developmentalism due to the income redistribution attribute. These policies, however, cannot be interpreted solely as a proactive and unilateral action from the PT governments. There was an accumulation of social struggles that had already begun as rejection and fight against the military dictatorship, which were resignified along the post-transition period as inequalities increased during those years. It was necessary to provide responses to the incapacity of the 1990s' neoliberal experience in reaching solutions for the deep social inequalities in Brazil. Still, it is important to realize that, as we describe next, the PT practiced profoundly conciliatory politics, and these redistribution policies also operated as tactics for social accommodation and demobilization of the working class (Zibechi 2007). Nevertheless, it is relevant to highlight that even with all the social weight of redistribution, it also presents a facet of economic strategy, since it generates growth for the national industry from consumption, taking into consideration that purchasing power increases and consequently there is more circulating income.

Another variation engendered the new developmentalism subtype (Bresser-Pereira 2009) which, instead of shedding light on redistribution, highlights exchange rate policy, suggesting it should be rather competitive instead. In Bresser-Pereira (2012, 20)'s words: "new developmentalism is not protectionist, it only emphasizes the need for a competitive exchange rate and identifies it with an *industrial balance exchange rate*"[12] (our emphasis), and continues saying that "a competitive exchange rate is fundamental for economic development because it makes the entire foreign market available to truly competitive national companies from a managerial and technological standpoint"[13] (Bresser-Pereira 2012, 11). As much as the author does not refer to a simple devaluation of the national currency, its relative depreciation would end up protecting domestic production – creating a barrier to the massive entry of foreign products – generating greater competitiveness of domestic products in the foreign market. New developmentalism does not deny the need for redistribution, nor its role as an engine of the domestic economy; nevertheless, it considers that in the context of the structure of contemporary and global capitalism, the exchange rate is more central than redistribution.

Notwithstanding, There is a Third Subtype:
Neo-Developmentalism (Boito Jr. 2017;
Boito Jr. and Berringer 2013)

Neo-developmentalism (i) presents an economic growth that, although is much higher than that of the 1990s, is much more modest than the one provided by old developmentalism; (ii) it bestows a lesser importance to the internal market; (iii) it ascribes less importance to the policy of developing a domestic industrial park; (iv) it accepts the constraints of the international labor division, promoting, under new historical conditions, a reactivation of the primary-exporter function of Brazilian capitalism; (v) it has a lesser income distribution capability; and (iv) new developmentalism is managed by a bourgeois fraction that lost all its will of acting as an anti-imperialist force (Boito Jr. and Berringer 2013, 32).[14]

For Boito Jr. and Berringer (2013), neo-developmentalism was possible in Brazil due to:

> (i) policies aiming to the recovery of minimum wage and cash transfer that increased the purchase power of the poorest strata, that is, those who present higher pretensions of consumption; (ii) elevating the National Bank for Economic Development (BNDES) budget allocation for financing a subsided interest rate for the greater national companies; (iii) a foreign policy of support to the greater Brazilian companies or installed in Brazil for products and capital exports; (iv) an anti-cyclical economic policy – measures towards sustaining aggregate demand in moments of economic crisis.
>
> (Boito Jr. and Berringer 2013, 32)[15]

Despite the outstanding efforts of the PT governments in regards to the formulation and implementation of policies aiming at income redistribution and social policies, when looking to reality from a neo-developmentalist standpoint, one cannot evade from ECLAC's main methodological contribution: the historic-structural method. The concept of neo-developmentalism is concerned with the unequal structure of global capitalism – more than either social-developmentalism or new developmentalism. Even when the 2000s were considered by part of the literature as being post-neoliberal, in the world context, neoliberalism never disappeared; instead, it became ever more oriented *by* and *for* rentier financial capitalism. As much as the local governments of the peripheral countries that shaped the *pink wave* were inspired by classical developmentalism, the contemporary constraints of the early 21st century were even greater and more perverse than those from the previous century.

The Differences between Classical Developmentalism (1946–1979) and the Developmentalist Trials (1930–1945/2003–2016)

Why did PT governments only achieve one developmentalist trial? Because, as was the case in the period from 1930 to 1945, there were not found all the attributes of the classical developmentalism concept in the Brazilian experience in the 2003–2016 period. If on the first period of the concept, the national project was of low intensity, in which there was some spotlight for State intervention that led to industrialization, although little planned; on the most recent period of developmentalism, it was experienced a low-intensity industrialization. Such low-intensity feature of the industrialization perceived during PT governments prevents us from thinking from the conceptual key of classic developmentalism. In addition to that, we perceive two new attributes in comparison to the original concept, as cited before: income redistribution and a competitive exchange rate. Thus, in order to use the classical concept of developmentalism, which reflects the Brazilian economic experience from 1946 to 1979, we would need at least a refined revision of the concept itself, in which we leave out a strict industrialization attribute and incorporate redistribution.

In a serious attempt to frame theory and practice and comparing classic and contemporary developmentalism, we could even associate ourselves with the subtype of social-developmentalism. This is because the policies of income redistribution seem to us to be those that most differentiate the period of old developmentalism from the period of recent developmentalism, from PT governments. This statement becomes valid, however, if we look strictly inward, at the proactive actions of the different domestic governments. We consider, nevertheless, that in the context of today's global capitalism, there is no geopolitically isolated economic policy. We do not think it is productive both for economics and politics to put aside what ECLAC taught before: that there is a differentiation between core and periphery, one in which peripheral countries are dependent on the ones at the core and that underdevelopment is a structural, not temporal, feature. These ECLAC's lessons gain stronger explicative power in the current context of neoliberalism.

We reproduce in Table 6.1, the data systematized by Prates, Fritz, and Paula (2017), showing that Lula and Dilma's developmentalist period was, in fact, strongly conditioned by the structure of global capitalism.

Orthodoxy was ever present in the macroeconomic policies of the PT governments and neoliberal orthodoxy is proof of a certain degree of national respect toward international markets and, obviously, powerful countries. This is also proof that even with an alleged political orientation for implementing a developmentalist project, there is a structural condition that disputes power with the national political will. Due to that reason, from the three subtypes of developmentalism presented, engendered out of the original/classical concept of developmentalism, we associate this period rather with the concept of neo-developmentalism.

As we understand it, the concept of neo-developmentalism – which finds similarities with the concept of dependent-associate developmentalism as defined by Fonseca (2015) – contributes more to the macro-structural understanding of economic policies in the Latin American context. It contributes more because its critical characteristic, inspired by ECLAC's thought, does not let us lose sight of the fact that domestic policies are crossed and conditioned by the desires of the international market and the countries at the core of the global structure. In the words of Bringel and Falero (2016, 39), the PT experiences were signed by a "corporative management with progressive government without any intent of transformation from an inherited State's shape"[16]. These authors' contribution is relevant insofar it shows that the Brazilian state had little transformations during these experiences. Besides, a corporative management could only deliver a scenario of maintenance of pro-market actions – neoliberal, by the way –, as the characteristics of the neo-developmentalism show and according to the systematization of developmental policies as presented in Table 6.1.

Table 6.1 Typology of Lula and Dilma's policies

	LULA *2003–2008*	*LULA* *2008–2010*	*DILMA* *2011–2014*	*DILMA* *2015–2016*
Monetary policy	ORT	ORT; ND; ORT	ND; ORT	ORT
Exchange policy	ORT	ORT; ND	ND; ORT	*ORT*
Fiscal policy	ORT	SD; ORT	ORT; SD	ORT
Social politics	SD	SD	SD	SD

Source: Adapted from Prates, Fritz, and Paula (2017, 210).

ORT = orthodoxy; SD = social-developmentalism; ND = new developmentalism.

From the classical concept of developmentalism, the industrialization characteristic is missing, whereas redistribution emerges as a novelty in the Brazilian experience during the PT governments. This lack of industrialization, or even deindustrialization, makes us think of rather neoliberal policies than of developmentalist ones – or, at most, in the merger of both kinds of policies, remissive of heterodoxy. The option of focusing on the agro-exporter economic sector is a trademark of the PT governments (Fonseca and Salomão 2017), notoriously influenced by the *commodities boom,* and which could have been followed by real investments in industrialization – whether through a new-developmentalist path or through higher public direct investment – and an aim on technological autonomy for the country. Nonetheless, for Latin American countries, being less industrialized and more agro-exporters while buying top-notch technologies from the countries at the core instead of investing in their internal development is a clear sign of the core-periphery structure of capitalism in its neoliberal phase. In synthesis, it is to say that, within neoliberalism, for the persistence of essential inequalities in the system, peripheral countries in the world-system are supposed to sell raw materials at a low price and buy high technology at high prices.

Finally, it is our understanding that even though it seems contradictory, what was experienced in the PT developmental exercise was, in fact, a kind of neoliberal developmentalism marked by low-intensity industrialization (or deindustrialization), by the novelty of income redistribution policies – which might be seen as tactics for class conciliation – and by non-disruptive (more or less intentional) responses to the conditions of global neoliberalism. We do not seek to create a new category – neoliberal developmentalism – but we intend to point out that the *neo* prefix in the formulation of neo-developmentalism brings to discussion the conditions of the structure of capitalism in its neoliberal phase.

Final Considerations

In the introduction of this text, we ask: What were the internal characteristics of the different forms of developmentalism in the two periods it was experienced in Brazil? Which were the main characteristics of the conceptual updates for contemporary developmentalism? In what context does neoliberalism gain space? What kind of economic policy does characterize the PT governments? Is it possible to think of a neoliberal developmentalism? We tried to show across this text the characteristics of the different periods of developmentalism in Brazil, besides briefly describing the non-developmentalist decades. We, as well, drafted attention to some political and international issues that we believe are useful in helping the comprehension of the historic development of the Brazilian economic formation.

We shared Fonseca (2015)'s reflections regarding the concept of developmentalism, considering the three main attributes of the concept: (i) a national project, (ii) industrialization, and (iii) State intervention in economic affairs. We dealt with the 1930–1945 period as a developmentalist trial because its national project attribute was low in intensity; and we dealt with the PT experience as also a trial given that its low-intensity industrialization, or deindustrialization, keeps that experience away from the classical concept, while sets it, among other reasons, closer to neoliberalism. However, we do not consider, as Fonseca and Salomão (2017) do, that, on the one hand, the lack of industrialization is a granted irreversible condition of our time; and that, on the other hand, due to that reason, the classical concept of developmentalism is a fixed concept in time (from 1946 to 1979).

What we do not know yet: Is it possible to have a developmentalism type with a high intensity of the original attributes to the concept, adding as well the novelty of redistribution, in the context of neoliberal capitalism? Specifically, on industrialization, is it possible to think of industrialization with high-tech aggregate for the countries of the geopolitical South in the hitherto permanent context of core-periphery dependency? Moreover, is it possible to think of high-intensity industrialization in the context of financial rentierism localized in the countries of the North? These few questions stimulate us to keep reflecting on the subject.

If Celso Furtado saw developmentalism as a way to overcome the condition of underdevelopment in the structure of global capitalism, perhaps we need to think about those terms, although transcending the premise that developmentalism is a way of doing economic policy only within the national margins of capitalism. None of the three basic attributes of the classical concept of developmentalism prevents us from thinking of a *Developmentalism for Latin American Integration*,[17] for instance. For that purpose, we would need to think more about finding answers from ourselves and from regional forms of integration, and less from the alignment to the conditions of neoliberal world capitalism.

Finally, is it possible to state that there was a neoliberal developmentalist trial in Brazil during the PT governments? Brazilian political-economic history shows that developmentalist actions were combined with orthodox actions, that is, neoliberal, during those government periods. The limits of that mix seem to have charged a high price from PT itself and from the population at large; it is sufficient to remember the tragic and casuistic way in which the PT was removed from the central government in 2016. It could be explained, among other reasons, by the end of the socio-political coalition that composed neo-developmentalism (Singer 2015; Ianoni 2017). We end this effort with several doubts and one certainty alone: the exit toward reaching an optimal combination of economic development and fair wealth distribution is still in construction and, as discussed throughout this text, we understand that the concept of neo-developmentalism is the one that represents best the experience that merges developmentalism and neoliberalism due to its structuralist outlook.

Notes

1. Portuguese to English translation by Daniel Sebastian Granda Henao.
2. Original in Portuguese: "sugerindo a convergência para um possível 'núcleo comum principal' ou core do conceito".
3. Despite the concrete possibility of framing the economic policies of Jair Bolsonaro's current government as ultra-neoliberal, we opt out to leave them outside this analysis, due to the temporal proximity between the event and the diagnosis, and due to the space limitations of this text.
4. Original in Portuguese: "política econômica formulada e/ou executada, de forma deliberada, por governos (nacionais ou subnacionais) para, através do crescimento da produção e da produtividade, sob a liderança do setor industrial, transformar a sociedade com vistas a alcançar fins desejáveis, destacadamente a superação de seus problemas econômicos e sociais, dentro dos marcos institucionais do sistema capitalista".
5. Original in English.
6. Original in Portuguese: "Foi a partir de meados dos anos 50 até o início dos anos 60 que a industrialização brasileira sofreu transformações estruturais decisivas. Esse avanço foi realizado sob impulso do Plano de Metas do governo Kubitschek (1956–1960) e caracterizou-se por uma intensa diferenciação industrial num espaço de tempo relativamente curto, articulada diretamente pelo Estado. Nesse período instalaram-se no país as indústrias automobilística, de construção naval, material elétrico pesado e outras de máquinas e equipamentos, permitindo uma significativa ampliação do setor de bens de capital. Ao mesmo tempo expandiram-se consideravelmente indústrias básicas como a siderúrgica, a de metais não ferrosos, química pesada, petróleo, papel e celulose. Para os avanços mencionados, afora os investimentos estatais em infra-estrutura e na produção direta de insumos, foram decisivos, como instrumentos de política econômica: (i) a Instrução 70 e o aumento da carga tributária e do déficit fiscal, como fontes de financiamento; (ii) a Instrução 113, como expediente para trair a curto prazo os investimentos estrangeiros diretos; (iii) o crédito oficial subsidiado para estimular a acumulação do setor privado nos setores considerados prioritários; (iv) a criação de grupos executivos com representantes da SUMOC, CACEX, BNDE e dos empresários, para organizar, incentivar (por exemplo, mediante concessões de terrenos industriais, isenções de importação e linhas especiais de crédito) e acompanhar a implementação das diferentes metas setoriais".
7. Original in Portuguese: "nacional-desenvolvimentismo, de ideologia mais nacionalista, [que] propunha maior papel ao Estado para alavancar recursos e realizar investimentos tidos como prioritários. A produção centrava-se nos bens de consumo populares, liderada pelo setor privado nacional. Como projeto, propunha avançar a industrialização para os bens de capital e intermediários; e politicamente, expressava-se como uma aliança entre este empresariado, segmentos das 'classes médias' (nestes incluídos a burocracia) e trabalhadores urbanos, propondo a 'incorporação das massas', cuja expressão política seria o 'populismo'".

8. Here understood as the synthesis between Marxist theory and the experiences of real socialism.
9. Currently BNDES (*Banco Nacional de Desenvolvimento Econômico e Social*, in Portuguese), the National Bank for Social and Economic Development.
10. For instance, Getúlio Vargas and Juscelino Kubitschek.
11. Original in Portuguese: "Tal frente reúne a grande burguesia interna brasileira que é a sua força dirigente, a baixa classe média, o operariado urbano e o campesinato. A frente incorpora, também, aquele amplo e heterogêneo setor social que compreende desempregados, subempregados, trabalhadores por conta própria, camponeses em situação de penúria e outros setores que compõem aquilo que a sociologia crítica latino-americana do século passado denominou 'massa marginal'".
12. Original in Portuguese: "O novo-desenvolvimentismo não é protecionista, apenas enfatiza a necessidade de uma taxa de câmbio competitiva e a identifica com a taxa de câmbio de equilíbrio industrial".
13. Original in Portuguese: "Uma taxa de câmbio competitiva é fundamental para o desenvolvimento econômico porque coloca todo o mercado externo à disposição das empresas nacionais realmente competentes do ponto de vista administrativo e tecnológico".
14. Original in Portuguese: "O neodesenvolvimentismo (i) apresenta um crescimento econômico que, embora seja muito maior do que aquele verificado na década de 1990, é bem mais modesto que aquele propiciado pelo velho desenvolvimentismo; (ii) confere importância menor ao mercado interno; (iii) atribui importância menor à política de desenvolvimento do parque industrial local; (iv) aceita os constrangimentos da divisão internacional do trabalho, promovendo, em condições históricas novas, uma reativação da função primário-exportadora do capitalismo brasileiro; (v) tem menor capacidade distributiva da renda e; (vi) o novo desenvolvimentismo é dirigido por uma fração burguesa que perdeu toda veleidade de agir como força anti-imperialista".
15. Original in Portuguese: "(i) políticas de recuperação do salário mínimo e de transferência de renda que aumentaram o poder aquisitivo das camadas mais pobres, isto é, daqueles que apresentam maior propensão ao consumo; (ii) elevação da dotação orçamentária do Banco Nacional de Desenvolvimento Econômico (BNDES) para financiamento da taxa de juro subsidiada das grandes empresas nacionais; (iii) política externa de apoio às grandes empresas brasileiras ou instaladas no Brasil para exportação de mercadorias e de capitais; (iv) política econômica anticíclica – medidas para manter a demanda agregada nos momentos de crise econômica".
16. Original in Portuguese: "gestão empresarial com governos progressistas sem intento de transformação da forma Estado herdada".
17. This is a hypothetical proposal to be developed in future works. What may be pointed now, however, in our understanding, is that it is possible to rearrange the structure of global capitalism, or even to transcend it through a Latin American reposition from intensive regional integration. In these terms, taking into consideration the formulation of the concept of developmentalism, industrialization would require a mix with investments in technological autonomy, the national project would not need substantial changes and the novelty of redistribution cannot be out of the scene. All the above do not mean, in the meantime, that there would be an automatic rearrangement of the labor-capital relation; for us, the transcendence from capitalism to another system yet in construction is the one that could rearrange that relation.

Bibliography

Arantes, P. (2016). Grandes Transformações na América Latina? A Onda Rosa, a Bolívia e o Contramovimento [Great Transformations in Latin America? Pink Wave, Bolivia and Countermovement]. Master's Dissertation. Pontifícia Universidade Católica de Minas Gerais (PUC-Minas).

Araújo, A. (2002). Estado e trabalhadores: a montagem da estrutura sindical corporativista no Brasil [State and workers: the assembly of the corporatist union structure in Brazil]. In *Do corporativismo ao neoliberalismo* [From corporatism to neoliberalism]. Araújo, Angela (Org.). São Paulo: Editora Boitempo.

Arretche, M. (2010). Federalismo e igualdade territorial: uma contradição em termos? [Federalism and territorial equality: a contradiction in terms?]. *Dados* 53(3).

Bielschowsky, R. (2000). Cinquenta anos de pensamento da CEPAL – Uma resenha [ECLAC's fifty years of thought – a review] (15–68). In *Cinquenta Anos de Pensamento da CEPAL*, Vol. 1 and 2 [ECLAC's fifty years of thought], edited by R. Bielchowsky. Rio de Janeiro: Record.

_____(2012). Estratégia de desenvolvimento e as três frentes de expansão no Brasil: um desenho conceitual [Development strategy and the three expansion fronts in Brazil: a conceptual design]. *Economia e Sociedade* 21.

Boito, Jr., A. (2017). O legado dos governos do PT [The legacy of PT governments]. In *Cinco mil dias: O Brasil na era do lulismo* [Five thousand days: Brazil in the age of Lulism], edited by J. Medeiros and G. Maringoni. São Paulo: Boitempo Editorial.

Boito, Jr. A. and Berringer, T. (2013). Brasil: classes sociais, neodesenvolvimentismo e política externa nos governos Lula e Dilma [Brazil: Social classes, neodevelopment and foreign policy in the Lula and Dilma governments]. *Revista de Sociologia e Política* 21(47).

Bresser-Pereira, L. C. (2009). From Old to New Developmentalism in Latin America. *Escola de Economia de São Paulo, Texto para Discussão* 193.

_____(2012). A taxa de câmbio no centro da teoria do desenvolvimento [The exchange rate at the heart of development theory]. *Estudos Avançados* 26(75).

Bringel, B. and Falero, A. (2016). Movimientos sociales, gobiernos progresistas y Estado en América Latina: transiciones, conflictos y mediaciones [Social movements, progressive governments and the State in Latin America: Transitions, conflicts and mediations]. *Caderno CRH, Salvador* 29(3).

Cardoso, F. H. and Faletto, E. (1977). *Dependência e desenvolvimento na América Latina: Ensaio de interpretação sociológica* [Dependency and development in Latin America: Sociological interpretation essay]. Rio de Janeiro: Zahar Editores.

Carneiro, R. (2002). *Desenvolvimento em crise: a economia brasileira no último quarto do século XX* [Development in crisis: The Brazilian economy in the last quarter of the 20th century]. São Paulo: Editora UNESP.

_____(2012). Velhos e novos desenvolvimentismos [Old and new developmentalism]. *Economia e Sociedade, Campinas* 21.

de Freixo, A. and Rodrigues, T. (2016). Sobre crises e golpes ou uma explicação para Alice [About crises and scams or an explanation for Alice]. In *2016, o ano do Golpe* [2016, the year of the coup], edited by A. de Freixo, T. Rodrigues. Rio de Janeiro: Oficina Raquel.

Fleury, S. (February 2011). The Hidden Welfare State in Brazil. Paper presented at the IPSA Seminar Whatever happened to North-South, *Panel "Development and Welfare Regime"*. São Paulo: USP.

Fonseca, P. C. D. (2015). Desenvolvimentismo: a construção do conceito [Developmentalism: The construction of the concept]. *Texto para Discussão IPEA* 2103.

Fonseca, P. C. D. and Salomão, I. C. (2017). O sentido histórico do desenvolvimentismo e sua atualidade [The historical sense of developmentalism and its relevance]. *Revista de Economia Contemporânea*. Special issue. https://www.scielo.br/j/rec/a/QbtqZ8BSPnMKWCdw4BfrgRt/?format=pdf&lang=pt

Furtado, C. (1965). Political Obstacles to Economic Growth in Brazil. *International Affairs* 41(2).

Gaudichaud, F. (January/June 2016). Fim de ciclo na América do Sul? Movimentos populares, governos "progressistas" e alternativas ecossocialistas [End of cycle in South America? Popular movements, "progressive" governments and eco-socialist alternatives]. *Lutas Sociais, São Paulo* 20(36).

Ianoni, M. (January/April 2017). Para uma abordagem ampliada das coalizões [Towards an expanded approach to coalitions]. *Sinais Sociais* 11(33).

Lafer, C. (2002). *JK e o Plano de Metas* [JK and the Goals Plan]. Rio de Janeiro: Editora da FGV.

Maricato, E. (2002). *Brasil, cidades: alternativas para a crise urbana* [Brazil, cities: Alternatives to the urban crisis]. Petrópolis, RJ: Vozes.

Marini, R. M. (1973 [2005]). Dialética da Dependência [Dialectic of Dependence]. *Marxists*. Retrieved from https://www.marxists.org/portugues/marini/1973/mes/dialetica.htm.

Menezes, T. and Vieira, M. (August 1–4, 2012). A "onda rosa" no Brasil e na Argentina sob o prisma das distintas morfologias políticas [The "pink wave" in Brazil and Argentina from the perspective of different political morphologies]. *Anais do 8° Encontro da ABCP*, Gramado, RS.

Monteiro, L. V. (March/June 2018). Os neogolpes e as interrupções de mandatos presidenciais na América Latina: os casos de Honduras, Paraguai e Brasil [The neo-coups and the interruption of presidential mandates in Latin America: The cases of Honduras, Paraguay and Brazil]. *Revista de Ciências Sociais. Fortaleza* 49(1).

Prates, D., Fritz, B., and de Paula, L. F. (July/December 2017). Uma avaliação das políticas desenvolvimentistas nos governos do PT [An assessment of developmental policies in PT governments]. *Cadernos do Desenvolvimento, Rio de Janeiro* 12(21).

dos Santos, W. G. (1985). O século de Michels: competição oligopólica, lógica autoritária e transição na América Latina [Michels' century: Oligopolistic competition, authoritarian logic and transition in Latin America]. *Dados* 28(3).

———(1986). *1964: Anatomia da crise* [Anatomy of the crisis]. São Paulo: Vértice.

Serra, J. (1982a). Ciclos e mudanças estruturais na economia brasileira do após-guerra [Cycles and structural changes in the post-war Brazilian economy]. *Revista de Economia Política* 2/2(6).

———(1982b). Ciclos e mudanças estruturais na economia brasileira do após-guerra: a crise recente [Cycles and structural changes in the post-war Brazilian economy: The recent crisis]. *Revista de Economia Política* 2/3(7).

Silva, F. (2014). Quinze anos da onda rosa latino-americana: balanço e perspectivas [Fifteen years of the Latin American pink wave: Balance and perspectives]. *Observador On-Line* 9(12).

Singer, A. (2015). Cutucando onças com varas curtas [Poking jaguars with short sticks]. *Novos Estudos* 102.

Tavares, M. da C. (2010). *Desenvolvimento e igualdade* [Development and equality]. Rio de Janeiro: IPEA.

Zibechi, R. (2007). *Autonomías y emancipaciones: América Latina en movimiento* [Autonomies and emancipations: Latin America on the move]. Lima: Fondo Editorial de la Faculdad de Ciencias Sociales UNMSM.

7 Capitalism and Labor Exploitation in Brazil

Human Trafficking and Slave Labor

Élio Gasda

Introduction

Material accumulation constitutes the principal engine of capitalism. The mere preservation of capital is impossible without its same-time expansion. In different stages of capitalism, the accumulation was made through the transformation of production relations creating new forms of labor exploitation.

A brief view of capitalism history demonstrates that it is a world-system, a world-economy, a system of totality (Wallerstein 1974). Capitalism elements are interdependent. The organic element that unites all historic processes and the mechanisms of the system is the division of labor. The division of labor surpasses cultural barriers and national frontiers. Its expansion goes up to the great geographic discoveries made during the European *Renaissance, Mercantilism,* and the great Spanish and Portuguese navigations. The conquest and colonization of America, the enslavement of the native Americans, and the traffic of African slaves would be its first and decisive stage. Its expansion absorbed mini-economic systems in Africa and America. Therefore, any economic, political, or cultural analysis must presuppose that capitalism was a world system since its origin.

The objective of this chapter is to introduce two forms of extreme labor exploitation in the history of Brazil: human trafficking and slave labor. Using the historic bibliographic method, the chapter goes through the history of Brazil in a chronological way, supporting itself with the reference literature on the subject. The last section, law based, offers a critical propositional view about the two forms.

The exploitation of labor has always been one of the pillars of capitalism. The first section demonstrates that human trafficking and slave labor are not practices restricted to the origin of capitalism. The exploitation of human work fed by human trafficking has been one of the capitalism pillars since its origin. The second section, divided into four items, examines the Brazilian case of human trafficking and slave labor. *The "meaning" of conquest and colonization of Brazil* describes

DOI: 10.4324/9781003045632-8

how capitalism was established while the consumer's markets were expanding, making commerce activity accumulate capital. The exportation of their products was all focused on the external market. That orientation generates a dependency on the slave workforce. Slavery was part of this historical moment, the birth of capitalism. The subsequent paragraphs of this section describe the type of people and the forms of expression of human trafficking and slave labor in this period of Brazil history: *traffic and enslavement of native people; traffic and enslavement of African people, "second slavery"; and exploitation of European immigrants.*

The third section – *contemporary manifestations of human trafficking and slavery in Brazil* – reports that four centuries of human trafficking and slavery leave deep scars in Brazil. The official slavery abolition act did not eliminate its own social, economic, and cultural problems. The independence of the country was made with the support of a proslavery oligarchy that kept the exploitation of slave labor. Thousands of African slaves continued arriving in Brazilian ports until the last quarter of the 19th century. Structural racism was radicalized.

The actual slave labor is characterized as contemporary slavery. It is not restricted to Africans and native American people but affects poor white people, immigrants, women, and children. Slave labor persists as a characteristic of contemporary capitalism. Having as a starting point the principle of human dignity, the fourth section emphasizes the function of *legal instrument* in the combat of human trafficking and slave labor. The approach is made by the view of international and Brazilian law.

Human Trafficking and Slave Labor: Permanent Reality

Since the primordium of capitalism and the colonization of America, black Africans were transported out of their countries and forced to work in many places of America. Native American people were also trafficked and subjected to slavery in the same period. Giving a time jump, in contemporary global capitalism, the practice of human trafficking and slavery is still observed.

Human trafficking is one of the three most lucrative illicit businesses in the world. Its market was intensified based on four activities: prostitution, traffic, pornography, and organs trade (UNODC, 2020). Slave labor follows up human history. Millions of people were sold and bought as slaves. Its vestiges are in the Great Wall of China, in the pyramids of Egypt, in the ruins of the coliseum of Rome, in the lap arches of Rio de Janeiro, and in the canals of Venezia. Today, the International Labour Organization (ILO) estimates that around 40 million people are being enslaved. Anti-slavery International, a British organization, calculates that currently there are more slaves in the world than in any other period. In Brazil, this would be about 400,000 people.

Human trafficking and slavery were raised around the beginning of the modern occident. The irruption of the Industrial Revolution and the market economy policy brought the comprehension that work is a merchandise. The exploitation of human work has been one of the capitalism pillars since its origin. It is estimated that around 1800 were approximately 45 million slaves all over the world (Alencastro 2000, 85, 144). Nothing was so everlasting, organized, lucrative, and gigantic as the slave trade between the African continent and America. It involved four continents, reconfigured the history, the economy, the society, and the culture of all countries implicated.

The characteristics of the enslaved individual: ripped of his territory and of his social environment; it is sold as a merchandise; it is a property; the relation between the lord and the slave is based on violence; always works for his owner; it is up to the owner to control his procreation, the slave children do not belong to the slave; the slavery is hereditary; social death: ripped of his culture, his family, his traditions, and his community. His existence totally depends on the will of his owner; loss of his original identity.

Brazil: Human Trafficking and Slave Labor in the Origins of Capitalism

The "Meaning" of Conquest and Colonization of Brazil

Capitalism is an economic, social, and political system that started with the decline of the feudal system in Europe. In feudalism, there were two distinct social categories: feudal lords, composed of the clergy and nobility; and the people, composed of free peasants and serfs who were subjected to serfdom because they worked on land that did not belong to them and gave the feudal lords a large part of their production. The latter were submitted to the regime of servitude for working in a land that did not belong to them and were obligated to give their lords a great part of their production.

With the development of commerce, initiated after the first crusades, the consumption of oriental products increased in Europe, enabling the creation of merchant companies and commercial routes. Capitalism was establishing itself as a system while the consumer market was growing, and commerce allowed capital accumulation.

In regards to maritime routes, the reactivation of the ports in the Iberian Peninsula was fundamental, contributing to the shift of the European commercial axis to Spain and Portugal. The discoveries of the islands of Cape Verde, Azores, Madeira, the American continent, and the occupation of the African coast are present in the same chapter of the history of the commercial enterprise since the 15th century (Prado Junior 1942). The colonization of American contributed to the growth of the capitalist economy.

In the Brazilian colonial period, in the context of Portuguese commercial expansion, it constituted a structure in which the objective was to export primary products to attend the external demand; it generated a dependency inclusive in the obtainment of the slave workforce, an "inevitable economic imperative" (Simonsen 1937). With the advent of the Industrial Revolution, agriculture and industry completed themselves economically.

The Brazilian economy was essentially commercial (Prado Junior 1942). The commercial expansion of Europe is the face of the process of the formation of capitalism. The colonization appears as a channel of mercantile capital accumulation in the center of the rising system (Novais 2002, 1114, 1115). In the colonial age, it is possible to identify the logic in "the meaning of colonization". The expansion was one of the components of the formation of capitalism. The colonial past of America founds its meaning in the system that promotes primitive capital accumulation. It means: the emerging of African slavery from the Atlantic slave trade promotes primitive capital accumulation. The rising capitalism introduced slavery in Brazil, which, on its way, contributed to the formation of the European industrial capital.

The work process in a proslavery sugar mill of the 16th century is similar to large capitalist husbandry. When inserted in this process of material production, the slave constitutes an anticipation of the modern worker. The modern proslavery system has important traces in common with capitalism. The slave workforce was a reinvention of capital in the era of discoveries. And the scarcity of a free workforce made the colonial capitalists use the slave workforce.

The slave labor was not seen as a cost but as an investment in production like any other else. Brazil needed a slave workforce to be exploited by capital to generate profit. These circumstances determined the type of exploitation adopted, that is, the large property and the monoculture to attend to the demand of the external market. The slave was a factor in the production and a merchandise.

The existing capitalism in Brazil was, since the beginning of its colonization, purely commercial; a National State did not exist and the production was destined to the external market. However, the country already presented the principal elements of a capitalist system: capital accumulation, market economy, currency exchange, companies that had profit as a single objective, and work exploitation as a source of capital to produce more capital. Slavery was a highly profitable business.

Traffic and Enslavement of Native People

The Europeans arrived in inhabited regions. Some villages had 5,000 residents. Their arrival in America produced one of the biggest humanitarian catastrophes in history. The genocide of 40 million native people corresponded to 8.9% of the world population at that time.

In Brazil, in 1500, the native population was approximately four million distributed in hundreds of different folks, speaking more than 1,000 languages. Three centuries later, this same population was reduced to 700,000. Wars promoted by the Portuguese, diseases, and slavery contributed to the annihilation of these proportions (Gomes 2019, 121–123). The Portuguese started to enslave the native immediately after their arrival in the territory. They captured natives from north to south. Their sale was the first large activity. The exploitation of native forced labor was utilized in the rural coffee sector and in the sugar cane, reaching a high degree of rentability.

The Portuguese crown legalized the slavery of native people via *the letter of donation of the hereditary captaincies*. The *provision* of October 17 of 1653 and the *provision* of March 9 of 1718 extended this concept, establishing a unique condition to slavery: the fact of being savages, in other words, any native people. The *paulista flags* (bandeirantes paulistas) were the main protagonist. Hunting native people was their principal objective. With a politic of scorched earth, they destroyed completely every village they found. It was one of the most predatory proslavery operations in modern history.

The *pombaline reforms* of 1755 and 1758 that abolished native people's slavery had no effect. The start of African slave trafficking, in the mid-16th century, did not interrupt the slavery of the native individual at least until the mid-18th century. Since then, they were substituted by Africans. Records of a sugar mill belonging to the society of Jesus in Bahia state, the Sergipe state of the earl, illustrates the transition of indigenous slave work to the African slave work. In 1574, Africans represented 7% of the enslaved workers. Around 1638 they would compose the totality of the workers.

Traffic and Enslavement of African People

The cradle of humanity, Africa, would have approximately 200 million habitants at the time of the European arrival. Only Mali would have almost 50 million habitants (Gomes 2019, 142, 143).

It is known with relative precision that 12,521,337 human beings boarded from Africa in around 36,000 trips in slave ships between 1500 and 1867. Of these, 10,702,657 arrived alive in America and 1,818,680 would be dead. Almost 2 million died on the cross.

The Portuguese found in African slave trafficking the solution to their problems. They searched a rapid enrichment. Unlike slavery in ancient Greece and Rome, where the defeated in wars were assigned to servitude, colonial slavery was assigned to the black race. Slave traffic was the fastest and most rentable solution that could break and explore the riches of the Brazilian lands. It was the nearest commercial activity to what they would call capitalism.

The aim of the slave traffic was always the profit. All aspects of life in America would gravitate around slavery. According to the historian Eric Williams, author of *Capitalism and Slavery,* the capital generated through trafficking would be enough to finance the Industrial Revolution (Williams 2015). Starting in the 19th century, the profits were raised in a substantial form. In this period, the return on the investments would have reached 300%.

The slave traffic involved the transport of people, merchandise, plants, and seeds between four continents: Africa, Europe, Asia, and America. The enslaved were captured and bought along the African coast, in a territorial extension of around 6,000 kilometers of length and 1,000 kilometers of width. Later this coastal strip would be extended for more 4,000 kilometers with the inclusion of Mozambique. The database Slave Voyages registers that there was a total of 188 ports of boarding slaves in Africa (Eltis and Richardson 2010, 37). Until the beginning of the 19th century, in the middle of the Industrial Revolution, slave traffic was the biggest business in the world. Selling slaves was so lucrative that it appeared as a business to reproduce captives with the objective of selling children the same way dogs and cows were sold in the market (Freyre 2019, 333).

"Brazil has its body in America and its soul in Africa" (priest Antônio Vieira). Slavery was a humanitarian tragedy. This horror was the historic phenomenon most determinant in the history of Brazil. No other event was so decisive for the national identity. Brazil was constructed by dark-colored people. Africa is in Brazil. The largest slave territory of capitalism for 350 years, Brazil received almost 40% of the 12.5 million Africans trafficked to America, 4.9 million. Received almost 40% of the total of 12.5 million Africans trafficked to America, 4.9 million. The number is ten times superior to the destined for the British colonies in North America. Portuguese and Brazilians were the biggest human traffickers in the history of mankind. One of three trips was organized in Brazil. Rio de Janeiro, principal organizer center of the traffic, corresponded to the transport of 1.5 million enslaved, followed by Salvador, with 1.4 million (the Trans-Atlantic Slave Trade Database). Rio de Janeiro was the biggest dark-colored slave port in history. Those numbers made Brazil the second country with a larger dark-colored population of the world, almost 120 million habitants, a number only inferior to the population of Nigeria, with 190 million habitants.

The traffic of enslaved people can be divided into four periods: cycle of Guinea, initiated after the arrival of Pedro Alvares Cabral in Bahia; cycle of Angola and Congo, up until 1850; Coast of Mina, in the 18th century; and cycle of Mozambique, in the 19th century. The kingdom of Portugal in the 15th century was created after a crusade against the Moors in the Iberian Peninsula. In 1418, a papal bull gave a surety to the Portuguese navigations, checking to them the status of a new crusade, this time against the unfaithful in Africa. The caravels boasted in their sails the cross of the Order of Christ, heiress of the Order of the Templar Knights. In 1317, the Portuguese king Dom Dinis welcomed all templars persecuted in Europe. Renamed as Order of Christ, the templars were in the rearguard of the great Portuguese navigations of the 15th and 16th centuries. A papal bull authorized the Order of Christ to hunt and commercialize slaves.

In 1444, the first auction of Africans happened in Portugal. In the village of Lagos, south of the country (Algarve), 6 caravels disembarked 235 Africans composed of men, women, and children to be sold in an auction. In 1455, Pope Nicholas V, through the bull *Romanus Pontifex,* authorized the Portuguese to enslave all non-Christians. More than 150,000 Africans were captured by the Portuguese between 1450 and 1500 (Gomes 2019, 51–56). At the start of the Lagos auction, the slave commerce helped to finance the conquest navigations of America. The most important economic activity of the Portuguese expansion was hunting, enslaving, and selling human beings. The true reason that the first large navigations profited was through this practice. It was an intimate relation between Italian merchants and bankers and the traffic of slaves.

The Spanish Christopher Columbus arrived in America in 1492, the same year of the construction of Saint George of Elmina castle, the first warehouse of slaves in Africa. The official start of slave traffic for America was marked by a decree of 1510, of King Fernando Catholic of Spain, in Valladolid. The arrival of the first Africans in Brazil coincides with the start of the sugar mill in the state of Pernambuco in 1535. The slave was considered entirely a work animal, as well as a horse. It was a disposable economic asset and replenished when its productive strength was exhausted. A horse was worth more than 15 human slaves.

The traffic of slaves interested not only merchants and colonizers but also the Portuguese crown, because it constituted an important source of revenue to the government. Between the 15th and 16th centuries, the Portuguese crown committed to the concretization of two tasks: catechize and incorporate, through baptism, the African pagans to Catholicism; extract the biggest possible number of Africans and transport them to Brazil to be enslaved.

Angola was consolidated as the providing territory of slave to America. Around 70% of the 4.9 million captives that disembarked in Brazil came from Angola. The crossing to Brazil was the most traveled traffic route between the 17th and 18th centuries (Ferreira 2012, 1). Luanda, the capital, was the biggest slave port in history. From there 12,000 trips left. The commerce between Brazil and Angola was stimulated by the ocean currents and the winds that impelled sail navigation. As a result of the traffic, around 1,600, the number of captives in Brazil was four times bigger than that of the Europeans. Of the 150,000 inhabitants of the colony, only 30,000 were white (Boxer 1969, 112). The Africans were the first merchandise of the commercial relations between Brazil and the neighboring countries.

In the middle of the 18th century, a healthy adult man was bought in Luanda for the price of fourteen pairs of silk socks or three barrels of gunpowder. A little time before, a man in the same condition could be bought for 45 liters of sugarcane liquor. A horse costs ten slaves. A barrel of 500 liters of sugarcane liquor bought ten slaves (Alencastro 2000, 49).

The life expectancy of an enslaved man was of only 18 years. The enslaved walked hundreds of kilometers famished and tortured up until the boarding ports. In the port, they waited half-naked, chained, stocked in filthy, dark warehouses without ventilation and hygiene, generally mixed with pigs, chickens, and dogs. The sanitarian needs were made inside the warehouse. They could wait weeks or months until the completion of the load. Before the boarding, they were baptized by a priest and marked with red-hot iron four times: with the symbol of the merchant, with the seal of the Portuguese crown, with the mark of the cross, and the name of the trafficker. Upon arrival in Brazil, they could receive a fifth mark of his owner. The fugitives were marked with a red-hot iron in the face.

Boarding a ship was an appalling experience. The majority of them had never seen the sea: many suicides. They were chained and collared like animals. It was documented that there were 600 revolts on the high seas. It was the most painful navigation ever registered in history – a horrendous portrait of human misery.

In Brazilian territory, the auction was the most common way of selling slaves. The transactions were similar to an animal fair. His value was compared to a pack animal. A young was worth three mules. The sickest and elderly who did not find a buyer were abandoned. If they are sold in an auction, the African starts going through the period of adaptation. If it was an urban slave, it would be installed on the ground floor of the house, dividing space with domestic animals. If destined to work in farms or sugarcane mills, it was taken to the slave house, a collective accommodation of slaves. Slave houses were warehouses without light, windows, floor, and sanitary installations and were covered with straw (Gomes 2019, 302–309). Domestic workers would come to the lord's house.

The colonial period was marked by the production of sugar. The slave work was responsible for the peak of sugar production. The arrival of Africans matches with the cycle of the economic prosperity of the sugar economy. This industry was characterized by the binomial lord house and slave house, the profound mark of the Brazilian identity. The biggest mills exploited up to 150 slaves. The captives were submitted to daily long, harsh, and dangerous journeys. The shift of work could last up to 18 hours. In the cane fields, individuals that could not accomplish the determined quota were tortured ruthlessly.

The "Second Slavery"

The "second slavery" can be divided into three phases: formation 1790–1830; apogee 1830–1870; greatness and crisis 1860–1888. The continuity of slavery attended to the economic interest of local elites and accomplished the requirements of an integration model with European capitalism. The importance of slavery for the consolidation of capitalism during the 19th century is indisputable. Until the middle of the 18th century, slavery was an accepted practice without more questioning.

At the beginning of the 18th century, the economy of sugar was in crisis due to the competitiveness of the Dutch, French, and British mills in the Caribbean. There were excess offers. The men of the state of São Paulo, responsible for the slavery of thousands of native people, turned their attention to the mountainous regions, until then called "Minas" (Mines). The discovery of gold provoked a large race in search of precious metals. Around 2 million enslaved Africans would arrive in "Minas" (Mines). The country would become the most dependent on slave work in America. The gold rush in "Minas" (Mines) was accompanied by a never-seen African occupation. It was the peak of slave trade in the Atlantic. In a period of only 100 years, more than 6 million human beings were trafficked from Africa to America.

The "second slavery" favored the proslavery process correlated to the demands of accumulation on the part of capitalism during the 19th century. The concept of "second slavery" was proposed by the British historian Robin Blackburn (Marquese and Salles 2016). Blackburn stipulates its beginning in 1790, reaching its peak in the middle of the 19th century, a spark of the Industrial Revolution in Europe.

Fundamental to the future of expansionist capitalism in Europe, the "second slavery" represents a proslavery regime more autonomous, more lasting, and, in terms of market, more productive. Unlike the first slavery, architected in colonial contexts, the second takes place in an economic context interconnected with the dynamics of production of merchandise in America as a crucial factor to the evolution of European industrial capitalism. Spawned from this are the relevance of cotton production in the United States, sugarcane in Cuba, and coffee in Brazil, merchandise produced by slavery basis. For its success, the "second slavery" required another role of the state (more support and incentive than supervision). The slaves were considered as "capital" and treated as a "function of production".

Semi Slavery of Immigrants

The capitalist system did not bear more slavery, and wage labor was necessary to the formation of a consumer market of industrialized products. The strengthening of the bourgeoises, above all after the Industrial

Revolution, boosted the conquest of new markets, making the English prohibit slavery. England stimulated the migration of mercantile capitalism to industrial capitalism. The English colonies, located in the Antilles, no longer used slave workforce. Therefore, the sugar produced there would become more expensive than Brazilian sugar. Beneficiated by the maintenance of slave work, prejudicated the economic interest of the English.

In 1831, due to external threats, mainly from England, it edited the *Law Feijó* prohibiting the slave trade. Others laws were created: *Viscount of Rio Branco Law* (Lei Visconde Rio Branco), of 1871, known as *Free Womb Law* (Lei do *Ventre Livre*); Saraiva Cotegripe Law (*Lei Saraiva Cotegripe*), called of *Sexagenarian Law* (Lei dos Sexagenários); *John Alfred Law* (Lei João Alfredo), of 1888, titled as *Golden Law* (Lei Áurea), declaring the abolishment of slavery in Brazil.

Around 1850 a political law of foreign immigration was promulgated. This workforce became utilized on a large scale after the *Golden Law*. The abolition of slavery came to occur only after the dominant class obtained from the state financial compensations for the liberty of the slaves. It does not speak about compensations for the enslaved, only to the enslavers. There had not been a social-economic integration of black-colored Africans. Marginalized, they faced a lack of housing and social and labor exclusion. The dominant Brazilian class demonstrated interest in the European immigrants. The European immigrants became the most utilized workforce and the African ex-slaves were discarded.

Contemporary Manifestations of Work Exploitation in Brazil

After the abolishment of slave work in 1888, what was observed during the following centuries was the restructuration of a labor exploring system analogous to the times of slavery. The Penal Code of 1890 did nothing but brought about the repression of slave work. This situation was acquiring its own contours while capitalism was expanding, but without losing its common base: the exploitation of human work.

Starting in the 18th century, society was drastically modified by the Industrial Revolution. The need for people to operate steam and textile machines imposed the substitution of slaves or servile to salaried work (Davis 2001). Contemporary slavery, different from the one that existed all around the world and especially in Brazil, with the Portuguese colonization and during the empire of Brazil, is a phenomenon conducted by the incessant search for profit that moves the big and medium corporations in search for the spotlight in the national and global economy.

Four centuries of slavery left profound marks in Brazil, with the main one being structural racism. The black-colored population lives in a permanent state of vulnerability and faces numerous difficulties to obtain access to social rights. The ex-enslaved were thrown in the margin of society without reparation for the centuries of violence. The abolition did not eliminate the economic, cultural, and social impacts of slavery. Many relations between boss and worker and the businessman and worker are still marked by the heritage left by slavery.

Brazil was born from human trafficking and slavery. The authoritarian state was configurated by the interests of proslavery colonial capitalism. The independence in 1822 was given by the support of the large slaveholders and oligarchs. The slave trade would make the traffickers and the Brazilian property owners increasingly richer, transforming them into true "empire magnates" (Nabuco 1977, 44). The same guaranteed, for more than six decades, the exploitation of the slave work. With the coffee sector expansion, thousands and thousands of Africans continued disembarking until the middle of the 19th century.

The economic elites used racism as a structuring element of the class division, income concentration, super exploitation of work, and repression against the poor. Not only was it given continuity, but it was also radicalized structural racism. Black people have less access to education, health, transport, and work, along with less access to security and worthy habitation, due to which they die first (Santos 1996/1997, 133–144). In capitalism, the workforce is a merchandise disciplined in a military manner.

The current slave work is characterized as contemporary slavery. It is not restricted to Africans and native people, but it is camouflaged and reaches poor white people, immigrants, women, and children. The low grade of schooling and personal qualification and the unemployment left them vulnerable to fictitious offers. The high level of illiteracy and the low human development index characterize the regions of most enslaved workers. These people are slaves of a penury economic situation. The economic disparity is translated into an enormous quantity of people that, for being so poor, are vulnerable to slavery.

Brazil started to act in the slave work combat only in 1995. Since then, the Ministry of Work has already freed more than 50,000 workers. Slave work was found in the following activities: coal-pits, mining companies, lumber companies, alcohol and sugar mills, distilleries, colonization companies, prospecting, farms, companies of reforesting/cellulose, agriculture, companies related to the production of tin, companies of the citriculture, pottery, coffee, seeds production and rubber plantations, clothing industry, fabrication of pirated products, drugs and arms dealing, and prostitution sector (Sutton 1994).

The slave work is a characteristic of contemporary capitalism in Brazil; it is one of the instruments of the system. The employers involved in this type of exploitation, most of the time, work with high technology and are inserted in the national and international markets. This slavery exists under the direct influence of the market economy and depends on it. The slave work is not a detour but a tool of the system (Sakamoto 2019).

As more capitalism require competitiveness, the exploitation of slave work appears as a cheap option to win the competition. Capitalism reconfigures its forms of exploitation in the function of profit. The less the companies spend, the more they can compete in the market. In this option, retired are the workers' rights.

The super exploitation of workers is one of the pillars of capitalism. The work relations are transiting from the exploitation mode to a spoliation regime. In the first, the employee has his capacities utilized beyond the minimal remuneration and protection conditions. He has rights that are not respected. When those rights are revoked, the spoliation regime is inaugurated. The workers are coerced to accept indecent working conditions: low wages, informality, precariousness, extenuating journey, no contract. The structure of the labor market reproduces the insertion in an unequal and more precarious way to the more vulnerable groups. The young, principally the poor, the women, and the black colored are the most affected. Outsourcing is the central aspect of spoliation. For the gigantic territories of people that do not have a chance of coming back to the labor market, capitalism offers a horizon: the "privilege of servitude" (Antunes 2019).

Capitalism continues depending on the sale of the workforce. Workers, each time more integrated by the productive global chains, sell their workforce as merchandise in exchange for hunger wages, not caring if the activities are not regulated. Labor exploitation is one of the principal causes of social inequality.

Legal Instrument

The Principle of Human Dignity

The values, the routine behaviors, and the law must emanate from the ethical principle of human dignity. Its comprehension is a consequence of a historical evolution made by the fight of the people for equality, liberty, and rights. Everything that does not has a price has dignity. The invaluable cannot serve as an exchange currency. When something has a price, it can be substituted for its equivalent. But when something is above all prices and does not permit equivalency, so it has dignity. The rights to life, honor, physical integrity, psychic integrity, and privacy are essential because without them, human dignity is not accomplished. All people must abstain from violating them (Kant 1986, 77). People are not things; therefore, no human being can be treated as private property or as an animal.

These and other ideas inspired the *Virginia Declaration of Rights* (*Bill of Rights* – 1776) and the *Declaration of the Rights of the Man and of the Citizen* (1793 – *proclaimed right after the French Revolution*). In the 20th century definitive recognition of human dignity was given with the *Universal Declaration of Human Rights*, of 1948. For the first time the welcome of human dignity as a source and axis of the rights occurred: Art 1° – All human beings are born free and equal in dignity and rights. They are endowed with reason and conscience and should act toward one another in a spirit of brotherhood.

Every individual has the dignity of a human being only by the fact of existing. Due only to their human condition, every human being is a holder of the rights that should be respected similarly (Sarlet 2002, 22). Every other right is only possible if accomplished when respected by the principle of human dignity. It is the base for the interpretation of all juridical rules.

The judicial consecration of human dignity remits to the vision of the human being as an axis of the law. As a constitutional category, human dignity must be expressed in the legislation. In this way, the repression and the severe criminalization of human trafficking and slave labor represent an application of the principle of human dignity in concrete situations.

Human Trafficking

Human trafficking has the *Palermo Protocols* as its international judicial mark of reference. National legislations about the theme are almost inexistent. The international community's concern with this crime led to the approval, together with the United Nations Convention against Transnational Organized Crime – called the Palermo Convention – of *the protocol to prevent, suppress and punish trafficking in persons, especially women and children*. The Palermo Protocols emerged to fill a gap in International Law. Until its entry into vigor, there were only treaties about specific criminal questions, like drug trafficking and money laundering.

The article 3 of the Palermo Protocol defines that: (a) the expression "human trafficking" means the recruitment, transport, transfer, accommodation, or host of people, using threats or the use of force or other forms of coercion, abduction, fraud, to deceit, to the abuse of authority or to a situation of vulnerability, or to the delivery or acceptance of payments or benefits to obtain the consent of a person that has the authority of other purposes of exploitation. Exploitation includes, at least, exploitation of prostitution or other forms of sexual exploitation, forced services or work, slavery or practices similar to slavery, servitude, and organ removal; (b) the consent given by the victim of human trafficking in view of any exploitation described in the point (a) of the present article will be considered irrelevant if it had been used any of the means referred in the point (a); (c) the recruitment, transport, transfer, accommodation, or host of people or a child for the purpose of exploitation will be considered "human trafficking" even if did not involve any of the referred means of the point (a) of the present article; and (d) the term "child" means any person with age lesser than 18 years (UNODOC).

The main instruments that preceded the *Palermo Protocol* in 2000 show the importance of the law as an instance to eradicate this crime. The legislation that started combating the African trafficking of slavery advanced to the repression of the trafficking of white women and children (1921) and ended up including any person as a victim, independent of sex, color, race, and age. In the *Palermo Protocol*, the victims who were, initially, just white women, after women and children, are, now, human beings, who maintained the special preoccupation of women and children.

The *Protocol* uses the clause for the purpose of exploitation, which includes any way of human exploitation, be it sexual, of work, or organ removal. Before, prostitution was mentioned as a unique category. Today, the genre is sexual exploitation, and types of it are sex tourism, child prostitution, child pornography, forced prostitution, sex slavery, and forced marriage.

The *Palermo Protocol* are documents of criminal nature that aim at the cooperation between the states, delegating them the competency to legislate under the best form to accomplish the propositions in the documents. The victims of human trafficking are eminently victims of violations, many times very severe, of human rights. Most parts of the states still do not possess legislation about human trafficking and, if possessed, it is insufficient. As victims do not receive enough protection the dimension of international human being protection– the International Law of Human Rights, the International Humanitarian Law, and the International Refugee Law – alternatives are searched for to suppress the gap presented in these treaties.

Human trafficking, in a broad sense, gained relevance in the last decades in reason of globalization. The victims of human trafficking, in many cases, found themselves in situations of vulnerability analogs of the refugees. In this way, a look at these victims under the optics of the International Refugee Law can guarantee the application of determinate benefits. For that to occur it is necessary to verify in what situations the victims of the traffics are refugees and, therefore, detainers of rights and prerogatives of this category of migrants. The *International Refugee Law*, being associated with the guarantee of human rights, shows up as a possibility of the guarantee of dignity to human trafficking victims in the absence of norms more favorable in the legislation of each country, when the application of it is possible.

Brazil, one of the signatories of the *Palermo Protocol*, committed to its implementation and ratified it in 2004, giving start to the creation of mechanisms of surveillance of and combat against this crime. The National Politic of Confrontation to the Human Trafficking (2006) was institutionalized, as was the promulgation of the First National Plan of Confronting the Human Trafficking (2008). The II National Plan of Confronting the Human Trafficking (2013) widens its range of action, reflecting the evolution of the treatment of this question and showing the mutual links between human trafficking and slave labor.

Slave Labor

The creation of the ILO in 1919 had established prospects of providing minimum standards of labor rights and preventing the slavery that persisted. The abolition of all forms of slave labor constitutes one of the fundamental principles to be observed independently of the ratification of the specific conventions (Miraglia, Hernandez, and Oliveira 2018). The ILO possesses two conventions on this theme. Both establish that the signatory countries should take measures to extinguish the slave labor: The Convention n. 29 – about forced labor – comprehends slave labor as "all work or service which is exacted from any person under the threat of a penalty and for which the person has not offered himself or herself voluntarily"; the disposal of the elimination of forced or obligatory labor in all its forms. The Convention n. 105 – about the abolition of forced labor – treats the prohibition of all forms of forced work or obligatory as a way of coercion or of political education; punishment for the expression of politic or ideological expressions; disciplinary measures in work, and punishment for participating in strikes as a measure of discrimination (ILO).

In Brazil, even with the abolition law of 1888, the *Penal Code* of 1890, nothing brought about the repression of slave labor. The practice of reduction to slavery only became a crime in the *Penal Code* of 1940, article 149: "Reduce someone to a condition analogue to slavery". The article had its composition changed in 2003.

The alteration was significant once it defined the crime in an embracing way. Slave labor is no longer determined as in the past model. In the new law, it is a crime to reduce someone to a condition analogous to that of a slave, in four situations: submit the person to forced labor or to an exhaustive journey or to degrading conditions, or restrict, by any means, the liberty of movement. There is no more need to have captivities. Degrading conditions of work are enough.

Article 206 of the *Penal Code* treats the grooming of workers to take them to foreign countries. The victims are brainwashed and taken to inhumane works. Article 207 of the Penal Code treats workers grooming in their own national territory. They are people in maximum conditions of poverty who live in locals extremely out of resources. Deceived by the enticers, they are taken from a region to another country in search of good salaries and good conditions of living. However, what they found was just the exploitation of their workforce.

The Constitutional Amend 81, approved on July 5 of 2014, defined a new composition to article 243 of the Federal Constitution, starting to rule in the referred article

> the urban and rural properties of any region of the country that were localized illegal cultures of psychotropic plants or the exploitation of slave labor by the law will be expropriated and destined to the land reform and programs of popular habitation, without any indemnity to the proprietary and without prejudice of any other sanction preview by the law, observing, in what applies, the disposed in the article 5.

The law, always when applied in these terms, will turn the crime disadvantageous to the criminals, who will have their profits depreciated with their expropriation of property and assets.

Still about the legislation, it is important to highlight the Normative Instruction n. 91 of 2011 of the Ministry of Labor that disposes the inspection for the eradication of work in analogous conditions to slavery. Its text defines the providences adopted and those that must be observed by the Fiscal-Auditors of work in the inspection to eliminate the practice, in any urban, rural, and maritime economic activity, and for any worker, natural or foreign. The Normative Instruction defines that labor working in analogous conditions to slavery is, among others, submission to the worker to forced labor or exhaustive journey; subjection to degrading labor conditions; restriction of locomotion of the worker, be it due to a debt contract, by the enclosure of the use of any means of transport by the worker, or by any other means of retaining him in the workplace; ostentatious vigilance of the workplace by the employer, or its representant, or possession of documents or personal objects of the worker, by the employer or its representant, with the objective to retain the worker in the workplace. Besides that, the employer is obligated to immediately paralyze the activities of workers found, regulate the labor contracts, perform the payment of labor credits by the Terms of Labor Contract rescission, proceed to the retreat of FGTS and of the Social Contribution, and accomplish the accessories obligations of the labor contract.

The first accusation about slavery was made only in 1971. The question was exposed through the Pastoral Letter of Pedro Casaldaliga, bishop of Saint Felix of Araguaia. It was only in 1995 that the country officially recognized the existence of slave labor in its territory. President Fernando Henrique Cardoso acknowledged the problem when he edited the decree 1.538/95, through which he created the Interministerial Group to the Eradication of Forced Labor. In the same year, the Special

Group of Mobile Inspection was instituted, the main instrument of combat of slavery. Another mechanism was the creation of a national register of offenders, more known as the *dirty list*, with the name of companies condemned by the use of slave labor.

The II National Plan for the eradication of the Slave Labor of 2008 contemplates the necessity to give legal and social assistance to the immigrants' workers in an irregular situation in the Brazilian territory as prevention of submission of these people to the slave labor.

Since 2017 the social and legal conjecture of the Brazilian state is representing a setback in the fight for human and social rights. The Labor Reform presented contradictions to the constitutional principles, intensifying the process of Labor precariousness and exploitation. The outsourcing of business activities in an unrestricted form potentializes the capacity of labor exploitation and rights extinction. Outsourced workers are submitted to a greater extent to exploratory regimes in comparison to those directly hired. Some alterations directly impacted the combat of labor in analogous conditions of slavery. The absolute portion of freed workers of the slave labor in the last 20 years was outsourced. The concept of slave labor counters the degrading labor that represents the lack of minimum guarantees of health and safety, housing, hygiene, respect, and nourishment. The labor analogous to slavery represents a genre of forced labor.

The labor reform promotes the precariousness of the labor relations, considering that it demotes the salaries significantly, magnifies the work journey, generates instability of employment bonds, aggravates the risks of accidents and deaths related to work, and, consequently, intensifies the labor exploitation, raising the number of workers submitted to modern slavery. When human rights are violated, people are transformed into disposable instruments of work. Degrading conditions of work are all conditions that humiliate the worker.

The super-exploitation of work in the actual stage of capitalism is slowly killing people. The 2019 version of the International Disease Classification includes the burnout syndrome related to the exhaustion of professionals in the workplace (NEXO). The worker that before was highly affectionately involved with work, in a given moment, gives up, losing the sense of his relation with the work. The syndrome is composed of three elements: emotional exhaustion; depersonalization; and decreased personal involvement in work. The risk of the syndrome is higher for all those that live the threat of compulsory changes in the work journey and significant declines in the economic situation. Factors of social and economic insecurity raise the risks of professional exhaustion. Generally present are the associated symptoms of insomnia, stress, fatigue, irritability, sadness, disinterest, anguish, and depressive syndrome. In short: the workers are getting sick and dying for a salary. This is the new slavery of the 21st century.

Final Considerations

The labor exploitation in sight of the accumulation of capital always has been one of the pillars of capitalism. The principle of capital accumulation constitutes its most important imperative. For that, it needs to expand. In different stages of its evolution, the accumulation was made through the transformation of the system of production in sight of new ways of labor exploitation, which was the contest of this chapter.

The text traced a framework of the history of Brazil around its two extreme forms of labor exploitation: human trafficking and slave labor. The first section demonstrates through statistical data that human trafficking and slave labor are not practices restricted to the origin of capitalism. Instead, they continue actually.

The Brazilian case of human trafficking and slave labor, described in the second section, is paradigmatic. Capitalism was consolidated in Brazil by combining in a structured way these two extreme exploitative forms. All production in the colony is focused on the external market. Already in the early days of capitalism the law of the market – the law of supply and demand – applied. The items of this section prove how indigenous and African slavery was a reinvention of capital in the era of conquest and colonization.

Contemporary manifestations of human trafficking and slavery in Brazil were the theme of the third section. Brazil carries deep and painful marks of the four centuries of human trafficking and slavery of indigenous people and Africans. The official abolition of slavery did not eliminate its social, economic, and cultural problems. The social, economic, and political history of Brazil translates to the division between the lord house and the slave house: the owners of capital and the workforce exploited by them. Since colonization, institutions have served as instruments of the defense of the privileged. The elite heir of slavery controls all the institutions of the state: parliament, judiciary, and executive.

Capitalism, at the extreme, has the unique ideology of the accumulation of wealth at its core. The wealthy decide the destiny of the country. Extreme poverty and illiteracy drive human trafficking and slave labor as strategies of contemporary capitalism and are instruments of capital accumulation. It is not a detour of the system.

The fourth and last section presented the law and rights sphere as a reference to confront these two forms of extreme exploitation. Reasoned with human dignity, the approach is made in light of International and Brazilian Law. People are not properties or animals. The principle of human dignity is the criteria for the interpretation of all the judicial norms. Impunity has been one of the biggest obstacles in the combat of the two crimes. The contemporary fetters are not always visible like they were before.

The victims of human trafficking are persons that are eminently victims of serious violations of human rights. In the sphere of International

Law, the *Palermo Protocol* is the mark of judicial reference. Brazil committed to the implantation of the protocol. It has created the National Politic of confrontation to the human trafficking and elaborated two National Plans of Confrontation.

In relation to work, the abolition of all forms of slave labor constitutes one of the fundamental principles of the ILO. In Brazil, the practice of slave labor has been criminalized by the Penal Code since 1940.

It is a crime to subject a person to forced labor or to an exhausting work day and to degrading conditions, or to restrict, by any means, the freedom of movement. Normative instruction n. 91 of the Ministry of Work disposes of the inspection of the eradication of labor in conditions analogous to slavery. In 1995, the Interministerial Group to the Eradication of Forced Labor and the Special Group of Mobile Inspection was created, the main instrument of combat to the slave labor and the "Dirty List", with the name of companies condemned due to the use of slave work.

Since 2017 the social and judicial conjecture of the Brazilian state has lived a setback in the fight for human, social, and labor rights. The labor reform intensifies the process of labor precariousness and significant demotion of the salaries. The end of the Consolidated Labor Laws (CLT) leaves the workers at the doorsteps of slave labor.

The best form of defining strategies to confront modern slavery involves the comprehension that it does not have the shape of the historical practice registered until the 19th century. Modern slavery is not limited to the restriction of the right to come and go. Workers are getting sick for a hunger salary. Burnout syndrome is one of the symptoms of the new slavery of the 21st century.

Bibliography

Alencastro, L. F. (2000). *O trato dos viventes: formação do Brasil no Atlântico Sul* [Trafficking in the living: The formation of Brazil in the South Atlantic]. São Paulo: Companhia das Letras.

Antunes, R. (2019). *O privilégio da servidão. O novo proletariado de serviços na era digital* [The privilege of servitude. The new service proletariat in the digital age]. São Paulo: Boitempo.

Boxer, C. (1969). *O império marítimo português, 1415–1825* [The Portuguese maritime empire, 1415–1825]. Lisboa: Edições 70.

Davis, B. (2001). *O problema da escravidão na cultura ocidental* [The problem of slavery in Western culture]. Rio de Janeiro: Civilização Brasileira.

Eltis, D. and Richardson, D. (2010). *Atlas of the Transatlantic Slave Trade*. New Haven: Yale University Press.

Fausto, B. (2019). *História do Brasil* [History of Brazil]. São Paulo: EDUSP.

Ferreira, R. (2012). *Cross-Cultural Exchange in the Atlantic World: Angola and Brazil during the Era of the Slave Trade*. New York: Cambridge University Press.

Freyre, G. (2019). *Casa-Grande & Senzala: a formação da família brasileira sob o regime da economia patriarcal* [Casa-Grande & Senzala: The formation of the Brazilian family under the patriarchal economy]. São Paulo: Global.

Gomes, L. (2019). *Escravidão. vol. I – Do primeiro leilão de cativos em Portugal até a morte de Zumbi dos Palmares* [Slavery. vol. I – From the first captive auction in Portugal to the death of Zumbi dos Palmares]. Rio de Janeiro: Globo livros.

ILO. Organização Internacional do Trabalho [International Labor Organization]. Retrieved from http://www.oitbrasil.org.br/node/449

Kant, I. (1986). *Fundamentação da metafísica dos costumes (1785)* [Metaphysical foundation of morals]. Lisboa: Edições 70.

Marquese, R. and Salles, R. (2016). *Escravidão e capitalismo histórico no século XIX: Cuba, Brasil e Estados Unidos* [Slavery and historical capitalism in the 19th century: Cuba, Brazil and the United States]. Rio de Janeiro: Civilização Brasileira.

Miraglia, L. M., Hernandez, J. N., and Oliveira, R. F. S. (2018). *Trabalho escravo contemporâneo: conceituação, desafios e perspectivas* [Contemporary slave labor: conceptualization, challenges and perspectives]. Rio de Janeiro: Lumen Juris.

Nabuco, J. (1977). *O abolicionismo* [Abolitionism]. Petrópolis: Vozes.

Novais, F. (2002). *Formação do Brasil contemporâneo* [Formation of contemporary Brazil]. In *Intérpretes do Brasil. vol. 3* [Interpreters from Brazil. Vol. 3], edited by S. Santiago. Rio de Janeiro: Nova Aguilar.

Prado Junior, C. (1942). *Formação do Brasil contemporâneo: colônia* [Formation of contemporary Brazil: colony]. São Paulo: Martins Fontes.

————(1980). *História econômica do Brasil* [Economic history of Brazil]. São Paulo: Brasiliense.

Sakamoto, L. (2019). *Escravidão contemporânea* [Contemporary slavery]. São Paulo: Contexto.

Santos, M. (1996/1997). *Cidadanias mutiladas* [Mutilated citizenships]. In *O preconceito* [The prejudice], edited by J. Lerner. São Paulo: IMESP.

Sarlet, W. I. (2002). *Dignidade da pessoa humana e direitos fundamentais na Constituição da República de 1988* [Human dignity and fundamental rights in the 1988 Constitution]. Porto Alegre: Livraria do Advogado.

Simonsen, R. (1937). *História econômica do Brasil: 1500–1820* [Economic history of Brazil: 1500–1820]. São Paulo: Nacional.

Sutton, A. (1994). *Trabalho Escravo: Um elo na cadeia da modernização no Brasil de hoje.* [Slave Labor: A link in the modernization chain in Brazil today]. São Paulo: Loyola.

The Transatlantic Slave Trade Database. Retrieved from https://www.slavevoyages.org

Thornton, J. (1992). *Africa and Africans in the Making of the Atlantic World, 1400–1800.* New York: Cambridge University Press.

United Nations. *The Protocol to Prevent, Suppress and Punish Trafficking in Persons.* New York: United Nations. Retrieved from http://www.odccp.org/trafficking_protocol.html

UNODC. (2020). Global Report on Trafficking in Persons 2020. https://www.unodc.org/documents/data-and-analysis/tip/2021/GLOTiP_2020_15jan_web.pdf

Wallerstein, I (1974). *The Modern World-System I: Capitalist Agriculture and the Origins of the European World-Economy in the Sixteenth Century.* New York: Academic Press.

Williams, E. (2015). *Capitalism and Slavery.* Philadelphia: The Great Library Collection.

8 The Latin American Economies Since c. 1950

Ideas, Policy, and Structural Change

Colin M. Lewis

Introduction

This chapter examines the macroeconomy of Latin America since the mid-twentieth century from a political economy perspective. Focusing on the "state" and the "market", it argues that modern development is associated with industrialization. Several broad questions frame the discussion about economy and industrialization: how the size and shape of the macroeconomy change over time; what was the role of policy in determining the pattern and rhythm of growth – and how capable was the state in managing both growth and crises; what was the "quality" of growth in terms of social delivery and sustainability? Many countries encountered bouts of volatility – imbalances in the fiscal and external accounts. Government deficits and balance of payments shock provoked demands for growth with stability. Analysts recognize a direct correlation between changes in rates of inflation and the incidence of poverty: poverty rises during macroeconomic meltdown; growth may yield a reduction in absolute poverty, while increasing equality is a function of policy.

Exploring the relationship between macroeconomy and policy compels consideration of the interaction between "state" and "market" – as well as an assessment of the nature of the state and its relationship with the market. Much writing about the economic performance of Latin America since the Second World War being cast in terms of "too much state" or "too much market", yet the interplay between the two should not be regarded as a zero-sum game, where more of one necessarily implies less of the other. Neo-liberal analyses attribute sluggish growth and repeated crises to excessive state intervention. Others view uneven development and structural imbalances as a function of untrammeled market economics. The principal argument here is that the blame-game between contending assessments of the long-run performance of the continent is gloomy, often neglecting substantial gains flagged by welfare indicators and evidence of structural modernization. The underlying problems may be to do with state capacity and shallowness of

DOI: 10.4324/9781003045632-9

markets – perhaps state and market failure as much as an "excess" of either. Such failures may account for periodic, abrupt policy changes – a further source of instability that impacted economy, polity and society. According to North, the state makes the market, the "... polity makes and puts in place the economic rules of the game ... a political structure that in turn puts in place an economic structure that shapes how society works" (North 2003, 3). Others would qualify and refine the dynamics: "The state is conceptually distinct from both economy and society, with inherent interests in expanding its scope for autonomous action, asserting control over economic and social interactions, and structuring economic and social relations" (Grindle 1996, 3, 4). Recent refinements recognize that previously there was an emphasized market failure and for the state to replace the market, and now a willingness to embrace the concept of the fallible state: there may be as much a deficit of the state as of the market (Foxley 2010, 11). From the 1950s to the 1970s, there was an emphasis on "more state". In the 1980s and 1990s, a stress on "more market". Since the early twenty-first century, a nuanced recognition of the importance of state capacity and effectiveness. The role of the state should be to correct market failure, not replace the market, while an efficient market can facilitate state capacity and effectiveness – delivering outcomes demanded by society. More than "bringing the state back in", this line of reasoning brings society into the matrix.

These ideas are explored in a stylized chronology of state-and-market arrangements that consider ideology, policy, and economic and social outcomes. Accepting differences of timing and process, five broad periods, marked by "growth cycles" and characterized by distinct state and market configurations are identified. First, a period of the economically and socially active state, from the 1930s to the 1960s/1970s: state-directed "growth from within" – aka import-substituting industrialization (ISI) triggered by external shocks. Second, a re-connection with the global economy – gradual in some countries, abrupt in others, partly rooted in disenchantment with inward-directed development in the 1960s, and partly challenges and opportunities consequent on the "first" oil crisis of 1973. There was growing external indebtedness and larger presence of transnational corporations. Presided over by authoritarian administrations in much of South America, technocratic military rule meant the consolidation of state-supported industrial deepening in some countries, the emergence of neoliberalism-cum-monetarism in others. The debt/loan crisis of the 1980s dealt a fatal blow to military regimes, facilitating a distinct period of democratization and heterodox economics that featured aspects of market economics as fragile democracies dealt with the economic chaos and social and political legacy of brutal dictatorships. This was the third period. The crisis of heterodoxy led to a fourth phase: the implementation of Washington Consensus prescriptions in the 1990s by democratic/electoral administration bent on capitalizing on global growth. This gave way to a fifth period during the early twenty-first century, when international economic crises and rising inequality elicited quite distinct responses: on the one hand, efforts to embed a broadly market approach to the economy through the implementation of progressive social programs; on the other, a rejection of economic internationalism, and emphasis on the role of government in economy, polity, and society.

Specific "state" and "market" labels may be applied to these phases. The populist state of the middle third of the twentieth century attempted "stabilizing development". The bureaucratic authoritarian state of the 1960s to the 1980s that enforced "discipline" to restructuring the real economy by applying neo-liberal or neo-structuralist strategies. Uncertain democracies of the 1980s that gave way to the "privatizing state" (or neo-populist state) of the late twentieth century based on a popular-business alliance that implemented Consensus remedies. Finally, "Pink Tide" states of the early twenty-first century that questioned Consensus delivery as growth-with-equity came to the fore, debating whether growth would be best achieved within a regional or global context. Some Pink administrations blended market economics and ameliorative social action – the social-market state; others emphasized state action in economy and society integrating neo-populism and neo-developmentalism – the national-populist state. Yet other administrations offered a different brand of populist politics: state-market capitalist economics and popular mobilization – a Blue Tide that both chimed with and differed from the Pink Tide.

The Populist State and Cepalismo[1]

Populism combined "open" politics (the main beneficiaries were "new" urban groups) with economic and social strategies indebted to structuralism or *cepalismo*. Elements of the strategy were observed in the inter-war decades, but the formalization of state-led, import-substituting-industrialization was institutionalized following the foundation of CEPAL/ECLA. *Cepalismo* was more than government-supported industrialization – the package came to include regional economic integration and agrarian reform. Regional integration was a mechanism to increase the productivity and efficiency of manufacturing firms through "fair" competition with enterprises in neighbor republics at a similar stage of development, which was preferable to exposure to unfair competition from overseas conglomerates. Agrarian reform served multiple objectives: land distribution would raise rural production and productivity; increase the supply of foodstuffs for local and regional markets, and of raw material inputs for industry – bottlenecks in the commodity supply chain were a major cause of inflation and balance of payments pressure; broaden and deepen markets for domestic manufactures; and ease inequalities in the distribution of income and wealth. Although the three elements constituted an integrated policy program for economic and social change, regional integration and agrarian reform were little acted upon before the 1960s as both entailed substantial political costs.

Policy prescriptions that evolved after 1948 drew on earlier national experiences. Love argues that industrialization was fact before it became policy and policy before it was a theory, and that in 1948 CEPAL was pushing at an open door when advocating state-led development spearheaded by industrialization. State intervention in economy and society became a well-established tradition by the 1960s, rooted in ideas and initiatives deriving from at least the 1920s (Love 1994, 395, 460; 2005, 103). CEPAL pioneered development economics, an approach to the discipline that rejected classical assumptions about a single, uniform pattern of growth grounded in hitherto dominant supply-side approaches. Drawing on historical data collated by its proponents, the Commission argued for a focus on demand. Economies such as the Latin American were distinct from those of the then advanced countries – they were structurally different. Structural heterogeneity – sophisticated processes existing alongside archaic institutions and socio-economic systems forged in the first age of globalization (1870s–1920s), inhibited "modernization". Market failure and immiserising growth resulting from distortions in the international economy constrained development. Export price volatility and uncertainty about future trends in the world economy – what Raúl Prebisch depicted as secular decline in the terms of trade, made state-led development a necessity rather than simply a preferred policy option.[2]

Potent forces working for change were nationalism ("patriotic rhetoric") and demands by mainly urban sectors for a greater "voice" in politics and economics, giving rise to the new "social politics".[3] These groups were particularly receptive to pro-industry ideas and policies – a compliant constituency for ideologues promoting populist, state-led development. Catering to the aspirations of a "thickening" middle class and "organizing" labor, regimes of the period placed an emphasis on expanding the social role of the state – supporting social protection coupled with a cautious expansion of labor legislation, while advancing the economic presence of government, often challenging foreign-owned utility, transport and energy monopolies (Weaver 1980, 111–115; Abel and Lewis 2015, 269, 270, 276, 277; Armendáriz and Larraín 2017, 149). Around mid-twentieth century, the main expressions of populist, state-led industrialization were *varguismo*, *cardenismo*, and Peronism in Mexico, Brazil, and the Argentine, respectively. Some administrations employed leftist rhetoric, some not. Urban groups were demanding accommodation in the political marketplace at the moment when the rate and rhythm of economic expansion were becoming erratic. When growth faltered, politics became messy: new groups could not be accommodated by distributing the proceeds of future growth; accommodation implied re-allocating existing resources, a more delicate operation that challenged the existence of a regime or even the state itself.

The economy became increasingly "managed" and the state grew in size and outreach. The "weight" of the state (government expenditure expressed as a share of GDP) increased from a high base of 22% in the Argentine in 1945 to 25% in 1960/1, remaining at around this level until the end of the decade. The "rise of the state" was even more dramatic in Brazil: public expenditure increased from 16% in 1945 to 25% in 1960/1 and to 33% in 1969/70. For Chile, the figures were 17%, 29%, and 35%; for Colombia (the least statized of the major economies), 15%, 11%, and 17%; for Mexico, 11%, 17%, and 22%; for Peru, 14%, 16%, and 19% (Fajnzylber 1983, 167). The state acquired

> a number of policy instruments, such as monetary discretion and a more diverse tax base [...] enlarged the economic infrastructure, established state enterprises and sought to promote entrepreneurship and entrepreneurs [...] often actually "creating" them under the umbrella of large government contracts.
>
> (Thorp 1998, 127)

The expansion of pre-existing manufacturing sectors and the stimulation of new industries, initially to reduce dependence on imports, later to promote "vital" and "strategic" activities, featured in many countries. Such projects capitalized on the advocacy and conceptualization of modernization emanating from CEPAL, which became a powerhouse for the formulation, rationalization, and diffusion of theory and policy (Love 1994, 423, 424, and 2005, 116–119; 2016, 276–280; FitzGerald 1998, 47, 48; Bértola, and Ocampo 2012, 159, 160).

The new institutional and ideological paradigm of the 1930s to the 1960s melded industrialism and welfarism just as population drifted from the countryside to cities. At its core, the model was "mixed", involving the state and private sector in which manufacturing would become an engine of growth and mechanism for wider structural transformation involving technical innovation and productivity gains. Economic and social interventionism was also necessary due to international economic volatility. Based on export pessimism, CEPAL theory presents a paradox. Many populist regimes – then and subsequently – implementing *cepalista* strategies relied on buoyant export prices driven by war-time scarcities and/or global commodity booms to underwrite interventionist programs. In different periods and in different places, the first phase in the cycle of populist, distributional politics depended on capturing windfall export rents (Skidmore 1978; Kaufman, and Stallings 1991; Bacha 2018). Windfall rents were critical for the social and economic aspects of the project under-pinning populist politics. "Open", if not democratic, politics facilitated the ordering of society and economy: economic rents and social reorganization ensured the viability of the state (Díaz-Alejandro 1979, 4–7; Sachs 1989a, 16–23; Cardoso, and Helwege 1991, 46–50; Dornbusch, and Edwards 1991, 11–12). The populist state was not a welfare state but presided over a substantial increase in social provision – especially for urban interests. The expansion of education, social insurance, and basic health care was instrumental to the economic and political arrangement (Malloy 1977; Mesa-Lago 1978; Lewis and Lloyd Sherlock 2009; Weyland 2013). Progressive social policy and modern macroeconomic management facilitated "representation" within the state and the construction of a modernizing coalition (Oszlak 1997). Aspects of what may be described as a Gerschenkronian position emerged as "ideology" or "national project" projected an image of administrative competence and efficacious management by the socially and economically active state directing a pro-state-led industrial alliance.[4]

By the 1960s, the CEPAL model was under threat – the development consensus dissolving. In retrospect, *cepalino* apologists identified three phases of ISI. The first, pragmatic phase from the 1920s to the 1940s involved *ad hoc* policy responses and consolidation of industrial bases mainly producing basic goods. The second phase, classic state-led industrial expansion from the 1940s to the 1960s, witnessed a gradual shift from the easy stage of horizontal industrialization (production of wage and consumer goods) to vertical industrialization (the production of intermediate items and some capital goods). The mature phase, expected to occur at some point during (or after) the 1960s, entailed the production of sophisticated capital goods – leading to fully integrated manufacturing sectors developing "homogenizing" linkages with other sectors of the economy, capable of supplying home and overseas markets (Cárdenas, Ocampo, Thorp 2000, 8, 9; Love 2005, 103, 104; Bértola and Ocampo 2012, 162–173). Transition to the third phase proved economically and politically challenging – open politics giving way to authoritarian politics. This broadly corresponds with the Dornbusch and Edwards schema. They describe "populist economics" as, "… an approach to economics that emphasises growth and income redistribution and de-emphasises the risks of inflation and deficit finance, external constraints and the reaction of economic agents to aggressive non-market policies". An inevitable sequences follows: (a) policy-driven growth with increased real wages and employment, which succeeds because controls ensure acceptable levels of inflation, but inventories and foreign exchange reserves are run down – helping curb inflationary pressure; (b) bottlenecks emerge as domestic stocks are exhausted and foreign exchange scarcity constrains essential imports, resulting in price adjustments and controls, exchange rationing and measures to protect incomes – but inflation and the budget deficit increase significantly; (c) shortages occur across the economy, inflation accelerates, the fiscal and exchange gaps widen dramatically – emergency measures like cuts in subsidies and exchange rate depreciation trigger falls in wages, consumption and welfare, while capital flight and demonetization indicate that the government is losing control of the economy; (d) regime change occurs and orthodox stabilization measures are applied amidst growing poverty and inequality – the economy is in a worst state than in the initial phase (Dornbusch, and Edwards 1991, 9–12).

Bureaucratic Authoritarianism: Industrial Deepening versus Neo-Liberal Monetarism

The scene was set for a new state-market model: bureaucratic authoritarianism and global re-engagement. There were two manifestations of technocratic authoritarianism: regimes pursuing neo-structural industrial deepening; others adopting monetarism; both entailed debt-led growth. Authoritarian systems "closed" politics to facilitate an "opening" toward the market.[5] Technocrats associated with some military regimes installed during the 1960s, notably in Brazil following the 1964 coup and in the Argentine in 1966, appeared committed to forcing industrial deepening, which could only be accomplished by dictatorship.[6] Radical reconstruction of civil society was required for economic "flexiibilization": de-politicization and discipline (euphemisms for political exclusion) were prerequisites for hard economic decision-making (Fishlow 1988, 118). Industrial-deepening incomes strategy favored select groups as consumers of durables and supply chain heavy industries, and as savers/investors to finance capital-intensive industrial complexes. The 1968 military regime in Peru also seemed to embrace a CEPAL-inspired pro-industry program, presenting itself as nationalist-cum-*indigenista* and radical (possibly syndicalist), championing statist-industrialization. By the late 1960s, politics in Mexico was also becoming more repressive. Whether espousing state-led industrial deepening, or the abandonment of ISI, several regimes from the mid-1960s to the early 1980s asserted that authoritarianism was essential for state- and market-reconfiguration. State violence was instrumental – a conscious policy to restore "efficiency" to politics and economics. By the 1970s, monetarist neo-liberalism was in the ascent – Chile the classic case, followed by the Argentine.

Retreat to the market was brutally observed in the most developed countries of the Southern Cone – the Argentine, Chile, Uruguay. In Chile, with the 1973 *glope* headed by General Pinochet; in the Argentine in 1976, with the *proceso de reorganización nacional* – the junta initially headed by Brigadier General Viola; in Uruguay with the autocratic civilian-military administration headed by democratically elected Juan María Bordaberry. (Elected in 1971, Bordaberry dissolved congress in

1973, relying on the support of the police and military until deposed by them in 1976.) Self-promoted "guardians of the nation", repressive military regimes embarked on "ideological and social cleansing". They dismantled and disarticulated working-class organization, restructured capitalism, and emasculated political institutions to enhanced state capacity to implement a new political economy – and "model" of society (Biglaiser 2002, 21; Undurraga 2015, 15). The new ideology was monetarism, an early expression of neo-liberalism that views tight control of the money supply and public spending as the principal mechanisms to stabilize an economy.[7] Kidnapping ("disappearances"), torture, and murder characterized institutionalized state terror. Possibly, because they were the most advanced economies and socially integrated countries of the continent, the degree of violence was greater and more intense than that observed elsewhere. Discipline in economics and politics underpinned strategy and policy in technocratic-authoritarian regimes as some transitioned from neo-structuralism to monetarism – a transition particularly observed in the Southern Cone: with distortions intensified by the 1973 oil crisis, the monetarist model was pursued with vigor and state violence (Corbo 1992, 30; Undurraga 2015, 15–17). There was state violence in Mexico and Brazil in the 1960s, but of shorter duration, less pronounced and less sustained. Neo-structuralist industrial deepening in Brazil and Mexico required a "disciplined" and compliant workforce, but possibly also as potential consumers (alongside the urban middle classes) of domestic manufactures. In the Southern Cone economies, wage compression served to cow the urban working class. Cheap labor and constrained consumption dovetailed with export promotion. State-led authoritarian modernization from the late 1960s to the 1980s, was partly indebted to *cepalismo*, and neo-structuralist "late industrialization" or "vertical industrialization" most observed in Brazil and Mexico – not that the term bureaucratic authoritarianism would have been applied in Mexico. The main objectives were industrial integration and capitalist transformation of the countryside; the defining feature, the triple alliance of state, national, and transnational capital – foreign corporate engagement "by invitation" in manufacturing and the rural economy, with a growing emphasis on production for export as part of a highly regulated foreign trade policy (Evans 1979; Goodman and Redclift 1982; Hewlett and Weinert 1982; Kline and Vidal Luna 2019). The history of Volkswagen in Brazil nicely captures the nature of "investment by invitation", and the melding of corporate overseas investment strategy with the evolving development objectives of a bureaucratic-authoritarian regime. The corporation engaged in motor vehicle production in São Paulo and re-invested locally accumulated profits in land purchases and the development of agro-industrial centers in Amazonia producing foodstuffs and, later, biofuel. By the time of the return to democracy in 1985, Volkswagen do Brasil had become the largest overseas subsidiary of the parent company, the fifth-largest conglomerate in Brazil, as well as the biggest fully integrated vehicle production complex in the country, and a large landowner (Kopper 2017, 2, 96–98).

Domestic and international contexts were similar for regimes applying neo-structuralist and monetarist programs: a continuing struggle with inflation and a search for political stability at a time of growing international liquidity. Policy changed significantly over time and from place to place – there was a drift from the orthodox to the heterodox between the late 1960s and early 1980s, but the defining common characteristic was growing dependence on foreign capital, which assumed a novel form. In the 1950s and much of the 1960s, capital inflows consisted mainly of investment by transnational corporations, supplemented by support from Washington – international financial institution (IFI) loans (the World Bank and the International Monetary Fund [IMF]), and from branches of the US administration. Borrowing from IFIs and foreign governments was long-term at low fixed rates of interest. Investment by corporations is lumpy and immobile. By the early 1970s, international banks (mainly based in the USA and Western Europe) had become the principal sources of credit. Transnational banks re-cycled euro-dollars and petro-dollars to Latin America after the 1973 oil shock. At the time, short-term loans from international banks were cheap and viewed as less politically sensitive than lines of credit from the Bank or the Fund – which were conditional and entailed supervision, and direct investment by foreign corporations – increasingly politically sensitive. This does not mean that domestic mechanisms of accumulation were abandoned, quite the contrary: credit creation, "borrowing" from social security funds, and forced/indexed savings remained important; wage constrains another source of domestic accumulation, though stabilization efforts reduced the "effectiveness" of inflation taxation. International liquidity funded bureaucratic-authoritarian regimes – and brought them down when there was a sharp reversal in the flow of credit. The 1980s debt/loan crisis paved the way for a return to democracy and experiments with heterodox economics and, subsequently, Washington Consensus neo-liberalism.

Debt, Democracy, and Economic Heterodoxy

Heterodox economics was framed by debt and democracy – another distinct state-market system. The timing and nature of the collapse of technocratic-authoritarian regimes varied, as did underlying domestic circumstances – it would be a mistake to attribute the retreat of the armed force as due exclusively to external events because local actors played a major role in democratization. The main ingredients of the debt/loan crisis were three-fold: a sharp rise in international interest rates – close to zero for much of the 1970s, rates turned abruptly positive around 1981–1982 when monetary authorities in global centers hiked central bank base rates to dampen inflation; a downturn in international trade which impacted growth; a marked deterioration in national terms of trade due to the collapse of overseas demand for exports. Most Latin American economies might have coped with one or two of these shocks, but not all three. Debt structure was also a problem: short- and medium-term lending, and the rolling over of bank loans, banks meant that repayment dates "bunched" in the late 1970s; borrowing at market rates meant that the cost of debt service was unpredictable and subject to sudden change – as occurred. The politics of lending/borrowing was similarly novel, as observed. Pre-1960s sovereign borrowing was government-to-government and multilateral agency to government; borrowing in the 1970s between governments in Latin America (or state entities – several authoritarian regimes encouraged state-owned enterprise to raise fund in global capital markets) and private banking corporations – multinational banks with multiple legal domiciles, subject to supervision by different regulatory authorities, which may explain deficient monitoring. Compounding the problem: much capital was squandered on "pharaonic" public works projects and military hardware; some was used to cover current expenditure. Government expenditure in Latin America rose rapidly after the late 1960s, revenue less so, particularly after 1974. Around 1974–1983, the gap between expenditure and revenue was between 2 and 3% points of GDP, reaching over 4% (possibly 5%) in the early 1980s (Gavin and Perotti 1997, 19–22; Thorp 1998, 212; Bértola and Ocampo 2012, 186, 187; Ocampo 2014, 108–110). Debts and deficits were a receipt for disaster, though facilitated democratization.

Latin America had been by far the largest international borrower, outstripping Africa and Asia combined, accounting for more than half total international bank lending to developing countries. In 1983, outstanding overseas debt equaled about half of continental GDP. But, in the early 1980s, average annual debt service ratios (fees, interest payments, and amortization relative to average export earnings) mushroomed. Peak ratios were: 447% in 1982 in the Argentinian case; 393% in 1983 for Brazil (Sachs 1985, 532–535; 1989b, 7; Reinhart, Rogoff, and Savastano 2003, 16). These were historically high debt thresholds. Multinational banks, the IFIs, and foreign governments feared Latin American debt would crash the international monetary order. In the event, there was no collective default, despite the formation of the Cartagena Group which called for solidarity on the part of regional sovereign borrowers and international agreement to share the costs of debt restructuring. Co-ordinated action by creditor banks and government actors in world centers prevented formal default. What emerged was a *de facto* creditor cartel, not a debtor cartel, the price of adjustment paid by the poor in Latin America through growth loss; austerity; and a decline in real wages, employment and living standards, and by tax payers in developed economies whose governments support private sector banks (Sachs 1989b, 14, 15; Devlin and Ffrench-Davis 1995, 127–132; Bértola and Ocampo 2012, 210).

The impact of the crisis, and the form of its resolution, explains the rise of heterodoxy. Orthodox IMF stabilization packages of the 1940s to the 1960s entailed wage freezes, cuts in subsidies, a reduction in government expenditure, and "corrective" currency devaluation to promote exports and curb imports. Underwritten by conditional bridging loans from Washington, such stabilization packages were remembered for economic contraction and protest that weakened government compliance and, in most case, abandonment of the policy package, as Dornbusch and Edwards observed. Given the context, an alternative to "stabilization-through-recession" was essential for emergent, fragile polities of the 1980s contending with popular expectations, economic disarray, and scarred civil societies – and restive armed forces fearing they would be held to account for the horrors they had inflicted. Some authoritarian regimes scuttled back to the barracks; others negotiated return. Disarray within the Peruvian military, economic turmoil, and mounting protest led to elections in 1980, and the installation of a weak civilian administration. The Argentinian military regime collapsed in 1982, following the Falklands debacle and economic meltdown; free elections led to a return to civilian rule in 1983. In Uruguay, a controversial agreement between civilian political parties and the armed forces facilitated cautious democratization. In Brazil in 1985, there was a similar negotiated, "orderly" retreat and conditional transition to democracy. Chile experienced an extended, monitored transition: surprise defeat in a plebiscite held in 1989 to legitimize the Pinochet regime led the general to retire in 1990, though the Constitution imposed by the armed forces ensure for them a strong "supervisory" role. A military coup in Paraguay in 1989 ended the Stroessner regime – the old general had held power since 1954; the transition was similarly extended, if somewhat less so than in Chile. After 1983, electoral politics in Mexico gradually democratized as the Partido Revolucionario Institucional (PRI)/Institutional Revolutionary Party, which in various guises had governed the country since the 1910s, was forced to give ground, but only in 2000 did it relinquish the presidency to an opposition candidate.

Political and economic uncertainty framed heterodoxy in the 1980s. Heterodoxy offered stabilization through growth, based on a domestic-demand-driven model, and the idea that the state should consolidate and stimulate the market to ensure "effective demand". Programs were presented as neutral, with costs and gains shared among social groups and sectors, hence politically low-cost and likely to be carried through (Kiguel and Liviatan 1992, 38–40; Weyland 2002, 81–84; Pérez Caldentey 2016, 67, 68). While national strategies differed, there were several common features. Firstly, plans were designed to break inertial inflation and inflationary expectations in societies where inflation was the embedded norm, transforming them into societies where price stability would be the new normal, and prices would become "real" indicators facilitating rational economic behavior. In order to achieve the desired objective, plans were usually introduced as a "shock" measure, with little prior consultation to pre-empt special pleading and/or resistance. Secondly, prices and income controls, fiscal discipline and a fixed exchange rate – orthodox packages had frozen wages but not prices. Income and price controls were intended as a transitional mechanism, to be phased out once stability had been achieved. Thirdly, as a confidence measure, a new currency unit was introduced, signaling a break with the past. The new unit usually provided the name of the new package. In South America, rebuilding democracy and promoting growth was also accompanied by renewed interest in regional economic integration. With the world economy in recession, international capital markets regarded Latin America as a no-go region – as was the case for most of the 1980s, little was to be lost in promoting regionalism as a substitute for global integration. What became the South American Common Market was launched in 1985 by Presidents Alfonsín and Sarney as a bilateral trade arrangement between the Argentine and Brazil.[8]

The principal heterodox programs were, the Austral Plan (the Argentine, 1985), the Inti Plan (Peru, 1985), the Cruzado Plan (Brazil, 1986). A near contemporary Pacto de Solaridad Económica, launched in 1987 in Mexico, partly to counter the impact of the Stock Market collapse in the United States, was broadly orthodox, generously supported by the IMF and US officials, which the others were not. Heterodox pacts initially succeeded in bringing down inflation, delivered growth, and attracted considerable political support, yet ultimately failed. Explanations for the collapse of the Austral Plan, which had served as something of a model for neighboring countries, include limited support (if not outright hostility) from Washington – a "democratic dividend" anticipated by President Raúl Alfonsín was not forthcoming, profound partisan opposition by the Peronist Party and allied trade unions – who blocked privatization and institutional reform, an unwillingness by the government to thaw the prices and incomes freeze – which was extended beyond its shelf-life for electoral purposes, perverse actor behavior, and miscalculations by the economic team. When the government attempted a "mini" heterodox program in 1988, it lost all credibility and control of the economy. Hyperinflation and electoral defeat ended the experiment.

The economic and political context of heterodoxy was different in Brazil. A negotiated return to the barracks in 1985 meant that elections were held under terms prescribed by the armed forces. Although debt overhang accompanied the democratic transition, the economic crisis was less acute than in the Argentine. The principal difficulties were political – continuing supervision by the military and unpopular indirect elections for the presidency. Widely respected liberal Tancredo Neves was nominated president, but died a few days before inauguration, resulting in his running mate, José Sarney taking office. Sarney was a little-known, and even less loved, politician: a right-wing nationalist who had supported the military regime, he lack legitimacy. To garner support, Sarney embarked on an expansionary program, which was derailed by inflation and opposition from Washington. Having observed the initial achievements of the Austral Plan, the Brazilian economic team embarked on a similar heterodox program in 1986. The Cruzado Plan was also based on a new monetary unit, a prices and incomes freeze, the de-indexation of the economy, and the application of a complex formula to adjust wages, prices, debts, and financial obligations, designed to combat inflationary expectations and deliver stabilization through "shared" growth. Because the underlying fundamentals were robust, the grace period between recovery and growth, when supply bottlenecks were likely to occur, was shorter for the Cruzado Plan than the Austral. Consumption rose, benefitting from generous adjustments to wages and salaries, but savings and investment declined. Sarney proved unable or unwilling to control expenditure – the public sector deficit was heading for 4% of GDP by the end of 1986, and the electoral cycle was out of sync with the economic. Sarney's party in the governing coalition lost ground to his erstwhile partner, further weakening the president's legitimacy. Hyperinflation kicked-in when the Plan came unstuck: an attempted re-launch failed, and the economy crashed. Again, there was a loss of confidence in Plan and administration. Further attempts at stabilization at the beginning of the short-lived administration of populist President Fernando Collor de Mello (1990–1992) met a similar end – an emergency package was launched at the beginning of the presidency disintegrated before the end of the year, leading to yet another plan in January 1991, which also failed, due to resistance in Congress, and a massive corruption scandal that further undermined president and project.

Heterodox stabilization plans acknowledged that fiscal, monetary, and exchange rate policies were essential tools: operated in concert and imaginatively, they would produce a stable macroeconomic environment leading to sustainable growth without the social hardships and political antagonisms generated by orthodox programs. Unfortunately, various forces conspired to disrupt what should have been the "natural" evolution of heterodoxy. Applying a wages and prices freeze proved to be easier than negotiating a return to market mechanisms. Electoral cycles weakened the political resolve to effect the essential move from wages and prices freeze to a thaw and return to collective bargaining and market price determination. Spectacular early successes – "excising inflation" – further reduced the political will to move from stabilization to economic restructuring. Currency reforms were not as socially neutral as promised. State reform was pursued with declining vigor – even in those countries where it was attempted, with inevitable budgetary implications. When plans unraveled, domestic support evaporated, opposition grew, and the political environment became more volatile. And the external environment was uncongenial; international financial organizations and institutions were unsympathetic – overseas debt re-structuring or forgiveness would have eased fiscal and external account deficits only came later; crisis and contraction in overseas markets constrained exports and foreign exchange earnings. An interesting, imaginative policy experiment that might have worked, failed, with inevitable consequences. As Kiguel and Liviatan argue, "… launching a heterodox program that is later abandoned can be dangerous – more costly, even, than postponing stabilization" (1992, 54). In modern times, the Latin American economies experienced their highest rates of inflation, often hyperinflation, around this time. In 1983–1985, continental annual average rates of inflation touched 300%, with national hyperinflation spikes registered between the mid-1980s and early 1990s. Peaks for individual countries were Brazil – 13,000% (1990), Bolivia – 12,000% (1985), the Argentine – 3,000% (1989) and Peru 2,000% (1988) (Tanzi 2000, 4). Hyperinflation killed heterodoxy in practice and the popular mind, if not in theory.

Washington Consensus and beyond: Contending Patterns of Stabilization – Neo-Liberalism, Neo-Populism, and Neo-Structuralism

Once again, collapse of an economic program prefigured a state-market experiment. Early success, followed by failure, of heterodox strategies shaped renewed effort to deliver growth with stability in the 1990s, generating support for the emerging Washington Consensus. Policymakers accepted that 1980s demand-led stabilization had increased consumption and growth as consumer confidence returned, but had not triggered an anticipated upsurge of savings and investment, thereby straining domestic productive capacity and the reserve position. Neo-liberal reformers were made aware of the need to strengthen the reserve position in advance of stabilization to ensure investment in capacity growth in the medium-term, and an "import cushion" in the short-term – imports would dampen inflationary pressure. Building up reserves was now easier. Commodity prices were improving, international liquidity returning, and confidence growing in global financial centers – for bankers, the crisis was over. IFIs and transnational banks adopted a more relaxed attitude to debt write-down as debt re-structuring and privatization promised lucrative profits. There was, too, an expectation among Consensus proponents that hyperinflation had induced greater patience on the part of electorates – that quick fixes were flawed.

The rise of the technopol was a novel feature of the new democratic environment in which Consensus programs were applied.[9] During the era of bureaucratic authoritarianism, technocrats implementing policy operated in isolation from the hurly-burly of politics, sheltered by military regimes. Technopols of the 1990s were technocratic apostles of the new ideology, for which they proselytized vigorously, many becoming politicians. They submitted themselves and their policies for electoral approval (Domínguez 1996). Advocating market economies, they competed in the political marketplace, expecting to generate program endorsement. The "ten commandments" of the Washington Consensus include: fiscal discipline – balanced budgets the aim, small deficit tolerated as long as they did not trigger inflation; tax reform – broadening the tax base, enhancing revenue-raising and avoiding disincentives and distortions; targeted (fiscally redistributive) government spending – pro-growth and pro-poor, focusing on economic and social infrastructure; trade liberalization – a low tariff regime; plus removal non-tariff restriction; financial market liberalization – abolition of controls on capital movements and interest rates; competitive/realistic unified exchange rates; deregulation of markets – including labor markets, save for essential regimes of social and consumer protection, along with prudent supervision of financial institutions; privatization – disposing of state corporations to increase macroeconomic efficiency and reduce public sector deficits; protection of property rights (Williamson 1990; 2004/2005; Kuczynski and Williamson 2003). Many governments subscribed to Consensus ideology and policy prescriptions, the main differences being between those that applied strategies abruptly as a bundle and those that adopted a phased approach. In the popular mind, the Consensus became associated with privatization, de-regulation, and "state retreat".

If Chile under Pinochet had been an early adherent to what became the Washington Consensus, the Argentine became the poster child of the Consensus period proper (Undurraga 2015, 11). Despite initial resistance by some senior members of the military, there is little dispute about the commitment of the post-1973 authoritarian regime and the Chicago boys to neo-liberalism. Having briefly favored a quasi-fascist, national corporatist approach to society and economy, the regime soon embraced technocrats advocating neo-liberalism to eradicate distortions in economy, society, and polity blamed on populism. Reducing the size of the state and redirecting government resources to the private sector would emasculate popular and sectoral interest opposed to the program and reward regime supporters – as would opening the economy to the "disciplining" forces of the market. Inflation would be excised; growth would affect an irreversible transformation (Angell 1991, 362–368; Undurraga 2015, 16–19). The Chicago Boys colonized key institutions of the state apparatus – the Central Bank and Budget Office. Many businesses nationalized under the ousted Allende (1970–1973) were returned to former owners or sold at knock-down prices. There was, however, a contradiction: contrary to the dominant discourse, the military government held on to profitable, strategic sectors and continued to intervene in factor and product markets. Despite emphasizing fiscal restraint and sound management, financial crisis and recession in 1982/1983 brought about private sector bankruptcies and the nationalization of private debt, leading to the re-statisation of businesses, only to be sold again. By 1988, all save 45 of the 400 enterprises held by the state in 1973 had been re-sold: companies retained by the regime were "strategic" enterprises. Yet it is worth recalling that in 1980, before the crisis, only 25 firms remained in public hands. Knock-down privatization led to the consolidation of business/financial *grupos* which, integrating finance, production, and commercialization, rapidly strengthen links with foreign consortia. Such *groupos* have dominated the Chilean economy ever since, pioneering the diversification of production and trade. Resource-based processed and industrial manufactures have increased their contribution to GDP and exports since the 1980s, as have services – notably finance. With the slow transition to democracy after 1990, a period of "pragmatic neo-liberalism", these conglomerates continue to exert considerable influence – their impact on public policymaking growing as state-business relations became more formalized and institutionalized (Ffrench-Davis 2000, 151–177; Muñoz Gomá 2015; Undurraga 2015, 27, 28). The influence of the *grupos* has been questioned by proponents of pragmatic neo-liberalism, and popular antagonism to the *grupos* partly fueled the explosion of protest against hikes in transport charges in Santiago in 2019.

Influenced by the fate of the Austral Plan, Washington was initially lukewarm about what would become the most audacious neo-liberal experiment in a democratic context – the Argentinian Convertibility Plan launched in 1991. Having campaigned on a neo-populist platform of wage increases and price controls, soon after being elected president in 1989, Carlos Saúl Menem did a volte face. Neo-populist/neo-developmentalist rhetoric was jettisoned: fiscal and financial discipline, the liberalization of product and factor markets, an opening to the global economy and sale of state enterprises – entities whose operating losses and poor services were driving the fiscal deficit and generating popular antipathy – were on the agenda. Yet the defining element of the Plan was the dual currency system: now called the "convertible peso", the peso and the US dollar were peg one-to-one (following a hefty devaluation of the austral). The dollar was granted equal status as legal tender and the Central Bank gained independence – its brief limited to that of a Currency Board (exchanging pesos or dollars on demand at the official rate), with very limited lender of last resort and monetary regulatory functions. Another salient feature: the arrangement was debated and inscribed in law, not introduced by government fiat or simply submitted for Congressional approval. This was a critical ploy, to give the project additional legitimacy, signaling the novelty of the arrangement while also seeking to embed it. As measures began to bight, inflation plummeted and growth resumed, and sections of a skeptical public came to embrace Convertibility. Menem assembled a "popular-business alliance" that delivered electoral victories until 1987. Some of his most ardent support was drawn from the poorest members of society, marginal groups seeking an existence in the informal sector. They had benefited little from previous growth spurts yet suffered most during contractions. Now they became consumers of credit and consumer durables. Convertibility weathered a number of political and economic challenges – the resignation of Economics Minister Domingo Cavallo (architect of the Plan) and international currency crises, as well as raising awareness of the social impact of state retreat in the area of social policy (Mussa 2002; Lewis 2002). Investment, consumption, and trade drove growth, along with debt. The inflation tax plummeted, but the "corruption tax" rose, especially after 1996. The rate of formal unemployment grew, but so did the number of jobs and the economically active proportion of the population. Poverty eased; inequality increased.

Notwithstanding the steady growth in open unemployment and inequality during the *menemato*, between 1989 and 1998, Argentinian GDP per capita increased by almost 40% – the continental figure a little less than 8% (Maddison 2001, 288, 291). Such growth for almost a decade, explains support for the Plan, despite disquiet about sleaze. When privatization receipts began to dry up and fiscal reforms stagnated, the project was increasingly financed by debt – domestic and external. Direct foreign investment eased pressure on the peso, which became overvalued. In the end, Convertibility was undermined by corruption – particularly shady, sweetheart privatization deals, which led to an evaporation of political support for Menem, and a failure to close the fiscal gap. Deficits, debt, and an over-valued currency proved a lethal combination. Politics and economic moved in parallel. Mounting scandals led to public disenchantment with the Peronist Party, while the inability of the Alliance government headed by Fernando De la Rúa, elected in 1989, to tackle structural fundamentals yielded the collapse of his administration and the Plan. A fixed exchange rate and lack of fiscal discipline – the fiscal deficit averaged around 2% per annum for almost a decade – proved unsustainable (Williamson 2004/2005, 199). Convertibility collapsed in 2001, and the economy shrank by around a quarter between 1998 and 2002 – approximately one half the population living in poverty. The mood changed: by 2005 it was clear that the electorate favored measures proposed by the Kirchner regimes (2003–2015), whose policy strategy shifted from Keynesianism-cum-neo-structuralism to neo-populism, by which time the administration would be counted among the new Pink Tide.

Similarities and differences between the Argentine and Chile are clear. In the Argentine, Consensus measures were applied by a democratically elected government. In Chile a government, democratically elected in 1990, continued Consensus strategies applied almost two decades earlier by a brutal regime drawing on contemporary monetarism (Undurraga 2015). There was no backsliding, even if the pace and focus of reforms evolved (Stallings and Peres 2011, 761). Despite differences in timing, in both countries, the strategy was initiated as an integrated package, aggressively applied over a short period, following a deep economic and political crisis. In Chile in 1973, hyperinflation (annualized monthly peak) was around 1,000% – then the highest in the world, a function of the US blockade and an explosion in money supply. Hyperinflation almost touched 5,000% in the Argentine in 1989, accompanied by a spike in poverty, the looting of supermarkets, and street protests – but no military coup. Chile and the Argentine were among the most "aggressive" reformers. Elsewhere, policymakers favored a gradualist approach: for example, in Brazil, Colombia, and Costa Rica. In these countries, first-wave reforms included trade liberalization, financial market liberalization, easing curbs on capital inflows, privatization, and tax reform, followed by a second wave that included deregulation, the reform of the state (designed to increase efficiency and transparency) and social policy reform. The critical changes driving investment and growth were trade liberalization and privatization Stallings and Peres 2011, 762–765).

In Brazil, initial successes and ultimate failures of a series of stabilization plans – there had been six between 1986 and 1993, again influenced later projects, notably the Plan Real launched at the end of 1993. Introduced by then Finance Minister and future president, Fernando Henrique Cardoso, the Real Plan attributed inflation to fiscal policy and inertial factors – economic actors had come to assume that inflation was systemic and behaved accordingly. Consensus-style reforms in Brazil were implemented in a less dramatic manner than in the Argentine and were less radical. The phased nature of reform may have been strategic, probably a function of the institutional structure. By 1990, political and economic elites agreed on the need for change, though there was little consensus about the breadth and scope of what was needed – particularly as regards state reform. Lack of agreement, and inchoate nature of the state apparatus, better explains the pace and phasing of reform (Manzetti 1999, 151–158; Weyland 2002, 220–225; Santiso 2003, 301). Recognizing that securing Congressional approval meant avoiding the severity of some previous reforms, Cardoso adopted a stage-by-stage strategy. First, during the latter part of 1993, he balanced the budget, increasing taxes and reducing expenditure. Secondly, at the beginning of 1994 monetary reform was essayed in ways that allowed for a phased adjustment of wages and prices – and debts and savings accounts. This facilitated the introduction of the real in mid-1994: the new currency unit was anchored to the US dollar – a narrow band of fluctuation prescribed. Privatization began in late 1994, and accelerated in 1995, beginning with the sale of minority stakes in state enterprises. Sale proceeds were applied to reducing public debt. The success of the Real Plan ensured a massive victory for Cardoso in the 1994 presidential election. By 1995, trade liberalization and capital account liberalization were on the agenda; privatization moved to center-stage, equaled by a commitment to the reform of the state, of which it was part. A Constitutional amendment allowed Cardoso to stand for a second consecutive term in 1988: he secured another major victory and aimed to deepen reform. He was not entirely successful. Phasing may have diluted the dynamics of the process, allowing opposition to organize, but the diffuse nature of the state probably made such a course inevitable. After leaving office, Cardoso declared that his life's ambition had been to make Brazil a more equitably society and, by the 1990s, had come to realize that market reform and reform of the state were the most effective means of doing so, and could be best delivered by incremental change that was most likely to embed and sustain change. Intellectually, he was convinced of the need for consensus, an approach that he regarded as likely to enhance democratic accountability and popular support (Manzetti 1999, 158; Santiso 2003, 301). Cardoso was largely correct.

Reform, recovery, and growth were near continental features of the ten years or so after the late 1980s. Regional economic integration was an accompanying institutional development. The Treaty of Asunción signed in 1991 strengthened the process initiated by Alfonsín and Sarney in 1985, recasting the ECLA project of the 1960s. The Central American Common Market (CACM) and the Latin American Free Trade Association (LAFTA) had been pressed by *cepalistas* as critical to the ISI package. Despite helping stimulate intra-regional trade in the 1960s, by the end of that decade, integration was moribund.[10] The South American Common Market formally created at Asunción proved to be more dynamic and enduring. In short space, the MERCOSUR/L morphed from a free trade association into something approximating a common market. One of the largest such organization in the world, the bloc has chalked up achievements. A large reduction in internal tariffs and growth in intra-bloc trade – the integration of supply chains allowed firms to specialize and scale up. Intra-regional import growth (as a share of total imports) was substantial, export growth less so, although the Brazilian industrial sector has been a notable beneficiary of export growth and diversification (Rosales and Herreros 2013: 39–40). Productivity increases and an expansion in intra-regional trade also benefitted small- and medium-sized national firms as well as transnational enterprises. Policy relating to inward external investment has been harmonized – with difficulty. Social benefits have been extended to nationals of one country living and working in another. There has been

institutional innovation: consultative agencies linking member government bodies (for example, economy and foreign affairs ministries and
central banks) have been established, as have arbitration courts, a governing secretariat, and regional parliament. Trade agreements with other
blocs and countries have been negotiated in attempts to integrate foreign economic policy, though countries continue to implement bilateral
commercial and financial deals with third parties. The North American
Free Trade Agreement was signed in 1992 by Canada, Mexico, and the
United States and implemented two years later, reducing tariffs and easing non-tariff barriers. For Mexican manufacturing, the consequences
were technology up-grading, an expansion of production, export
growth, and diversification, as well as job-creation. Mexican agriculture benefitted less. Even the Central American project revived around
2005, and there have been other initiatives such as the Pacific Alliance,
formed in 2011. These point to a commitment to economic regionalism
and global engagement (Malamud 2015; Peña 2015). Arméndariz and
Larraín describe post-1991 MERCOSUR/L tariff reductions as "enormous", citing how Brazil's tariffs with partners nearly halved, and how
intra-regional trade between the Argentine and Brazil experienced "fast"
growth, and how NAFTA facilitated significant increases in the range of
Mexican exports, notably in such sectors as motor vehicles, communications equipment, and high-tech products (Armendáriz and Larraín 2017,
253, 254, 258). MERCOSUR integration has been tested, and faltered,
yet survives. Further north, positive tendencies for Mexico deriving from
NAFTA have weakened with the re-negotiation of the treaty demanded
by President Donald Trump of the United States.

While the *cepalista* regional initiative was revived as part of heterodox
stabilization programs in Brazil and the Argentine, integration projects of the 1990s evolved along lines that were consistent with the new
orthodoxy, at least until the early twenty-first century when an alternative anti-global, anti-capitalist proposal was advanced. The Bolivarian
Alliance for the Peoples of Our America (Alianza Bolivariana para los
Pueblos de Nuestra América – ALBA) attracted some new left-leaning
governments.[11] The ALBA proposal was seen at the time as confronting
and likely to reverse Washington Consensus reforms. This expectation
was premature. Despite disenchantment with some elements of the package, Consensus-indebted reforms were a basis for high growth during
the early years of the twenty-first century. Reform enabled countries to
maximize opportunities yielded by the China-related commodity boom,
which they prefigured and, in several cases, modulate impact of the meltdown of the global financial sector around 2007/2008. In this respect,
regional trade blocs, international commercial, and financial agreements
between groups of Latin American countries and overseas customs
unions and regional groups, and participation in international organizations and fora, cannot be underestimated. Participation in international

organizations and inter-bloc commercial and financial treaties have "locked in" elements of national reform packages. For instance, in such areas as tariff reductions, government regulation, investment strategy, and a range of domestic procedures that impinge upon treaty-regulated external financial and commercial relations.

Social Democracy and Populist Nationalism: "Pink" Variants of State and Market

With challenges to the Washington Consensus, there was speculation about the future shape of polities and economies. Would strategies of the 1990s be abandoned and new economic and state formations emerge, typified by the Bolivarian project in Venezuela. Among others, Panizza, Stallings, and Peres produced a robust response. They maintained that in many parts of Latin America, public opinion broadly supports the underlying thrust of reform – to "restore" the market economy. Support for the market has been sustained in countries where left-leaning administrations have buttressed reform with employment-generating growth and distributive social programs, as well as among sectors of the population in others where neo-populist governments have rejected market capitalism (Panizza 2009, 194; Stallings and Peres 2011, 773–775). Despite disenchantment with elements of the Consensus package, as reforms were a basis for high growth during the early years of the twenty-first century, principles of fiscal discipline, market liberalization, and economic openness continued to command popular approval, notwithstanding global volatility. Questioning social outcomes of reforms did not imply an outright rejection of them.

The term "Pink Tide" was coined to reflect a socialist, rather than communist, position. Most left-leaning administrations were center-left and left of center, though Red was the emblematic color of the Chávez years, a hue continued by his anointed successor Eduardo Maduro. Hugo Chávez did little to secure the future of oil production in Venezuela, but while prices were high, he channeled windfall profits into social and health projects – which had a huge impact on the welfare of the poorest sections of society, to the military and security services, and to friends of the regime at home and overseas. The onset of the Pink Tide has been dated from 1998, when Chávez was elected president – he took office at the beginning of 1999, remaining in power until his death in 2013 (González 2019, 1). Given Chávez domestic economic program and international position, it is debatable whether he represented the onset of the Pink Tide or a revival of old-style populism. Sometime coup leader and democratically elected president, Chávez was immensely charismatic and his language socialistic, pioneering "socialism for the twenty-first century" – his approach was populist (not neo-populist), anti-capitalist and pro-state-socialism. Chávez became even more radical as the economy faltered, domestic protest rose, and right-wing groups, with foreign support, attempted to oust him. It is more appropriate to date the turn-to-the-left from the election of President Ricardo Lagos in Chile in 2000 (Panizza 2009, XXX Chaps. IX, X).

Lagos is a social democrat whose predecessors, after the return of democracy, had been members of the center-right Christian Democrat Party – Patricio Aylwin (1990–2004) and Eduardo Frei (1994–2000). Lagos was followed by others. Alejandro Toledo was elected President of Peru in 2001, heading a new center-left grouping formed in 1994. In effect, Toledo displaced Alberto Fujimori (1990–2000), later convicted of corruption and violating human rights, who had been forced out of office some months before the election by demonstrations orchestrated by Toledo. (Fujimori assembled a popular-business alliance and implemented a mix of heterodoxy and "raw" neoliberalism to stabilize the economy, assuming dictatorial powers to combat insurgency). Luiz Inácio Lula da Silva (popularly known as Lula), elected President of Brazil in late 2002, he took office the following year. Leader of the Partido dos Trabalhadores (PT – the Workers' or Labour Party), he headed a center-left/left-of-center party committed to poverty reduction and sustainable growth. Lula served two presidential terms (2002–2010) and was succeeded by Dilma Rousseff, also of the PT. Elected in 2010, she assumed office in January 2011. Néstor Kirchner, who became president of the Argentine in 2003, is difficult to categorize. An active member of a left-wing Peronist group during his youth, by 2003, he projected the image of a reformist Peronist. During office, he assumed a more rightist, nationalist and neo-populist stance, taking back into state control enterprises privatized during the *menemato*. His economic program was broadly Keynesian and distributionist. The language of the administration was decidedly radical, sometimes socialistic, generally anti-global. He was succeeded by his wife, Cristina Fernández de Kirchner, in 2007. She was re-elected in 2011. Fernández de Kirchner is easier to categorize. Neo-populist in political style and in approach to the economy, for much of her period in office enjoying windfalls from the global commodity boom (with Cuba, the Kirchners were the principal beneficiaries of Chávez's largesse). In 2005, Tabaré Vázquez of the Frente Amplio (a broad, progressive center-left/left coalition) was elected President of Uruguay. Hailing from the center of the coalition, he was re-elected in 2015. Between Vázquez's two terms, José "Pepe" Mujica, a former left-wing guerrillero who had served as a minister under Vázquez, was elected president. In office, he described himself as a pragmatic socialist and lived modestly. On stepping down, he bequeathed his successor a healthy economy and a society at ease with itself. The year 2006 witnessed two quite different Pink Tide presidents elected: Michelle Bachelet in Chile and Evo Morales in Bolivia. Bachelet, a socialist, became the first female president of the republic. Morales was also an avowed socialist. An ethnic Aymara, he was the first indigenous president of Bolivia. Bachelet was re-elected president in 2014; Morales served from 2006 until 2019 – re-elected in 2009 and 2014 following the introduction of a new Constitution. His image and legacy were badly dented when he sought the constitutional change to run for a fourth term in 2019. He left the country at the end of the year amidst massive protest that gained military support. Raúl Castro was nominated President of Cuba in 2008, succeeding brother Fidel; Raúl had been Acting President since mid-2006. Whether these appointments represent a consolidation of the Tide is a moot point: modest "capitalistic" economic reforms were introduced after 2008 to encourage the private sector and foster inward foreign investment in 2011. The Pink Tide reached Mexico in 2018 when Andrés Manuel López Obrador (commonly known by his initials, AMLO) gained the presidency. A highly popular, reformist head of government of the federal district, he narrowly failed to secure the presidency in 2006 and 2012.

Tides flowed and ebbed. Pundits inclined to interpret the victory of Sebastián Piñera in the Chilean presidential election of 2010 as marking the turning of the Pink Tide were premature, as revealed by the stunning victory of Mrs Kirchner in the Argentinian presidential election the following year. Populist economics remained alive and well in Venezuela and Bolivia and would continue to do so for some time. The election of Mauricio Macri in the Argentine occasioned further predictions of an ebb in 2015, perhaps more realistically. Macri was a trenchant champion of neo-liberalism. His electoral success was followed by the return of Piñera to the presidency of Chile in 2018. On 1 January 2019, Jair Bolsonaro became President of Brazil, having campaigned on a Consensus-inspired program. Later the same year, Luis Lacalle of the National Party narrowly gained the presidency of Uruguay, taking office in 2020. Lacalle's win ended the seeming stranglehold on the presidency of the center-left/left-of-center Frente Amplio – it had won all post-2004 elections. Yet the pendulum swung in more than one direction, as AMLO's victory in Mexico showed and, in 2019, Alberto Fernández of the Peronist Party defeated Macri, who was seeking a second term. Fernández campaigned on neo-populist program; his running mate was none other than Cristina Fernández de Kirchner (no relation). Furthermore, at the time of writing, it is unclear if Piñera will complete his term, due to end in 2022. The jury is out on the Blue Tide as much as the Pink.

How "prink" or "red" was the Pink Tide? In Washington, the "left turn" was regarded as threatening free-market reforms and assumed connection between economic progress and democratic governance, but Castañeda provides a nuanced typology, later refined by others. The turn left witnessed the emergence of social democratic regimes and national populist alternatives, pursing quite different economic strategies, albeit with some shared characteristics. The change may be more about politics than economic policy. Given levels of extreme poverty and acute concentration of wealth and power, the combination of inequality and democracy made a move to the left inevitable. Democracy, coupled with electoral competition, ensured that parties and coalitions of the left would pay special attention to universalist social programs to reduce poverty and inequality (Pribble 2013, 13, 173–179). Population growth, the dismal employment prospects of cohorts of young people entering the labor market, and corruption also made a lurch to the left likely. The key question is, what kind of left? For Castañeda, there is the "good", democratic left, marked by a commitment to macroeconomic stability, market economics, and economic internationalism, while emphasizing social distributionism. The "bad" left melds socialistic rhetoric and populist policy; it is nationalistic, anti-capitalist, anti-imperialist (aka the USA) and anti-globalization, favoring instead co-operative internationalism and the promotion of "non-exploitative" commercial and financial relations. Panizza would differentiate regimes as social-democratic and national-populist. Locating individual regimes on the Pink spectrum around 2010, Colombia and Mexico might be described as conservative reformers – defending and extending Consensus-style policies – decidedly un-leftist. Brazil, Chile, Costa Rica, Peru, and Uruguay would be "centrist" – convinced of the importance of maintaining macroeconomic stability, yet critical of social outcomes of the Consensus agenda, therefore given to interventionist state action in the social sphere – consequently the good left. Bolivia, Ecuador, and Venezuela categorized as anti-reform – definitely the bad left, though administrations in Quito have recognized gains from economic openness and global engagement. The Argentine of the Kirchners defies easy categorization: official rhetoric was anti-globalization and anti-imperialism, yet policy was often conducive to international commercial engagement. The language of the regime is socialistic accompanied by solidarist internationalism. At the core, however, in politics and economics, the so-called "K-model" mimics mid-twentieth century corporatist populism (Castañeda 2009; Stallings and Peres 2011; Falleti and Parrado 2018).

An additional method of categorizing regimes and policy is the ALBA litmus test: which administrations have shown commitment to the project; which have been lukewarm? The founding principles of ALBA, then Alternativa Bolivariana para las Américas, were established in 2004: "democratic growth" and "social solidarity", ensured by state action and international collaborative exchange based on non-exploitative commercial and financial relations that respected the environment and cultural diversity. A radical alternative to previous models of integration, as the name signals, that would better enable Latin Americans to confront the evils of imperialism and globalization through co-operation and solidarity (Yaffe 2011). The founder members – the only members for some time, were Cuba and Venezuela. Subsequently, Ecuador and Bolivia affiliated, along with some Central American republics and Caribbean states. Ecuador withdrew in 2018; a year later Bolivia announced that it would leave. The membership of a related organization, the Union of South American Nations (Unión de Naciones Suramericanas – UNASUR) set up in 2008 is/was more extensive: all South American republics ratified the treaty that year, save Uruguay which joined in 2009. Six countries suspended membership in 2018: the Argentine, Brazil, Chile, Colombia, Paraguay, and Peru, protesting about political repression in Venezuela; later in the same year, Colombia withdrew. In 2019, Brazil and Ecuador withdrew. Internal disagreements over procedure and policy pronouncements, in addition to the turn of events in Venezuela led to cooling enthusiasm for UNASUR in several capitals, where the organization came to be viewed as much a *chavista* project as ALBA. While Buenos Aires was below hot and cold, Bogotá, Brasília, and Santiago de Chile came to regard the organization as an irrelevance – peddling an ideology that did not resonate with politics and economics in much of the continent. These developments further endorse arguments that many center-left and left-of-center administrations maintain economic policies broadly in keeping with the Consensus, supplemented by innovative social programs. Degrees of engagement with ALBA and the UNASUR are a reference for government domestic and international economic policy.

Many Pink Tide governments were undermined by corruption and centralization of power (González 2019, 2). Not that such tendencies were peculiar to left-wing administrations. Yet the cult of personality was especially pronounced among nationalist-populist regimes advancing an alternative agenda, often accompanied by a tendency to authoritarianism as growth faltered, triggering debate about the legacy of such. A significant feature of the period was the election of female heads of state. In Chile and Brazil, Bachelet and Rousseff were the first women to be elected president. Cristina Fernández de Kirchner was not the first woman president in the Argentine – that was Isabel Peron who, as Vice-President, assumed the presidency on the death of her husband, but she was the first directly elected to office. Other notable advances were in the areas of human rights, gender equality, poverty reduction, and democratic consolidation. As many left-of-center administrations took office after periods of military rule, it was inevitable human rights became a priority. New Constitutions promulgated in the early twenty-first century emphasized human and social rights – not that all administrations were scrupulous defenders of human rights. Similarly, commitments to environmental projections varied, depending on the role ascribed to energy security and energy production and export in national development plans. Despite extolling a new solidarist alternative economic model, nationalist-populist regimes favored an extractivist program of development founded on energy (or rural commodities) exports and relied on foreign capital – from China instead of traditional sources of finance and investments, a strategy that narrowed the productive base by undermining industry and services (González 2019, 12, 13). Nevertheless, the political economy of these regimes will be assessed by their record on poverty and inequality reduction – an explicit compact with society.

Cash transfers became a notable policy feature of several administrations. Designed to reduce poverty, combat hunger and ill-health, improve access to government social services, they served to upgrade human capital and had an impact on employment and the labor market, performing quasi Keynesian functions during economic downturns. Started as modest, local government initiatives in Brazil in 1995, Mexico was the first country in Latin America to inaugurate a nation-wide program of conditional transfers in 1997, albeit one aimed at the rural families in food poverty. New schemes were launched after the turn of the century, with dramatic increases occurring around 2004–2006. From c. 2005 to 2015, the number of new cash-transfer schemes inaugurated each year averaged around 27. A common characteristic was that all schemes promised regular, guaranteed cash payments to poor or extremely poor households, with mothers usually named as the beneficiary. By 2012, a varied mix of conditional transfer programs was operating in 16 countries. Increasingly, with few exceptions, programs were run by national social development agencies or ministries. Coverage peaked between 2009 and 2013, when recipient households represented an average of 22% of the continental population, declining somewhat thereafter. Coverage was greatest in the Argentine, Bolivia, Brazil, Colombia, Mexico, and Peru. Expenditure on programs represented an average of 0.33% of Latin American GDP in 2015; the highest was Ecuador at virtually 1%. In terms of level of funding and effectiveness of administration, the Brazilian scheme was deemed to be the most sustainable; the Argentinian, the most generous (Cecchini and Atuesta 2017, 15–18, 21–23, 30). Redistributive cash transfers are the main cause of welfare improvements in Latin America during the twenty-first century – key to both inequality and poverty reduction. Programs became more institutionalized and more universalized, with more positive and sustainable results under new left governments than neo-populist (Lustig, López-Calva, Ortiz-Júarez 2012, 6, 7, 12, 13; Pribble 2013, 170, 171, 173–181).

Conclusion

Aggregate continental GDP in constant U$S grew approximately six-fold from 1950 to c. 2020; GDP per capita doubled. The longest uninterrupted growth run occurred during the formative and classic "CEPAL decades" from the mid/late 1930s to c. 1980 – the Brazilian economy grew continuously until 1980, the Mexican until 1981, the Peruvian until 1982. Chilean growth stalled around 1972/1973; Argentinian

1975/1976. Many economies contracted during the "lost decade" – but not all: Colombian growth continued uninterrupted. Contraction was deeper and recovery more hesitant in such countries as the Argentine and Peru, with many economies not registering strong recovery until the latter part of 1980s. Structural change was reflected by industrialization and urbanization. In 1930, approximately one-third of the population of Latin America lived in cities; in 1980, almost two-thirds – an unprecedented change within the space of two generations (ECLAC Population Division/Data Bank). Annual average rates of growth in manufacturing during the twentieth and twenty-first centuries were at their highest between 1938 and 1973, with the contribution of industry to GDP peaking in the 1970s (CEPAL Historical Data; Bénétrix, O'Rourke, Williamson 2012, 7, and 16). The mid-twentieth century witnessed considerable catch-up with core industrial economies in terms of the contribution of manufacturing to the economy – with further convergence in the post-1970s period largely attributed to industrial policy (Williamson 2011, 199, 200–203; Bénétrix et al. 2012, 8, 9, 22–25; Bértola and Ocampo 2012, 127–131; Della Paolera, Durán Amorocho, Musacchio 2018, 1; Santarcángelo, Schteingart, Porta 2018, 1).

Welfare indicators tell a similar story: literacy rates and life expectancy at birth convergence within the continent and catch-up with the advanced economies, especially from around mid-twentieth century. An average of major country literacy rates was 29% of the US rate in 1900, 47% in 1950, and 83% in 2000. Data on life expectancy is even more impressive: 64% in 1900, still 64% in 1950, yet 87% in 2000 – remembering that the USA was a moving target. Southern Cone countries had virtually caught up with the United States by 2000 (Astorga, Bergés, FitzGerald 2005, 776–778). Further corroboration is provided by comparison with a broader mix of countries. Expressed as a proportion of a composite index for the advanced economies (France, Germany, the UK, and the USA), the average Historical Human Development Index (HHDI) for Latin America was 39% in 1900, 46% in 1930, 55% in 1950, 61% in 1960, 64% in 1970, 68% in 1980, 71% in 1990, and 73% in 2000 (Bértola, Hernández, Siniscalchi 2011, 86, 87). Convergence was again greater and faster in the Southern Cone. The picture regarding living standards was less rosy, but there was similar catch-up after c. 1950.

Issues of market efficiency and international competitiveness dominated the policy debates in Latin America from the 1980s until the early twenty-first century, trumping the 1940s–1960s paradigm that emphasized state-led structural change. Concerns that were initially voiced by authoritarian, military regimes; later, fitfully, by fragile democratic administrations; later still by resurgent neo-populist and market-friendly left-leaning democratic governments. The new development ideology brought with it a reduction in the rhetoric of nationalism and welfarism.

For neo-liberal and neo-structuralists regimes – authoritarian and democratic, growth was a legitimizing force. Regimes pursuing neo-liberal and neo-structural strategies borrowed abroad and promoted export growth. De-industrialization in the Southern Cone republics meant a resurgence of traditional exports and/or a diversifying mix of new commodities. Further north, an increased participation of manufactures in exports. Was industrial export growth a direct response to authoritarian policy measures, or a "natural" outcome of earlier macroeconomic change? Persuasive evidence suggests the difficult transition to industrial deepening, including modest growth in the participation of manufactures in exports, was already underway before the bloody action of technocratic-military regimes (Kaufman 1979, 203–217, 235–239; Serra 1979, 118–127, 133–135; Bértola and Ocampo 2012, 170, 182, 183). Less open in doubt is the sharp contraction in manufactured output and exports in countries like Chile and the Argentine in the 1970s, following abrupt opening, in contrast to industrial deepening in Mexico and Brazil. It is also clear that the debt/loan crisis of the 1980s undermined authoritarianism and, coupled with the failure of heterodox stabilization programs, prepared the way for the hegemony of the neo-liberal Washington Consensus "remedy" of the 1990s – key elements of which continue to be applied by social-democratic administrations in the twenty-first century. There were various democratic manifestations of Consensus neo-liberalism and post-Consensus political economy: some entailed the re-emergence of neo-populism – a re-configured state defined by "delegative democracy" and a privatizing business-populist alliance; another, the left-leaning, democratic "socially responsive state" that combined market economics and social activism. And there were national-populist states pursuing an anti-Consensus, anti-global agenda – whose commitment to democratic governance has been questioned, if not their rejection of market capitalism.

In the second quarter of the twentieth century, the rise of urban middles classes contributed to messy politics and state-led developmentalism. At the end of the century and in the early twenty-first, the growing presence of the middle classes probably facilitated political and macroeconomic stability. Analyzing data from a sample of Central and South American countries, Birdsall finds that the presence of "indispensable" middle classes increased from around one-fifth to more than a third of the total population between 1990 and 2010, while their share of national income grew from two-fifth to around one-half. Tending to be in regular employment, experiencing rising living standards and patterns of consumption, and enjoying greater access to education and other public services, the middles classes supported economic and political reform (Birdsall 2014, 259, 261–267, 283–285). The middle classes were not the only constituency voting for change. Other sectors of society also fought corruption, favored the rule of law, and clamored for stronger and more representative political institutions. More reliant on an effective state (and an efficient economy) than the wealthy, middle- and working-class groups were likely to support market-friendly economic reform and policies that targeted poverty reduction and social inclusion. This probably accounts for the appeal of neo-liberalism in some countries in the 1990s, and Consensus-indebted macroeconomic policy combined with innovative social interventionism after c. 2000.

Notes

1. Terms such as *cepalistas, cepalino, cepalismo* derive from the acronym CEPAL, the Spanish and Portuguese versions of the initials for the United Nations Economic Commission for Latin America (ECLA) established in 1948. In 1984, the agency became known as ECLAC when "and the Caribbean" was added to its regional remit. The Portuguese and Spanish acronyms remained unchanged – CEPAL.
2. Sometimes head of the Research Division of the Banco de la Nación Argentina and founding president of the Banco Central de la República Argentina, Prebisch would subsequently become Secretary-General of CEPAL and go on to head the United Nations Conference on Trade and Development (UNCTAD). Earning the moniker, the "father" of structuralism, in association with Hans W. Singer, Prebisch would devise what became known as the Prebisch-Singer thesis, a core element of the emerging discipline of development economies.
3. For an introduction to the new social politics of the interwar period and emphases on state action, especially the reconfiguration and strengthening of the state provoked by economic turmoil, see Drinot and Kinght (2014).
4. The term derives from the work of Alexander Gerschenkron, in particular, his theories about economic backwardness and "later" industrialization, which argue *inter alia* that the later the process of industrial development occurs, the greater the role of the state, and the likely use of an "ideology" of development to build a political coalition to support policies promoting rapid industrial development – and accepting the costs involved.
5. The term and concept of Bureaucratic Authoritarianism were devised by the Argentinian lawyer and political scientist Guillermo O'Donnell. The main features of "BA" regimes, as they became known, were a general restructuring of political and economic institutions. This entailed: strong, institutionalized systems of power; technocratic decision-making; the proscription of political parties and autonomous representative organization – political compression and demobilization; a focus on economic modernization. BA regimes were also characterized as a civil-military alliance and as tripartite transnational alliances, involving national industrial bourgeoisies, state capital, and international business and finance. See O'Donnell (1973).
6. The 1964 Brazilian military regime, which continued until 1985, at first proposed a broadly orthodox, austerity anti-inflationary stabilization program based on monetary and fiscal policies. When this failed, following opposition from associates of the regime, and massive popular demonstrations, there was an abrupt change around 1967/1968 in favor of industrial deepening and diversification, leading to the so-called Brazilian miracle (high growth and relatively low inflation, coupled with structural change) resulted between 1968 and 1974, and continued in attenuated form until

c. 1980, when it was accompanied by a slow retreat from authoritarianism. In the Argentine, the authoritarian experiment achieved much less – and policy moved in the opposite direction. The 1966–1973 military regime initially attempted industrial deepening, blending political nationalism and economic internationalism in an orthodox stabilization program. When this failed, the armed forces returned to the barracks, only to re-emerge in 1976, launching a neo-liberal experiment, applied in an exceptionally brutal manner.

7. Modern monetarism is associated with Milton Friedman, an enthusiastic advocate of free-market capitalism, based at the University of Chicago. He argues that inflation is caused by the growth of money supply, as opposed to structural distortions in an economy, as maintained by *cepalista*. Chile, during the early years of the military regime headed by General Pinochet, was a pioneer of monetarism, as the so-called "Chicago Boys". Argentina was another early test case, following the coup of 1976: the team headed by Minister of Economy José Martínez de Hoz attempted to reign-in government spending and the printing of money. Later exponents were Margaret Thatcher in the UK in 1979 and, in the USA, Ronald Reagan – hence Reaganomics.

8. In Spanish, Mercado Común del Sur (MERCOSUR; in Portuguese Mercado Comun do Sul (MERCOSUL). Initially formed as a Free Trade Area between the Argentine and Brazil, the Treaty of Asunción signed in 1991, by which time the founder members had been joined by Paraguay and Uruguay, changed the bloc into a Customs Union. Other countries joined or became associate members, though the process of integration has proved problematic.

9. The principal technopols, whose served as presidents and ministers, are Pedro Aspe, Domingo Cavallo, Fernando Henrique Cardoso and Alejandro Foxley. Most were social scientists and academics, zealous advocates of the reform packages with which they were associated.

10. LAFTA was established in 1960 by the Treaty of Montevideo, signed by the Argentine, Brazil, Chile, Mexico, Paraguay, Peru, and Uruguay – all the other South American countries subsequently joined. As the name implies, the focus was on increasing intra-regional trade through external tariff harmonization and internal tariff reduction. Stimulating intra-bloc trade was regarded as a partial substitute for sluggish world trade growth and as a vehicle for future closer regional economic integration that would be brought about by policy alignment and through the improvement of continental physical infrastructure. The CACM, with active intervention of CEPAL policy advisors, aimed at integration among members from the beginning; intra-bloc trade growth was viewed as an outcome of integration rather than a mechanism to promote it – an inversion of the LAFTA schema. The bloc emerged from a series of bilateral and multilateral agreements effected during the 1950s. These were harmonized and integrated at the Managua Conference, held in 1960, which brought together the five Central American republics and Panama. Other blocs were: the Andean Pact established by the Cartagena Acord of 1969 (Bolivia, Chile, Colombia, Ecuador, and Peru – Venezuela subsequently joined only to leave, and Chile withdrew) – in effect a quasi-common market sub-grouping within LAFTA created by countries that favored faster and closer integration; River Plate Basin Group (the Argentine, Brazil, Paraguay, and Uruguay) formed in 1969, largely confined to improving fluvial and terrestrial transport links and realizing hydroelectricity generating potential. Largely dormant after the 1970s, these organizations experienced something of

a renaissance in the 1990s, reinvigorated by a renewed commitment to regional integration epitomized by MERCOSUR/L dynamics.
11. Until 2009, known as the "Alternative" – Alternativa Bolivariana para las Américas.

Bibliography

Abel, C., Lewis, C. M. (eds.). (2015). *Latin America: Economic Imperialism and the State*. London: Bloomsbury Press.

Angell, A. (1991). Chile since 1958. In *The Cambridge History of Latin America. Volume VIII: Latin America since 1930: Spanish South America*. Cambridge: Cambridge University Press.

Armendáriz, B., Larraín, B. F. (2017). *The Economics of Contemporary Latin America*. Cambridge, MA: Massachusetts Institute of Technology Press.

Astorga, P., Bergés, A. R., FitzGerald, V. (2005). The Standard of Living Debate in Latin America during the Twentieth Century. *Economic History Review* 58(4).

Bacha, E. (2018). On the Economics of Development: A View from Latin America. *PSL Quarterly* 71(286).

Benavente, J. M., Crespi, G., Katz, J., Stumpo, G. (1996). Changes in the Industrial Development of Latin America. *CEPAL Review* 60.

Bénétrix, A. S., O'Rourke, K. H., Williamson, J. G. (2012). The Spread of Manufacturing to the Poor Periphery, 1870–2007. NBER Working Paper 18221. Published as "Measuring the Spread of Modern Manufacturing to the Poor Periphery". In *The Spread of Modern Industry to the Periphery since 1871 (13–32)*, edited by K. H. O'Rourke, J. G. Williamson (2017). New York: Oxford University Press.

Bértola, L., Hernández, M., Siniscalchi, S. (2011). *Un índice histórico de Desarrollo humano de América Latina y algunos países de otras regiones: metología, fuentes y bases de datos*. Montevideo: Universidad de la República, Facultad de Ciencias Sociales, Serie Documento de Trabajo.

Bértola, L., Ocampo, J. A. (2012). *The Economic Development of Latin America since Independence*. Oxford: Oxford University Press.

Biglaiser, G. (2002). *Guardians of the Nation?: Economists, Generals and Economic Reform in Latin America*. Notre Dame: University of Notre Dame Press.

Birdsall, N. (2014). A Note on the Middle Class in Latin America. In *Inequality in Asia and the Pacific: Trends, Drivers and Policy Implications (257–287)*, edited by R. Kanbur, C. Rhee, J. Zhuang. New York: Asian Development Bank/Routledge.

Cárdenas, E., Ocampo, J. A., Thorp, R. (2000). Introduction. In *An Economic History of Twentieth-Century Latin America: Vol. III: Industrialisation and the State in Latin America: The Postwar Years (1–35)*, edited by E. Cárdenas, J. A. Ocampo, R. Thorp. Basingstoke: Palgrave/Macmillan.

Cardoso, E., Helwege, A. (1991). Populism, Profligacy and Redistribution. In *The Macroeconomics of Populism in Latin America (45–74)*, edited by R. Dornbusch, S. Edwards. Chicago: Chicago University Press/National Bureau of Economic Research.

Castañeda, J. (2009). Latin America's Turn Left. *Foreign Affairs* 85(3).

Cecchini, S., Atuesta, B. (September 2017). *Conditional Cash Transfer Programmes in Latin America and the Caribbean: Coverage and Investment Trends.* Santiago de Chile: ECLAC. Social Policy Series Working Paper No. 224.

Corbo, V. (1992). *Development Strategy and Development Policies in Latin America: A Historical Perspective.* San Francisco: International Center for Economic Growth, Occasional Paper No. 22.

Della Paolera, G., Durán Amorocho, X. H., Musacchio, A. (February 2018). The Industrialization of South America Revisited: Evidence from Argentina, Brazil, Chile and Colombia, 1890–2010. NBER Working Paper 24345. Published as Industrialization in South America: Argentina, Brazil, Chile and Colombia, 1890–2010. In *The Spread of Modern Industry to the Periphery since 1871* (318–344), edited by K. H. O'Rourke, J. G. Williamson. New York: Oxford University Press.

Devlin, R., Ffrench-Davis, R. (1995). The Great Latin American Debt Crisis; A Decade of Asymmetric Adjustment. *Revista de Economía Política* 15(3).

Díaz-Alejandro, C. (1979). Southern Cone Stabilization Plans. Yale Center for Economic Growth Discussion Paper No. 330.

_____(1984). Latin American Debt: I Don't Think We Are in Kansas Any More. *Brookings Paper in Economic Activity* 2.

Domínguez, J. (ed.) (1996). *Technopols: Freeing Politics and the Market in Latin America in the 1990s.* University Park: Pennsylvania State University Press.

Dornbusch, R., Edwards, S. (1991). The Macroeconomics of Populism in Latin America. In *The Macroeconomics of Populism in Latin America (7–14)*, edited by R. Dornbusch, S. Edwards. Chicago: Chicago University Press/National Bureau of Economic Research.

Drinot, P., Knight, A. (2014). Introduction. In *The Great Depression in Latin America (1–21)*, edited by P. Drinot, A. Knights. Durham, NC: Duke University Press.

Economic Commission for Latin American and the Caribbean (ECLAC) (n.d.). History of ECLAC. Retrieved from https://www.cepal.org/en/historia-de-la-cepal

_____(2007). Reduction of Infant Mortality in Latin America and the Caribbean: Uneven Progress Requiring a Variety of Responses. *Challenges* 6.

Evans, P. B. (1979). *Dependent Development: The Alliance of Multinational, State and Local Capital in Brazil.* Princeton: Princeton University Press.

Fajnzylber, F. (1983). *La industrialización trunca de América Latina.* México, DF: Editorial Nueva Imagen.

Falleti, T. G., Parrado, E. A. (2018). Introduction. In *Latin America since the Left Turn (1–10)*, edited by T. G. Falleti, E. A. Prado. Philadelphia: University of Pennsylvania Press.

Fishlow, A. (1988). The State of Latin American Economies. In *Changing Perspectives in Latin American Studies (87–119)*, edited by C. Mitchel. Palo Alto: Stanford University Press.

FitzGerald, V. (1998). CEPAL y la teoría de industrialización. *Revista de la CEPAL. Número Especial. CEPAL: cinquenta años, reflexciones sobre América Latina y el Caribe.* Santiago de Chile: CEPAL.

Foxley, A. (2010). *Market versus State: Postcrisis Economics in Latin America.* Washington: Carnegie Endowment.

Ffrench-Davis, R. (2000). *Reforming the Reforms in Latin America: Macroeconomics, Trade, Finance.* Basingstoke: Macmillan/St Antony's Series.
———(2016). Neostructuralism and Macroeconomics for Development. In *Neostructuralism and Heterodox Thinking in Latin America and the Caribbean in the Early Twenty-First Century (117–138),* edited by A. Bárcena, A. Prado. Santiago: ECLAC Books.

Gavin, M., Perotti, R. (1997). Fiscal Policy in Latin America. *NBER Macroeconomics Annual* 12.

González, M. (2019). *The Ebb of the Pink Tide: The Decline of the Left in Latin America.* London: Pluto Press.

Goodman, D., Redclift, M. (1982). *From Peasant to Proletarian: Capitalist Development and Agrarian Transition.* New York: St Martin's Press.

Grindle, M. (1996). *Challenging the State: Crisis and Innovation in Latin America and Africa.* Cambridge: Cambridge University Press.

Hewlett, S. A., Weinert, R. S. (eds.) (1982). *Brazil and Mexico: Patterns of Late Development.* Philadelphia: ISHI Press.

International Monetary Fund. (2016). *IMF Country Report No. 16/169: Argentina: Economic Developments.* Washington, DC: International Monetary Fund.

Kaufman, R. (1979). Industrial Change and Authoritarian Rule in Latin America: A Concrete Review of the Bureaucratic-Authoritarian Model. In *The New Authoritarianism in Latin America (165–253),* edited by D. Collier. Princeton: Princeton University Press.

Kaufman, R., Stallings, B. (1991). The Political Economy of Latin American Populism. In *The Macroeconomics of Populism in Latin America (15–43),* edited by R. Dornbusch, S. Edwards. Chicago: Chicago University Press/National Bureau of Economic Research.

Kiguel, M. A., Liviatan, N. (1992). When Do Heterodox Stabilization Programs Work?. *The World Bank Research Observer* 7(1).

Kline, H. S., Vidal Luna, F. (2019). *Feeding the World: Brazil's Transformation into a Modern Agricultural Economy.* Cambridge: Cambridge University Press.

Kopper, C. (2017). *VW do Brasil in the Brazilian Military Dictatorship, 1964–1985: A Historical Study.* Wolfsburg: Quensen Druck & Verlag.

Kuczynski, P. P., Williamson, J. (2003). *After the Washington Consensus: Restarting Growth and Reform in Latin America.* Washington: Institute for International Economics.

Latin American Post. (2018). Informal Working in Latin America: Is It a Real Alternative. Retrieved from https://latinamericanpost.com/22788-informal-working-in-latin-america-is-it-a-real-alternative

Lewis, C. M. (1986). Industry in Latin America before 1930. In *The Cambridge History of Latin America. Volume IV. c. 1870–1930 (267–323),* edited by L. Bethell. Cambridge: Cambridge University Press.

———(2002). *Argentina: A Short History.* London: One World.

Lewis, C. M., Lloyd-Sherlock, P. (2009). Social Policy and Economic Development in South America: An Historical Approach to Social Insurance. *Economy and Society* 38(1).

Love, J. (1994). Economic Ideas and Ideologies in Latin America since 1930. In *The Cambridge History of Latin America. Volume VI Pt. 1. 1930 to the Present (393–460),* edited by L. Bethell. Cambridge: Cambridge University Press.

_____(2005). The Rise and Decline of Economic Structuralism in Latin America; New Dimensions. *Latin American Research Review* 40(3).

_____(2016). CEPAL, Economic Nationalism and Development. In *The Political Economy of Latin American Independence (276–291)*, edited by A. Mendes Cunha, C. E. Suprinyak. London: Routledge.

Lustig, N., López-Calva, L. F., Ortiz-Júarez, E. (2012). *Declining in Inequality in Latin America in the 2000s: The Cases of Argentina, Brazil and Mexico.* Washington, DC: World Bank Policy Research Working Paper No. WPS 6248.

Maddison, A. (2001). *The World Economy: A Millennial Perspective.* Paris: Organisation for Economic Co-operation and Development (OECD).

Malamud, C. (2015). Regional Integration in Latin America: A Diagnosis of the Crisis. In *A New Atlantic Community: The European Union, the US and Latin America (199–207)*, edited by J. Roy. Miami: Thomson-Shore.

Malloy, J. (1977). Authoritarianism and the Extension of Social Security Protection to the Rural Sector in Brazil. *Luso-Brazilian Review* 14(2).

Manzetti, L. (1999). *Privatization South American Style.* Oxford: Oxford University Press.

Mesa-Lago, C. (1978). *Social Security in Latin America: Pressure Groups, Stratification and Inequality.* Pittsburgh: Pittsburgh University Press.

Muñoz Gomá, O. (2015). Public-Private Relationships in Chile after 1990. In *The Impact of Globalization on Argentina and Chile: Business Enterprise and Entrepreneurship (215–247)*, edited by G. Jones, A. Lluch. Cheltenham: Edward Elgar.

Mussa, M. (2002). *Argentina and the Fund: From Triumph to Tragedy.* Washington, DC: Institute for International Economics.

Naím, M., Toro, F. (March/April 2020). Venezuela's Problem Isn't Socialism: Maduro's Mess Has Little to Do with Ideology. *Foreign Affairs* 99(2).

North, D. (October 2003). *The Role of Institutions in Economic Development.* Geneva: United Nations Organisation, Economic Commission for Europe, Discussion Paper Series, UN/ECE.

Ocampo, J. A. (2014). The Latin American Debt Crisis in Historical Perspective. In *Life after Debt: The Origins and Resolutions of Debt Crises (87–115)*, edited by J. E. Stiglitz, D. Heyman. Basingstoke: Palgrave/Macmillan.

O'Donnell, G. (1973). *Modernization and Bureaucratic Authoritarianism: Studies in South American Politics.* Berkeley: University of California Press.

O'Rourke, K. H., Williamson, J. G. (2017). Introduction. In *The Spread of Modern Industry to the Periphery since 1871 (1–12)*, edited by K. H. O'Rourke, J. G. Williamson. New York: Oxford University Press.

Oszlak, O. (ed.) (1997). *Estado y Sociedad: Las Nuevas Reglas del Juego.* Buenos Aires: CEA-CBC.

Panizza, F. (2009). *Contemporary Latin America: Development and Democracy beyond the Washington Consensus: The Rise of the Left.* London: Zed Books.

Peña, F. (2015). Regional Integration in Latin America: The Strategy of "Convergence in Diversity". In *A New Atlantic Community: The European Union, the US and Latin America (189–198)*, edited by J. Roy. Miami: Thomson-Shore.

Pérez Caldentey, E. (2016). A Time to Reflect on Opportunities for Debate and Dialogue between (Neo)structuralism and Heterodox Schools of Thought. In *Neostructuralism and Heterodox Thinking in Latin America and the Caribbean in the Early Twenty-First Century* (31–83), edited by A. Bárcena, A. Prado. Santiago de Chile: ECLAC Books.

Pribble, J. (2013). *Welfare and Party Politics in Latin America*. Cambridge: Cambridge University Press.

Reinhart, C. M., Rogoff, K. S., Savastano, M. A. (August 2003). Debt Intolerance. NBER Working Paper 9908. https://www.nber.org/papers/w9908

Rosales, O., Herreros, S. (2013). Trade and Trade Policy in Latin America and the Caribbean: Recent Trends, Emerging Challenges. *Journal of International Affairs* 66(2).

Sachs, J. (1985). External Debt and Macroeconomic Performance in Latin America and East Asia. *Brookings Papers on Economic Activity* 16(2).

———(March 1989a). Social Conflict and Populist Policies in Latin America. NBER Working Paper 2897.

———(July 1989b). New Approaches to the Latin American Debt Crisis. *Essays in International Finance* 174.

Santarcángelo, J. E., Schteingart, D., Porta, F. (2018). Industrial Policy in Argentina, Brazil, Chile and Mexico: A Comparative Approach. *Revue Interventions économiques [Online]* 59. Retrieved from http://journals.openedition.org/interventionseconomiques/3852

Santiso, C. (2003). Another Lost Decade? The Future of Reform in Latin America. *Public Administration and Development* 23.

Serra, J. (1979). Three Mistaken Theses Regarding the Connection between Industrialization and Authoritarian Regimes. In *The New Authoritarianism in Latin America (99–163)*, edited by D. Collier. Princeton: Princeton University Press.

Skidmore, T. E. (1978). *Politics in Brazil, 1930-64: An Experiment in Democracy*. New York: Oxford University Press.

Stallings, B., Peres, W. (2011). Is Economic Reform Dead in Latin America? Rhetoric and Reality since 2000. *Journal of Latin American Studies* 43(4).

Tanzi, V. (2000). Taxation in Latin America in the Last Decade. University of Stanford, Center for International Development Working Paper No. 76.

Thorp, R. (1994). The Latin American Economies, 1939–c.1950. In *The Cambridge History of Latin America, Volume VI, Pt. 1: 1930 to the Present (117–158)*, edited by L. Bethell. Cambridge: Cambridge University Press.

———(1998). *Progress, Poverty and Exclusion: An Economic History of Latin America in the Twentieth Century*. Washington, DC: Inter-American Development Bank.

Undurraga, T. (2015). Neoliberalism in Argentina and Chile: Common Antecedents, Divergent Paths. *Revista de Sociologia e Política* 23(55).

Weaver, F. (1980). *Class, State and Industrial Structure: The Historical Process of South American Industrial Growth*. Westport: Greenwood Press.

Weaver, F. (2000). *Latin America in the World Economy: Mercantile Colonialism to Global Capitalism*. Boulder, CO: Westview Press.

Weyland, K. (2002). *The Politics of Market Reform in Fragile Democracies: Argentina, Brazil, Peru and Venezuela*. Princeton: Princeton University Press.

———(2013). Populism and Social Policy in Latin America. In *Latin American Populism in the Twenty-First Century* (117–145), edited by C. de la Torre, C. Arnson. Baltimore: The Johns Hopkins University Press.

Williamson, J. (1990). What Washington Means by Policy Reform. In *Latin American Readjustment: How Much Has Happened (7–20)*, edited by J. Williamson. Washington, DC: Institute for International Economics.

_____(2004/2005). The Strange History of the Washington Consensus. *Journal of Post Keynesian Economics* 27(2).

_____(2011). *Trade and Poverty: When the Third World Fell Behind*. Cambridge, MA: Massachusetts Institute of Technology Press.

Yaffe, H. (2011). The Bolivarian Alliance for the Americas: An Alternative Development Strategy. *International Journal of Cuban Studies: Special Issue: A New Dawn? ALBA and the Future of Caribbean and Latin American Integration* 3(2/3).

9 The Dependency Hypothesis
A Theoretical Moment in Latin American Thought

Felipe Lagos-Rojas and Edward L. Tapia

Introduction

The set of analyses and debates that is commonly known as "dependency theory" was epistemological shifting, and in many ways, seminal ground from which Latin American and other anti-colonial and anti-imperialist movements in the global South have borrowed and found inspiration. The discussion about the structural nature of dependency in Latin America as well as other former colonial or semi-colonial regions in Africa and Asia was groundbreaking in both the realm of social sciences and left-wing political orientations, hence shaping the cultural landscape and furnishing its language and imaginary. Although there were dependency debates across the whole continent – and actually the world –, the location of many of the most salient was in Santiago de Chile, which transformed this city into a political and cultural hotspot, a type of internationalist hub for radical thinkers and source of hope for non-Western regions.

Nonetheless, it is misleading to keep referring to the dependency debate in terms of a theory or school, as if we could identify a single common thread, be it in terms of theoretical architecture, method, or political conclusions. In this vein, some commentators indicate that the dependency realm worked more as a critical perspective on traditional conceptions of capitalist modernization and development, and not much as a coherent set of theses and/or policies (Larraín 1989; Domingues 2011). The emphasis of this chapter's title precisely stresses the evidence of a common hypothesis, but the versatility of formulations allows no coinage such as school nor theory. As a matter of fact, a rough division of *dependentista* thinkers would easily distinguish between a very heterogeneous group of Marxist approaches and more heterodox perspectives, also reformist ones (Munck 1984; Kay 2010). However, the centrality of many of Marx's categories and considerations makes it fair to say that this realm is as much a Marxist contribution to Latin American intellectual history as it is to affirm the other way around – the Latin American contribution to Marxism and liberation paradigms.

DOI: 10.4324/9781003045632-10

This chapter offers a reconstruction of the dependency hypothesis outlining both the common threads and main differences among the authors encompassed under such an umbrella. First, we present a brief account of the two currents from which it borrowed the most, namely the *desarrollista* (developmentslist) or *estructuralista* (structruralist) school that emerged within the UN's Economic Commission for Latin America and the Caribbean (ECLAC), on the one hand, and the different versions of imperialism argued through a Marxian prism, on the other. Next, we introduce the most important arrangements, general consensuses, central categories, and main debates and internal divisions of the dependency debate. In it, we identify three main groups: the proponents of "dependent-associated development" (Fernando H. Cardoso, Enzo Faletto, José Serra), the "super-exploitation" and "sub-imperialism" camp (Ruy Mauro Marini, Theotonio Dos Santos, Vania Bambirra), and the authors focused mainly on unequal exchange (André Gunder Frank, Samir Amin, although the latter was also an advocate of super-exploitation). Finally, we offer a reinterpretation of the thesis of unequal exchange from the vantage point of Marx's law of value, which attempts to go beyond the straitjackets of circulation and super-exploitation thesis. As a way of conclusion, we argue that the dependency hypothesis was prematurely dismissed and declared as passed away by pointing out some contemporary debates in which it still haunts present-day affairs.

The Race for "Development": Historical and Conceptual Antecedents of the Debate on Dependence

After almost a century of independent political life, the catastrophic effects of the Great Depression in 1929 and the following years of the Second World War made it apparent for an important number of Latin American countries that the conditions for the local bourgeoisie to gain national control of the local economies by fostering industrialization was an achievable goal. By 1940, many of the economies of the region had created or strengthened national industrial sectors, a path that was conceived of as *the* road to development. In an increasingly post-colonial world, many countries were attached to the goal of industrial development as a recipe to catch up with the West. The governments of Getulio Vargas in Brazil as early as 1930, and later of Lazaro Cárdenas in Mexico in 1934, Pedro Aguirre Cerda in Chile in 1938, Romulo Betancourt in Venezuela in 1945, and Juan Domingo Perón in Argentina in 1946, promoted national industrialization, agrarian reform, and the invigoration of internal markets. Consequently, during the late 1940s and the 1950s development through industrial growth was established in the agendas all over the subcontinent (see Ward 2004, 20–37).

As we will see below, the dependency debates were crisscrossed by a general critical evaluation of both the actual policies and the conceptual assumptions that supported the industrialization efforts to catch up to Western standards, crucially the establishment of an expanded internal market. Particularly significant were two lines of thought prominent at the time. First, it was the conceptualizations on the deterioration in terms of trade that characterized the ECLAC approach that served as a conceptual mantra in the organization of processes of import-substitution industrialization. Second, there was an array of Marxist theories of imperialism with which some exponents of dependency analysis draw lines of dialogue and of commitment. Indeed, we can actually talk of a "Marxist" department or position within the dependency debate (Chilcote 1982; Larraín 1989; Kay 2010).

Cepalino Approach: ECLAC and the Prebish-Singer Thesis

Created by the UN Assembly in 1948 with headquarters in Santiago de Chile, the ECLAC (CEPAL in the Spanish acronym) had as its mandate the contribution to economic development in the region through the combination of high-standard analysis and strategic provision of intellectual and technical advice to Latin American governments. Mainly consisting of economists with Keynesian leanings (Grigera 2015), the approach that will become to be known as *Cepalino, desarrollista* or *estructuralista* strongly promoted a process of import-substitution industrialization that will become known by its acronym – the "ISI model". This approach was based on the thesis of the deterioration of the terms of trade elaborated during the late 1940s by Raul Prebisch and Hans Singer. Prebisch (1950), who would become president of ECLAC the next year, presented in 1949 the paper "The Economic Development in Latin America and its Principal Problems", which will come to be considered the "ECLAC manifesto" (Hirschman 1971, 280). Strongly influenced by his colleagues in the UN Economic Department, particularly by Hans Singer's influential article "Economic Progress in Underdeveloped Countries" (Singer 1949; also Toye and Toye 2003), these ideas prompted the adoption of industrialization strategies to stimulate economic growth as a means to overcome underdevelopment.

Prebisch's argument portrayed an international system composed of developed centers, that is, economies formed by a large industrial sector based on technological innovation, and peripheries or satellite economies that remain undeveloped, with minimal or no industrial sector. In a nutshell, the Prebisch-Singer thesis portrayed Latin American countries as dual-economy societies (see Chilcote 1974), arguing that such a condition was structural and explaining this by a secular tendency for the price of primary commodities to fall relative to manufactured commodities. In other words, while technical progress increases incomes in developed nations, this leads to lower the demand and consequently lowers the prices for primary commodities in the underdeveloped nations.

Therefore, if a nation gets stuck producing sugar or copper, the purchasing power of its imports will decrease over time and its ability to invest, grow, and develop will remain implausible (Birkan 2015, 157). Therefore, it was believed that the interests of multinational corporations exporting primary commodities to the metropole did not lie with general economic development of the periphery. Prebisch et al. (1969, 18) later coined the idea of "deterioration in the terms of trade" to describe the structural situation of Latin America within the world market.

Challenging mainstream neo-Ricardian theories of "comparative advantages" for extractive economies, the recommended policy that derived from Prebish's diagnosis was the need for greater diversification of Latin America's national industries through a process of import-substitution industrialization, popularly known as ISI model. In its main outlines, the model was conceived as the successive passages from a soft or easy phase of substitution (related to the import of non-durable consumer goods) to a harder stage of substitution in the import of intermediate (durable consumer) goods and of capital (machinery and technology) and hence to "development". Accordingly, the augmentation of the aggregate value to be exchanged was considered the way to secure control of the national economy and the surplus generated therein. In doing this, the Prebisch-Singer thesis coupled industrialization, the achievement of development and national autonomy. Cristobal Kay (2010, 2) considers the dependency debate so imbricated with the *Cepalino* framework that he prefers to take both *desarrollismo* and *dependentismo* as an internal distinction within a single main current of Latin American "theories of development".

Marxist Theories of Imperialism

Among the reasons for considering dependency arguments as a different but related strand of thought is the significant influence of Marxist categories, particularly the theory of imperialism formulated above all by Vladimir Ilyich Lenin, and especially the relationship between oppressor and oppressed nations. Drawing a critical synthesis between John Hobson and Rudolf Hilferding's arguments, Lenin's (1996 [1915]) pamphlet *Imperialism, The Highest Stage of Capitalism*[1] established that there was not enough of a domestic market for the accumulation of capital in imperialist countries, hence capital sought opportunities for new investment abroad through the export of capital to colonial and semi-colonial countries. The starting point of his *Imperialism* was thus the outward movement of capital from its point of origin in imperialist countries to the colonial and semi-colonial world. Lenin identified imperialism as capitalism in its monopoly stage, in which the conditions of competition among individual capitalists have entered a new phase underlined by giant cartels that have concentrated production into the hands of a financial oligarchy. Against the reformist sector of the Second International, which considered imperialism as a policy that could simply be reversed, he argued that imperialism was a necessary historical development of capitalism and highlighted how the export of capital to foreign areas required a corresponding level of political control, in the sense that the giant cartels of finance capital carved up the world into different political spheres of influence.[2] Therefore, Lenin's argument connects imperialism and monopoly to the export of capital, the political annexation of colonies, and the outbreak of wars between competing capitalist powers.

In political terms, Lenin argued that the split in the working-class movement as a result of the collapse of the Second International was fundamentally bound up with the objective conditions of imperialism, with the development of a "labor aristocracy" (understood as a bribe of a part of the Western proletariat, especially in England and Germany) made possible by monopoly profits from imperialism. However, this new stage also contained its opposite – revolutionary opposition from the non-compromised strata of the proletariat in imperialist countries, and the national liberation struggle in the colonial and semi-colonial countries. Anti-imperialist and national liberation movements appear in this light as the dialectical opposite of monopoly and imperialism, which allowed his theory to go beyond the mere economic dimension of analysis in the recognition of renewed revolutionary subjects arising from imperialism (Anderson 1995).[3]

With the partial Stalinization of many of the Communist Parties in Latin America over the 1930s and 1940s, the official version of Marxism established that the weak conditions of the local bourgeoisie demand a national-popular and anti-imperialist alliance in order to overcome feudal social relations of production and achieve a well-defined capitalist stage, thus transforming Lenin's insights on the concrete imperialist conjuncture back into a historical teleology of sequential stages. Important exceptions to this official trend were Sergio Bagu, Luis Vitale, Caio Prado Jr., and Rodolfo Stavenhagen. This situation suffered a dramatic shift with the triumph of the Cuban Revolution and the subsequent Second Declaration from Havana, in which it was declared a Socialist revolution. In this sense, Steve Stern (1988) argues that dependency analyses emerged not only as a response to the exhaustion of the developmentalist roads and *Cepalino* concepts but also as part of the intellectual and political energies unleashed by the Cuban Revolution.

The Monthly Review School

To an important extent, the dependency debates drew upon arguments and concepts elaborated within the Monthly Review School of thought pioneered by neo-Marxist economists Paul Baran and Paul Sweezy and hosted under the journal of this name. In particular, Baran's (2010 [1957]) *The Political Economy of Growth* contributed importantly to Marxist theories of imperialism from a conception of monopoly capitalism that was contemporaneous with Prebisch in its focus on the underdeveloped world as an object of analysis. Baran argued that monopoly capitalism assures the polarity of developed and underdeveloped nations; the so-called backwardness of the latter corresponds, indeed, to a type of development fostered by capitalism and deepened by imperialism. The central mechanism of this structural unevenness is the drain of what he calls "economic surplus" from peripheral to central economies, a mechanism that reinforces the places already assigned in the world division of labor.

Replacing Marx's concept of surplus-value with the more abstract category of economic surplus, defined by Baran as the difference between total output and the socially necessary cost of producing total output (see Baran 1953; also Foster 2014), allowed this perspective to differentiate between a society's actual current output and actual current consumption versus the potential output that could be produced and the potential consumption that could be realized to satisfy the needs of society. The aim of this intervention is to highlight the part of surplus value that is actually being accumulated, while also taking account of what is not encompassed by Marx's concept of surplus-value, the output lost to the mismanagement of productive resources – that is, unemployment, unproductive labor, and excess consumption.[4] Summarizing, Baran describes an imperialist system tending not toward a homogeneous capitalist world but to the simultaneous and correlative processes of development at one pole and underdevelopment at the other.

Dependency and Its Arguments: Main Concepts and Discussions

By the early 1960s, the optimism of *Cepalino* perspectives was given way to a more pessimistic climate, in account of the by and large poor economic indicators of much of the formerly runners-up of industrialization. W. W. Rostow's (2017 [1960]) "take-off" – meaning the beginning of a modernizing trajectory toward economic growth and similar, or mirror in essence, to metropolitan countries, and that was transformed into a mantra of "non-communist" modernization theories – was not happening. This evidence gave room for the replacement of the question of development by that of dependence.

The dependency debate was also the reunion of several Latin American intellectuals and scholars who formed a new intellectual milieu in Santiago de Chile. In 1962, the Latin American and Caribbean Institute for Economic and Social Planning (ILPES in its Spanish acronym) was inaugurated in Santiago as ECLAC's "sociological complement" (Love

1996, 191). Two years later, in Brazil, a coup against Joao Goulart initiated a series of right-wing military takeovers that led many leftist politicians and intellectuals to exile, Chile being an important destination given the institutional and intellectual hub formed there. At the time, the Andean country was under an increasing climate of reforms, first with the promising but at the end of the day disappointing government of Eduardo Frei Montalva and the Christian Democracy (1964–1970), and then with Socialist politician Salvador Allende and the Popular Unity bloc coming into power by ballot six years later. The "Chilean road to socialism" was an unprecedented process of social mobilization and political radicalization fostered from below (with manifold manifestations of people's power) and above (as the formation of a political coalition declared transversally as Marxist, from its president down). It is safe to say that the dependency debate was one of the most salient paradigm-shift outcomes of this continental moment of arouse.

Holding an argument similar to that of this paper, Fernanda Beigel (2010; also 2006) offers a useful classification of the ranks of the dependency debate, making it apparent that it was more an assemblage of questions and ideas in motion than a discussion organized in definite or stable frameworks. A centripetal assemblage to be sure, as it revolved around the concept of "dependence" and took place mainly in institutional locales and academic niches. Beigel organizes the diversity of perspectives comprised in the dependency field around three main institutional frames: (1) ECLAC itself; (2) ILPES, and subsequently the Latin American Faculty of Social Sciences (FLACSO); and (3) the Centre of Socio-Economic Studies (CESO) at Universidad de Chile together with the Centre for Studies of the National Reality (CEREN) at Universidad Católica.

ECLAC was the place of the early criticism of the Prebisch-Singer thesis – say, criticism from within. Brazilian economist Celso Furtado and Chilean economists Aníbal Pinto and Osvaldo Sunkel represent a sort of internal radicalization of the ECLAC paradigm. Furtado (Furtado 1964) was among the firsts to argue that, rather than reducing it, the ISI model increased dependency. In what latter will be termed "new dependency", he argued that foreign capital (in the form of multinational corporations) takes control over local industries and thus reinforces underdevelopment. On the other hand, ILPES hosted the partnership between Chilean sociologist and historian Enzo Faletto and Brazilian sociologist Fernando H. Cardoso. The latter arrived in Chile in 1964, and a couple of months later, a significant draft of what would be *Dependency and Development in Latin America* (1979 [1969]) commenced to circulate among dependency intellectuals. Once published, it became an indisputable landmark in the debate for its combination of Marxist "structural" considerations and a Weberian focus on agency capacity within an institutional system of domination. The proposed method stressed "the socio-political nature of the economic relations of production" (1979, ix), and from the very beginning, disqualified attempts to construct a formal theory out of dependency categories.

Conversely, CESO was the place of the more radical approach to the dependency debate. Formed in 1965, the Center based on Universidad de Chile's School of Economics was rapidly filled by dependency topics at different levels of analysis, particularly from Dos Santos's creation of the Group of Dependency Research. Along with him, Orlando Caputo, Roberto Pizarro, Vania Bambirra, André Gunder Frank, Ruy Mauro Marini, and Tomas Amadeo Vasconi were part of this hub. Conversely, CEREN hosted a heterogeneous circle of intellectuals reflecting on cultural imperialism and the ideological dimensions of the condition of dependence. A well-known outcome was Ariel Dorfman and Armand Mattelart's (2019 [1971]) *How to Read Donald Duck*, which analyzes Disney's ideological naturalization of subjugation and exploitation over Latin America and the rest of the Third world. Also part of CEREN in different moments were Michele Mattelart, Paulo Freire, Hugo Zemelman, Norbert Lechner, and René Zavaleta Mercado. In October 1971, CESO co-organized the symposium "Transition to Socialism and the Chilean Experience" in collaboration with CEREN; an event in which the majority of *dependentista* intellectuals attended.

Santiago worked as the "laboratory" of the dependency hypothesis – to borrow Beigel's insightful image (2010) –, and in this sense, they were part of the momentum of Chile's discussions on the transition to socialism through a democratic process, but certainly, neither a city nor a country restricted the scope of the intellectual exchange, in which also participated names as important as Anibal Quijano, Helio Jaguaribe, Pedro Paz, Augusto Salzar Bondy, Enrique Dussel, Pablo Gonzalez Casanova, Agustin Cuevas, and Edelberto Torres-Rivas (to call out some Latin American ones), or Arghiri Emmanuel, Samir Amin, Dudley Seers, Johan Galtung, Giovanni Arrighi, and Immanuel Wallerstein (to bring names from elsewhere). There was also a Caribbean dependency theory (Girvan 2006; also Green 2001).

Although not a well-centered "paradigm" or systematic theory, what this brief survey shows is a heterogeneous intellectual assembling gathered around some intellectual and political concerns that went from the actual existence of a structural dependence (that is, an accountable and somehow measurable penetration of foreign capital and technological subordination of the periphery) to the external and internal (political, institutional, cultural) dynamics that were specifics to such international arrangements. Pivotal to the urgency of the debate were the questions on the level of generality and formalization possible for the dependency framework (i.e. the problem of transforming the dependency categories into a formal theory of capitalist underdevelopment), and its alignment with identifiable political positions, first and foremost revolutionary Marxism.

A Tale of Two Poles: On Centers and Peripheries

German-born economist Andre Gunder Frank is one of the proper names that comes to mind more quickly when referring to dependency debates"; however, his work is more related to the ideas of centers and peripheries – or alternatively metropolises and satellites – than to the specificities of the category of dependence. His name was worldwide popularized with the publication of the article "The Development of Underdevelopment" in *Monthly Review* (Frank 1966). Being himself a participant of the Monthly Review perspective, and borrowing from the conclusions drawn by Paul Sweezy in his much-discussed debate against Maurice Dobb on the primacy of "internal" versus "external" conditions for the establishment of a capitalist mode of production (Baran et al. 1961 for a view on the debate; also Sweezy 1986), it is unsurprising that Frank's main argument is elaborated from the perspective of a single and inter-connected world system wherein a chain of metropolises and satellites were unequally distributed. According to this perspective, the unequal structure of the world economy was only rendered possible insofar as the relations conditioning the underdevelopment of the periphery are profit-able for the development of the metropolis. Consequently, the interests of the latter are the freezing of the international division of labor so that peripheral economies continue to produce primary commodities.

Given this situation – Frank goes on – peripheral countries are inca-pable of recapitulating the developmental trajectory of the metropolitan ones, which makes underdevelopment a stable rather than exceptional form of participation in the international market, with basis on the absence of access to a surplus for local bourgeoisie. In a nutshell, this is the "development of underdevelopment" thesis, in which a causal or structural relationship between underdevelopment and dependency is suggested. Frank was criticized all along the *dependentista* camp by his rather loose use of concepts, historiographic methods, and eco-nomic analyses. Hinkelammert (1972) perhaps summarizes the discon-tent among dependency authors with Frank's formulations when he indicated that "the periphery" must not be taken as synonymous with "underdevelopment", and instead it becomes necessary to explain both the satellization tendency of the first industrial center toward the rest of the world and the maintenance and variations of this unbalanced global structure, giving thus room to the demand of a better conceptualization of dependency itself. Yet, even with this criticism, Frank's ideas about the inherent duality of the world capitalist system remained highly influ-ential within dependency debates.

What Is Dependency?

In a paper that has not transcended but had its influence back in the time, Tomas A. Vasconi (1969) argued that the framework of depend-ency allows social sciences to grasp centers and peripheries as part of a single capitalist structure, in which the peripheries are incorporated to the world system only as a function of the centers' own expansion. Conversely, the much-cited 1970 article "The Structure of Dependence" written by Theotonio Dos Santos summarized in a similar vein some half-decade of reflections about the subject and its centrality for a proper comprehension of the economic realities of Latin American countries. In a famous paragraph, he argued that:

> By dependence we mean a situation in which the economy of certain countries is conditioned by the development and expansion of another economy to which the former is subjected. The relation of interdependence between two or more economies, and between these and world trade, assumes the form of dependence when some countries (the dominant ones) can expand and can be self-sustaining, while other countries (the dependent ones) can do this only as a reflection of that expansion. (1970, 231)

This definition had a huge circulation but also gained criticism because of its formalism, i.e. lack of historical content (e.g. Palma 1978). Nonetheless, it helps bring to the fore the basic analytical commitments of dependency analysis. First, we have the consideration of the condition of underdevelopment neither as a belated capitalist stage nor as merely "lack" of some elements, but rather as a concrete aspect or face of the global capitalist development. In a similar vein, Hinkelammert (1972, 33) referred to "the structural presence of development's absence" as an explanation to the ongoing disadvantage of Latin America vis-à-vis Western capitalist countries. Consequently, both development and underdevelopment are redefined in terms of a relational, uneven, and combined process whose foremost dynamics are situated at the level of the international division of labor. Second, as a critique of Frank's, Dos Santos' (1970, 234) argument points out the need of a deeper consideration of the dialectics between "external" conditions and the "internal" social structures formed under dependence relationships: "the unequal and combined character of capitalist development at the international level is reproduced internally in an acute form". We are not dealing simply with processes of "satellization" – Frank's hypothesis – but with the formation of domestic structures that give internal disposition to the external impositions characteristic of the dependency condition.

The correction of Frank's schemes also helps clarify the conception of capitalism at work in dependency analysis, amounting to the specification of the dialectical – and not causal-mechanical – relations between global forces and local arrangements. While Frank's characteristic focus on market-centered exchange relations would state that Latin America has been capitalist since the sixteenth century (allegedly from the 15th century, when the region was incorporated into commercial capitalism), dependency theorists referred to the modern capitalist system only from the early 1800s on, when the post-colonial hegemony of laissez-faire policies found the newly politically independent countries in a position to assure the provision of raw materials and foodstuffs necessary to maintain the industrialization process of the metropolis. Dos Santos identifies three historical types of dependence: colonial, financial-industrial, and the new, technological-industrial one.

A more historically accounted version of the dependency hypothesis was offered by Cardoso and Faletto (1979, xviii and Chapter 3), who argued that the late-nineteenth-century economic re-articulation of the world allowed some countries to gain certain control over internal production, while others were not able to compete with foreign companies and thus became "enclave" economies. Making the case for concrete analysis (rather than an abstract theoretical formalization) of the historical formation of internal structures of exploitation and domination, they highlight that the deterioration in the prices of raw materials and foodstuffs and world-market instabilities led to the crisis of dominance in which local oligarchies were politically challenged by middle classes that therefore pressed for institutional arrangements and social mobilization; this was largely the political base for national industrialization projects (1979, Chapter 4; also Bambirra 1978, 68).

In Cardoso and Faletto (1979, 5) argument, conditions for a solid capitalist development were apparent in countries such as Argentina, Brazil, Chile, Colombia, Mexico, and Venezuela, countries of internal markets that might be further expanded and incipient industrial production of light-consuming goods, with abundant foreign trade and incentives to economic growth. The subsequent failure of the ISI model is mainly explained by what was referred to at the time as the "new character of dependence" (Cardoso and Faletto 1979, 130; also Cardoso 1972), in which, as the peripheral industrialization advances, metropolitan capitals begin to directly invest in the periphery's productive systems. In a similar argument, Osvaldo Sunkel (1972) pointed out the simultaneity of international integration and "national disintegration" that the industrialization processes bring to Latin American economies, with dramatic effects in low wages and the increasing poverty and marginalization (see also Quijano 1977).

A more Marxist-based approach was offered by Brazilian economist Ruy Mauro Marini (1977 [1972], chapter. 2), who in his magnum opus *Dialectic of Dependency* drew a distinction between two central mechanisms at the heart of a structure of dependence. The first and more commonly acknowledged one is the transference of value from peripheral to central economies by means of international trade – namely, unequal exchange. We will return to unequal exchange immediately. However, Marini points out that unequal exchange is just the most apparent feature of dependence, and that a dependent structure becomes fully expressed only in its last, most fulfilled stage, once capital has built in the peripheral country its own spheres of reproduction of the conditions for its own accumulation. It is, therefore, only partially fair to consider Marini's theorization as a mere repetition of Rosa Luxemburg's schemes of expanded reproduction of capital (which are at the basis of her theory of imperialism), as Gabriel Palma (1978, 901) does.

The central thesis here, and the one which Marini (1977, 30, 58) will be acknowledged for, is that the second, less identified feature of dependence corresponds to the presence of "the super-exploitation of the laborer" as a mechanism for the local bourgeoisie to compensate the flow of surplus-value from the periphery to the metropolis. Super-exploitation is characterized by the combination of three different mechanisms: an intensification of the labor process, the extension of the working day, and the expropriation of part of the socially necessary labor of the worker; therefore, it "tends to be expressed in the fact that the labor-power is remunerated for under its value". Marini does not clarify whether this entails a structural hindering to the extraction of relative surplus-value, or we are before a sui generis form to do so. Be that as it may, drawing upon Marx's (1976, 747–748) Chapter XXIV of *Capital, Vol. I*, indicates that the dependence condition converts part of the worker's fund of consumption into a fund for capital's accumulation. Therefore, super-exploitation lies at the basis of the impossibility to build an industrial sector and a correspondent internal market in the periphery. At a theoretical level, it demonstrates that industrialization accompanies rather than helps overcome dependence; the decoupling of Frank's conflation of satellization, underdevelopment and dependence produced an analysis in which industrialization was but another trajectory to dependence, expressed in economic imbalances and more super-exploitation. From these coordinates, Marini (1977, 81) went as far as to attempt the clarification of the "laws of development of dependent capitalism" in Latin America.

The Role of Unequal Exchange

The term "unequal exchange" has a special place in dependency debates. Although it was employed by Marx and post-Marx-Marxists long before it was popularized by the *dependentistas*,[5] and in the 1960s, its main proponent was Greek economist Arghiri Emmanuel (1972, see also 1962), who as early as in 1962 held that the international transfer of value between the core and periphery, at least since the late nineteenth century, has been linked to differential wage costs. In a perspective that will be shared (explicitly or otherwise) by most of his Latin American colleagues, he argued that Prebisch's thesis of the worsening in terms of trade is an "optical illusion" (Emmanuel 1972, xxx), that is, the latter would be the manifestation or consequence of unequal exchange.

Emmanuel's version of unequal exchange situated differential wage costs on a higher order than differences in labor productivity to the extent by which the latter is nearly equal to developed countries, while the former is unequal and forms the grounds of trade imperialism. The assumption here is that international trade operates as an equalizing mechanism for prices of production, whereby general mobility of capital exists across markets relative to immobility of labor-power. Emmanuel made an attempt to contest the Ricardarian theory of comparative advantages by asserting that, while on the one hand, the international mobility of capital generates an equalization in the rate of profit, on the other it disconnects national labor markets creating significant differences in monetary wages between developed and underdeveloped economies. This coincides with Marini's analysis, in which the main factor conditioning the unequal hierarchy of exchange is when the differential between the rewards to labor is greater than productivity (cf. Emmanuel 1972, 265; Marini 1977, Chapter 2; also Larraín 1989, 133). Therefore, this argument purports that the main mechanism of imperialism is the super-exploitation of workers in the periphery through depressing wages below the value of labor-power.

This analysis was also shared by Samir Amin – a world-renowned Marxian economist and leading theoretician of the global South. Amin agreed that capital (which is mobile) is marked by a tendency toward equalizing the rate of profit, while the remuneration of labor (which is immobile) is marked by a tendency toward inequalities across countries. Yet Emmanuel made no real effort to explain the origin of these differences in wage levels other than to attribute them to institutional factors such as the trade union power of workers in developed countries (Ricci 2016, 3). By contrast, Samir Amin elaborated a more precise line of argumentation which held that the rate of exploitation is higher in the periphery than in the core because in the latter social relations of production tend to approximate a pure capitalist form, whereas in the former, a more heterogeneous character is preserved, namely, an inflow of peasants and non-capitalist workers which tend to depress wages at costs below the value of labor-power. Under these conditions, Amin argued that ISI industrialization begins from a distorted premise in an attempt to replicate development in the core, at the expense of mass consumption for the domestic market in the periphery. According to Amin, this process will not give rise to internal demand to produce these commodities in the periphery but only reinforce underdevelopment through dependence on exports at cheap labor costs.

Dependency, Imperialism, and Marx's Law of Value

Now that we have briefly outlined the concept of unequal exchange and its importance within the dependency hypothesis, we turn to express this process in more concrete terms. We offer in this section a critique of the mechanisms pointed out by the dependency analysis, attempting at the same time to demonstrate that, despite the fact that super-exploitation may play a role in the unequal exchange, the main factor conditioning the flow of surplus-value between the core and periphery is technological competition among capitals. This demonstration corrects the logical inconsistencies of Amin and Emmanuel's models by highlighting that peripheral capitalists initiate super-exploitation, as a means to overcome technological differentials, that is, a lower level of labor productivity. By means of this critique, we advance a conception of imperialism grounded in Marx's law of value, in particular, the tendency for capitals to employ labor-saving technologies by way of competition to produce commodities with the lowest amount of socially necessary labor-time.

In all of our three models, the core appropriates surplus-value from the periphery. We start from Marx's formula of the organic composition of capital, in which (c) corresponds to constant capital (raw materials and means of production); (v) is variable capital (living labor-power in the production process expressed as the value of labor-power in the form of wages); (s) is the surplus-value (the excess value produced above the necessary labor, i.e. the time required for the reproduction of labor-power.); and (p) corresponds to the final production price. Also, ROP indicates the rate of profit (s/c+v) and RE corresponds to the rate of exploitation (s/v).

Unequal Exchange Independent of Super-Exploitation

In the first equation below, we formulate a model to represent foreign trade between the core and periphery, in which the rate of exploitation is measured in value terms and is the same in both core and periphery (s/v) = 100%, indicating thus the existence of unequal exchange without super-exploitation. Therefore, the core capitalists employ advanced technologies (80c) in order to gain an edge over their competition by reducing the time necessary to reproduce the value of labor-power (20v). In the periphery, on the other hand, capitalists employ less technology (30c) and rely on cheaper labor (70v). Hence, we arrive at

$$\text{Core} = 80c + 20v + 20s = 120v \text{ ---} \text{ROP} = 20s/(80c + 20V)$$

$$= 20\% \text{ ---} \text{RE} = 20s/20v = 100\%$$

$$\text{Periphery} = 30c + 70v + 70s = 170v \text{ ---} \text{ROP} = 70s/(30c + 70v)$$

$$= 70\% \text{ ---} \text{RE} = 70s/70v = 100\%$$

$$\text{Total} = 110c + 90v + 90s = 290v \text{ --Average ROP}$$

$$= 90s/(110c + 90v) = 45\%$$

The capitalists in the core squeeze (120v) in value out of their workers owing to a higher level of labor productivity and higher organic composition of capital corresponding to it, which enables them to produce commodities with lower units of socially necessary labor-time. Whereas, in the periphery, capitalists squeeze more value out of their workers (170v), insofar as less technology (30c) is applied owing to a lower level of labor productivity resulting in higher units of socially necessary labor-time. However, through competition on the world market, the rate of profit equalizes to form an average rate of profit of (45%) and a market price of production of (145p). Since capitalists in the core produce commodities whose individual value (120v) stands below the market price of production (145p), consequently they realize an extra surplus-value transfer of (25v). Conversely, since the individual value of commodities produced in the periphery (170v) stands above the market price of production (145p), they are unable to realize a part of their surplus value (25v), which is transferred to the core.

$$\text{Core} = 80c + 20v + 45s = 145p \text{ --Total value of 120, value transfer of 25}$$

$$\text{Periphery} = 30c + 70v + 45s = 145p \text{ --Total value of 170, value loss of 25}$$

Unequal Exchange through Super-Exploitation

The model now assumes that super-exploitation operates in regard to foreign trade, in which the rate of exploitation in the periphery = 300% versus 100% in the core. Subsequently, the value of labor-power (70v) in the periphery is decreased by half to (35v) and surplus value is increased to (105s). We now arrive at,

$$\text{Core} = 80c + 20v + 20s = 120v; \text{ROP} = 20s/(80c + 20V) = 20\%;$$

$$\text{RE} = 20s/20v = 100\%$$

$$\text{Periphery} = 30c + 35v + 105s = 170v; \text{ROP} = 105s/(30c + 35v)$$

$$= 162\%; = 105s/35v = 300\%$$

$$\text{Total} : 110c + 55v + 125s = 290v;$$

$$\text{Average ROP} = 125s/(110c + 55v) = 76\%$$

The capitalists in the periphery are driven to depress wages below the value of labor-power, in reaction to the loss of surplus-value to the core evidenced by the first model. Super-exploitation is thus put in place by the periphery as a countermeasure to the superior efficiency of technology in the core. As a result of super-exploitation, the average rate of profit has increased from (45%) to (76%) and the rate of profit in the periphery has increased from (70%) to (162%).

Core = 80c + 20v + 45s = 145p. Total value of 120, value transfer of 25

Periphery = 30c + 35v + 80s = 145p. Total value of 170, value loss of 25

It is therefore evident that super-exploitation increases the profits of both capitalists in the core and periphery, however, the wages of workers in the core remain unchanged by this process. The higher wages and social benefits of workers in the core may indirectly derive from the super-profits of the multinational corporations they work for – but that is the result of the class struggle over the share of value going to wages, not directly as a result of imperialist exploitation. Therefore, it is incorrect to maintain that capitalists in the core simply reward a part of surplus value to their workers in the form of higher wages through the super-exploitation of low-wage workers in the periphery. What determines exploitation in Marxist terms is the *ratio* between surplus value or profits and the value of labor power or wages. Therefore, what matters is whether the wages of workers in developed nations *exceed* the value they create. We are not at all suggesting that super-exploitation does not exist, but rather expressing our doubts as to the extent that it operates as the main factor of imperialism and benefits workers in developed nations.

Explaining Super-Exploitation and Imperialism

We have presented the process of unequal exchange as a function of uneven levels of labor productivity and how this procedure can be exacerbated through super-exploitation in the periphery. Nonetheless, Amin and Emmanuel argued that unequal exchange does not merely exist in traditional sectors where productivity is low but in modern industrial sectors where productivity is equal to that of the core, whereby the reward to labor is still unequal on account of super-exploitation. Let us follow this line of reasoning in the following equation:

Core = 80c + 20v + 20s = 120v; ROP = 20s/(80c + 20V) = 20%;

RE = 20s/20v = 100%

Periphery $= 80c + 20v + 60s = 160v$; ROP $= 60s/(80c + 20v) = 60\%$;

RE $= 60s/20v = 300\%$

Total $= 160c + 40v + 80s = 280v$;

Average ROP $= 80s/(160c + 40v) = 40\%$

In Marxist terms, the productivity of labor is measured from one particular sphere of production to another according to the quantity of means of production set in motion in relation to the value of labor-power in the form of wages. Therefore, in the model above, we assume capitalists in the core and periphery employ equal levels of advanced technology (80c) and an equal value of labor-power (20v). However, provided that super-exploitation exists in the periphery surplus-value is doubled (60s) resulting in a rate of exploitation $= 300\%$.

Core $= 80c + 20v + 40s = 140p$. Total value of 120, value transfer of 20

Periphery $= 80c + 20v + 40s = 140p$. Total value of 160, value loss of 20

As a result of competition in the world market, the rate of profit now equalizes to an average of (40%) and a market price of production of (140p). Therefore, as shown by the previous models, since the core produces commodities with an individual value (120v) below the market price of production (140p), they appropriate a surplus profit of (20v) from the periphery. As opposed to the periphery, which produces commodities with an individual value (160v) above the market price of production (140p) resulting in a value loss of (20v) to the core.

Further Remarks on Dependency and Imperialism

We have attempted to show that, while super-exploitation may play an important role in foreign trade, the argument constructed by Amin and Emmanuel is logically inconsistent with the reality of imperialist exploitation. Such a model suggests that super-exploitation is the main factor conditioning unequal exchange independent of technological competition. In other words, they abstract their analysis from the tendency for capitals to employ labor-saving technologies by way of competition to produce commodities with the lowest amount of labor-time socially necessary. Hence there is no motivation for capitalists in the periphery to implement super-exploitation as a means to overcome technological differentials if the productivity of labor is equal to the core. What the models demonstrate is that technologically advanced countries make a surplus-profit at the expense of technologically less-advanced countries to the extent that they can produce commodities with lower units of socially necessary labor-time. Yet given that Amin and Emmanuel ultimately ignore differences in the organic composition of capital and assume capitalists in the periphery impose super-exploitation for an unidentified reason, they fall short of formulating an actual theory of imperialism.

In light of our reading, the lens to view imperialism should be that of Marx's law of value, in which capitalism is increasingly driven into imperialist expansion as an effort to restore the rate of profitability. As seen above, the price of any given commodity generally deviates from its value, because abstract labor is measured by a social average that is always fluctuating, especially because of technological innovations. This occurs through the continual transfer of capital between spheres of production, in a process that generates rising and falling profit rates which tend to balance the rate of profit to an equal level across industries on the world-market (Marx 1981, 297). The equalization of the rate of profit across industries to form an average is simply the manner by which the surplus value extracted from workers is distributed among capitalists. The fundamental law which determines imperialist expansion is what Marx observed in *Capital, Vol. 3* as the tendency for the rate of profit to decline, determined by the *relative* diminution of the variable portion of capital in comparison with constant capital. Since capital is driven by the incessant strive to produce ever more amounts of value and surplus-value, new labor-saving technologies are applied, thereby increasing the organic composition of capital at the expense of living labor-power, the only source of value and surplus-value. Confronted with a decline in the rate of profit, on the one hand, and an overaccumulation of capital, on the other, capital is driven toward imperialist expansion as a means to overcome the breakdown tendency.

As we have written elsewhere, the dependency arguments had a tendency toward stressing the quantitative side of value – that is, the unequal hierarchy of exchange which transfers "surplus" between the core and periphery – as opposed to the qualitative side, the specific social relations which create value as such. This to a large extent is more apparent in the works of Andre Gunder Frank and Samir Amin, who understood in general the priority of social relations of production over exchange and the market, but when it came to their specific enumeration of the dynamics of capitalism, they emphasized the unequal transfer of "surplus", even to the point of conflating socialism with overcoming the anarchy of the market, and not abstract value production. This is perhaps the result of interpreting capitalism as a system external to social relations of production, and conceptualizing value and surplus-value in subjective terms (that is, the manner in which capitalists react to the law of value, i.e. their subjective search for profits). What they missed is the whole significance of Marx's analysis is that, irrespective of the subjective will of its agents, capitalist society is governed by the law of value: capitalists are a mere personification of the immanent laws of capitalist production, which operate outside their control (Dunayevskaya 1943).

Dependency Is Not a Dead Dog! As a Way of Conclusion

The dependency debates were epistemological shifting in developing a new mode of analysis within the social sciences focused on the conditions and nature of development in non-Western regions. The intellectuals who participated in this field were, almost with no exception, fully committed to leftist political projects, in a gesture that certainly defied the almost oligarchic dominance of more traditional disciplines such as economics or law, as more heterodox disciplines such as sociology and politics were being performed. The rise of a wave of civic-military dictatorships throughout Latin America put a significant number of them together first in Santiago and later in Mexico City; to no little extent, the dependency hypothesis is the child of exile's stories. The latter hosted a new shift in the social sciences toward a more academic-oriented study of "transitions to democracy". Paradoxically, this shift occurred in the 1980s during the midst of the Third World debt crisis and the new industrial division of labor, which created new forms of dependence and underdevelopment in the global South. This was the context for the surprisingly quick, and profoundly wrong, dismissal of the dependency framework altogether. Even when some of the analysis pointed precisely to stress such a trend in transnational arrangements, the more optimistic view on globalization and neo-Ricardian interdependence prevailed.

As we hope to have clarified, the flaws and shortcomings of the dependency analysis this does not diminish the enormous contribution of these debates in the sphere of economics and politics, and furthermore at the level of knowledge production as such. As Fernanda Beigel (2010) argues, the epistemological shift championed by the "dependency moment" took the form of an endogenous process of scientific paradigm-building in Latin America, reaching global-Southern dimensions (also Connell 2007). The dependency hypothesis inspired a significant turn in the imaginary of a more "autonomous" (i.e. regionally determined) production of knowledge. The influences of the dependency debates go to world-system analysis on the one hand, and to the discussions on Latin America's coloniality (e.g. Mignolo 2007, 2012; Quijano 2008), and more broadly on the project of decolonizing thought as a whole (Young 2001; Go 2013; Bhambra 2014).

Finally, dependency analysis is still very useful for observing important features of the economic performance of Latin American countries, especially in those cases in which efforts to break with forms of structural dependence have faced barriers that are intimately connected to some aspects of the arguments made by the *dependentistas*. For example, the Pink Tide movement in South America was propelled into power by a wave of social movements in opposition to the region's neoliberal governments after the exhaustion of the previous ISI model. In this wave, the Bolivarian Alliance for the Peoples of Our America (ALBA) was promoted by the more radical Pink Tide governments, with the explicit aim of overcoming historical dependent features, most importantly the terms of trade (Arellano 2009; Yaffe 2011). But once these governments came into power, they demobilized and co-opted these popular social and political mobilizations into the existing state apparatus through an acceleration of dependence on raw material exports, with the redistribution of rent from this sector of the economy being the most prominent progressive policy. Much of these policies across the region were made possible as a result of a global commodity boom – to a large extent driven by the Chinese economy – but once prices began to recede, especially since 2011, the whole project fell into shambles and hence confirming the dependency hypothesis regarding the structural factors conditioning the international division of labor.

The dependency debates were aborted, on the one hand, due to the silencing of radical thought in several countries; on the other, due to the academic subject-shifting toward democracy and the transitional process that accompanied the generalization of the neoliberal "Washington consensus" as the dominant economic doctrine across Latin America. We hope the introduction and analysis presented in this chapter to build toward a more concrete conception of the function and laws of motion of imperialism in Latin America.

Notes

1. The original Russian language title was *Imperialism: The Latest Phase of Capitalism*. This is an important distinction since the English translation incorrectly suggests that Lenin viewed imperialism as the highest or last stage of capitalism. Rather the aim of his analysis was to establish a brief purview of the political dimensions of power shaping the capitalist world-economy on the eve of the first imperialist world war.
2. Contrary to some mistaken but frequent assumptions, this reasoning does not imply that imperialism ends competition altogether; rather, competition reappears in a higher form. It is the dialectical analysis of imperialism – namely his grasp of the unity of opposites – what separated Lenin's theory to fellow Bolshevik Nikolai Bukharin who argued imperialism and monopoly had replaced competition or Karl Kautsky who reduced imperialism to a mere policy of finance capital that led to the annexation of agrarian lands by industrial capital. For Lenin, imperialism reflects a transformation into opposite and thus shows how the competition engendered by monopoly capitalism has the economic effect of "sharpening class antagonisms, by worsening the conditions of the masses through trusts and high costs of living", while the political effect of, "the growth of militarism, and frequent wars which intensify national oppression and colonial plunder" (1916).

3. There are some major weaknesses to Lenin's theory of imperialism. The one we need to highlight here is that Lenin failed to see imperialism as a counteracting factor to the tendency for the rate of profit to decline, in which capitalism is increasingly driven into imperialist expansion as an effort to restore the rate of profitability. This is because like many of the Marxists of his generation, Lenin's economic writings, to a large extent, focused on the sphere of circulation through the prism of *Capital, Vol. II*. In this regard, one of the main problems with Lenin's theory of imperialism is that it failed to draw a connection between imperialism and the law of value, that is, the tendency toward the endless augmentation of value and surplus-value.

4. For Baran and Sweezy, the capitalist society organizes existing productive resources in a wasteful manner to the extent that total output and distribution among consumption are regulated by the anarchic character of exchange. This analysis suggests that the contradictions of capitalism arise from a lack of effective demand (the inability to absorb or utilize actual surplus) and socialism as a state-planned economy (reutilizing potential surplus to satisfy the consumption requirements of society). It is equally true that under so-called "monopoly capitalism", profit is expressed as the part of the labor process in which surplus-value or surplus labor is added to a commodity above the necessary labor, i.e. the time required for the reproduction of labor-power. Therefore, Baran and Sweezy found it vital to develop the term "surplus", that is, a measure of wasted output insofar as their theoretic position holds that the aim of capitalist production is consumption as an end in itself.

5. Marx's writings conveyed the importance of foreign trade as a means for advanced countries to exploit less-advanced countries; see for instance Chapter 20 of *Theories of Surplus Value* (Marx 1972), entitled "Disintegration of the Ricardian School", where the international effects of the law of value are highlighted. Moreover, in Chapter 14, "Counteracting Factors" of *Capital, Vol. 3*, Marx (1981) argues that foreign trade acts as a countervailing tendency for the rate of profit to fall. In addition, Marxist economist Henryk Grossman (1992 [1929]) developed a theory of unequal exchange in his book *The Law of Accumulation and Breakdown of the Capitalist System* well before the concept was taken up by the dependency debates.

Bibliography

Anderson, K. (1995). *Lenin, Hegel, and Western Marxism: A Critical Study*. Urbana, IL: University of Illinois Press.

Arellano, F. G. (2009). Nacimiento, evolución y perspectivas de la alianza bolivariana para los pueblos de nuestra América [Origins, evolution, and perspectives of the Bolivarian Alliance for Peoples of Our America]. ILDIS-FES. Retrieved from https://library.fes.de/pdf-files/bueros/quito/06815.pdf

Bambirra, V. (1978). *Teoría de la dependencia : una anticrítica* [Dependency Theory: An Anti-Critique]. Mexico City: Ediciones Era.

Baran, P. A. (1953). Economic Progress and Economic Surplus. *Science & Society* 17(4).

_____(2010). *The Political Economy of Growth*. New York: Monthly Review Press.

Baran, P. A., Bettelheim, C. O., Dobb, M., Galbraith, J. K., Kronrod, Y. A., Strachey, J., Sweezy, P., Tsuru, S. (1961). *Has Capitalism Changed? An International Symposium on the Nature of Contemporary Capitalism.* Tokyo: Iwanami Shoten.

Beigel, F. (2006). Vida, muerte y resurrección de las "teorías de la dependencia" [Life, Death, and Resurrection of "Dependency Theories"] (287–326). In *Crítica y teoría en el pensamiento social latinoamericano* [Criticism and Theory in Latin American Social Thought], edited by B. Levy. Buenos Aires: CLACSO.

_____(2010). Dependency Analysis: The Creation of New Social Theory in Latin America (189–200). In *The ISA Handbook on Diverse Sociological Traditions*, edited by S. Patel. London: SAGE.

Bhambra, G. K. (2014). *Connected Sociologies.* London: Bloomsbury Publishing.

Birkan, A. Ö. (2015). A Brief Overview of the Theory of Unequal Exchange and Its Critiques. *International Journal of Humanities and Social Science* 5(4).

Cardoso, F. (1972). Dependent Capitalist Development in Latin America. *New Left Review* 1(74).

Cardoso, F., Faletto, E. (1979). *Dependency and Development in Latin America.* Berkeley and London: University of California Press.

Chilcote, R. H. (1974). Dependency: A Critical Synthesis of the Literature. *Latin American Perspectives* 1(1).

_____(1982). *Dependency and Marxism: Toward a Resolution of the Debate.* Epping: Bowker.

Connell, R. (2007). *Southern Theory: The Global Dynamics of Knowledge in Social Science.* Inglaterra: Polity.

Domingues, J. M. (2011). Revisiting Dependency and Development in Latin America. *Ciência & Trópico* 35(2). Retrieved from https://periodicos.fundaj.gov.br/CIC/article/view/905

Dorfman, A., Mattelart, A. (2019). *How to Read Donald Duck: Imperialist Ideology in the Disney Comic.*

Dos Santos, T. (May 1970). The Structure of Dependence. *The Latin American Economic Review*, Eighty-Second Annual Meeting of the American Economic Association 60(2).

Dunayevskaya, R. (1943). A Restatement of Some Fundamentals of Marxism against "Pseudo-Marxism". Retrieved from https://www.marxists.org/archive/dunayevskaya/works/1943/reification.htm

Emmanuel, Arghiri (1962) Échange inégal. In *Echange inégal et politique de développement*, Arghiri Emmanuel and Charles Bettelheim. Paris: Ecole Pratique des Hautes Etudes. Centre d'étude de planification socialiste.

_____(1972). *Unequal Exchange: A Study of the Imperialism of Trade.* London: New Left Books.

Foster, J. B. (2014). *The Theory of Monopoly Capitalism.* New York: Monthly Review Press.

Frank, A. G. (1966). The Development of Underdevelopment. *Monthly Review* 18(4).

Furtado, C. (1964). *Development and Underdevelopment.* Berkeley: University of California Press.

Girvan, N. (2006). Caribbean Dependency Thought Revisited. *Canadian Journal of Development Studies/Revue canadienne d'études du développement* 27(3).

Go, J. (2013). *Postcolonial Sociology.* Bingley: Emerald Group Publishing Limited.

Green, C. (2001). Caribbean Dependency Theory of the 1970s Revisited: A Historical-Materialist-Feminist Revision. In *New Caribbean Thought: A Reader*, edited by B. Meeks, L. Folke. Kingston: University of the West Indies Press.

Grigera, J. (2015). Conspicuous Silences: State and Class in Structuralist and Neostructuralist Thought (193–210). In *Crisis and Contradiction. Marxist Perspectives on Latin America in the Global Political Economy*, edited by S. J. Spronk, J. Webber. Leiden and Boston: Brill.

Grossman, H. (1992). *The Law of Accumulation and Breakdown of the Capitalist System: Being Also a Theory of Crises*. London: Pluto.

Hinkelammert, F. J. (1972). *Dialéctica del desarrollo desigual* [Dialectics of Uneven Development]. Valparaiso and Chile: Ediciones Universitarias de Valparaiso, Universidad Católica de Valparaiso, Centro de Estudios de la Realidad Nacional, Universidad Católica de Chile.

Hirschman, A. O. (1971). *A Bias for Hope: Essays on Development and Latin America*. New Haven: Yale University Press.

Kay, C. (2010). *Latin American Theories of Development and Underdevelopment*. New York: Routledge.

Larraín, J. (1989). *Theories of Development: Capitalism, Colonialism and Dependency*. Cambridge: Polity.

Lenin, V. I. (1916). The Socialist Revolution and the Right of Nations to Self-Determination. Retrieved from https://www.marxists.org/archive/lenin/works/1916/jan/x01.htm

———(1996). *Imperialism: The Highest Stage of Capitalism. A Popular Outline*. London and Junius: Pluto.

Love, J. L. (1996). *Crafting the Third World: Theorizing Underdevelopment in Rumania and Brazil*. Stanford, CA: Stanford University Press.

Marini, R. M. (1977). *Dialéctica de la dependencia* [Dialectics of Dependency]. Mexico City: Ediciones Era.

Marx, K. (1972). *Theories of Surplus Value*. London: Lawrence and Wishart.

———(1976). *Capital: A Critique of Political Economy. Volume One*. London: Penguin Books & New Left Review.

———(1981). *Capital: A Critique of Political Economy. Volume Three*. London: Penguin & New Left Review.

Mignolo, W. (2007). Introduction. Coloniality of Power and De-Colonial Thinking. *Cultural Studies* 21(2–3).

———(2012). *Local Histories/Global Designs: Coloniality, Subaltern Knowledges, and Border Thinking*. Pbk Reissue with a New Preface. Princeton, NJ: Princeton University Press.

Munck, R. (1984). *Politics and Dependency in the Third World: The Case of Latin America*. Jordanstown, Newtonabbey, and Co. Antrim: Ulster Polytechnic.

Palma, G. (1978). Dependency: A Formal Theory of Underdevelopment or a Methodology for the Analysis of Concrete Situations of Underdevelopment? *World Development* 6(7–8).

Prebisch, R. (1950). The Economic Development of Latin America and Its Principal Problems. United Nations. Retrieved from https://repositorio.cepal.org//handle/11362/29973.

Prebisch, R. et al. (1969). *El pensamiento de la CEPAL* [The Thought of ECLAC]. Santiago de Chile: Editorial Universitaria.

Quijano, A. (1977). *Imperialismo y "marginalidad" en America Latina* [Imperialism and Marginality in Latin America]. Lima: Mosca Azul editores.

————(2008). Coloniality of Power, Eurocentrism, and Social Classification. In *Coloniality at Large. Latin America and the Postcolonial Debate*, edited by M. Moraña, E. Dussel, C. Jauregui. Durham and London: Duke University Press.

Ricci, A. (2016). Unequal Exchange in International Trade: A General Model. Working Papers Series in Economics, Mathematics and Statistics, 16/05, Urbino: University of Urbino.

Rostow, W. W. (2017). *The Stages of Economic Growth: A Non-Communist Manifesto*. Eastford, CT: Martino Fine Books.

Singer, H. W. (1949). Economic Development in Underdeveloped Countries. *Social Research* 16(1).

Stern, S. J. (1988). Feudalism, Capitalism, and the World-System in the Perspective of Latin America and the Caribbean. *The American Historical Review* 93(4).

Sunkel, O. (1972). *Capitalismo transnacional y desintegración nacional en América Latina* [Transnational Capitalism and National Disintegration in Latin America]. Buenos Aires: Ediciones Nueva Visión.

Sweezy, P. M. (1986). Feudalism-to-Capitalism Revisited. *Science & Society* 50(1).

Toye, J. F. J., Toye, R. (2003). The Origins and Interpretation of the Prebisch-Singer Thesis. *History of Political Economy* 35(3).

Vasconi, T. A. (1969). De la dependencia como una categoría básica para el análisis del desarrollo latinoamericano [On Dependence as a Basic Category for the Analysis of Latin American Development]. In *Hacia una crítica de las interpretaciones del desarrollo latinoamericano* [Toward a Criticism of the Intepretations of Latin American Development], edited by T. A. Vasconi, C. Lessa. Caracas: Centro de Estudios del Desarrollo/Universidad Central de Venezuela.

Ward, J. (2004). *Latin America: Development and Conflict since 1945*. London: Routledge. Retrieved from http://public.eblib.com/choice/publicfullrecord. aspx?p=200420

Yaffe, H. (2011). The Bolivarian Alliance for the Americas: An Alternative Development Strategy. *International Journal of Cuban Studies* 3(2/3).

Young, R. (2001). *Postcolonialism: An Historical Introduction*. Oxford: Blackwell.

10 The Transnational Endeavor of ECLAC for the Latin American Development

Veridiana Domingos Cordeiro

Introduction

In a Mexican expedition in 1862, Napoleon Bonaparte III created the term "Latin America" to identify the homogeneity among the Iberian countries in America, which he wanted to conquer over the Spanish crown (Morse 1988). From an external view, it was easier to draw this unity. However, from inside, Latin America could not consolidate this "fictitious" unity because each people were fighting for their independence. Despite the term "Latin America" being created by a European in the 19th century, it magnetized ideas of a common identity among the region's countries that came to flourish in the further century. At the turn of the 20th century, on the one hand, Latin America was obsessed with modernization; on the other hand, it was concerned with nationalism. Many intellectual contradictions emerged at this time, and the racial richness of Latin America became a threat to its development. The Latin American cultural melting pot, at this point, was cooking ideas such as the inferiority of mestizos concerning the "pure races". These ideas took the heart of the Latin American intelligentsia. For example, in Brazil, authors such as Nina Rodrigues considered that the miscegenation (white, black, and indigenous people) would hinder the country's cultural and biological development (Cordeiro and Neri 2019). These positivist approaches (with evolutionist and social Darwinist influences) fall apart during the further decades, and the valorization of the miscegenation spread among the intellectuals. The essayist Gilberto Freyre (1900–1987), for example, stood for the valorization of the mixed racial relationships, arguing that Brazil had a real racial democracy (Freyre 2010). Although the valorization of miscegenation proved to be a theoretical statement and the racial democracy was nothing but a mere "myth" (Fernandes 1965), the social and cultural domains were still at the center of the modernization debate in the 1950s.

From the 1950s onward, the modernization debate focused on the economic domain. At that time, the rural world was deemed as backwardness, and the urban world became the target to be pursued. The

DOI: 10.4324/9781003045632-11

"new", expressed both in the culture (in movements, such as "Bossa Nova"[1] and "Cinema Novo"[2]) and the economy (such as the "Plan of Goals" by Juscelino Kubitschek[3]), flooded not only the Brazilian but also the Latin American intelligentsia as a whole. In what follows, progress and modernization started to work in order to overcome the underdevelopment. Instead of "underdeveloped", "developing" started to be used to characterize countries that had the potential to become industrialized, such as the Latin American ones. Most of these economic ideas and theories were developed by the Economic Commission for Latin America (ECLAC/CEPAL in Spanish and Portuguese), a United Nations body created in 1948 and headquartered in Santiago de Chile. ECLAC had considerable relevance to Latin America's economic ideas and policies during the second half of the 20th century, mainly because it was one of the few times Latin America gathered together to think about issues regarding the region. Unlike today, in its first phase, ECLAC worked more as a school of thought than a multilateral international body. This first phase was crucial for academia (esp. Sociology and Economy), and it deserves to be revisited by highlighting aspects of its legacy. The first phase of ECLAC broke with the dominant economic approach of that time, being a huge innovation in the economic domain. At odds with the dominant economic approach, the arguments elaborated by ECLAC in its first decades marked its historical role of paying attention to the structural and historical condition of Latin America, which would not be merely overcome by the free regulation of the markets. ECLAC has been positioning itself in a different way comparing to its historical arguments lately. ECLAC works less as a "school of thought" (as it did during the 1950s to 1970s) nowadays. Instead, it works as a multilateral organization with a different theoretical and practical orientation, accepting the idea of development as an outcome of the market operation (Almeida Filho and Corrêa 2011). In this manner, the article provides an overview of how ECLAC emerged in the Latin American scenario, its original arguments, and its legacy to Brazilian intellectuals.

An Overview on ECLAC

Right after World War II, the United Nations set an economic commission to plan the long-run development of Europe under the supervision of the Swedish sociologist and economist Gunnar Myrdal and the Hungarian economist Nicholas Kaldor. The Latin American countries (esp. Mexico and Chile) have also pushed the UN to create a commission dedicated to Latin America. Despite the contrary position of the United States (which was trying to strengthen the OAS, Organization of American States), the UN ended creating an economic commission for Latin America. In 1948, the Economic Commission for Latin America and the Caribbean (ECLAC) was settled by the United Nations Economic and Social Council in Santiago de Chile[4] to investigate the development and promote economic cooperation among its members. After WWII, the debate on the underdevelopment of the "peripheral" countries emerged. Topics such as "national security" and "nuclear weapons" left room for topics not deemed as "high politics" so far. For understanding the situation of these countries, the United Nations created a temporary observatory focused on economic issues. Thus, ECLAC emerged as a way to put forth ideas regarding the cooperation and industrial-technological development of Latin American countries to ensure that they become emergent potencies. The commissions were temporary and had one year to furnish the first economic overview analysis of the region. After that period, ECLAC was permanently settled (because of the suggestion of the Chilean UN delegate Hernán Santa Cruz), and it has been working for the past 70 years to analyze the underdevelopment of the Latin American economies.

The unique and privileged group of intellectuals which formed ECLAC at the first moment lighten the future steps taken by the institution. The most important economist and the first head of the project was the Argentinian economist Raúl Prebisch. He took over ECLAC's secretary in 1950 and directed it until 1963.[5] Prebisch was in charge of assembling a qualified team, and he did it by recruiting young and talented economists such as the Chilean economist Aníbal Pinto Santa Cruz; the Chilean economist Osvaldo Sunkel; the Chilean sociologist Medina Echavarría, the Luso-Brazilian economist Maria Conceição Tavares, and the Brazilian economist Celso Furtado. Likely, Furtado excelled at the others at the expense of some conflicts with Prebisch and his consequent withdrawal of ECLAC. Prebisch was an admirable leader who could articulate institutions, movements, and thoughts (Dosman 2012). After his period as General Secretary of UNCTAD (United Nations Conference of Trade and Development), Prebisch took over the Latin American and Caribbean Institute for Economic and Social Planning (ILPES), a permanent body of ECLAC to support the Latin American countries with planning and public administration through training, advisory services, and research (Jackson and Blanco 2020). As ILPES was part of ECLAC, Prebish remained as an advisor to ECLAC. Later, in the 1970s, Prebisch was editor of ECLAC Review for ten years, when he passed away.

In the next decades, ECLAC reviewed its arguments and positions many times. It might be worthwhile to note that all of them were trying to make sense of Latin American issues. Thus, its legacy for economic policies and academia was primarily oriented to Latin America. At the outset of ECLAC, a real school of thought was formed, providing a unique interpretation for the development of Latin America, which was opposed to the dominant economic view from that time (Bielschowsky 1998). The dominant view understood that the expansion of productive activities would overcome the differences regarding development. Thus, underdeveloped countries were just some steps behind the developed economies. As we will see later, contrarywise, ECLAC argued that the international division of labor after WWII structured a condition of underdevelopment that was beyond the production capacity because it was based on the terms of trade between countries. This way, the State would be crucial to regulate this situation, given that the market would not do it for itself. This rough idea drove many theories, studies, and pubic policies.

ECLAC's arguments evolved across time to adjust itself to the new economic and political scenarios. ECLAC has suffered across the decades due to the dictatorships in Latin America; thus, it started to furnish new solutions for new problems. In 1980, the Commission had to shed light on new paths and assume the new globalized situation. ECLAC focused deeper on the technical progress and the international competition, which had been a claim since the 1950s. This new approach proposed by ECLAC was primarily based on the concept of systemic competitivity by the Chilean economist Fernando Fajnzylber (1988). During the 2000s, ECLAC started to work more as a multilateral body than a school of thought. ECLAC also furnished new arguments behind the State's emphasis and left the room for the interpretations and policies based on the action of markets.

ECLAC Economic Arguments for Interpreting Development

One may name the "ECLAC school of thought" as a set of socio-economic theories and studies first developed at ECLAC that followed the original ideas of Raúl Prebisch. The ECLAC school of thought began with identifying and cracking the puzzle that was the common economic reality of the Latin American countries of the 1950s. After the Crash of 1929, the primary good importation model collapsed because the external demand plummeted. The high prices of the imported goods appeared to be a long-term tendency and not only an outcome of the crisis. This way, the primary commodities increasingly sloped up relative to the price of the manufactured goods. The economies based on commodities exportation (such as the Latin American economies) should sell much more to buy/import the same number of products. In what follows, Prebisch identified four main problems in the Latina American economies: a.) the necessity of protecting the domestic industry; b.) high levels of unemployment because of the low foreign demand; c.) structural unbalance of the Balance of Payments because of the deterioration of the terms of trade; d.) an economy based on specialized primary goods.

The orthodox economy's general interpretation laid on the idea that development follows phases. Once the national economies expanded their productive activities, they would achieve new steps of development. This way, these problems Latin America was facing were the consequence of limited production capacity. Prebisch (and ECLAC) used a historical deductive method to understand the development issue in the region. Prebisch developed a train of thought within the economy known as "Latin American Structuralism", which had significant consequences and followers. Most of these ideas are gathered in the book *El desarrollo económico de la América Latina y algunos de sus principales problemas* (1949) [The economic development of Latin America and some of its main issues]. At odds over orthodox economic ideas, Latin American structuralism stuck to the strategies for developing Latin American countries focusing on the power of the State. Prebisch was deeply influenced by John Maynard Keynes's ideas, even though he developed a theory utterly different from the European and North American thoughts. His foremost claim regards the lower Latin American average income compared to developed countries. He divided the countries based on their economic aspects between two groups: the core (the industrialized countries) and periphery (the non-industrialized countries). Both groups had a subordinated relationship in which the periphery should attend to the necessities of the core. Instead of transferring the core's productivity to the periphery, the periphery transferred most of its productivity to the core. That is, the price of the primary goods produced in the periphery was always devalued. Contrariwise, the prices of the industrialized goods produced in the core have never stopped increasing. To overcome this condition, Prebisch believed that Latin American countries should increase labor productivity to withhold income. The point is that this situation was structural and beyond the peripheral countries because there was a continued loss in international trade, which harms the peripheral countries. This structural situation lay on the unequal international trade in which the peripheral countries were restricted to import manufactured goods and export commodities. Thus, local conjectures or the mere evolution of prices could not explain the disadvantage between the core and the periphery. Instead, it was an outcome of trading capitalism that bounded the homogeneous industrialized core countries to the heterogeneous and specialized periphery. A possible expansion of the productive activities in a specialized economy would lead to a wider gap of development because the terms of trade would increasingly deteriorate. The economic condition would never improve because the Latin American underdevelopment is part of a specific historical condition. It is worth emphasizing that ECLAC's arguments are not the same as those of the Theories of Imperialism, which stated that the inequality and dependency between core-periphery was a mere political-economic imposition from the core to the periphery. In this view, the dependency condition would be immutable. Nevertheless, the solution would emerge, for instance, with a revolution, such as the proposed by socialism. From these problems, the "ECLAC school of thought" synthetized a developmental approach that praised industrialization as capable of substituting the importations and national state interventionism for work on the backwardness of industrial technology.

Prebisch's structuralism was more sophisticated than that. He understood that a process of development has a crucial element: productivity gains, which are impossible without scientific and technological development, and capital accumulation. Prebisch also understood that, on the one hand, the classical theory would not work because the labor's union of the industrialized countries increasingly has been holding the domestic product, and the State wanted more taxes to build more public services. On the other hand, the agricultural exportation economies of the peripheral countries were limiting and deforming. For Prebisch, the way to solve this contradiction is the State's domain. Once the market could not self-regulate the accumulation capital, the State should do it. Instead of channeling the production for the foreign market, the State should support the market to strengthen the domestic production to the domestic market itself. For that, the State would promote domestic and foreign investments through an accurate public policy plan. After that, the Import Substitution Industrialization (ISI) is the proposal of a trade and economic policy that replaces imports with domestic production. This strategy would avert the dependency condition by locally producing industrialized goods in peripheral countries. For implementing such a model, the State should establish public companies to protect the nation against the external market. By doing that, the State assures the accumulation of capital inside the country. The State is also in charge of regulating the exchange rate and increase the technical coefficient to promote productivity.

His central thesis and his proposals were correct; however, he dismissed the structural heterogeneity of the Latin American countries because they are different regarding (i) size, (ii) wealth, (iii) productive matrix, and (iv) actual insertion in the globalization process. Even though his economic matrix influenced other intellectuals working at ECLAC, they were in charge of honing and complementing his arguments by adding other perspectives and aspects. Next, we discuss how these economic ideas on development were already being disseminated in other intellectual spaces in Brazil and how they were hefted and put forth by two influential Brazilian intellectuals.

The ECLAC's Thinking by Brazilian Intellectuals: Cardoso's Sociology and Furtado's Economy

ECLAC's thinking had a significant impact in Latin American in the 1950s and 1960s, both in public policies and academia. Here we will highlight two Brazilian scholars who worked on and put forward

ECLAC's. In the 1950s, Brazil was already going through a promotion of development much influenced by ECLAC. Juscelino Kubitschek (Brazil's president between 1956 and 1961) drew a plan, based on ECLAC's studies, for overcoming the economic backwardness, called the "Plan of Goals", the motto of which was "development of 50 years in 5 years". ECLAC also signed a cooperation agreement to join a study group to support the *Banco Nacional de Desenvolvimento Econômico* (BNDES) [National Bank for Economic Development] – a federal body established in 1952 to obtain and parse out economic data and prepare public policy proposals.

ECLAC also had a reasonable influence and synergy with Brazilian academic institutions, e.g. The *Instituto Brasileiro de Estudos Sociais e Políticos* (IBESP) [Brazilian Institute for Social and Political Studies] and the *Instituto Superior de Estudos Brasileiros* (ISEB) [Superior Institute for Brazilian Studies]. Those were institutions where ideas related to national developmental projects could flourish. Both institutes assumed a similar perspective to ECLAC. They believed that the State should be the principal agent for promoting both economic development and democracy. There must happen for such the population's integration by unions and a constant process of industrialization.

Such requirements lifted nationalism as a political ideology deemed as capable of overcoming the forces of backwardness and people's exploitation. Although both institutions followed a nationalist path in consonance with ECLAC, they served much more to convince groups to struggle for a new social reality (Bresser-Pereira 2005) than constituted a robust theoretical framework. In this regard, ISEB rejected the neutral position of science, esp. Social Sciences, which should support activism and be politically engaged. ISEB and IBESP had a more potent political claim compared to ECLAC's propositions.

From the 1950s onward, Latin American in general, and Brazil were marked by an engaged *intelligentsia*. The emergence of a common set of issues led to an exchange between different professionals and intellectuals from Latin American countries. Besides that, the ongoing process of modernization drove the development of Sociology as a scientific discipline. At that time, Sociology in Brazil got into its "golden era", when the discipline could finally be recognized and institutionalized (Cordeiro and Neri 2019). At that point, the Brazilian Sociology of Development was highly influenced by ECLAC's thinking. The idea of development turned to be interpreted under the idea of "social change". Sociologists wanted to understand the social conditions of development as resistances to change from the archaic to the modern. In what follows, social problems, such as personalism and patrimonialism, explain the challenges and differences in the development stages of these countries.

Such requirements lifted nationalism as a political ideology deemed as capable of overcoming the forces of backwardness and people's exploitation. Although both institutions followed a nationalist path in consonance with ECLAC, they served much more to convince groups to struggle for a new social reality (Bresser-Pereira 2005) than constituted a robust theoretical framework. In this regard, ISEB rejected the neutral position of science, esp. Social Sciences, which should support activism and be politically engaged. ISEB and IBESP had a more potent political claim compared to ECLAC's propositions.

From the 1950s onward, Latin American, in general, and Brazil were marked by an engaged *intelligentsia*. The emergence of a common set of issues led to an exchange between different professionals and intellectuals from Latin American countries. Besides that, the ongoing process of modernization drove the development of Sociology as a scientific discipline. At that time, Sociology in Brazil got into its "golden era", when the discipline could finally be recognized and institutionalized (Cordeiro and Neri 2019). At that point, the Brazilian Sociology of Development was highly influenced by ECLAC's thinking. The idea of development turned to be interpreted under the idea of "social change". Sociologists wanted to understand the social conditions of development as resistances to change from the archaic to the modern. In what follows, social problems, such as personalism and patrimonialism, explain the challenges and differences in the development stages of these countries.

Two prominent intellectuals brought to Brazil and put forth many ideas on development after working on ECLAC during the 1950s-1960s: the sociologist and former Brazil's President Fernando Henrique Cardoso (1931-present) and the Argentinian historian and economist Enzo Faletto (1935–2003). They enriched ECLAC's ideas with a sociological approach. Faletto was involved with Medina Echavarría, a Spanish sociologist who introduced a sociological perspective into ECLAC (Jackson and Blanco 2020) focused on the differences among the Latin American countries ignored by Prebisch so far. Cardoso worked at ILPES (as aforementioned, an ECLAC's institute for researching and training) during his exile in the 1960s.[6] Before that, he was a professor at the University of São Paulo, linked to Professor Florestan Fernandes, who had a contrary position to the Marxist thinking present at ISEB at that time. While the interpretation advocated by ISEB and ECLAC was the national-developmental of Brazil was closely tied to the idea of national revolution, Florestan Fernandes' sociological school was closer to one of the three versions of the dependency theory: the associated dependency version. Whereas the ISEB group was placed within the State's apparatus and was not concerned with the empirical research, Florestan's group adopted a cosmopolitan and anti-dualistic viewpoint that emphasized class struggle by rejecting the possibility of national pacts. Much of this approach marks Cardoso's interpretation of development.

During the period Cardoso spent at ILPES, he and Faletto wrote a book of the uttermost importance for Sociology, *Dependência e*

*Desenvolvimento na América Latina: Ensaio de interpretação soci-
ológica* [Dependency and development in Latin America: essay of
sociological interpretation] (1969). In this book, many ideas brought
from the University of São Paulo by Cardoso could be better developed and expressed. Cardoso and Faletto discussed the differences
regarding the economic systems of each country and its socio-political
contexts. Although most Latin American countries had some common
economic aspects inherited by the colonization, they had specific political processes of Independence and Nation-State's formation during the
19th century (Jackson and Blanco 2020).

They furnished an analysis that considered each country's characteristics, stressing out the domestic aspects and how they interplayed with
the "core countries". Throughout the study, they highlighted the political and historical elements to understand how the peripheral and core
countries had been differently constituted. They classified two modes
of insertion of the Latin American countries in the international system: (i) when production for exportation was controlled by the domestic
producers or (ii) when the foreign capital controlled the domestic production. Both are cases of inevitable dependency. The dependency was not
a mere external imposition, rather the outcome of the interplay between
internal and external factors. They concluded that, in general, domestic
production was controlled by domestic producers. The Latin American
middle classes just benefited from the exchange dynamics of internal and
external factors when they used the State as a collector and redistributor
of the taxes. Thus, the workers depended on the owners, who could later
accumulate capital and diversify the industrial production. The domestic
accumulation and the diversification of the production were keys for the
development. From that, Cardoso and Faletto drew a new horizon for
the possibility of economic growth of the dependent countries.

From the 1960s onward, one observes the tendency of association
between domestic capital and foreign capital for the local industry and
services. The foreign capital in the industrial investment was prominent, esp. in Brazil and Mexico. This new form of "dependency" would
be further known as "globalization". In this situation, the domestic
market grew because of the external capital invested in producing non-
exportable goods. Thus, the peripheral countries could keep growing if
they reach the international market with manufactured goods. At odds
over the previous ECLAC arguments, Cardoso and Faletto believed that
the economic growth of the periphery would come from the external
market instead of the domestic market growth.

Cardoso and Faletto focused on the cases of their native countries,
Brazil and Argentina, by directly comparing them. Both economies are
based on the production and exportation of commodities and livestock.
From an economic standpoint, the outperformance of Brazil compared
to Argentina would be explained through the size of its productive

capacity. However, Cardoso and Faletto stressed the political aspects acknowledging that Brazil had a nationalist government during Getúlio Vargas' administration[7] which highly invested in the national industry, allowing economic growth.

The book became a reference for the theory of dependency. Because it foresaw the possibility of development even in a condition of dependency in the academic environment, Latin American dependency was deemed immutable and structural. Moreover, the only way to overcome it would be through a socialist revolution. Contrariwise, Cardoso and Faletto understood that the dependency condition does not hinder the transformation, which is possible through State's investment in education to build a diversified industry at a level to compete with the core countries.

Their theory spread out over Latin America; it was very important for the Sociology of Development and still had commonalities with the ECLAC perspective – esp. in avoiding the mechanical transposition of existing theories (Faletto 1996). The main difference compared to ECLAC's approach was the attention given to the variability of growth opportunities among the peripheral countries. As they focused on the domestic factors instead of the external factors, Cardoso and Faletto could better understand that the conditions of growth in Latin America depended on the variability of the national autonomy, the role of the State in charge of development, and the general conditions of capitalism.[8]

In the 1960s, the economic debate on development was also heated in Brazil, and ECLAC was in its center. ECLAC organized some courses of planning and economic development in Brazil in 1965, and former members disseminated and debated its ideas. Celso Furtado was one of them. He was in charge of developing the *Plano Trienal* [Triennial Plan], a plan of economic development deployed in 1963. The plan was based on the principle of progressive import substitution, blaming the rise of prices on the Brazilian economy's structural imbalances.

Although the industrialization project proposed by ECLAC has worked during the 1950s and early 1960s, it fizzled out during the late 1960s. The region witnessed the exhaustion of the process of industrialization. Marginalization and unemployment started to increase over Latin America, and industrialization seemed to be not enough to overcome the underdevelopment. In the same way, Furtado understood what Cardoso and Faletto did, i.e. the underdevelopment relied on other aspects other than economic ones.

Furtado assumed a methodological basis dialectics, as proposed by Karl Marx. It means that he considers the antagonistic forces of relations of production within the historic social-economic development and the relationship between infrastructure and superstructure. As Furtado (1964, 19) points out, "whenever technology advances and material bases develop, all other elements will be called upon adjustment". In this sense, the author concludes that changes in the social structure (superstructure) are conditioned to changes in the economic structure (infrastructure). Therefore, economic development must also be understood as a process of social change in which human needs are achieved through changes in the production system resulting from technological innovations. Bearing in mind that technological innovations cause an increase in the economic surplus and can be used to expand the capacity of production or in the immediate improvement of social well-being, the excess appropriation mechanism itself derives from social conflict. More precisely, as titled by Marx, it results in the class struggle. According to Furtado (1964), such a conflict does not cause economic development to be stopped, but it acts as an engine of capitalism.

The pressure from workers who wanted to increase their participation in the socio-economic development outcome does not compromise the performance of capitalists under penalty of reducing their savings since the capitalists can counterattack with the use of technological innovations capable of compensating the margin for wage increases. Therefore, the class struggle fosters innovation esp. technical and technological advancements. Core countries were quick to notice the benefits of this conflict, allowing this process to be institutionalized with unions and other mechanisms. As a result, the pressure for higher wages and the demand for less workload by the working class required an improvement in the innovation process. For Furtado, being in charge of technical progress is of the utmost importance. Since underdeveloped/peripheral countries consume technology from core countries, the former countries suffer from the problem of dealing with inherited structures. In other words, since the process of peripheral industrialization occurred late and without the total elimination of the pre-existing economic sector, the adaptation of the new (technological) process becomes a complex issue. These countries ended up with a dual structure in which the deployment of technological processes leads to the labor-saving mechanism, which creates an obstacle in the absorption of the labor force. Hence it produces underemployment.

Consequently, the fact that peripheral countries are not in charge of their technical progress avert them from using technology, which is appropriated to its course of development – a conclusion analogous to that presented by Prebisch. This position shows Furtado's concern with the historical development of different countries. Hence, there would not be any homogenous process of socio-economic development for neither core countries nor peripheral countries. This situation would also reflect the difficulty in resolving the class struggle as pressures for increasing wages end up being resolved in the political field; therefore, losing one of the essential factors of capitalist dynamism. Such contradictions in the peripheral structure lead Furtado to a reformist diagnosis by shifting the problem to the internal structure. Since economic development "is fundamentally a process of incorporating and propagating new techniques, it implies structural changes, both in the production and distribution systems" (Furtado 1964, 61). Given this theoretical exposition, in Furtado's perception, the crisis's cause would be structural and related to anachronic forms of income distribution present in Latin America.

Finally, as exposed by Furtado, throughout the 1960s, the experience in Latin America has shown that this type of substitutive industrialization tends to lose momentum when the "easy" substitution phase ends and eventually causes stagnation. Given such conclusions, Furtado's prescription for the new panorama of development in Latin America would not reside in a purely economic domain proposal but would involve social-political issues and changes throughout the institutional framework (Medeiros and Consentino 2020). For Furtado (1969), massive reforms in the land structure – land reform – and effective measures of income distribution should be made feasible, resuming, and expanding the State's role in what concerns.

Conclusion

ECLAC thinking had a considerable impact on Latin America academia and public policies. Besides being a theoretical framework, ECLAC thinking dealt with the empirical reality pushing it to constant evolution. As it was a transitional endeavor that gathered together intellectuals from different countries and fields, ECLAC could be a rich crib for branches of ideas on development.

Furtado and Cardoso's approaches are examples of how ECLAC thinking deeply impacted intellectuals over Latin America. As both authors joined the endeavor between the 1950s and the 1960s, it is possible to see how their passage influenced their academic production through ECLAC. Cardoso's *Dependency and development in Latin America: essay of sociological interpretation* (1969) and Furtado's *The Economic Formation of Brazil* (1969) are still crucial works for understanding Brazilian thinking. Both are mandatory books in undergraduate courses, providing an overview of Brazilian social-economic evolution inside a broader Latin American context. Their ideas may not fit anymore in the actual context and provided directions on how Latin America has been built over the years.

During the 1980s, the process of import substitutions collapsed. The exhaustion of the process gave room for the neoliberal ideology, which changed the dynamics of the peripheral countries. Although some of ECLAC's ideas proposed in the 1950s and the 1960s must be overcome, the "new developmentalism" still accepts the main idea that the underdevelopment has a structural basis that leads to a deterioration of the terms of trade, negatively impacting the wages, for instance, example. The new developmentalism proposes the overcome of three theses of its original conception: (i) the tariff protection for the domestic industry –

because the industry could already compete with the external industry (ii) the existence of structural inflation – because the peripheral countries could grow with stable inflation, (iii) the mitigation of the external restriction – because the peripheral countries could grow with external savings. Thus, instead of prioritizing closed industrialization driven to the domestic market, the new developmentalism considers a competitive insertion to the international market. In this manner, we may say that the additional thesis of the new developmentalism regards the exchange rates, which allow the growth of the external demand, stimulates economic growth, and creates internal savings (Bresser-Pereira 2014).

The new developmentalism has less tolerance for inflation; on the other hand, it admits the challenges only to prioritize price control. That is because the high interest rates focused only on controlling inflation, weakening the growth, and the capacity of the State's economic policy, which must be strong enough to implement countercyclical policies when necessary. In this sense, the new developmentalism praises the stability of the State (Bresser-Pereira 2014).

Comparing the two original developmentalism, the new developmentalism understands that the public sector should put forward a national coalition and boost the "catch up" of the peripheral countries (the approach of underdeveloped economies to the accumulated wealth of the developed countries). Strictly to a neo-Schumpeterian approach, the new developmentalism emphasizes a productive transformation to insert the peripheral countries in the international market, such as the original developmentalism proposed by ECLAC (Lopes 2018).

Despite the empirical changes over time and the new theoretical propositions, the core ideas of ECLAC, proposed by Prebish and affirmed by his critics and followers (such as Cardoso and Furtado), are still legacies for contemporaneity and the future. Development with equality, diversification of production, regional integration, and the insertion of Latin America in the international order will not leave the international agenda soon.

Notes

1. Bossa Nova is a Brazilian musical movement that emerged in Rio de Janeiro in the 1950s as a renovation of "samba".
2. Cinema Novo is a Brazilian cinematographic movement that emerged in the 1960s that focused on topics such as "social inequality" and "intellectualism".
3. Juscelino Kubistchek was president of Brazil between 1956 and 1961.
4. Nowadays, ECLAC has four headquarters over Latin America, in Brasília (Brazil), in Bogotá (Colombia), in Montevideo (Uruguay), and in Buenos Aires (Argentina)
5. Prebisch withdrew ECLAC in 1963 to head a commission for *the United Nations Conference on Trade and Development* (UNCTAD), an intergovernmental body for the promotion of trade and investment in developing

countries, which had just been created at that year. At UNCTAD, Prebisch could disseminate his ideas for the world because right in the year after, the commission became permanent inside the UN's structure, and Prebisch became the general secretary of it.

6. During the Military Dictatorship, Fernando Henrique Cardoso was exiled in Chile and France for four years.
7. Getúlio Vargas was Brazil's president from 1930 to 1945 and from 1951 to 1954. During his first administration, there were ample nationalist policies.
8. It is worth emphasizing that at that time, the role and autonomy of the multinational companies, as well as the power of international organizations (such as the International Monetary Fund and the World Bank), was also essential to stabilize the economic growth of developing countries.

Bibliography

Almeida Filho, N. and Corrêa, V. (January/April 2011). A CEPAL ainda é uma escola de pensamento? [ECLAC is still a school of thought?] *Revista de Economia Contemporânea* 15(1).

Bielschowsky, R. (1998). Evolución de las ideas de CEPAL [The evolution of ECLAC's ideas]. Revista de la CEPAL, special issue. Santiago de Chile.

Bresser-Pereira, L. C. (2005). Do ISEB e da CEPAL à Teoria da Dependência. [From ISEB and ECLAC to the Theory of Dependence]. In *Intelectuais e política no Brasil: a experiência do ISEB [Intellectuals and politics in Brazil: ISEB's experience]*, edited by C. Navarro de Toledo. Rio de Janeiro: Editora Revan.

_____(2014). *Do antigo ao novo desenvolvimentismo na América Latina* [From old to the new developmentalim in Latin America]. Retrieved from http://www.bresserpereira.org.br/papers/2012/12.Do_antigo_ao_novo_desenvolvimentismo.pdf

Cardoso, F. (2007). Análise e Memória: recordações de Enzo Faletto [Analysis and Memory: remembrances of Enzo Faletto]. *Tempo Social Revista de Sociologia* 19(1).

Cardoso, F. and Faletto, E. (1969 [1977]). *Dependência e desenvolvimento na América Latina: Ensaio de interpretação sociológica [Dependence and development in Lation America: an essay of a sociological interpretation]*. Rio de Janeiro: Zahar.

Cordeiro, V. and Neri, H. (2019). *Sociology in Brazil: An Institutional and Intellectual History*. London: Palgrave McMillan.

_____(2020). Essayism as a Sociological Research Tradition in Brazil: A Definition of Essay and Essayism for Sociology. *The American Sociologist Journal*. Retrieved from https://link.springer.com/article/10.1007%2Fs12108-020-09438-0

Dosman, E. (2012). *Raúl Prebisch (1901–1986): A construção da América Latina e do Terceiro Mundo [The construction of Latin American and the third world]*. São Paulo: Contraponto.

Fajnzylber, F. (1988). Competitividad Internacional: evolución y lecciones [International competition: Evolution and Lessons]. *Revista de la CEPAL 36*. Santiago de Chile.

Fernandes, F. (1965). *A integração do negro na sociedade de classes: no limiar de uma nova era [The black's integration in a within class society: in the brink of a new era].* Volume II. São Paulo: Dominus/Edusp.

Fernández López, M. (April/May 2001). Biografía de Raúl Prebisch [Raúl Prebisch's Biography]. *La Gaceta Económica.* Buenos Aires.

Freyre, G. (2010). *Casa-Grande e Senzala [The Masters and the Slaves].* São Paulo: Graal Press.

Furtado, C. (1964). *A dialética do desenvolvimento [Development's dialetics].* São Paulo: Editora Fundo de Cultura.

_____(1969). *A Formação Econômica do Brasil [The economic formation of Brazil].* São Paulo: Cia das Letras.

Jackson, L. C. and Blanco, A. (2020). A Transnational Book: Dependency and Development in Latin America. *The American Sociologist Journal.* Retrieved from https://link.springer.com/article/10.1007/s12108-019-09426-z?shared-article-renderer

Lopes, H. C. O. (September/December 2018). Brasil no novo milênio: regulação, progresso técnico e novo desenvolvimentismo [Brazil in the millennium: Regulation, technical progress and the new developmentalism]. *The Sociedad y Economía Journal* 27(3).

Morse, R. (1988). *O espelho de próspero [The prosperous mirror].* São Paulo: Cia das Letras.

Medeiros, F. and Consentino, D. (2020). Celso Furtado e Raúl Prebisch frente à crise do desenvolvimentismo da década de 1960 [Celso Furtado e Raúl Prebisch on the developmentalism crisis in the 1960s]. *Revista de Economia* 41(74).

Oliveira, L. L. (2001). A redescoberta do Brasil nos anos 50: entre o projeto político e o rigor acadêmico [The rediscovering of Brazil in the 1950s: between the political project and the academic rigor]. In *Descobertas do Brasil [Brazil's Discoveries]*, edited by A. E. Madeira and M. Veloso. Brasilia: UnB.

Prebisch, R. (1949). *El desarrollo económico de la América Latina y algunos de sus principales problemas* [The economic development of Latin America and some crucial issues]. Retrieved from https://repositorio.cepal.org/bitstream/handle/11362/40010/4/prebisch_desarrollo_problemas.pdf

Tavares, M. C. and Cardoso, F. H. (2000). *Além da estagnação: uma discussão sobre o estilo do desenvolvimento recente do Brasil* [Beyond stagnation: A debate on the freshly Brazil's development]. In *Cinquenta anos da CEPAL*, edited by R. Bielshowsky. Rio de Janeiro e São Paulo: Conselho Federal de Economia.

11 The Evolution of Capital Markets in Latin America

John C. Edmunds

Following the independence achieved at the beginning of the 19th century, each national financial system in Latin America has had a turbulent history, with periods of euphoria, crises triggered by external shocks, and a litany of collapses brought on in large part by home-grown misdeeds. This unsettled underpinning has been a persistent obstacle to the development of capital markets throughout the region. This summary of this lurid and dramatic history will only touch on watershed events and reforms that are exemplars of the many waves of reform that have rolled through the region. These waves of financial reform and innovation are still coming. In each country, debate still simmers about what is the best way of organizing and regulating each national financial system.

A national financial system should gather the savings of the citizenry and allocate those savings to the most productive uses. That ideal is very hard to achieve. In every country in every part of the world, there are critics pointing out that their national system does not live up to that lofty goal. This occurs because every financial transaction implies a future commitment, which requires that the institutional framework be stable and foreseeable. Too often, this dependable framework has not been present, which has generated a lack of confidence and deterred risk-taking on the part of providers of funds and also users of funds. Latin American capital markets have been criticized for being unable to finance many projects that would have been profitable, and for allocating too little capital to new businesses, and also for allocating too little to people from the lower socioeconomic strata. The region's capital markets are tagged as handmaidens of large existing businesses and as supporters of the status quo. They are, consciously or unconsciously, sources of financing for oligopoly businesses and public expenditure, and less helpful in launching fast-growing new sectors. The looming presence of state banks has implied that frequently the national capital markets have been constrained by the actions of pressure groups linked to political operatives (on the case of the Brazilian State Banks see: Salviano Junior 2004).

DOI: 10.4324/9781003045632-12

Data reported by the International Monetary Fund illustrate the underperformance of Latin American and Caribbean capital markets. In 2012, the value of listed common stocks and bonds including corporate and government issuance was only 107% of the region's aggregate GDP. For the entire world that ratio was 210%. Only the Middle East and North Africa, another aggregate that the IMF tracks, had a lower ratio.[1] Some examples of Latin America's low stock market capitalization (in May 2020) are: Argentina 32% of GDP, Colombia 41%, Mexico 34%. At the same time, Canada had 113% and Australia 106% (over of nominal GDP, see CEIC n/d).

The Colonial and Early Independent Period

During the colonial period, there was an incipient development of the financial markets in Latin America. In the Spanish empire, this development was facilitated by the stable currency based on the silver coin of eight *reales*. The quality of this coin was safeguarded by the Spanish Crown and therefore it was used in international trade by many nations (on colonial currency see: Marichal 2017).

The rich silver mines in what it today Mexico, Peru, and Bolivia would produce the metal used in large part of the globe. The silver from Potosi went by tortuous routes to Seville, over the Andes to Buenos Aires to the Atlantic, or down to the Pacific coast to Callao, then to Panama, then to the Caribbean, the Atlantic, and at last to Seville. Once there, it was paid to moneylenders to settle the king's debts and expenditures, and in that way, it entered into circulation in Europe, triggering inflation and episodic waves of prosperity. The monarchs spent most of their windfalls of silver and gold on European endeavors and adventures, not on building up the productive capacity of the Latin American colonies (Braudel 1985, passim).

Given monetary stability and low or non-existent inflation in the colonial period, there was long-term credit, generally granted by religious establishments. The mercantilist scheme applied in the Spanish Empire, however, implied that the financial resources be restricted to local or Spanish sources, so colonial trade had to be conducted only through mercantile houses of the Iberian Peninsula or their local representatives. The meager financial development of Spain implied restricted and expensive sources of funds. In turn, within each Latin American country, there were small local markets. Those intermediated the financing offered by wealthy individuals, commercial houses, and long-duration mortgage loans offered by religious institutions. The supply of credit offered by these institutions was adversely affected by several measures that were applied to them during the Bourbonic period. The first of these was the confiscation of the credit assets of the Jesuits in 1776. That entailed the gradual collection of these credits, with the proceeds being applied to cover public expenditure. The second was called "consolidation of Vales Reales", by which the Spanish government, beginning in 1804, forced institutions with endowments to exchange their loans to third parties for public debt securities, which lost their value over time. These funds were, in that way, withdrawn from the local capital markets. That quasi-confiscatory action was carried out and was later repeated. In the colonial era, there were almost no proper banking institutions. An exception was the Monte Piedad de Aminas of Mexico, founded in 1775, which granted loans (on colonial capital markets see: Quiroz 1995, 275–288; Bauer 2009).

After independence, sooner or later, the nations began to issue fiat currency and to abandon the colonial metallic system. Given the constrained fiscal capacity caused by internal and external wars, some states tried to cover a part of their fiscal deficits by issuing paper currency, generating inflationary pressures. Inflation would have negative consequences for the supply of credit. A paradigmatic case was the Buenos Aires Bank, which caused inflation of more than 600% between 1825 and 1860. Other countries, such as Chile, Bolivia, Peru, Mexico, and Colombia, would be more conservative and would keep the metal-based system, which held their price indexes more stable. In these countries, from the middle of the 19th century, private commercial banks appeared that, in addition to offering credit, began to issue banknotes supported by their reserves. In the second half of the 19th century, concomitant with the generalization of fiat currency, inflation became more endemic and widespread. Between 1861 and 1893, the price level rose 150%; in Chile, it rose 115% and in Peru 50%. In the same period, Brazil and Venezuela had stable prices. Then, in the last decades of the 19th century, all the nations that had not yet done so moved on to issue paper currency. Between 1886 and 1913, Mexico and Argentina experienced inflation of around 100%, while in Chile, inflation exceeded 200%. It is clear that the inflationary track record discouraged the development of financial instruments denominated in local currency (on the evolution of inflation see: Gaviria Cadavid 1985; Braun-Llona et al. 1998; Barba 1999; Gómez-Galvarriato and Musacchio 2000; Cuesta 2012; Arroyo Abad 2016).

Local financial services achieved incipient development, highlighted by the creation of stock and bond exchanges in various capital cities starting in the second half of the 19th century. However, their size was small and the array of listed companies was narrow. Investment from outside the region was most important, especially investment originating in England. Starting in the 1820s, European financiers, seeking the high returns that they could obtain on their investments, channeled funds toward mining and loans to governments, especially those of Buenos Aires, Brazil, Chile, Peru, Colombia, and Mexico, which were often searching for funds to support their local expenditures. The British soon would learn that working in Latin America was not easy. Many of the loans soon went into default due to fiscal deficits. After 1850 and given an upward trend in exports, investments in incoming loans from abroad would begin to accelerate, funding government expenditure, infrastructure, and railways. Argentina was the most important attractor of foreign investment. At the end of the 19th century, two-thirds of the external funds received by the Latin American region were borrowed by the public sectors and one-third by private companies. Approximately one-third of the capital formation was financed by funds originating outside the region. The region remained risky. In 1890, Argentina triggered a financial crisis that spread to the other nations of the region and reached Great Britain. The pattern of serious crises began with unsustainable monetary and fiscal policies, generating a speculative boom, followed by a steep fall in the markets, followed by a notable depression. A few years later, a similar crisis would occur in Brazil, leading to a default (on the capital markets and foreign lending in the 19th century see: Taylor 2003; Marichal 2014).

The 20th Century

The first three decades of the 20th century, with the exception of World War I, were a period of economic growth for the region, financed as before by foreign investment. Some Latin American nations intermittently adopted the gold standard, which they hoped would achieve monetary stability and consequent stability in local capital markets. These were Brazil, Chile, Mexico, and Argentina. Only Argentina was able to adhere to the gold standard for a relatively long period, from 1899 to 1914. For the other countries, macroeconomic instability did not allow maintaining gold convertibility. After the forced abandonment of the gold parity during World War I, the gold standard would again be adopted by Argentina and Brazil during the end of the 1920s, but countries had to abandon it once again with the advent of the Great Depression.

The experiences that Latin American countries during the 20th century had with issuing paper money continued to be overdone and ultimately unsuccessful. Most credit expansions came unraveled, sometimes disastrously. Inflation, prior to triggering surprise devaluations of local currencies, would raise the demand for imports, including luxury imports. The country would inexorably run out of foreign exchange, then have to go through a period of austerity and belt-tightening, with rounds of debt renegotiations, finally allowing access to international capital markets once again. Then the country, with its credit restored, could commence the expansionary cycle once again. During the austerity phase, the country's paper money had to be backed up by a credible promise that paper money was continuously redeemable in gold at a stable exchange rate. That convertibility became a watchword for conservative, Europe-oriented governments. Guatemala, for example, had a fixed exchange rate vis-à-vis the US dollar for the period 1933–1985. Until 1914, many Latin American countries tried to fix the exchange rate of their local currency to the British pound, and after 1919 to the US dollar. The debates over the exchange rate were a theme that pulled the Colombian elite into warring camps, the Liberals and the Conservatives. The underlying issue was that if a country could issue currency that did not have to be convertible into gold, the local businesses could expand, and give work to the Campesinos who had migrated to the city. With that possibility frequently in view, like a gleaming, enticing alternative to the entrenched economic and social order, the demands for the issuance of local currencies were intense. Those demands often succeeded, but then the increased money supply produced a disparity between the stated value of the local currency and its value in unregulated exchange markets. Devaluation had to occur to readjust the parity. Unfortunately, the devaluation was usually drastic and unannounced. These traumatic shocks had unintended consequences and caused collateral damage. Among the most famous shocks that rocked financial markets when a currency was devalued, two are from Mexico. President José Lopez Portillo's hollow promise to "defend the peso like a dog" led to derisive nicknames and presaged the defeat of the PRI, the party that dominated Mexican politics for seven decades. A second rude shock was the devaluation of December 1994, quickly labeled the "Tequilazo" (see Griffith-Jones 1997).

The region's checkered history with monetary experiments was, in broad attributes, similar to the monetary experiments of the fledgling United States, or of pre-1848 Europe. To capture the essential features of this long, colorful period, a touchstone is the tension between centralization and regionalism, and the tension between vying elites. Latin American countries are regionalized; some regions see themselves as the creators of the national wealth, footing the bills for carrying the unproductive bureaucracy of the central government. Ecuador's economic activities, and in particular its exports of bananas, shrimp, and crude oil, come from the coast and the Amazon regions. Its government sits in Quito, three thousand meters higher in altitude, with little contribution to the physical production of export goods. Its tourist attractions earn an important share of the GDP, but when there is a national election, the result is often so closely divided between the coast and the altiplano that the winning candidate can barely govern. Argentina has suffered many elections that did not deliver a decisive victory. The Pampa, and in particular the province of Buenos Aires, producer of grain and meat exports, finds itself subsidizing the provinces of the interior, where public employment is predominant in influencing voting preferences. Throughout the 20th and 21st centuries, the central governments wrestled with the issue of how to capture and allocate the proceeds of export sales, and some-times discouraged investment in those richly profitable activities.

A related issue was how to create a local currency that would work to facilitate local production of non-traded goods and services. Inevitably, for reasons of communication and economies of agglomeration, there was centralization of financial activity in the capital city. What var-ied from country to country was how much local autonomy the banks in the provinces had. Trading firms in the provincial cities could issue scrip and gain some liquidity from that issuance, but they ran the risk of having their notes presented to them all at once, which would tip them into default. The classic bank-centered system that Latin American countries copied from Europe was vulnerable to both exogenous and endogenous shocks. Latin American countries suffered from bouts of financial instability because any crisis in Europe promptly depressed the prices of Latin American export commodities. But in addition to those exogenous shocks, the region's political systems were unable to prevent overexpansion of credit during times of export-driven prosper-ity. European economies could rebound from crises more easily than Latin American countries could because European economies were more diversified. Latin American countries were much more linked to a small set of export goods, or to a single export good, so the recovery of domes-tic production, for example, from a good harvest of grain and other food crops, was often not of sufficient magnitude to offset the losses in the export sector (on the economic history of Latin America see: Bulmer-Thomas 1994; Bulmer-Thomas, Coatsworth, and Cortés Conde 2006; Bértola and Ocampo 2012).

The Evolution of Capital Markets

Borrowing money has always been expensive and difficult in Latin America. Opportunities to invest have come in waves, as commodity prices rose, or as economic policy favored infrastructure investment including railroads, highways, telecommunications, and electric power generation and distribution. Real rates of return on investment could be high, though volatile. Argentina's storied expansion from 1870 is the exemplar of these booms (della Paolera and Taylor 2003). The rub-ber boom in the Amazon region, which famously financed the Manaus opera house, is another similar, though more regional, episode. Loans were issued if the borrower had sufficient collateral, usually in the form of land or commodity exports ready to be shipped.

Export goods, when they reached European ports, could be sold for hard currency. Those payments were the source of hard cash to repay the bonds. It sometimes happened that the export proceeds were inadequate to repay the bonds. In the Caribbean and Central America, there were occasions where the bondholders were able to assert their claim by taking over the customs house and channeling half the export tax proceeds to the bondholders until the bonds were paid off. The Dominican Republic and Nicaragua both went through this forced repayment regime (see Bartlow 1966; Millett 1973).

During most decades of the 20th century, the price system did not allocate foreign exchange optimally. There were usually two markets for foreign exchange, the official market and the informal market (also called the black market, the parallel market, and other names). Importers wishing to acquire foreign exchange could apply at the central bank and could sometimes obtain foreign exchange at the official rate. Those who did not qualify, or did not wish to wait, could go to the informal market and obtain foreign exchange but would have to pay more. In some countries, governments were so determined to gather and allocate all the foreign exchange that came into the country, they made it illegal for their citizens to own foreign currency, or to have a foreign bank account (on the management of Exchange rates in Argentina see: FIEL 1989).

Capital markets could not operate to their fullest extent in countries with monetary regimes that were so vulnerable to unanticipated devaluations or bursts of inflation. Capital markets operate best when there are clear rules and a stable unit of account. Investors were willing to lend money for short periods of time, if the loans were secured by adequate guarantees or collateral, and if the interest rate was high enough to compensate them for the risk, but would not lend for longer periods of time.

Throughout the entire post-independence period until 1998, it was difficult for Latin American companies to issue equity securities. One major reason was the rule imported from the Napoleonic Code, a set of laws promulgated in France, then adopted in Madrid, then adopted in Latin America. That rule gave majority shareholders too much power over minority shareholders. Any individual or group who owned 51% of the shares of a company had absolute control, and could aside the wishes of any individual or group who owned 49%. This rule meant that investors would not buy any shares of a corporation unless they could buy 51%. Founders were extremely reluctant to sell enough shares to put their control in jeopardy. That impasse made it difficult to do initial public offerings of common stock. The impasse could be overcome with a legal remedy, called a shareholder agreement, but in many countries, there was an ingrained reluctance on the part of investors, wary of stepping into a role where they had so little power. A shareholder agreement (called a pacto de accionistas) is a legal arrangement, akin to a voting trust in the Anglo-Saxon legal tradition. When it works properly, it protects minority shareholders from being abused by majority shareholders (see Lefort 2005).

Another reason why it was difficult to issue equity securities in Latin American stock markets was the absolute priority rule. When a company goes bankrupt and is liquidated, the absolute priority rule requires that all senior claims be paid in full before the junior claims receive any of the proceeds. Shareholders are always junior claimants, and Latin American companies are often operating in volatile markets, so bankruptcy is a risk that has to be taken seriously. In consequence, Latin American capital markets mostly intermediated short-term debt instruments, smaller amounts of intermediate-term debt instruments, and very small amounts of equity securities (OECD 2013).

Following World War II, many countries in the region had a strong desire to industrialize. Raul Prebisch, a noted Argentine economist, advocated strongly for industrialization as a way of moving beyond the region's dependence on commodity exports (See Prebisch 1950). He was the most influential advocate of import substitution, and his urgings found willing listeners, because most Latin American countries, and especially the biggest ones, had a national aspiration to industrialize. The policy was to foster the creation of national manufacturing industries. It was an updated version of Alexander Hamilton's "infant industry" argument. Local industry could not survive or prosper without protective tariffs to make foreign goods more expensive. The nascent industry could compete successfully as long as the foreign good was expensive enough. Tariff protection was to be temporary, to be rolled back gradually as the local manufacturing companies became more efficient (McCrawm 2012).

The national strategy of import substitution had financing costs. The nascent industry was supposed to learn how to make manufactured goods that were of high enough quality and low enough cost to compete successfully with foreign goods. That would take time, and in the meanwhile, the import substitution industries would need to finance their operating losses. In the early stages, those industries would need infusions of cash, both local currency and foreign exchange. After the nascent industry achieved maturity, it would become profitable and then would pay back the financing it had received. The country's economy would have become more diversified, its international trade accounts would have become more stable, and its population could break away from the monoculture export social hierarchization (see Baer 1972).

The national financial systems, regrettably, were not suited to finance industrialization. The composition of financial intermediaries was, in appearance, similar to the national financial system of France or Spain. There were stock brokerage firms, insurance companies, leasing companies, a stock exchange, foreign exchange shops in tourist areas, an almost-full gamut. But most national financial systems were dominated by a few commercial banks. The institutions that were missing were those that handled long-term loans and long-term bonds. The commercial banks financed international trade using the time-honored instruments such as letters of credit, bills of lading, and marine insurance policies. They also made short-term loans to large, well-established local companies. They could not make long-term loans because their deposits were mostly short-term. Depositors could withdraw their money on short notice if there was a threat of devaluation, inflation, or an unscheduled change of government.

Import substitution remained the chosen path to economic progress until the 1970s, when it gave way to a new doctrine termed export substitution. Regrettably, both import substitution and export substitution took longer than the local capital markets could support. The industrial sector of most economies chronically consumed more foreign exchange than it earned. Traditional export industries were the source of foreign exchange to fund the needs of the industrial transformation. The local tax burden fell more heavily on the traditional export industries. Meanwhile, local prices of manufactured goods were high to maintain the viability of the fledgling manufactured industries. In consequence, foreign exchange accounts were chronically out of balance. Many countries bridged the financing gap by borrowing abroad. Those foreign debts became onerous when the performance of the import substitution industries fell short of the hoped-for benchmarks. Refinancing the foreign debt became expensive, and debt service consumed more of many countries' foreign exchange earnings. For example, Costa Rica's debt service payments to foreign lenders consumed 41% of its export revenues in 1978. Paying that much to foreigners left too little to pay for essential imports like pesticides and pharmaceuticals, and too little to pay for the imports that the import substitution industries needed. Import substitution, the entire region learned to its chagrin, entailed importing an unending stream of capital goods, foreign experts, intermediate goods, and raw materials. Ideally, the push to industrialize delivered manufactured local substitutes for foreign manufactured import goods, which would become good enough and cheap enough to export. That ambitious strategy usually implied importing more in the early years to jump-start the local manufacturing business, in hopes of importing less in the future and fulfilling the aspiration of exporting a more sophisticated, diversified mix of goods and services in the more distant future.

The government institutions of national financial systems were a replica of the conventional monetary architecture of the European national financial systems. There was a treasury and a small number of commercial banks. There was also a mint that issued coins to facilitate transactions in the local economy. The power to issue paper money was claimed by central governments, provincial governments, commercial banks, and cooperatives. Fiat money (i.e. paper money that was not convertible into gold or silver) was gradually introduced, often in conjunction with a change of government. For example, the Mexican Revolution of 1910 led, by 1913, to the de facto abandonment of convertibility. With the advent of central banks and independent management of monetary aggregates, paper money gained acceptance. Most national currencies in Latin America came to be managed in a similar fashion to the major fiat currencies of modern decades, such as the euro, the Japanese yen, or the New Zealand dollar. They are no longer theoretically convertible into gold or silver, but are valuable because they command purchasing power in their own territory, are legal tender for payment of debts and taxes, and are useful for conducting local commerce. There was also a central bank, which performed the usual roles of holding the cash reserves (encajes) of the national commercial banks, and acted as lender of last resort. What varied, and continues to vary, was the degree of independence of each country's central bank. The institution of a central bank acts as a restraint on national governments to prevent them from borrowing directly from the treasury – i.e. to finance its expenditure without having to borrow from sources that would later demand repayment. Each country's treasury collected taxes and spent the money as it was directed to do by the president and the legislature. If the president and the legislature authorized expenditure in excess of tax revenues, the extra expenditure would need to be financed by borrowing; or, if lenders would not lend, then by the issuance of more of the national currency. Such issuance of additional local fiat money can stimulate increases in economic activity, but if the issuance exceeds the market's demand for the national currency, the result will be inflationary pressure. Too much issuance can lead to hyperinflation, especially if local market participants do not see how the issuance would be controlled or retracted later. The central banks, usually headed by respected, technically trained managers, were sometimes able to restrain the distortions associated with inflation, by continuing to monitor the commercial banks to make sure they were solvent and that their loan portfolios were not over-concentrated in loans to a single sector or family group.

Capital Markets Emerge from Turbulent Times

By the end of the 1960s, the Bretton Woods system of fixed exchange rates was showing its central defect, the immutable link between the US dollar and gold. The Bretton Woods agreement was a pillar of the post-World War II world economy. It suffered a fatal blow in August 1971, when Richard Nixon was forced to abandon the convertibility of the US dollar into gold at the fixed price of $35 per ounce. Then in 1973, the International Monetary Fund formally abandoned the gold standard. Exchange rates, including those of the rich countries, fluctuated well outside their pre-1971 bands.

That traumatic departure from gold happened at the same time as the first oil crisis, when crude oil rose from US$2.50 a barrel to US$10.00 a barrel. The result was a deep worldwide recession in 1974–1975. The rise in the price of oil benefited a few Latin American countries but hurt more of them. Most were net importers of oil. For many countries, their oil import bill went up much more than their income from exports. Those countries suffered severe shortages of foreign exchange and had to make gut-wrenching adjustments to their economies (on the impact of the petrol crisis in Latin America see Federal Deposit Insurance Corporation 1997, chapter 5).

Then a huge opportunity appeared. The OPEC oil-exporting countries had always deposited the proceeds of their oil exports in banks in London. Suddenly, from 1973 to 1979, those banks found themselves with unprecedented amounts of money to lend, because the OPEC countries did not spend their huge new inflows of cash immediately. Many Latin American enterprises, including government and quasi-government entities, proposed large investment projects to the London banks. The banks granted loans to finance those projects. Usually, the proponents of each project were able to obtain the guarantee of their nation's government.

The London banks made the loans because the large projects, taken one by one, looked promising. After it became clear that there were too many projects aiming to increase the production of the region's traditional exports like sugar, coffee, and cacao, the outlook turned negative, and the Latin American Debt Crisis commenced. The bank-lending officers in London, New York, and Zurich comforted themselves by asserting that a country could not go bankrupt.

Unfortunately, many of the loans financed increases in the production of goods that came on stream as the world economy was going into recession. The dream of China's consumers switching to coffee soon encountered the hard reality of oversupply. Coffee's price peaked in 1977 at the unheard-of price of US$3.40 a pound. New high-yielding varieties soon replaced the delicate-flavored Bourbon variety, and the price commenced a slide that took it below US$1.00 a pound. It never rose again to its previous peak price. Once again, the national financial systems were unable to allocate credit to projects that would not aggravate the oversupply. The local financial institutions were also unable to finance schemes for withholding the excess prediction of storable commodities. They could not diversify their portfolios enough nor hedge their risks enough, so they gradually fell victim to the region's particularly deep recession of 1982. Many had to be rescued or nationalized.

The foreign-debt-fueled expansion led to what became known as the Lost Decade of the 1980s (Devlin and Ffrench-Davis 1995). The dream of updating and diversifying the economies of the region died a slow death, exacerbated in the press and in the popular perception by the slow working down of the debt burden. The two deep recessions of 1974–1975 and 1982–1983 obscured the progress that some countries in the region were able to make in fostering new activities, like offering inexpensive, comfortable retirement living for old people from rich countries. Exports of services were less conspicuous than exports of physical goods and seemed a less promising way of providing long-term employment for workers.

Social scientists of every specialization struggled to find ways of reforming the national financial systems that failed so frequently. It was particularly distressing that the financial systems, though quite small, could wreck so much collateral damage to sectors of each country's economy that had no proximate linkages to the finance sector. Many businesses and their employees suffered without ever having enjoyed the periods of bonanza in between the recessions.

There were proposals that ranged from nationalization to dollarization. The banks did a poor job of allocating loans, the central banks did a poor job of controlling the money supply, and the tax authorities were chronically unable to collect the full amounts of taxes that the legislatures had decided should be collected. Jamaica and Mexico, among other countries, both nationalized the banks, and El Salvador and Ecuador both abandoned their local currencies, using US dollars instead. Panama had abandoned its local currency in 1948. The stage was set for reforms.

Reforms Arrive Stealthily

In any nation's financial system, the rewards to savers need to be commensurate with the profitability of the investments that their savings finance. The return on investment, if measured in terms of units of input required to yield units of output, is usually high. The costs and returns, however, when measured in net monetary returns, are often lower, and too often negative. If risks of external shocks are high, it is justified for savers to demand high returns, and it is acceptable that returns can be reduced or wiped out if external shocks occur. Investment would still flow into the most advantageous projects. But if internal shocks or defectively designed local institutions also lower returns to investors, the results are less optimal. Among the internal impediments to optimal allocation, inflation is the most often cited.

Inflation distorts financial incentives, penalizing long-term investments and favoring short-term investments. Most obviously, it diverts preferences away from productive investment and favors quick-turnaround short-term investments. In countries with high inflation, young, enterprising, talented people are drawn into activities that reward opportunistic behaviors. Hoarding, trading with privileged information, and abuse of legally chartered institutions are often more profitable and less risky than traditional productive activities.

The harm that inflation causes is more pernicious than that, however. Inflation makes it difficult for companies to match the maturities of their liabilities to the maturities of their assets. Fixed assets should be financed with long-term debt, not with short-term debt. Businesses should be financed with a mix of short-term debt for their circulating assets, long-term debt for their more durable assets, and equity. With that mix, the returns to short-term lenders, long-term lenders, and equity investors should come out, over time, in the proper relationship. Each kind of financing should earn returns commensurate with the risk, and suited to the type of investor. In countries with high inflation and weak protections for minority shareholders, however, the mix of financing is usually not properly matched to the assets. Businesses rely too heavily on short-term debt. Or they can choose to finance their expansion entirely from internal cash flow and profit. In consequence, the businesses grow more slowly than the opportunities would allow, and too many businesses fail when credit markets do not provide new short-term loans to pay off the ones that are maturing.

Latin American orthodox economists always knew that inflation is destructive, and they worked hard to persuade elected officials to avoid inflationary policies. But their voices had little effect until the 1980s. During the decade of the 1980s and for the first half of the 1990s, Brazil and Argentina struggled to break free of the inflationary mindset that had gripped them for so long. Both countries succeeded, and so did Chile and Colombia. Mexico and Peru took longer, but all eventually succeeded (Loría and Ramírez 2011). Success came after high-profile schemes awakened hope but then stumbled. Most famous of all was Domingo Cavallo's plan de convertibilidad, which set the Argentine peso equal to the US dollar, and backed up the convertibility with a reserve of US dollars. Brazil had tried a scheme of its own that was called the Plan Real.

Success in controlling inflation brought more benefits than the quick windfalls that most market participants expected. In the early days of monetary stability, it was difficult to imagine how each national economy would function with a stable national currency. Market participants were accustomed to dealing in a world with hard currencies and soft currencies. They were wary of soft currencies, because those often lost purchasing power rapidly, and sometimes catastrophically. As month after month of low inflation happened, investors and business people reoriented their expectations and preferences. At first, they took tentative steps to hold the local currencies longer, even if only for a few days longer. They no longer felt the urgency to convert their extra local currency into foreign currency, and they no longer made extra effort to send the foreign currency out of the country to safe havens like the United States, Panama, and Switzerland. Instead, business people reinvested their profits locally, postponing when they would convert the profits into dollars and send them out of the country. The returns on local investments remained high because there was still a risk premium that people wishing to borrow local currency had to pay. With local rates of return remaining high, and no immediate prospects of sudden increases in inflation or surprise devaluations, market participants increased their investments in local-currency-denominated assets. Some local investors began to bring back the money they had spirited out of the country to take advantage of local investment opportunities.

The single reform that did the most to control inflation was central bank independence. Central banks had been subordinate to the public-works priorities of presidents. Central bank presidents had taken orders from the presidents of the countries. Central bank presidents could be fired and replaced on short notice and without recourse. That traditional authority that presidents had over monetary policy dissipated rapidly. In a short span of time, central banks achieved their independence, and then the technocrats who managed them were able to maintain the purchasing power of the local currencies (Jácome 2001).

Another big step in controlling inflation was that most Latin American countries abandoned their attempts to have fixed exchange rates. For the half-century following World War II, fixed exchange rates had seemed prudent. The argument, classically expounded by Milton Friedman, was that importers and exporters faced many uncertainties, so would not conduct as much international trade if exchange rates were not fixed (Hanke 2008). In practice, however, exchange rates in some countries did not remain fixed for long periods of time. Business people often had to try to be one jump ahead of currency traders. In Argentina, they called that "la bicicleta" [the bicycle] to imply that playing the inflation rate, the local interest rate, and the rate of depreciation of the currency were more important skills than producing products or services. In the time frame when "la bicicleta" was dominant, the finance manager of a company was the most important contributor to the business's profits and survival.

The early experiences with floating exchange rates were turbulent. Countries abandoned fixed exchange rates abruptly when the country's foreign exchange reserves ran out. Devaluations usually came as rude surprises. Middle-class families lost a fraction, and sometimes a large fraction, of their savings. Worse, they sometimes found that the loan documents they had signed included dollar escalator clauses. Costa Ricans could suddenly find, as happened in 1982, that their monthly car payment jumped by so much that the monthly payment exceeded their entire monthly salary. The exchange rate of the Costa Rican colon, for example, shot up from 8.5 per US dollar to over 40 per US dollar. The borrower had been paying 1700 colones per month, equivalent to US$200, and then suddenly had to pay 8000 colones per month – with no increase in salary. Fixed exchange rates, as they operated in practice, after the turbulence of the 1970s, were not providing enough certainty to exporters and importers to be worth the disruptions they caused when devaluations became necessary. Fixed exchange rates were also seen as a subsidy to rich, well-informed people, who could use their superior information to know when to sell the local currency for dollars, hold the dollars until after the impending devaluation, and then buy back the local currency at a much lower price. The middle classes and the poor had no such advantages. For them, the adoption of floating exchange rates was an improvement. After governments stopped trying to maintain fixed exchange rates, the local currencies lost purchasing power vis-à-vis the US dollar and other hard currencies, as expected. But with floating exchange rates, the devaluation process was gradual, not sudden and traumatic. Local interest rates adjusted to take into account the expected inflation and devaluation. Market signals were more aligned with future prospects. Rewards to savings and investing were more uniformly allocated to market participants.

There was a gradual improvement in debt markets. During the era of fixed exchange rates, many business people wanted to borrow the local currencies. They would use the loans to buy imported durable goods, then hope that a devaluation would occur before they would have to repay the loans. If a devaluation occurred, the borrowers would owe much less than the replacement cost of the durable goods that they had purchased.

After exchange rates were allowed to float, it became possible for businesses to borrow money for longer periods of time. Chile was able to create a long-term bond market, where companies were able to borrow to buy fixed assets (Committee on Financial Markets 2001). The bonds in that market were indexed, meaning that the borrower had to repay the original amount and also an adjustment for inflation. The interest payments also had to be adjusted for inflation. Before floating exchange rates, long-term loans were scarce, and were mostly, in effect, subsidized. The borrower proposed using the long-term, fixed-rate financing for a project that was a national priority, like a hydroelectric dam. Many such long-term loans for major infrastructure projects were for periods of time as long as 40 years, with as much as 10 years of grace before payments would be due. These often came from the Inter-American Development Bank, the World Bank, or the national economic development agencies of the rich countries.

National Pension Systems and National Stock Markets

Every country in Latin America faces the challenge of how to provide for the retirement of its citizens. Pension systems have been at the forefront of the national debate in many countries, most notably Brazil. The controversy has been that some retirees get much more than others, even if they did similar kinds of work. The famous pension system is Chile's. The Chilean model was copied in Argentina, Peru, Colombia, and Mexico (on the private pension systems in Latin America see: Tuesta 2011. On the Peruvian pension system see: Bernal et al. 2008). The Chilean model was, for its first decade and a half, a brilliant success. It not only gave future retirees the hope of having a comfortable retirement. It also fueled strong economic growth, financed by the national savings of Chileans. Then, after the worldwide financial crisis of 2008–2009, its performance lagged. Its rules came under scrutiny, and finally, it became embroiled in controversies.

The Chilean pension law was approved in 1981, as a replacement for the pre-existing state-run pension system (on the Chilean pension system see: OCDE 1998). The new pension fund system was centered around private pension fund administration companies. These were regulated and audited, and quickly were accepted by Chileans. Employees contributed part of their salaries to the pension funds, which then invested the savings in bonds. At first, the pension fund administrators were only allowed to invest in very safe bonds, because the legislature and the regulators did not want savers to face the risk of losing money, especially after the turbulence of the worldwide recession of 1974–1975 and the currency fluctuations associated with the country's lengthy maneuvers to repay its foreign debt.

The new pension system did not have much effect until 1983 because it started just at the worst moments of the severe worldwide recession of 1982–1983. Then from 1983 until 1996, Chile's pension funds took off. They fueled rapid economic growth, raising the country to the ranks of the high-middle-income category.

The pension funds successfully attracted local savings, which otherwise might have gone into unproductive investments or might have gone out of the country into capital flight. Savers who previously might have tried to buy foreign currency, to send to safe investment havens abroad, instead followed the guidelines and put their savings into the private pension funds. Chileans trusted their national institutions enough to entrust their savings to the pension fund administrators. Their trust was rewarded. The rate of return on Chilean pension funds in 1983, as the system took over, was 21.2%. The strong performance continued, ringing up gains of 15.6% and 29.7% in 1990 and 1991. All returns are quoted after adjusting for inflation.

The brilliant success of the Chilean pension system was the springboard for an economic leap forward. That traditional economy was vying to become a Pacific Rim Tiger. The rate of return on investments could be so high because there were good opportunities to build infrastructure including fiber optics and long-distance electricity transmission lines. Those investments were profitable enough to compensate the bondholders adequately. The pension funds were the bondholders, so they could press for adequate returns more powerfully than individuals might have been able to.

Shareholder returns were as spectacular in the early years following monetary stabilization, but the stock markets were riskier because of the weak protections for minority shareholders, and because individual investors could not press effectively for equitable treatment at the hands of the majority shareholders. The privatized pension funds became the de facto protectors of individual common stock investors. The majority shareholder (who in Mexico is colloquially called *el dueño*), could act dictatorially, in defiance of the wishes of the minority shareholder. But after each country instituted pension funds that bought common stocks, the majority's preemptive rights were constrained. The landmark improvement in shareholder rights was la Ley de OPAs in Chile in 1998. That stated that in the case of a takeover offer (oferta pública de adquisición), the acquirer could not buy only 51% of the shares, but instead had to buy 100%, paying the same price for the non-controlling shares as for the control block.

The next landmark improvement in minority shareholder rights was Brazil's Novo Mercado law passed in Brazil in 2000 (on the development of the Novo Mercado see: Santana 2008). That law stated that any new issuance of equity securities in Brazil had to conform to rules that outlawed super-voting shares. The Novo Mercado law also required truly independent audits, and truly independent boards of directors. Those differences attracted new investors, who bought new issuances of common stocks on the Bovespa, the main Brazilian stock exchange. The Brazilian stock market, which had been a sleepy, insignificant part of the Brazilian financial system, and an almost-irrelevant part of the Brazilian economy, took off. The magnitude and steepness of the takeoff were unprecedented in the recent history of Brazil. To cite the magnitude in US dollars, the total stock market capitalization of the listed common stocks on Brazilian stock exchanges was US$60 billion in the third quarter of 2002. That was a depresed level because Lula had just been elected, and market participants did not know how prudent his policies were going to be. By the middle of 2007, the stock market capitalization of Brazil had risen to US$1.5 trillion, or rovement 1,500 billion of US dollars.

The Novo Mercado reform was the catalyst to attract foreign portfolio investors to Brazilian stocks. During that same time frame as foreign investment was flowing into Brazil, the exchange rate of the Brazilian real strengthened from 4 reais per US dollar to 1.55 reais per US dollar for a US dollar.

The gargantuan Brazilian stock rally was happening in synchronization. It seemed, for a brief dazzling moment, that the Latin American economies were going to experience a quantum improvement in their capacity to finance the full range of productive activities that are present in the country at a given time (on the evolution of financial markets during the last 20 years in some countries of the region see: OECD 2019).

Chile launched the next two major initiatives. Those were the Bolsa Emergente [Emerging Stock Market] and the Ley de Multifondos

[Multifund Law]. La Bolsa Emergente was a simpler set of documents that a company had to present in order to be allowed to sell shares to the public on the Chilean stock exchange. It was a good gesture but did not produce a wave of new issuances of common stock. The Ley de Multifondos had a much more visible and widespread impact. It allowed Chileans to choose to assign a higher portion of their pension fund accumulation to a fund that invested solely in common stocks. That was Fondo A, and it had a profound effect on the entire economy. Prices of Chilean common stocks rose, as short-term traders bought, anticipating that the pension funds were going to have to buy to fulfill the mandate of Fondo A.

During the heady years of 2005–2007, the flow of money into venture capital investments should have been high. And it was. There was hope that Chilean venture capital would finance a startup, which would achieve success and then make an initial public offering on the Bolsa Emergente of Chile. That would complete the entire cycle of financing that has been the aspiration of reform-minded individuals in Latin America, but which has eluded those countries most of the time.

The *Fiesta* Ends

The world financial crisis of 2008–2009 hit the Latin American region hard (on the regional impact of the Great Recession see: Ferrari-Filho, and de Paula 2016 and Arroyo Abad 2016). Foreigners stopped investing as they pulled money back to attend to needs at home including margin calls. Optimism gave way to pessimism. The dizzying rallies of the past gave way to stagnation, but not to collapse. The premier names in each stock market retained much of their value. The fundamental socioeconomic order was not threatened. The crisis was an external shock and did not trigger large, unexpected local shocks.

Reforms continued in each country but had little effect compared to the landmark reforms in the preceding decades. The results could not have been dramatic because pension funds were still constrained in the mix of securities they could buy. Following the financial crisis, bond yields fell and remained low. In consequence, the private pension funds gradually lost prestige and were tagged as charging fees that were too high in comparison with the low and declining yields that they were delivering.

The financial system lost prestige and became identified as a prime offender in the wealth concentration process. In the riots of 2019–2020, large financial institutions were targeted, with the complaints being inadequate access to financial services and excessive fees for services being delivered, with high returns for high-status people, earned by delivering bad service.

Resilience and Reinvention

Having suffered from widespread riots as the rest of the world was celebrating the tenth year of a long, slow recovery from the financial crisis of 2008–2009, the Latin American region was dealt a massive external shock.

The current challenge can be an opportunity. The existing financial institutions will be over-stressed to finance the recovery of the national economies. People in business will be seeking financing to reactivate viable businesses that ceased operations during the period of quarantine caused by the pandemic in 2020. Local observers can take note of which businesses reopen and which remain closed, and can find out if the lack of financing was the key input that was lacking. Opportunities for non-traditional financing should be considered, as should crowdfunding and cyber currencies. The current crisis will give opportunities to a new generation of innovative individuals, who will find ways of operating in the new environment.

Note

1. Ratio computed from regional aggregate figures in World Capital Markets summary page for 2012, in International Monetary Fund 2012, 11. Statistical Appendix.

Bibliography

Arroyo Abad, L. (July–December 2016). Despegue frustrado: costo de vida y estándares de vida en el Perú durante el siglo XIX. *Economía* XXXIX(78).

Baer, W. (1972). Import Substitution and Industrialization in Latin America: Experiences and Interpretations. *Latin American Research Review* 7(1).

Barba, F. (1999). *Aproximación al estudio de los precios y salarios en Buenos Aires desde fines del siglo XVIII hasta 1860.* La Plata: Ediciones UNLP.

Bartlow, M. J. (1966). *Overtaken by Events: The Dominican Crisis from the Fall of Trujillo to the Civil War.* New York: Doubleday.

Bauer, A. J. (2009). The Church in the Economy of Spanish America: Censos and Depósitos in the Eighteenth and Nineteenth Centuries. *Hispanic American Historical Review* 63(4).

Braudel, F. (1985). *The Mediterranean and the Mediterranean World in the Age of Philip II.* California: University of California Press.

Braun-Llona, J., Braun-Llona, M., Briones, I., Díaz-Bahamonde, J., Lüders, R., and Wagner, G. (1998). *Economía Chilena 1810–1995. Estadísticas Históricas.* Documentos de Trabajo 187. Santiago de Chile: Instituto de Economía. Pontificia Universidad Católica de Chile.

Bernal, N., Muñoz, A., Perea, H., Tejada, J., and Tuesta, D. (2008). A look at the Peruvian Pension System. In *Diagnosis and Proposals.* Lima: BBVA.

Bértola, L. and Ocampo, J. A. (2012). *The Economic Development of Latin America since Independence.* Oxford: Oxford University Press.

298   *J.C. Edmunds*

Bulmer-Thomas, V. (1994). *The Economic History of Latin America since Independence*. Cambridge: Cambridge University Press.

Bulmer-Thomas, V., Coatsworth, J., and Cortés Conde, R. (2006). *The Cambridge Economic History of Latin America*. Cambridge: Cambridge University Press.

CEIC. (n/d). Indicators. Retrieved from https://www.ceicdata.com/en/indicator/brazil/market-capitalization–nominal-gvdp

Committee on Financial Markets (CMF, OECD). (2001). Chile: Review of the Financial System. Retrieved from https://www.oecd.org/finance/financial-markets/49497488.pdf

Cuesta, M. (2012). Precios y Salarios en Buenos Aires durante la gran expansión, 1850–1914. *Revista de Instituciones, Ideas y Mercados*.

della Paolera, G. and Taylor, A. (eds.) (2003). *A New Economic History of Argentina*. Cambridge: Cambridge University Press.

Devlin, R. and Ffrench-Davis, R. (1995). The Great Latin American Debt Crisis: Ten Years of Asymmetric Adjustment. In *Poverty, Prosperity and the World Economy*, edited by G. Helleiner, S. Abrahamian, E. Bacha, R. Lawrence, and P. Malan. London: Palgrave Macmillan.

Federal Deposit Insurance Corporation. Division of Research and Statistics. (1997). *History of the Eighties: Lessons for the Future*. Washington, DC: FDIC.

Ferrari-Filho, F. and de Paula, L. F. (2016). The Impact of the Great Recession and Policy Responses in Latin America: Was This Time Different? In *Emerging Economies During and After the Great Recession*, edited by P. Arestis and M. Sawyer. International Papers in Political Economy Series. London: Palgrave Macmillan.

FIEL. (1989). *El Control de Cambios en la Argentina*. Buenos Aires: FIEL.

Gaviria Cadavid, F. (1985). *Moneda, banca y teoría monetaria*. Bogotá: Fondo de Promoción de la Cultura del Banco Popular.

Gómez-Galvarriato, A. and Musacchio, A. (2000). Un Nuevo índice de precios para México, 1886–1929. *El Trimestre Económico* LXVII(1).

Griffith-Jones, S. (May 1997). Causes and Lessons of the Mexican Peso Crisis. Wider. Working paper 132. Retrieved from https://www.wider.unu.edu/sites/default/files/WP132.pdf

Hanke, S. (September 2008). Milton Friedman: Float or Fix? *Wainwright Economics*. https://www.cato.org/sites/cato.org/files/articles/hanke_IFr-friedman-float.pdf

International Monetary Fund. (October 2012). *Global Financial Stability Report*. Statistical Appendix. Washington: International Monetary Fund.

Jácome, L. I. (2001). Legal Central Bank Independence and Inflation in Latin America During the 1990s. IMF Working Papers 01/212. Washington: International Monetary Fund.

Lefort, F. (2005). Ownership Structure and Corporate Governance in Latin America. *Revista Abante* 8(1).

Loría, E. and Ramírez, J. (2011). Inflation, Monetary Policy and Economic Growth in Mexico. An Inverse Causation, 1970–2009. *Modern Economy* 2.

Marichal, C. (2014). *Historia mínima de la deuda externa de Latinoamérica*, México: El Colegio de México.

———(2017). El peso de plata hispanoamericano como moneda universal del antiguo régimen (siglos XVI-XVIII) (37–76). In *De la plata a la cocaína. Cinco siglos de Historia Económica de América Latina, 1500–2000*, edited by C. Marichal et al. México: Fondo de Cultura Económica.

McCrawm, T. K. (2012). *The Founders and Finance: How Hamilton, Gallatin, and Other Immigrants Forged a New Economy*. Boston, MA: Harvard University Press.

Millett, R. L. (1973). The History of the Guardia. Nacional de Nicaragua. Unpublished Ph.D. dissertation. U.S.: University of New Mexico.

OECD. (1998). The Chilean Pension System working paper. Ageing Working Papers 5.6. Paris: OECD.

———(2013). *Trends and Factors Impacting on Latin American Equity Market Development*. Paris: OECD.

———(2019). *Equity Market Development in Latin America: Enhancing Access to Corporate Finance*. Paris: OECD.

Prebisch, R. (1950). *The Economic Development of Latin America and Its Principal Problems*. New York: United Nations.

Quiroz, A. (1995). Crédito de origen eclesiástico y deuda pública colonial en el Perú, 1750–1820 (275–288). In *Iglesia, Estado y Economía. Siglos XVI al XIX*, edited by M. P. Martínez López-Cano. Mexico: UNAM.

Salviano Junior, C. (2004). *Bancos estaduais: dos problemas crônicos ao PROES*. Brasília: Banco Central do Brasil.

Santana, M. H. (2008). *Novo Mercado and Its Followers: Case Studies in Corporate Governance Reform*. International Finance Corporation.

Taylor, A. (2003). Foreign Capital in Latin America in the Nineteenth and Twentieth centuries. NBER. Working Paper 9580. Retrieved from http://www.nber.org/papers/w9580

Tuesta, D. (2011). A Review of the Pension Systems in Latin America. Research Working Papers, Number 11/15. BBVA.

12 Workers' Self-Management in Latin America

From the First Cooperatives to the Workers' Recuperated Enterprises

Andrés Ruggeri

The process of recuperation of enterprises by workers that began in Argentina in the 1990s and expanded during the great crisis of 2001–2002 attracted worldwide attention for its massiveness and the radical nature of its practices, in a context where it was growing the debate about globalization and its consequences. The "occupied factories" appeared, as intellectuals from Europe or North America such as Naomi Klein or James Petras (Petras and Veltmeyer 2002) pointed out, as a creative and bottom-up response to the most negative effects of neoliberal globalization. From Argentina, where the phenomenon was occurring, the vision was less idealized. Up close, what we could observe was that the workers occupied the factories that the bosses abandoned in the midst of the crisis to try to preserve the jobs and, in doing so, they unwittingly activated the resurrection of *autogestion* (self-management), a concept that symbolized the "new left" of the sixties and seventies. However, the term was almost absent in the tradition of the Argentine labor movement, so the name "recuperated enterprise" was the one that prevailed.

However, this reappearance of self-management and worker cooperativism that contrasted with the traditional cooperative, represented by stagnant and conservative institutions, led to an update of debates on labor democracy, workers control, and workers self-management that seemed to be abandoned years ago. The nineties, both in Argentina and in most countries of Latin America, had been the stage of the triumph of neoliberalism, embodied in the Washington Consensus, with a series of governments that carried out an almost traced economic plan of privatizations, deregulation, destruction of the Welfare State and massive precariousness of work, wiping out labor gains and little union resistance. The emergence of groups of workers occupying factories and forming cooperatives to restart the production was a revival of old traditions, in a new and devastating context of crisis.

Once the first wave of recuperated enterprises and the first moment of academic attention to this process had passed, the memory of

DOI: 10.4324/9781003045632-13

previous experiences began to emerge. Most of the background on self-management cited in the first studies corresponded to European experiences: the Paris Commune, the Russian Revolution, collectivizations in the Spanish Civil War, or Yugoslav socialism. In relation to Latin American experiences, there were only some distant references to the factory outlets in Chile during the brief government of Salvador Allende. However, the history of worker self-management processes in the region is rich and complex, although little known.

The emergence of recuperated enterprises contributed to us wondering some questions about the history of workers' self-management in Latin America. In this article, we sketch the history of these processes in this part of the world, based on the experience of the Argentinian recuperated enterprises.

Workers' Self-Management and Recuperated Enterprises

The expression "recuperated enterprises" – which for our purposes refers more precisely to "worker-recuperated enterprises" (WREs) – did not exist prior to 2001, neither in Argentina nor anywhere else in the world. It was born in this country during the 2001 struggles, coined by the workers themselves, whose intention was to underline that their principal interest was to recover a source of employment that would have remained forever lost in the absence of some form of resistance. This recuperation of individual employment also represented a recovery for the embattled national economy. Generally speaking, WERs have little in common with the anti-capitalist, international labor movement, instead of drawing more immediately on the traditions of Argentina's powerful labor movement, which has been deeply intertwined, since the middle of the 20th century, with the history of Peronism. Albeit situated within this historic continuum, it is difficult to see points of rupture punctuating an otherwise uninterrupted period of continuity. Such ruptures demonstrate the real threats posed by the WREs to the prevailing capitalist logic that make them irreducible to another instance of the typical disputes of the country's organized labor movement.

Although the "recuperated enterprise" label had never previously been used, we should in no way assume that Argentina's recuperated enterprises were a historical first. As we shall see, there are those WREs that trace their roots back to the 1990s and beyond, and, even among those historic attempts that never prospered, records show that they championed similar causes and expounded similar methods that would live on in the practices of the future WREs. Additionally, given the definition of the WREs we are using here, we will find any number of similarities between the recuperated enterprises and other cases at different stages in history, even going back to the initial stages of industrial capitalism, and particularly in the first workers cooperatives that were founded during the Industrial Revolution in England.

The Argentine case is not only unique for the denomination it would give to such workers' occupations, that we are provisionally defining as economic entities in transition from capitalist management to collective worker control. Instead, it consisted in the sheer scale of the phenomenon, such that it amounted to a whole movement with its own organizational structure, identity, and autonomy. While we can find similar WREs in many countries, those cases not only have not cohered into a specific, delineated social movement but also tend to get lost among the different organizations that form part of the traditional cooperative movement. The denomination used by the Argentine workers to describe their own experiences also allows us to distinguish it from other cases in which the formation of a cooperative is the stated goal from the outset, and in which, generally speaking, there is no moment of worker expropriation (although, as will become clear, in the majority of cases in Argentina the capitalist actually abandons the business).

To advance a further definition, we can say that:

> the recuperated enterprises are a social and economic process that presupposes the prior existence of a business functioning along the lines of a traditional capitalist model (including, in some cases, with the legal status of a cooperative), and whose bankruptcy, closure, or insolvency created the motivation for its workers to fight in order to restore it to full functionality under worker self-management.
>
> (Ruggeri, Martínez, and Trinchero 2005)

Workers' Self-Management and the Cooperatives

As Peixoto de Albuquerque has pointed out (2003, 20–26), the concept of self-management enjoyed resurgence along with the concrete instances of collective management of businesses that had been bankrupted by neoliberal globalization; at the same time, "the return of the political and ideological struggles that originally gave birth to the concept have simultaneously spurred the return of the self-management idea" (2003, 22). Nevertheless, the same author admits that the concept remains ambiguous, remitting at once to an idea of collective social and economic activity that can mean virtually anything to anyone. This author makes an essential distinction between self-management "in a restricted sense", that is, in the strictly economic field, and "generalized" self-management, in which the notion of self-management is extended to the social and the political aspects, as a project for society as a whole. From our point of view, most of the experiences of workers' self-management should be analyzed as cases of restricted self-management, which, however, has or may have a projection beyond purely economic practices. In this sense, the debate on self-management traverses the history of workers' struggles within the framework of capitalism, especially regarding the relationships between both dimensions of self-management (restricted and generalized), the relationships between the processes of workers' self-management and the general economy, the relationships of these processes and the State and, also and mainly, with the capitalist market.

Then, we can establish that for our purposes, self-management consists of the management of an economic body by its workers – with no capitalists or managers – who organize their own methods of labor within non-hierarchical structures. In other words, the workers are responsible for collectively setting the norms that regulate production, organizing the labor process, deliberating over the use of any surplus, and determining their overall relation with the rest of the economy and society. Self-management is essentially a permanent dynamic of relationships within the workers that constitute it, which is all to say that it can never be reduced to a determinant legal business schema, such as would be the case if we equated self-management with cooperativism. Furthermore, self-management implies that the workers assume control of the labor process, altering the basic operating manual common to all capitalist enterprises and going against the tendency toward the exploitation of labor by capital (Ruggeri 2014).

Cooperativism in Latin America

The first cooperatives emerged in Great Britain in the late 18th century, most as consumer associations, but some were also resistances against extreme labor exploitation and because of social conflict. There were an estimated 350 cooperatives operating in England and Scotland before the famous Rochdale Pioneers Cooperative, founded in 1844 and widely known as the first cooperative, although in reality, it was the cooperative that systematized the so-called "principles" of cooperativism (Cole 1957; Ruggeri 2018).

Cooperatives spread in the first decades of the century to other European nations that began to develop their industry and in which, at the same time, the working class began to be born. Both unions and cooperatives were forms of organization that arose in the heat of workers' resistance to the brutal conditions of exploitation of industrial capitalism in formation. The systematization of Rochdale principles was subsequently, and with few variations, adopted by the International Cooperative Alliance founded in London in 1895. However, that cooperative began to mark the distance of a part of cooperativism from the most radicalized fractions of the labor movement, especially those grouped by the international workers' association (Ruggeri 2018).

In Latin America, the labor movement appeared later than in Europe, as its incorporation into the world market has become deeper and, through this process, the expansion of capitalist production relations in some linked economic sectors to the export of agricultural raw materials or minerals was having taking place. The development of sectors related to foreign trade and basic infrastructure to increase the capacity to supply raw materials to the industrial powers of the time facilitated the emergence of an incipient labor movement in countries that were firmly inserted in the international division of labor, such as Argentina, Uruguay, Brazil, Chile, or Mexico.

At the end of the 19th century and the beginning of the 20th century, unionism and cooperatives or mutual aid societies, framed in these first organizations, began to organize in these nations.

In Argentina, for example, the first cooperatives emerged in much the same way as the early days of European cooperativism, mostly composed of migrant workers who brought the experience of their countries of origin (Montes and Ressel 2003). That first period of activism dominated by socialist and anarchist movements marked the evolution of cooperativism for much of the 20th century. Cooperatives of small rural producers were formed to defend the work of poor farmers in a field dominated by large exporting landowners of the agrarian oligarchy, together with the struggle of rural peons expressed in the "grito de Alcorta" [cry of Alcorta], which gave rise to the rural cooperativism as early as 1912 (Martínez and Ruggeri 2016). The mutual aid societies that formed the unions and migrants from the different communities formed powerful cooperatives such as "El Hogar Obrero" [The Worker Home], linked to the Argentine Socialist Party and which became the largest commercial chain in the country until it went to bankruptcy in the 1980s (Montes, and Ressel 2003; Ronchi 2016). These first Argentine cooperatives were not yet regulated by laws and had multiple forms, all of them linked to the workers' organization.

In Mexico, for mentioning another case, the first cooperatives appeared at the beginning of the 20th century (Pacheco Reyes 2018), when the Mexican Revolution produced an enormous transformation and led to a deep modification of social relations, first in rural areas with a process which culminated in the agrarian reform implemented along with great nationalizations in a consolidated and pacified State under General Lázaro Cárdenas, but also with some major strikes by mine workers, as was the case of the famous Cananea mine strike (Hernández 1996). In the 1930s, along with the consolidation of the modern Mexican State, large worker cooperatives also appeared with the Cardenas's government (Pacheco Reyes 2018).

Cooperatives proliferated and began to consolidate as a form of economic organization although, as in Europe, they were the object of mistrust by the most radical political and worker parties. A clear example is the opinion of José Carlos Mariátegui on cooperativism, which expresses the same kind of mistrust that Vladimir Lenin had raised a few years earlier at the Congress of the Second International in Copenhagen in 1910, among others (AA.VV. 1969) or Rosa Luxemburg (1967) in her book *Reform or Revolution?* Mariátegui, for example, stated in a 1928 article that "the cooperative, within a regime of free competition, and even with a certain favour from the State, is not opposed, but on the contrary, useful to capitalist companies" (Mariátegui 1986).

In Argentina, the cooperativism developed with force after obtaining, in 1926, the first cooperative law that allowed state recognition (Montes and Ressel 2003). The development of agricultural, consumer, service, and credit cooperativism grew in volume and in economic importance during the following decades, but the separation with the labor movement became ever deeper with the rise of Peronism and the reconfiguration of a powerful union movement, strongly integrated with the State, which privileged it as a form of labor organization and expanded union membership to levels that doubled its representativeness and power (Antivero and Elena 2011). Most cooperativism, on the other hand, continued to be linked to the expressions of the left that were formerly majority in the Argentine working class (Ronchi 2016).

That does not mean that Peronism has ignored cooperativism. In fact, during the first and second governments of Juan D. Perón, there were several cases of worker cooperatives that emerged from private companies that transferred their assets to their workers, such as the case of the Cooperativa Industrial Textil Argentina (CITA, Argentine Textil Industry Cooperative), possibly the first company recuperated in the country. In his second term, Perón gave an important speech highlighting cooperative as a form of economic organization (Jaramillo 2012).

In other South American countries, meanwhile, cooperativism failed to form a strong stream. In Venezuela, for example, although cooperativism recognizes origins in the early 20th century, its organizations had little development until Hugo Chávez came to power (Azzellini 2013). In Mexico, the PRI (Institutional Revolutionary Party, IPR) government promotes several important worker cooperatives. The most notorious case for its subsequent significance was the Cruz Azul cement plant, which emerged in the 1930s from a labor struggle whose consequence was the transfer of the company to the workers' cooperative, in other words, to a recuperated enterprise (Pacheco Reyes 2018).

Argentine cooperativism, like in other countries in the region, has become a relatively important economic actor as an alternative to capitalist companies and even to state management, through relatively strong agricultural and food production cooperatives and cooperatives that provide basic services in many small and medium-sized cities of the country (Martínez and Ruggeri 2016). Thus, cooperatives providing electricity, gas, and water to numerous urban centers were formed at the same time that the emergence of a credit cooperativism, with savings banks that fulfill the role of providing financial support to small cooperatives and family businesses in places in which banks were not present or did not serve small savers or entrepreneurs. The Argentine cooperative credit system, like the Uruguayan and, in part, the one of Brazil, became an important factor in the credit system until it was the object of destructive policies by the military dictatorships of the 1960s and 1970s (Plotinsky 2018).

However, the importance of the workers' cooperatives on the movement was increasingly reduced. Most of these organizations did not respond to the concept of worker self-management, although a type of associativism did exist in general. The workers' movement and cooperatives followed increasingly separate paths, which were finally consolidated with the passing of Law 20367 in Argentina in 1973, a law that remains in force to this day.

Workers Control and Self-Management in Revolutionary Processes: Cuba, Chile, and Peru

Unlike the cooperativism already institutionalized within the capitalist economies of the region, the different revolutionary crises that took place in post-World War II generated experiences of workers' power that did not adopt the cooperative forms and generated other political and theoretical premises.

The radicalization of social and political struggles led to revolutionary processes in some countries, of which the clearest and most radical was in Cuba, whose influence in the rest of the region extended during the 1960s and 1970s. The Cuban Revolution provoked a violent response from the United States, the hegemonic imperial power in the hemisphere that, at the time, had established itself as the first world power. Bolivia underwent a revolution in the early 1950s, led by mine workers and peasants, which led to the dissolution of the armed forces and the existing political regime, an agrarian reform, and the nationalization of mines under the control of the workers, but which soon gave way to a regime that distorted the achievements and demands of that revolutionary movement (Plá 1980).

Peru, during the military government led by Velazco Alvarado, underwent a process of reforms "from above" that concluded in an agrarian reform and the establishment of a self-management regime for companies that were nationalized through a participation regime for their workers and, in other cases, cooperativization (Iturraspe 1986).

In Chile, the short and intense period of government of Salvador Allende and the Popular Unity (UP) was characterized by an enormous social mobilization and the creation of an area of social ownership of the economy, in which the companies considered strategic were nationalized and co-managed with unions. However, the most interesting process was that of the so-called "industrial cords" (cordones industriales), in which workers occupied factories where employers had interrupted production as a form of boycott against the government of the "Chilean road to socialism" (Gaudichaud 2004, 2016; Winn 2004; Kries 2013). Industrial cords were the most complete form of what the Chilean left called "popular power" (poder popular), most of them going beyond what was desired by the Allende government itself.

In other countries of the region, it was a period of intense popular struggles: the Mexican 1968, the *Cordobazo* and the radicalization of the masses in Argentina until the establishment of state terrorism in the second half of the 1970s, the factory commissions in Brazil, among other cases, in addition to the heyday and subsequent defeat of most of the attempts at armed struggle inspired by the Cuban Revolution. Finally, it was in Cuba that the role of workers in building a non-capitalist society was further discussed.

Although the organizations and leaders of the Cuban Revolution, including Fidel Castro himself, had not made explicit formulations about a socialist path during the process of the revolutionary war against the dictatorship of Fulgencio Batista, the victory of the guerrilla fighters of the Movimiento 26 de Julio [Movement 26th July] and other allied organizations accelerated times and quickly radicalized the process based on the decision to expropriate large companies and corporations, overwhelmingly US-owned, and to advance agrarian reform (Arboleya Cervera 2008; Buch and Suárez 2009). In that spiral of events that led the revolutionaries to quickly seal an alliance with the Soviet Union, reject the attempted invasion at Playa Girón, and be at the center of a crisis that put the world on the brink of nuclear war and the beginning of the North American blockade that continues to the present day, Cuban workers on numerous occasions anticipates the leadership of the revolution by taking foreign-owned companies and putting them into operation pending for their nationalization (Buch, and Suárez 2009; Cushion 2018). In those first moments of great mobilization and hostility by the United States, the debate on the role of workers in socialism building was led by Ernesto Che Guevara, who was in charge of the Ministry of Industries until his departure to head others guerrilla attempts in the Congo and, finally, in Bolivia.

Che Guevara's stage as a minister is perhaps the one least known of his career, although a number of his writings about economy and his actions in the area were rescued from oblivion by different authors (Tablada 2005; Guevara 2006; Yaffe 2011). Guevara's vision of the economy and workers' economic participation was a fundamental part of his vision of revolutionary change and gave rise to original debates in relation to the rest of the countries of the so-called "real socialism". Che was very critical of the economy of these countries, especially of the USSR (in which he saw tendencies that were to lead to the restoration of capitalism, especially in the self-financing system of companies submitted to the state planning of the economy, which he called "economic calculation") and of the priority given to material stimuli to achieve the best labor performance for workers (Tablada 2005; Guevara 2006; Yaffe 2011). Faced with this, Guevara proposed the "budget financing system", consisting of a general assessment of the needs of planning rather than a standardized calculation, the permanent participation of workers in improvements in production and in management and prevalence of "moral encouragement" based on worker consciousness rather than on material rewards according to productivity (Yaffe 2011; Tablada 2005).

Just as he criticized the Soviet Union for these tendencies and for what he judged as the lack of solidarity of the then socialist superpower with the anti-imperialist struggles and the development of third world countries (for example, in the famous "Algiers speech"), which was interpreted so many times in favor of a supposed and non-existent rupture of Che with Fidel. Guevara had an even worse image of the self-management system of Yugoslavia, also a socialist country, but rehearsing an alternative way to the Soviet one. It is precisely in Yugoslavia that the word "self-management" was born, when, following the break between Tito and Stalin at the end of the 1940s, the Communist Party of Yugoslavia began to build a system with workers' participation in the management of enterprises, described by Yugoslav leaders as a return "to the origins of Marxism" in the face of the bureaucratic deviations of Stalinism (Djordjevich 1961; Laserre 1966). Che's opinion about Yugoslavia following a visit in 1959 – the same year that the Cuban Revolution triumphed – was quite negative, seeing in the market competition system of Yugoslavia's self-managed companies and other mechanisms of management of these companies as a precedent for a mixed system with capitalism that was rejected outright (Yaffe 2011, 41).

Evidently, the conception developed by Che was not a self-managed position, but it did include an idea of the role of work and workers that is extremely active and far from the passivity of the employee who receives instructions and orders that are alien to him, proposing participation and active commitment, including the presentation of productive, organizational and even commercial proposals by workers, in addition to the rotation of volunteer work and the obligation of managers to share one month of annual work with base workers in industries (Guevara 2006; Yaffe 2011). All measures quickly began to be dismantled before his departure from the ministry and his departure from Cuba in 1964. Beyond the fundamental presence of Commander Guevara in the discussion on the construction of socialism against Cuban supporters of importing the Soviet model without major adaptations, it was fully implemented in Cuba, but not until the 1970s.

The Chilean case is more related to other Latin American experiences of that time and later, as it occurred in circumstances of political struggle in a framework of access to government through elections, the "Chilean way to socialism". The Popular Unity (UP) government program, led by the socialist leader Salvador Allende and also formed by the Communist Party and other left-wing formations, included the nationalization of the strategic sectors of the economy (copper mines, industrial companies, communications, banks) and the building of the "Social Area of the Economy" (Gaudichaud 2016). In the Social Area, in addition to the government cadres, union delegates, generally aligned with the Communist Party, were granted considerable participation. It was a kind of co-management. The frontal opposition of the right and the support of the US government to a coup against Allende quickly led the country to a notorious political crisis in which the opposition quickly radicalized against the government, which had to face shortages, employer lockouts, permanent conspiracies to boycott the government and eventually expel it by force (Kornbluh 2003; Moniz Bandeira 2011; Kries 2013). During these lockouts, thousands of workers began to occupy the stopped plants because their owners were betting on the economic breakdown of the UP government, to form bodies of delegates and to put them back into operation. This process, in spite of the doubts of Allende himself (who in the face of pressure from the right did not judge it opportune) became massive and the "cordones industriales" [industrial cordons] ended up occupying hundreds of companies of all types and organizing themselves to manage them collectively. The *cordones industriales* not only took care of keeping the factories operating and, therefore, sustaining the country's economy despite the employer boycott, but they began to consolidate this principle of self-management. From the political level, the experience was supported by the radicalized left of the MIR (Movement of the Revolutionary Left) and the left-wing of the Socialist Party, while they were not well regarded by the other more moderate of the party, and by the Communist Party (despite which, there were not a few *cordones* led by communist workers leaders) (Kries 2013; Gaudichaud 2016). The MIR and the bulk of the Chilean left developed the concept of "popular power" to characterize all the experiences of autonomous organization of the popular sectors, from the peasant communities and the supply of cities to the industrial cords (Mazzeo 2014; Gaudichaud 2016). From there, they came to have debates with President Allende himself about the political situation, discussing the timing of the tactical concessions with which the president was trying to calm the right-wing coup's desire. Finally, the coup d'état took place on September 11, 1973, ending the lives of Allende and thousands of Chileans, causing the exile and imprisonment of many more, and ending with the various experiences of popular power, including the *cordones industriales*.

Factory Occupations in Argentina

After the coup d'état against the Peronist government in 1955, the workers' struggle in Argentina was radicalized in the face of the reaction of the dictatorship of the so-called "Revolución Libertadora" [Liberating Revolution], which aimed from the first moment to break the Peronist unions. In the period known as the "Peronist resistance", recourse to factory occupation was used as one more form of struggle. Among these cases, the most notorious was the taking of the Frigorífico Lisandro de la Torre [Lisandro de la Torre Refrigeration Plant], in the Mataderos neighborhood of Buenos Aires. The occupation of the factory led by a union commission of what was later called the "Peronist left" and the communists, occurred in opposition to the privatization of the company announced by the government of Arturo Frondizi, which, paradoxically, had won the elections with the support of Perón himself. The occupation was a massive event accompanied by the neighborhood, where most of the workers lived, and ended in a massive repression led by Army tanks (Salas 2015). In 1964, in another period of civil government between dictatorships (although with Peronism still proscribed), the Confederación General del Trabajo [General Confederation of Labour-CGT] declared a general strike and called for the massive occupation of factories. It is estimated that some 8000 establishments were occupied, in general by the impulse of the union base commissions (Schneider 2005; Basualdo 2010).

In the late 1960s, the Argentine working class experienced a period of political mobilization and radicalization that led to major rebellions against the military dictatorship of Juan Carlos Onganía, the most important being the *Cordobazo* of 1969, in which thousands of workers and students maintained the city of Córdoba in their power for three days until they were suffocated by the Army. As early as the 1970s, this period of mass struggle generated a series of episodes of factory occupation, amidst great political tension that included the proliferation of left-wing guerrillas (Peronists and Marxists) and the reaction of far-right paramilitaries and, subsequently, the coup d'état that led to the genocidal dictatorship of 1976–1983. In that turbulent period, especially during the short term of the government of Héctor Cámpora and the third and inconclusive government of Perón, hundreds of factories were occupied in the midst of union conflicts, and in some cases, such as Petroquímica PASA, a brief "workers control of production". The peak of the workers' mobilizations came in August 1975 in response to the shock plan known as the "Rodrigazo", in which a general strike of all union tendencies forced the government to expel the most repudiated ministers (Rodrigo himself and José López Rega, organizer of the far-right Triple A, responsible for more than 1,500 murders of leftist leaders and militants). It was, strictly speaking, the last great mobilization before the imposition of a massive and tragic State terrorism.

In the 1980s, with the return of the democratic regime in 1983, the country quickly recovered its unions, although the left wing of unionism had been decimated and weakened by the dictatorship. Amid a great economic crisis that was the prologue to the imposition of the radical neoliberalism of the Carlos Menem government since 1989, some union sectors led strikes with factory occupation. The most notorious was that of the largest automotive plant of Ford, which went as far as to put the assembly lines into production before being defeated by the intransigence of the government and the company with the complicity of the SMATA union. In the case of the Lozadur factory, the workers went on to form a cooperative that operated for a couple of years before the final closure during the hyperinflation unleashed in 1989.

Workers' Self-Management in Mexico

In the decades that followed the Mexican Revolution, the working class grew, in the context of an economy strongly oriented by the State, achieving from the presidential term of Lázaro Cárdenas a strong union presence and labor legislation (Gilly 2017) that, among other things, it favored in later years some recovery processes in the context of major manufacturing conflicts. We already mentioned one of these cases, the huge Cruz Azul cooperative, which was followed, already in the 1980s, by the Pascual soft drink factory. Cooperativism expanded in some sectors of the economy favored by government policy, such as in the fishing sector (Domínguez Carrasco 2007). Fishing cooperatives were privileged by the State with exclusive fishing zones for fishermen's cooperatives and the purchase of their production, but that State agency ended up sealing their fate when President Salinas de Gortari undertook a neoliberal turn and took away those benefits to allow the entry of large fishing companies to the market, causing the bankruptcy and massive disappearance of cooperatives (Anguiano 2010; Trejo 2012).

Despite these antecedents, the Mexican working class does not recognize a strong tradition of self-management and cooperatives. The youth political radicalization represented by the Mexican 68, bloody repressed by the Echeverría government in the tragic massacre of Tlatelolco, did not incorporate self-management as one of its premises, as it did in France or Italy in the same year (much less bloody processes, on the other hand). Furthermore, along with the labor tradition, in Mexico, the peasantry predominates as an important factor in popular struggles, in which the ideas of industrial self-management were logically absent. However, indigenous cultural traditions, based on the rural community, were expressed throughout the 20th century through peasant struggles, especially the agrarian reform pursued by the leaders of the Revolution of the early 20th century, mainly Emiliano Zapata. This was translated, when the agrarian reform was effectively carried out by the Cardenismo, in recognition of the *ejidos* and communal lands, which contributed to reinforce a tradition of communal organization in the rural areas that was transmitted to the poor neighborhoods and the Worker colonies in big cities (Gilly 2017).

The case of Refrescos Pascual in 1985 has to do with a company recovered after a two-year strike that in any other country would have been almost impossible to imagine, but that the Mexican labor legislation allowed (Taibo II 2010). Pascual is a witness case of what we would currently call, based on the Argentine example, a recuperated enterprise, and which in Mexico, on the other hand, could be distinguished as cooperatives stemming from union conflicts. Both the old Cruz Azul and Pascual and, more recently, TRADOC, respond to this typology (Pacheco Reyes 2018). However, these are the most notorious cases, large factories with hundreds or thousands of workers and extreme conflicts that attracted great attention at the time, while there are no records or researches to identify other less notorious cases, which, if they exist (and everything presumes that they do) are intermingled in the mass of the rest of the cooperatives. The Pascual conflict began as a strike for layoffs and claims typical of a union conflict and culminated with the workers who were left after two years of struggle (about 300) making a cooperative due to the inability of the company to resume activities because of losses caused by the prolonged strike. The cooperative managed to expand despite competing against global giants such as Coca-Cola, reaching the present day with thousands of workers and retaining a leading role in supporting workers' struggles despite the passage of time, being part with other unions of the foundation of the Nueva Central de Trabajadores [New Central of Workers] (Pacheco Reyes 2018).

Another similar case was the conflict of the Continental tire factory, formerly Euzkadi, in the city of Guadalajara, which after a conflict even more prolonged than that of Pascual and with the support of the union in Germany got the transfer of the plant and formed TRADOC [Trabajadores Democráticos de Occidente, Western Democratic Workers Cooperative] (Gómez Delgado 2008; Luna Broda 2011). This cooperative, in order to maintain the level of investments of the company, made an agreement with an American company to be able to export to the United States and, finally, the workers sold their shares for not being able to sustain the level of investments necessary to match the company associated, becoming employees of their previous peers. This happened after more than ten years of co-management, keeping the cooperative (which did not dissolve) the marketing of its own line of tires in the Mexican market anyway.

The most important and most recent conflict is that of the Sindicato Mexicano de Electristas (SME) [Mexican Electricians' Union], one of the oldest union organizations in Mexico and representing the workers of the state-owned electric power company that supplied Mexico City, Luz y Fuerza del Centro [Light and Power of the Center] (Montes de Oca 2019). During the government of President Felipe Calderón, of the right-wing National Action Party (Partido de Acción Nacional, PAN), the union had become one of the strongest opponents of the government's neoliberal policy. Calderón decreed in late 2009 the "extinction" of the company, taking all its facilities with the police and the Army to avoid resistance from the union and its 44,000 workers. A prolonged struggle followed and, in very difficult conditions, in which some 20,000 workers did not accept the compensation and followed the intransigent position of the SME, and which included demonstrations, camping at public spaces ("plantones"), hunger strikes, judicial appeals, and all kinds of measures, which were systematically ignored by Calderón and his successor Enrique Peña Nieto. Toward the end of the latter's government (the presidential terms in Mexico are six years), the SME obtained through negotiation the authorization to form a cooperative with its affiliates who had not settled their dismissals (at that point, about 15,000) and the transfer of the former LyF facilities to capitalize on the new company. In this way, the Luz y Fuerza del Centro Cooperative became one of the largest worker cooperatives in the world, managing several workshops of the enormous former state company and even several hydroelectric power plants in the surroundings of Mexico City (Pacheco Reyes 2018). However, they have not yet managed to re-employ all of the company's former employees and must compete against other companies in a deregulated and privatized electricity market, concentrating on repairs, installations, and maintenance work, as the electricity supply is carried out by the other public company that took care of the rest of the country (Montes de Oca 2019). The SME has been debating the complex transition internally from being a union organization of a public company to developing a self-managed enterprise, with the particularity that it wants to preserve its status as a union organization. The association with a Portuguese company for the joint management of the hydroelectric plants, in addition to the capitalization, as in the case of TRADOC, has the purpose of keeping the union active. The SME leads this transition without difficulties, which continues at the time of writing this text.

Workers' Control and Consejos Comunales in Venezuela

One of the least known aspects of the Bolivarian Revolution in Venezuela is the existence of processes of worker control and recovery of different factories and enterprises by workers. While the edges of the political and economic dispute for state control and the development of state policies that advance toward what Hugo Chávez called "21st century socialism" have been widely discussed and analyzed, the other process – which has been developing in the workplace and in the construction of the working class power in different areas of the economy – appears in a second or third level, not only in the political discourse but even in the theoretical formulation and academic research.

As a first attempt to advance the economic transformation by giving broad participation to the popular sectors, Chávez adopted several tools, one of which was the massive formation of cooperatives, giving a strong impetus to the so-called "popular economy". The creation of a ministry and the promotion of cooperatives and endogenous development centers (Núcleos de Desarrollo Endógeno) at the communal level were the main tools of this policy, much more important in rural than in urban sectors. Although later highly criticized because this massive promotion of coop-erativism did not have the desired effects, among other things because an overestimation of the transformative capacity of the cooperative tool itself – isolated from a policy of promoting a new logic of collective economic relationship –, and due to the proliferation of cooperatives that armed themselves for the sole purpose of perceiving the abundant lines of state financing, it was the first Chávez trial (and error) toward an economy under workers' control. The result was that between 2001 (the new cooperatives law) and 2008, more than 260,000 cooperatives were created, of which an estimated 70,000 of them came into operation. According to official data mentioned by Azzellini (2013, 6, 7), almost 50% correspond to the service sector, and only 25% to production, including food and other products, among which the industrial sector occupies an extremely low portion.

The government's interest in the processes of workers' self-manage-ment was accelerated by the successive attempts at the coup d'état in 2002 and 2003, which made the Venezuelan government and popular organizations subject of a test of force where social, political, cultural, and economic contradictions and their expressions were strained to the maximum. It was in the context of the sabotage of the country's econ-omy led by the technical and administrative bureaucracy of the state oil company (PDVSA) that Venezuelan workers began to demonstrate their ability to try the self-managed path. It was the oil workers who won the decisive battle in that conflict by managing to put the gigantic company into operation, despite the sabotage and the absence of managerial and technocratic sectors of the firm.

It is from this moment on that the Chavez' government begins to see in the experience of the Argentine recuperated enterprises a source of inspiration. The government began expropriating companies that had been abandoned or closed by their owners in the context of the conflict and that continued to boycott the Venezuelan economy until mid-2005, many of them already occupied by its workers. With approximately 40 companies recuperated through this procedure, the most notorious cases were the INVEPAL paper mill (ex Venepal), INVEVAL (ex Constructora Nacional de Válvulas/National Valve Builder), and Sanitarios Maracay (a later process, started in November 2006) (Azellini 2012, 171). Unlike the cases of other Latin American countries, the Venezuelan recuperated enterprises went through complex processes of relationship with the State that included a workers' cooperative integrated into a co-management company, in which the State held 51% of the capital and the cooperative the 49% remaining, although in general the practical resolution was more complex and went through different forms and conflicts around the formation of the boards of directors, the participation of the workers and the type of economic contributions from the State, in a dispute that, under different forms, was repeating thereafter.

The difficulties in the recovery of the expropriated factories added to the economic need for a quick start-up and an intention to move quickly toward a model of the socialist economy (which from different government sectors continued to think basically of a planned and administered economy in centralized form, with little room for worker participation) gave way to a series of more or less explicit questions to the experience of both cooperatives and recuperated enterprises. The usual insight was based on classical Marxist ideas against cooperatives, as an economic expression that benefited a set of workers who became owners and who did not articulate their company to the general needs of the economy. Likewise, some cases of internal corruption, in which workers were involved but also state administrators or managers (Azzellini 2013, 17, 18) and conflicts between state administrators and workers that began to occur in co-managed companies collaborated to re-discuss the issue and started talking about a new model, the "socialist company or factory".

In 2005, the somewhat confusing figure of the EPS – the Social Production Company – appeared, i.e., companies whose objective should be the integration of social needs and the articulation with cooperatives, the contribution of 10 to 15% of the profits to investment and internal democracy (Azzellini 2013, 7). When the idea of a "socialist company" was re-discussed (especially when trying a new constitutional reform, rejected by very little in a referendum in 2007) as part of the advance toward socialism of the 21st century, the EPS became an Empresa de Propiedad Social [Socially Owned Company], which began to mark its articulation with the communal councils first, and the communes, later (Azzellini 2012, 248). The new EPS can be an indirect EPS (administered by the State) or direct one, case in which they respond to the communes and the so-called socialist factories, but in practice, they are state factories with different modalities or attempts at workers' control.

In 2007, it took place the first experience of the so-called workers' control system, a co-management formed by an elected leadership and a council with the participation of workers, which led to the launch of the policy of "socialist factories" as the second stage of the struggle within the companies for giving more power to workers, subsequently giving rise to a call for the formation of socialist workers' councils, inspired by the traditions of workers' control and councils of the post-World War I and other historical experiences. Chávez declared on numerous occasions that socialism could not be limited to a part of economic activity or to the state organization, and that it should become a system of self-government, of general self-management (citing Mészaros). When, as of 2007, Chávez began to re-estate the large companies that were privatized public in the 1980s and 1990s, he promoted the creation of the workers' control movement in order to strengthen a process of transformation in the management of these companies in the sense of advancing transformations of the Venezuelan economy in a socialist sense. Thus, the first major milestone in this process occurred with the launch, in May 2009, of the Plan Guayana Socialista 2009–2019, in the industrial complex of the region, where the re-nationalization of the enormous steel company SIDOR and other factories had already taken place. Along with the call to develop workers' control, Chávez did the same with the communes, territorial organizations of popular power, in which not only would political authority be decentralized and an alternative power to the State itself would begin to be formed, but elements of community economic management would also be developed. Approved the plan by the president, the administrative and political bureaucracies of the different companies delayed its implementation until the personal intervention of Chávez himself, who uttered the phrase "I'm playing for the workers" and appointed workers to the management of all the companies. However, the experience collided with the corruption installed for years in the companies, and the opposition of the political leadership and, especially, of the unions. Chávez's illness and subsequent death ended this experience, which faced fierce resistance and could not be sustained over time. Although corruption and complicity between political leaders (among them the governor of the Bolívar State), the old managers, and the unionists was the knot of power that the workers' councils failed to untie, it was in Guyana that the most powerful worker control was developed, especially from the Alcasa factory. It was there that, in 2011, the first meeting of socialist workers 'councils met, in which 900 delegates from all over Venezuela discussed the political and economic conditions of the process and formed the National Movement for Workers' Control.

By that time, the workers' councils had extended to hundreds of Venezuelan companies and factories, driven by the call of Hugo Chávez himself. The workers' council was the basic body for workers' control that was sought to be promoted. In the words of Chávez, quoting the then Minister of Planning Jorge Giordani, "the productive accumulation in the transition (to socialism) would be given by [...] the incorporation of productive self-management mechanisms at the collective level", as one of the conditions for its realization. The workers' control councils were, in this scheme, a fundamental element for the factories and companies of state property or direct social property to advance toward the socialist company model.

The councils, then, were thought of as tools for workers' control and not for the union or vindictive struggles in which the union makes sense and in which its structure developed. However, in a few places (one of the exceptions was the companies in Guyana, notoriously Alcasa), the workers understood the councils and the practice of co-management in this way, but they generally presented the councils as a new union type organization, whose utility was in solving problems or claiming and pursuing claims. In this way, the difference between the council and the union was blurred, therefore, in cases where the union was very weak or had no presence, the council began to play its role, and where the union was strong, it entered into collision.

This situation of competition and dispute between councils, unions, and business management was repeated in numerous cases. The weakening of the policy of promoting and supporting the councils after the death of Hugo Chávez only exacerbated those disputes where they existed, and rapidly caused the existence and power of the councils to decline in the rest. President Maduro, who comes from unionism, did not continue to give impetus to the policy of the workers' councils. Without legality, its legitimacy came from the impulse of the bases and from the explicit support of Chávez. Although the Movement for Workers' Control continues to exist, its main force continues to reside in Guyana, where the most powerful experiences occurred (although the workers who had managed to place in the presidency of the companies have been displaced) and have weakened in the rest of the country. But, despite this setback, the idea and objectives of workers' control have remained in the memory of the Venezuelan working class, and they continue to manifest themselves both in conflicts within state companies and in the most recent experiences, linked to the idea of the communes.

Workers' Recuperated Enterprises in Argentina

In June of 2020, according to data from Open Faculty Program of the University of Buenos Aires, 407 recovered enterprises existed in Argentina, occupying 15,783 workers. Since the appearance of the first cases at the beginning of the 1990s, the WREs have grown in quantity and in diversity, as the previous works of the research program have shown (Ruggeri 2014; Ruggeri et al. 2011, 2016, 2018). The growth trend has remained steady after the rise of recovery processes during the late 1990s and the crisis of 2001, after a stagnation during the years of greater economic recovery in the Kirchner period (there is a notable slowing of recoveries after 2005 until the middle of 2008, although new cases never stopped appearing; this is also the period in which the most closures of WREs were verified). As of 2008, recoveries and conflicts about the closure of enterprises again begin to proliferate, and they maintained a sustained pace from then on that, while far from the massiveness of the period 2001–2003, is close to an annual average of about 15 cases per year. According to data from the fourth survey of the Open Faculty Program of the UBA, between 2010 and 2013, 63 factories and companies of all kinds distributed throughout Argentine territory were recovered (Ruggeri 2014). An update of the general data carried out in mid-2016 shows 43 recoveries for the following two years (between January 2014 and early 2016), bringing the total WRE in Argentina to March 2016 (as soon as the Macri government has just started) some 370 with almost 16,000 workers. By the beginning of 2020, after the Macri government was overcome, with political and economic difficulties different from those experienced in the previous period, the ERT continued to grow in quantity (407 as recorded in the report) but the number of workers had decreased slightly (around 15,700). The new recoveries were 39 since the arrival of the government of the Cambiemos alliance, but there had also been closings (the report established 20 cases) and many other stoppages, evictions, or closings, which had the effect of reducing the growth of the total (Ruggeri et al. 2018).

We can distinguish different stages in the curve of the emergence of WREs that are connected to changes in macroeconomic, political, and social context. The first cases of business recovery by the workers (excluding some historical cases that are still working, like the COGTAL print shop, which comes from the 1950s), take place in a neoliberal context, during the 1990s. A second period, that of the expansion, consolidation, and increasing visibility of the phenomenon, happened in the crisis of 2001 (between the years 2000 and 2003). We can identify the third stage as the consolidation of the post-convertibility economic recovery, between 2004 and 2008. The fourth stage was defined by the throes of the global financial crisis and the framework of the countercyclical policy and protection of the internal market by both governments of Cristina Fernández de Kirchner, a sustained and constant growth of recoveries (with a peak in 2008–2009, a decline in the second stage of growth and a new increase during 2012), but concentrated in non-industrial sectors or, among manufacturers, in highly precarious sectors with weak unions or vulnerable to technological changes that require large investments. The last phase encompasses the government of Macri, marked by a context of neoliberal economic policies that seriously harmed the internal market and, therefore, the operating environment of the ERT, coupled with political and judicial hostility not seen in previous periods.

The characteristic common to the majority of the WREs at their origins is that owner conduct tended to include asset stripping and labor fraud at the cost of jobs and productive capacity. It is also important to take into account that macroeconomic context, influenced largely by the economic policy enacted by the government, has an enormous importance as the context of the possibility of the existence of recovered enterprises or processes that may lead to their formation, though that does not mean that they are formed through State policies. However, a hostile State policy can make conditions exceedingly difficult for the development of these processes or even put an end to those that show weakness. In that sense, since December of 2015 until December of 2019, we have been in a stage of a return to neoliberal policies that led to recession and massive job losses, but with the addition of a change in the attitude of the State toward the WREs, which went from social support to aggressiveness.

In relation to the profile of the ERT in Argentina according to the activity sector, the data collected for 2018 indicate that 52% belonged to manufacturing industries, 25% to the food industry (including gastronomy), and the rest to services such as health, education, and hospitality, among an enormous diversity of branches of activity (Ruggeri et al. 2016, 10–12). Despite the fact that industrial manufactures are half of the cases, among these metallurgical factories, even though they continued to be the most numerous sector their relative importance in the total decreased since the first registration in 2002 (from 30 to 17%). On the other hand, a great diversification of economic sectors was observed, turning the recovery process of companies less and less into a mainly industrial phenomenon. In other words, it already appears as a process that affects all sectors of the economy where there is wage labor. This takes him beyond the well-known image of the "occupied factory", which seduced activists and intellectuals in the 2001 crisis, and closer to the deep reality of the diversity of the working class of contemporary capitalism.

Basically, the worker of a recuperated enterprise remains a vulnerable worker, whose level of social and labor inclusion depends on his collective abilities to adapt to the competitive market in the area in which the company operates. It is a worker who has not managed, despite his efforts, to constitute his company as a total reinsurance for his permanence in the labor market, both due to the legal vacuum regarding WREs as economic and labor units as well as due to the ambiguity about the legality of the collective property that they exercise and to the lack of social security and legislation for their particular conditions.

Another important feature of ERTs is their legal conformation as worker cooperatives. According to our figures, 95% of cases were formed under this legal form, while the remaining 5% is made up of other types of cooperatives, undefined cases that are involved in conflicts, and cases of co-management between workers and former owners or other business people. The cooperative form is favored for several reasons, such as lower taxes and the possibility of being recognized by a bankruptcy judge as "continued production" of a factory or business that has been declared bankrupt. As a cooperative, the members can operate legally on the market and enjoy protection over ownership of facilities, machinery, or other assets of the former company. Moreover, in forming a cooperative, workers can control the plant without being held responsible for the generally large, sometimes multimillion-dollar debts left by former owners.

In short, it is a complex and multifaceted process, which highlights the reappearance of self-management processes of labor in different circumstances from that the classic examples generally mentioned as historical antecedents, such as the Paris Commune or Tito's Yugoslavia. These are not revolutionary exercises but expressions of resistance to the process of excluding a large part of the working class from the labor market, characteristic of the economies that went through periods of neoliberal hegemony and, more generally, of global capitalism in the late of the 20th century and the beginning of the 21st century. The self-management of the recuperated enterprises arises from the need and organization for resistance rather than in the framework of a revolutionary crisis, so that the concept of worker self-management (as well as others that we can assimilate as worker control or popular power) goes from to be an advanced idea or a project of revolutionary social transformation to the analytical description of a practice that arose from the struggles rather than from theory and conscious political action. And this practice has a long history in Latin America.

Bibliography

AA.VV. (1969). *Congresos de las internacionales socialistas, selección de documentos* [Congresses of Socialist Internationals, Selection of documents]. Buenos Aires: Siglomundo, CEAL.

ACI. Alianza Cooperativa Internacional. La historia del movimiento cooperativo [International Cooperative Alliance. The history of the cooperative movement]. Retrieved from https://www.ica.coop/es/cooperativas/historia-movimiento-cooperativo

Anguiano, A. (2010) *El ocaso interminable. Política y sociedad en el México de los cambios rotos* [The endless twilight. Politics and society in the Mexico of broken changes]. México: Ediciones Era.

Antivero, J. and Elena, P. (June 9–11, 2011). Sindicatos y Empresas Recuperadas en Argentina: continuidades, rupturas e innovaciones surgidas a través de las experiencias autogestionarias de los trabajadores [Unions and Recuperated Enterprises in Argentina: continuities, ruptures and innovations through the workers' self-management experiences]. II Encuentro Internacional La economía de los trabajadores. México DF.

Arboleya Cervera, J. (2008). *La revolución del otro mundo. Un análisis histórico de la revolución cubana* [The revolution of the other world. A historical analysis of the Cuban revolution]. La Habana: Editorial de Ciencias Sociales.

Azzellini, D. (2013) From Cooperatives to Enterprises of Direct Social Property in the Venezuelan Process. In *Cooperatives and Socialism. A view from Cuba*, edited by C. Piñeiro Harnecker. London: Palgrave Macmillan.

_____(2012) De la cogestión al control obrero. Luchas de clases al interior del proceso bolivariano. Ph.D. Thesis in Sociology [From co-management to Workers' Control. Class struggles within the Bolivarian process]. Mexico: Benemérita Universidad Autónoma de Puebla.

Basualdo, V. (2010). Los delegados y las comisiones internas en la historia argentina: 1943–2007 [The delegates and internal commissions in Argentine history: 1943–2007]. In *La industria y el sindicalismo de base en la Argentina* [Industry and grassroots unionism in Argentina], edited by M. Schorr et al. Buenos Aires: Atuel.

Buch, L. and Suárez, R. (2009). *Gobierno revolucionario cubano. Primeros pasos.* [Cuban revolutionary government. First steps]. La Habana: Editorial de Ciencias Sociales.

Cole, G. D. H. (1957). *Historia del pensamiento socialista, vol. I, The precursors 1789–1856* [A History of Socialist Thought 1789–1856]. México: Fondo de Cultura Económica.

Cushion, S. (2018). *Movimiento obrero revolucionario* [Revolutionary Workers Movement]. Santiago de Cuba: Editorial Oriente.

Domínguez Carrasco, J. G. (2007). *Las cooperativas. "Polos de desarrollo regional en México"* [Cooperatives. "Regional development poles in Mexico"]. México: Red Bioplaneta.

Djordjevich, J. (1961). *Yugoslavia, democracia socialista* [Yugoslavia, Socialist Democracy]. México: Fondo de Cultura Económica.

Gaudichaud, F. (2004). *Poder popular y cordones industriales* [Popular Power and Industrial Cordons]. Santiago: LOM Ediciones.

_____(2016). *Chile 1970–1973. Mil días que estremecieron al mundo. Poder popular, cordones industriales y socialismo durante el gobierno de Salvador Allende* [Chile 1970–1973. A thousand days that shook the world. Popular power, industrial cordons and socialism during the government of Salvador Allende]. Santiago: LOM Ediciones.

Guevara, E. (2006). *Apuntes críticos a la economía política.* [Critical notes on political economy]. La Habana: Centro de Estudios Che Guevara/Editorial Ciencias Sociales.

Gilly, A. (2017). *El Cardenismo. Una utopía mexicana* [Cardenism, a Mexican Utopia]. México: Ediciones Era.

Gómez Delgado, E. (2008). *Ellos sí pudieron mirar el cielo. La victoria obrera en Euzkadi* [They were able to look at the sky. Workers' victory in Euzkadi]. México: Ediciones El Socialista.

Hernández, S. (1996). Tiempos libertarios. El magonismo en México: Cananea, Río Blanco y Baja California [Libertarian times. Magonismo in Mexico: Cananea, Río Blanco and Baja California]. In *La clase obrera en la historia de México. De la dictadura porfirista a los tiempos libertarios* [The working class in the history of Mexico. From the Porfirian dictatorship to libertarian times], edited by Cardoso et al. México: Siglo XXI Editores/UNAM.

Iturraspe, F. (ed.) (1986). *Participación, Cogestión y Autogestión en América Latina/2* [Participation, Co-management and Self-Management in Latin America/2]. Caracas: Editorial Nueva Sociedad.

Jaramillo, A. (ed.) (2012). *Cooperativismo y Justicialismo* [Cooperativism and Justicialism]. Remedios de Escalada: Ediciones de la UNLA.

Kornbluh, P. (2003). *Los EE.UU. y el derrocamiento de Allende. Una historia desclasificada* [USA and the overthrow of Allende. A declassified story]. Santiago: Ediciones B.

Kries, R. (ed.) (2013). *Los viejos del cordón industrial. Reflexiones sobre poder popular y movimientos de base en Chile (1972–1973)* [The old men of the industrial cordon. Reflections on popular power and grassroots movements in Chile (1972–1973)]. Caracas: Celarg.

Laserre, G. (1966). *La empresa socialista en Yugoslavia* [The Socialist enterprise in Yugoslavia]. Barcelona: Editorial Nova Terra.

Luna Broda, S. (2011) Apuntes para la discusión sobre autogestión obrera y la precarización laboral en empresas trasnacionales a partir del caso de Euzkadi en México [Notes for the discussion on Worker self-management and Labour insecurity in transnational companies from the case of Euzkadi in Mexico]. *Osera* 4.

Luxemburg, R. (2010). *Writings of Rosa Luxemburg: Reform or Revolution, the National Question, and Other Essays*. Florida: Red and Black Publishers.

Mariátegui, J. C. (1986). El provenir de las cooperativas [The future of cooperatives]. In *Participación, Cogestión y Autogestión en América Latina/2* [Participation, Co-management and Self-Management in Latin America/2], edited by F. Iturraspe. Caracas: Editorial Nueva Sociedad.

Martínez, C. and Ruggeri, A. (2016). El cooperativismo rural argentino. Una breve historia [The Argentine rural cooperativism. A brief history]. In *Questao agraria, cooperaçao e agroecología* [Agrarian question, cooperation and agroecology], edited by A. Mazin et al. Sao Paulo: Outras Expressoes.

Mazzeo, M. (2014). *Introducción al poder popular. "El sueño de una cosa"* [Introduction to popular power. "The dream of one thing"]. Santiago: Tiempo Robado Editoras.

Moniz Bandeira, L. A. (2011). *Fórmula para el caos. La caída de Salvador Allende (1970–1973).* [Formula for chaos. The fall of Salvador Allende (1970–1973)]. Buenos Aires: Corregidor.

Montes, V. and Ressel, B. (2003). Presencia del cooperativismo en Argentina. [Presence of cooperativism in Argentina]. *Revista UniRcoop* 1(2).

Montes de Oca, H. (2019). Formar una cooperativa fue la forma de no abandonar la lucha [Forming a cooperative was the way not to abandon the fight]. Interviewed by A. Ruggeri. *Revista Autogestión para otra economía 8.*

Pacheco Reyes, C. (2018). Mudanza: sindicalismo y cooperativas de trabajo en México [Moving: unionism and worker cooperatives in Mexico]. In *Empresas recuperadas y cooperativas de trabajadores en América Latina* [Recuperated enterprises and worker cooperatives in Latin America], edited by F. Partenio and A. Ruggeri. Buenos Aires: Red Latinoamericana de Investigadores de Empresas Recuperadas. SPU.

Peixoto de Albuquerque, P. (2003) Autogestão [Self-management]. In *A outra economía* [The other Economy], edited by A. D. Cattani. Porto Alegre: Veraz Editores.

Petras, J. and Veltmeyer, H. (2002). Auto-gestión de trabajadores en una perspectiva histórica [Self-management of workers in a historical perspective]. In *Produciendo realidad. Las empresas comunitarias* [Producing reality. Community businesses], edited by E. Carpintero and M. Hernández. Buenos Aires: Editorial Topia.

Plá, A. J. (1980). *América Latina siglo XX. Economía, sociedad, revolución* [Latin America 20th century. Economy, society, revolution]. Caracas: Ediciones de la Biblioteca de la Universidad Central de Venezuela.

Plotinsky, D. (2018). *El dinero de los argentinos en manos argentinas. Historia del cooperativismo de crédito* [The money of the Argentines in Argentine hands. History of credit cooperatives]. Buenos Aires: Ediciones Idelcoop.

Ronchi, V. (2016). *La cooperación integral. Historia de "El Hogar Obrero"* [Comprehensive cooperation. History of "El Hogar Obrero"]. Buenos Aires: Ediciones Fabbro.

Ruggeri, A. (2014). *¿Qué son las empresas recuperadas? Autogestión y resistencia de la clase trabajadora* [What are recuperated enterprises? Self-management and resistance of the working class]. Buenos Aires: Continente/Peña Lillo.

———(2018). *Autogestión y revolución. De las primeras cooperativas a Petrogrado y Barcelona* [Self-management and revolution. From the first cooperatives to Petrograd and Barcelona]. Buenos Aires: Ediciones Callao.

Ruggeri, A. et al. (2011). *Las empresas recuperadas en la Argentina. 2010. Informe del tercer relevamiento de empresas recuperadas* [Recuperated Enterprises in Argentina. 2010. Report of the Third survey of Recuperated Enterprises]. Buenos Aires: Ediciones de la Cooperativa Chilavert.

———(2016). *Worker-recovered enterprises at the beginning of the government of Mauricio Macri. State of the situation as of May 2016.* Buenos Aires. Cooperativa Cultural Callao/Programa Facultad Abierta.

———(2018). *Las empresas recuperadas por los trabajadores en el gobierno de Mauricio Macri* [Worker-recovered enterprises at the government of Mauricio Macri]. Buenos Aires. Cooperativa Cultural Callao/Programa Facultad Abierta.

Ruggeri, A., Martínez, C., and Trinchero, H. (2005). *Las empresas recuperadas en la Argentina. Informe del Segundo relevamiento de empresas recuperadas por los trabajadores* [Recuperated Enterprises in Argentina. 2010. Report of the Second survey of Recuperated Enterprises]. Buenos Aires: Facultad de Filosofía y Letras, UBA.

Salas, E. (2015). *La Resistencia peronista. La toma del frigorífico Lisandro de la Torre* [The Peronist Resistance. The occupation of the Lisandro de la Torre factory]. Buenos Aires: Punto de Encuentro.

Schneider, A. (2005). *Los compañeros. Trabajadores, izquierda y peronismo, 1955–1973* [The comrades. Workers, left and Peronism, 1955–1973]. Buenos Aires: Imago Mundi.

Tablada, C. (2005). *El pensamiento económico de Ernesto Che Guevara* [The economic thought of Ernesto Che Guevara]. La Habana: Ruth Casa Editorial.

Taibo, II, P. I. (2010). *Décimo round* [Tenth round]. México: Sociedad Cooperativa de Trabajadores de Pascual.

Trejo, R. (2012). *Despojo capitalista y privatización en México, 1982–2010* [Capitalist dispossession and privatization in Mexico, 1982–2010]. México: Ítaca.

Winn, P. (2004). *Tejedores de la revolución. Los trabajadores de Yarur y la vía chilena al socialismo* [Weavers of the Revolution. Yarur workers and the Chilean road to socialism]. Santiago: LOM Ediciones.

Yaffe, H. (2011). *Che Guevara. Economía en revolución* [Che Guevara. Economy in Revolution]. La Habana: Editorial José Martí.

13 Economic Policies and Development in Chile

From Dictatorship to Democracy, 1973–2013[1]

Ricardo Ffrench-Davis

Chile has Latin America's highest per capita income (GDPpc). It achieved this in democracy, principally between 1990, when democracy was restored, and 1998. In 1989, at the end of the dictatorship, GDPpc was below the regional average. In fact, the annual growth of per capita GDP reached 1.5% in the first half of the dictatorship (1974–1981) and 1.2% in its second half (1982–1989) but then jumped to 5.5% in the first nine years after the restoration of democracy (1990–1998), before dropping gradually up to figures close to one-half that in the last sub-period (2008–2013) covered in this chapter (see Figure 13.1). We close in 2013, the last year in which potential GDP and actual GDP were close to each other; since then it has prevailed a significant output gap in between.

Since the development of a country is not only a matter of comparison of each country itself along time, but it is also relative to that of other countries in the world. Has Chile been converging toward development? On the basis of World Bank data, the evolution of the Chilean GDP per capita is compared with that of the larger developed nation, the United States that is not the one with higher Gaps: in 2017, it was only the 14th one. Figure 13.2 shows how the gap between Chile and the United States has evolved. During the dictatorship, Chile moved away from development since its GDPpc dropped from 26% of the GDPpc of the United States in 1973 to 23% in 1989. In the return to democracy, between the 1990s and 1997, it had increased 9 points and, albeit more slowly, by a further 9 points over the next one-and-a-half decades. The financial crisis that began in 2008 helped in this latter convergence because it particularly affected the most developed economies where it had a high cost in terms of economic contraction and increased inequality, although from a position that, on both these fronts, was far superior to that of Chile. The two figures indicate that, by 2013, the Chilean economy needed pro-growth and pro-inclusion reforms going beyond the significant reforms implemented soon after the restoration of democracy. By 2013, Chile was much closer to development than in 1990 but still had a long way to go and had been losing speed.

DOI: 10.4324/9781003045632-14

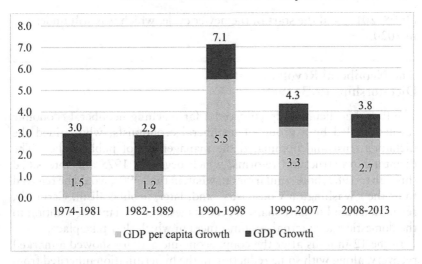

Figure 13.1 GDP and GDP per capita growth by economic cycles, 1974–2013 (annual rates of change %).

The summary that follows is inevitably brief and refers only to the most salient events. For details and hundreds of references to other authors, see Ffrench-Davis (2010, 2018) and the list of diverse authors at the end of the chapter. The summary is divided into three periods: the dictatorship (1973–1989), the early years of democracy (1990–1998) and the period between 1999 and 2013. As said, the latter year was chosen because it marked the end of recovery from the last full cycle

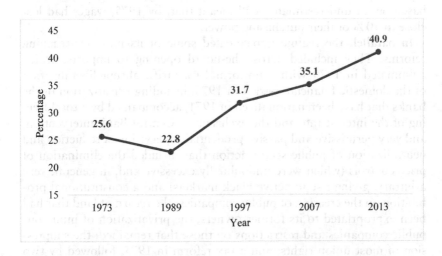

Figure 13.2 GDP per capita in Chile: as percentage of the United States, 1973–2013 (PPP, USD 2018).

(2008–2013) and the start of the newer cycle, which was still underway in 2020.

The Neoliberal Revolution of the Dictatorship, 1973–1989

The Pinochet dictatorship enforced a far-reaching neoliberal economic revolution, led by a group of neoliberal economists, who gained the dictator's trust and dominated the management of public policy. The dictatorship's structural reforms, which began in 1975 and intensified through to 1982, bore similarities to what, in the 1990s, would be referred to as the "Washington Consensus" and, later, neoliberalism. Certainly, revolutions tend to have many facets, stages, and variants in addition to the domestic and external circumstances in which they take place.

In the 12 months after the coup, economic activity showed a marked recovery, along with some reduction in the hyperinflation inherited from before the coup. Labor discipline imposed through union and social repression, the update of lagging prices and tariffs, devaluation of the currency, and a very high copper price eliminated bottlenecks that had hampered utilization of potential GDP. In 1973–1974, the large increase in the copper price was mostly captured and spent by the government. However, at the end of 1974 and in 1975, the copper price fell sharply and, along with the persistence of inflation, this led the government to take drastic fiscal and monetary adjustment measures in 1975. That year, industrial production fell by 28% and GDP by 17% while unemployment climbed to 20% of the labor force. At the same time, harsh repression of union activity, high unemployment, and wage adjustments based on an underestimated CPI meant that, by 1975, wages had lost close to 40% of their purchasing power.

In parallel, the regime implemented some of its most far-reaching reforms. They included across-the-board opening to imports, which culminated in 1979 with a uniform 10% tariff; abrupt liberalization of the domestic financial market in 1975, including privatization of the banks that have been nationalized in 1971, accompanied by a total freeing of the interest rate and the exclusion of Central Bank intervention, and very permissive and passive prudential supervision; a reduction and neutralization of public sector action that included the elimination of price controls (which were undoubtedly excessive and, in general, very arbitrary, giving rise to active black markets) and a constitutional prohibition on the creation of public companies; the return of land that had been expropriated to its former owners; the privatization of numerous public companies and restrictions on those that remained; the suppression of most union rights; and a tax reform in 1975, followed by two others in 1984 and 1988, which not only removed some distortions (for example, the cascading effects of the sales tax, which was replaced by a value-added tax [VAT]) but also significantly reduced progressive taxes and fiscal revenue.

In 1981, this was followed by the privatization of the pension system and partial privatization of the health system. The public pay-as-you-go pension system was replaced by one based on individual accounts managed by private pension fund administrators (AFPs) and the contribution rate was cut to 10% of wages. Without solidarity mechanisms, the new system capitalized on existing inequality. Moreover, the public sector continued to be responsible for paying current pensions and for a *bono de reconocimiento* payable to those joining the new system on account of their past contributions to the pay-as-you-go system. As a result, the state lost its inflow of contributions while continuing to have outflows, with a negative impact on the fiscal accounts.

By 1981, inflation had shown a marked drop, activity had recovered from the 1975 recession and the large fiscal deficit of 1973 had been replaced by a significant surplus. At the same time, however, an enormous foreign trade imbalance had developed and a current account deficit of 21% of GDP was being financed through heavy overseas borrowing by local banks (used principally for consumer lending) and by local economic groups (used to acquire firms being privatized). This was accompanied by weak productive investment and, associated to this weakness, annual growth of actual and potential GDP was running below 3% (in the 1960s, growth of potential GDP reached 4.6%, based on a net productive investment ratio that doubled that in the dictatorship). The external imbalance, which had built up gradually as imports exceeded exports (despite their very vigorous growth), widened further in 1979 when, in a new effort to curb inflation (which was already down to just over 30% per year), the government decided to freeze the price of the dollar. In this, it followed a *new fashion* in neoliberal economics known as the Monetary Approach to the Balance of Payments.

Meanwhile, international financial markets continued to boom and inundate most Latin American countries with lending from banks located in developed economies. The outcome of the accumulated imbalances in Chile began to become evident in 1981 with a general decline in exports and an increase in the external deficit. The government explicitly assumed that, since it had achieved a fiscal surplus and the foreign debt was private, a currency crisis could be ruled out. Reflecting its fervent belief in *automatic macroeconomic adjustment*, the government was confident that the *real* exchange rate would automatically depreciate, thanks to the contraction of monetary liquidity in response to the loss of international reserves, which the Central Bank began to suffer in 1981. However, the resulting drop in domestic prices fell short of the government's expectations. This implied that the exchange rate continued to revalue (cheap price of the dollar in pesos) and the highly freed imports accelerated their climbing.

The situation worsened further during the first half of 1982 but it was not until June, with a change of minister, that a minor devaluation was announced. This was obviously regarded as insufficient by the markets, which naturally responded with a run on Central Bank reserves. This marked the start of an economic and social debacle that only deepened in August when Latin America – led by Mexico – entered the *Debt Crisis* or *lost decade*. Chile had the region's largest current account deficit and highest external debt in relation to GDP and suffered its deepest banking and currency crisis: a 14% drop in output and an unemployment rate above 30%, accompanied by a severe worsening of poverty and income distribution.

The second half of the dictatorship (1982–1989) was marked by a more pragmatic approach, forced on the government by the depth of the crisis. It took various measures to balance the country's external accounts, such as renegotiations of the foreign debt, higher import tariffs, and "selective" incentives for non-traditional exports. It once again began to manage the exchange rate and the Central Bank began to "suggest" the interest rate to the banks.

The most far-reaching measure was the direct intervention of most of the collapsed financial system. The government committed the equivalent of 35% of annual GDP to rescuing the worst affected sectors, diverting these resources from public investment and social spending (wages in education and the public health system). With the nationalization of the private foreign debt, the public sector, which a few years after the coup had been in surplus, became a large overseas borrower.

By the end of the 1980s, the economy had recovered from the deep recession of 1982–1983, albeit with a sharp deterioration in distribution on top of that already seen in the 1970s.

GDP showed a vigorous recovery, particularly in 1988 and 1989. However, if the previous recessionary gap is taken into account – it is remarkable how often it is ignored in evaluations of the dictatorship years – average annual growth in the second half of the Pinochet regime was 2.9%, a figure similar to that recorded in the first half. This average includes the strong recovery registered during its last two years when a dramatic temporary increase in the international price of copper enabled it to overcome financial constraints and the shortage of dollars that persisted by 1987 due to the debt crisis.

Figure 13.3 illustrates the intensity of the two downturns and the two recoveries, with a very modest 2.9% annual growth.

How the evolution of the economy travels between 1973 and 1989 is very relevant for investment, growth, and income distribution. In each of the two sharp downturns, it was between 20% and 21% below capacity, implying that labor and capital were significantly underutilized (for example, includes the 31% unemployment rate in 1983). Underutilization of both factors tends to be very unequally distributed in society, with

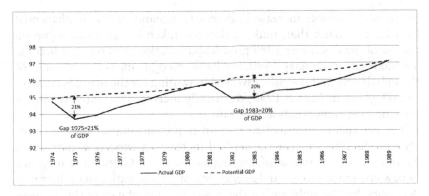

Figure 13.3 Actual and potential GDP, 1974–1989 (log scale, potential GDP 1996: 100).

higher unemployment focused in lower-skilled workers and in smaller firms, and increased informality takes place. Moreover, the prevalence of a gap between the two curves (the recessionary or output gap) discourages productive investment given that then several private firms are not using its installed capacity: what for to expand it.

As had also happened in the late 1970s, the 1982–1986 recession was used as propaganda for the dictatorship's neoliberal model. Local and international media gave extensive coverage to the vigorous recovery of GDP. Even today, it is common for economic evaluations of the regime to measure growth as from 1986, ignoring the huge gap that then existed between actual and potential GDP because of the severe underutilization of available capacity in 1982–1985.

Moreover, given the regime's policy approach, the economy's performance in 1988 and 1989 would probably have been very different if the copper price had maintained its trend level. Thanks to temporary income from copper, captured mainly through the state copper producer, CODELCO, taxes were reduced, wages and employment risen, imports were freed, and the peso appreciated; all financed with *temporary* income. Given the gap that still existed between potential and actual GDP, this led to an important reactivation in 1988-89, with an increase in employment and output that enabled the regime to hand over an economy with clearly positive figures in the margin.

However, as in the 1970s, the reuse of existing capacity had been achieved with macroeconomic imbalances that soon had to be corrected, more pressingly so because inflation in several other Latin American countries was beginning to turn into hyperinflation. In 1990, average inflation in the region climbed to a staggering 1,600%.

This explains the severe monetary adjustment implemented in Chile in January 1990 – when the newly elected democratic government had yet to take office – in order to curb an overheating which had been led by an unsustainable increase in domestic demand. It was implemented by a Central Bank that, under a decision taken by the dictatorship on the eve of the December 1989 presidential election, had recently become autonomous. In January 1990, the Bank, recognizing the seriousness of the imbalances and the risks involved in waiting for the new government to take office in March 1990, drastically increased the interest rate by offering long-term bonds at that rate.

The neoliberal reforms had had an important impact on the country's production structure: a marked increase in exports accompanied by an abrupt drop in manufacturing as a share of GDP. The emergence of new economic groups and executives, more innovative than their predecessors, had brought with it the modernization of part of the business sector. However, the vast majority of companies had not modernized and this accentuated the structural heterogeneity (or inequality) between businesses (large and small) and between workers (high and low skilled). In short, the downside of the remarkable progress of some was the marginalization of many. This explains why the modernization and expansion of some sectors coexisted with mediocre economic growth – the average of 2.9% per year in 1974–1989 – and an average investment rate similar to that seen in 1971–1973 and notably lower than in the 1960s.

Income distribution deteriorated significantly in the 1970s and, again, in the 1980s. Indeed, the relationship between the average income of the richest and poorest quintiles rose from 13 times in the 1960s, to 15 times in 1974–1981, and to 20 times in 1982–1989. This reflected the worsening of wages, high unemployment and increased informality, as well as a reduction of the space for small and mid-sized enterprises (SMEs), and the regressive tax cuts.

Politically, a significant phenomenon in this period was the reorganization of social movements and political parties, enabling them to press for the return to democracy, even within the rules of the game imposed by the dictatorship. After the victory of the *Concertación de Partidos por la Democracia* coalition in the 1989 presidential election, President Patricio Aylwin took office in March 1990 amid the recessionary adjustment that had begun in January.

Reforms for Growth with Equity, 1990–1998

When Chile returned to democracy in 1990, the government of President Patricio Aylwin sought to achieve sustained growth and increase equity. It was necessary to increase tax revenues, restore labor rights, increase public and private investment and avoid recessionary situations (the dictatorship had the two severe crises in 1975 and 1982) and hyperinflationary processes (experienced by new democracies in countries like Argentina, Brazil, and Peru). The new government attempted to respond to the most urgent social demands and begin to reduce the extremely high poverty rate inherited from the dictatorship (45% of the population, according to the first National Survey on Economic and Social Attributes – CASEN – a survey in 1987).

From the very beginning, the new government sought to correct the serious deficiencies of the dictatorship's neoliberal reforms. A labor reform to reinstate workers' rights and reduce the anti-union bias of labor legislation was accompanied by tax reform to increase revenues, strengthen progressivity and support the growth of social spending. In addition, substantial changes were made in macroeconomic (fiscal, monetary, exchange rate, and regulatory) policies, with strong countercyclical regulation, in a bid to achieve a sustainable macroeconomic environment, which the new authorities considered functional to economic development and employment. In this new context, investment and employment increased significantly in 1990–1998 and annual GDP growth averaged 7.1% (Table 13.1), while social indicators also improved. These improvements were associated not only with social policies but with the increased growth of the domestic economy; that is, the output produced and used in the domestic economy. While growth of exports was similar in this period to that achieved by the dictatorship (9.9% and 10.7%, respectively), the performance of the rest of GDP was notably different: 6.2% in 1990–1998 versus 1.8% during the dictatorship. It must be stressed that, notwithstanding the vigorous growth of exports, this non-exports sector covered about ¾ of total GDP.

Table 13.1 Economic growth, exports, and rest of GDP, 1974–2013 (annual average rates of growth)

	GDP	Exports[a]	Rest of GDP[b]
1974–1989	2.9	10.7	1.8
		(1.8)	(1.1)
1990–1998	7.1	9.9	6.2
		(2.5)	(4.6)
1999–2007	4.3	6.4	3.5
		(1.9)	(2.4)
2008–2013	3.8	1.0	4.9
		(0.3)	(3.5)

Source: Central Bank and Ffrench-Davis (2018).

Notes

[a] The figures correspond to gross percentage changes in exports of goods and services, but the estimate of their contribution to GDP (in brackets) corresponds to the domestic value-added by exports to GDP.
[b] The rest of GDP changes are equal to those of total GDP minus the domestic value-added of exports.

Macroeconomic, Tax, and Labor Reforms in 1990–1995

This superior performance was achieved despite the different obstacles faced by the democratic government: (i) although having won the parliamentary elections of 1989, it did not have a majority in the Senate due to the presence of senators *appointed* by Pinochet; the center-left coalition, Concertación, had won a majority of the elected seats, despite the binomial electoral system imposed by the 1980 constitution under which pro-Pinochet candidates needed only 34% of the votes to take one of a constituency's two seats; (ii) despite important changes to the constitution negotiated in 1989, it still contained numerous obstacles to democratization, to productive development and to the reduction of inequality due, for example, to the high supermajorities required in Congress for some reforms; (iii) the hyperinflation experienced by Argentina, Brazil and Peru in their transition to democracy in the 1980s was used by pro-Pinochet sectors to argue that the Concertación's program also pointed in this direction; (iv) the media were largely controlled by economic groups that had emerged under the Pinochet regime and had strong neoliberal leanings; (v) pro-democracy think-tanks were weakened by the emigration of personnel to the government and its mistaken decision not to contribute to strengthen those institutions; and (vi) Pinochet remained commander-in-chief of the army until 1998.

The tax reform approved by Congress included the reinstatement of corporate tax, which had been abolished in 1988, and this was set at 15% of profits, up from its earlier 10%. In addition, VAT, which the dictatorship had reduced in the year of the plebiscite, was raised from 16% to 18%. The labor reform sought to reestablish the role of the Central Unitaria de Trabajadores (CUT), the main trade union federation, and to strengthen unions and balance the bargaining powers of employers and employees.

In order to obtain approval of its bills, including the labor and tax reforms (Pizarro, Raczynski, and Vial 1996), the government had to negotiate with the right-wing opposition. Indeed, it was able to veto many bills, preventing the solution of problems that were to be at the heart of the social explosion of October 2019.

In 1990, the government reached an agreement with representatives of unionized workers (the previously prohibited Central Unitaria de Trabajadores, CUT) and employers (the Confederación de la Producción y del Comercio, CPC) under which the real minimum wage increased gradually. By 1995, it was 39% above its level in 1989. In this constructive climate (albeit with narrow limits), important progress was made in the early 1990s on income distribution and poverty. Indeed, the poverty rate fell from 45% in 1987 (the last available figure for the dictatorship) to 27.5% in 1994 and 22% in 1998.

The tax reform of 1990, the dynamism of economic activity and a reduction in tax evasion were reflected in a three-point increase in the tax burden to 18% of GDP. Thanks to this, the government was able to increase social spending and public investment while also running a fiscal surplus that averaged 1.8% of GDP in 1990–1997 and reducing a public debt that had its origins in the 1982–1983 financial crisis and was due to face large amortizations in the early 1990s.

Neoliberal economists had predicted that the tax reform would discourage private productive investment, but this was not borne out by events. In fact, an increase in capital formation was decisive in the acceleration of growth from the annual average of 2.9% in 1974–1989 to 7.1% in 1990–1998. Private investment tends to show a very close correlation with real macroeconomic equilibria. The evolution of demand must be consistent with the productive capacity that is being generated, while key macro prices (such as the exchange rate) must be "sustainable" and relatively stable (Agosin 1998; Ffrench-Davis 2006). During these years, both conditions were met.

As explained above, the macroeconomic imbalances created in 1988–1989 forced the Central Bank to implement a severe adjustment at the beginning of 1990. Its contractionary impact on domestic demand was subsequently reversed by a boom in capital inflows to emerging economies. Initially, the increased inflow contributed to the reactivation of domestic markets but soon began to press for an appreciation of the peso (cheap price of the dollar). However, the economic authorities managed to avert a destabilizing appreciation, protecting the competitiveness of the tradable sector and avoiding external and exchange-rate imbalances (both of which had been present in the serious crises of 1975 and 1982).

To this end, the economic authorities implemented a set of counter-cyclical policies. The Finance Ministry and the Central Bank worked closely together on their design and implementation, despite "the autonomy of the Central Bank" determined by the dictatorship a few days before having to hand overpower. Key macroeconomic policy reforms, for which the approval of Congress was not required, included a flexible exchange rate managed by the Central Bank and a reserve requirement on incoming credit and other financial inflows, containing what was considered an oversupply of these funds by raising their cost. When the inflow became excessive, the Central Bank further tightened controls, either by modifying the rate of the reserve requirement or its coverage or eliminating loopholes through effective monitoring of the evolution of financial markets.

These policies successfully controlled the financial inflows, creating space for monetary policy, while avoiding the destabilizing effect of exchange rate appreciation, keeping the current account deficit at a sustainable level (2.3% of GDP in 1990–1995) and preventing imbalances of the real macroeconomy. These were key in enabling the economy to make broad use of its productive capacity without overheating, thereby encouraging productive investment and export diversification. The effectiveness of this set of countercyclical policies became evident after the outbreak of the 1995 Mexican crisis from which the Chilean economy emerged unscathed (Ffrench-Davis 2006, chap. VIII).

In the six years between 1990 and 1995, GDP growth reached 7.8%. One of the salient features of this period was the close coordination that existed between the Finance Ministry and the Central Bank: I insist on this because this coordination is crucial for achieving sustainable growth and inclusion. It was greatly to their credit that the authorities avoided the temptation to accelerate abatement of inflation through greater absorption of external financial capital and appreciation of the exchange rate. Even without this, annualized inflation showed a persistent decrease, dropping from 31% at the end of 1989 to 8.2% in 1995.

However, the key to growth with inclusion goes far beyond sound management of the exchange rate and the capital account. Indeed, a broad set of positive results played a role: (i) GDP growth was sustained, instead of becoming exhausted after a few years; (ii) sustained growth was based on vigorous productive investment; and (iii) a fiscal surplus prevailed.

As well as maintaining successful policies and adapting them if required, other policies became ever more necessary in order to ensure sustainability over time: for example, productive development policies, with support for research, job training, and SMEs; reforms of the capital market which was extraordinarily weak in financing small business; and the application of significant royalties to capture the great economic rent generated by Chile's wealth of natural resources.

Gradual Return to Pro-Cyclical Vulnerability, 1996–1998

In this period, there was progress on social policies, particularly increases in the minimum wage and expenditure in in education and health, maintaining fiscal responsibility underpinned by strong GDP growth and rising tax proceeds. By contrast, countercyclical policies to stabilize the real economy began to weaken as from 1996, giving way to a destabilizing appreciation of the exchange rate, a rise in the private external debt and a larger external deficit in 1996–1997. Chile was being influenced by an international and academic fashion, with its origins in the Anglo-Saxon world: liberalization of the capital account and of the exchange rate.

A number of other factors also help to explain this policy deterioration. Firstly, the strength shown by the Chilean economy in the face of the Mexican crisis in 1995 obscured the fact that this was the result of a consistent countercyclical approach that had avoided: (i) an excessive exchange-rate lag; (ii) a large external deficit; (iii) an unsustainable accumulation of liquid external liabilities; and (iv) an *excess* of financial inflows for speculation and to finance a fast-rising consumption of imports.

Secondly, there was a clear shift in the Central Bank's priorities from 1996 when it began to exercise its autonomy and focus on the fight against inflation to the detriment of other macroeconomic objectives. In other words, it increasingly adopted the approach then dominant in Washington, led by the IMF, and US academic circles in a context of abundant financial flows into emerging economies, with the Central Bank gradually distancing itself from the macroeconomic policy of the previous period. As a result, although the avalanche of capital made it advisable to strengthen countercyclical regulation, it was weakened.

Thus, when the Asian crisis began to be felt in 1998, Chile found itself with a real exchange rate that had appreciated by 16% between 1995 and 1997, a private external debt that had nearly doubled between 1995 and 1998 as a share of GDP and with a current account deficit that, in 1996–1997, was also the double of its level in 1990–1995. The Chilean economy had become vulnerable to changes in international markets in contrast with the set of stabilizing policies in the first half of the 1990s. That vulnerability was put in action under two negative shocks in 1998-1999: a sharp drop in the price of copper and an outflow of financial capital associated with the Asian crisis.

By contrast, thanks to responsible fiscal management, higher expenditure was being financed with resources from the tax reform, reduced evasion, and a still fast economic growth. In fact, in 1996 and 1967, the government ran a budget surplus equivalent to 2.1% of GDP. Despite the deterioration in macroeconomic policy and the resulting vulnerabilities to eventual negative external shocks, the economy continued to operate at around potential GDP until 1998. This was decisive in a sustained increase in capital formation, which was an average eight points higher than during the neoliberal experiment (21.4% of GDP in 1990–2008 versus 13.6% in 1974–1989, at 2003 prices). Although foreign direct investment rose fast, 82% of productive investment in 1990–1998 was domestic.

Even though the 7.8% GDP growth recorded in 1990–1995 was not repeated, the average for 1990–1998 still reached a high 7.1%, with a decreasing contribution of non-exports to GDP growth, from 5.3 percentage points in 1990–1995 to 3.2 points in 1996–1998 (see Table 13.2); a significant drop, but still more than doubling the most 1.1 points contribution to the meager 2.9% economic growth during the dictatorship.

The high growth is linked not only to a higher labor force participation and the important increase in capital formation but also to progress on productivity, which rose by between two and three percentage points per year. As said, growth was led by exports, which showed an average 9.9% annual expansion, a rate close to that exhibited during the

Table 13.2 Economic Growth, Exports, and Rest of GDP, 1990–1998 (annual
average rates of growth)

	GDP	Exports	Rest of GDP
1990–1995	7.8	10.1	7.1
		(2.5)	(5.3)
1996–1997	7.0	11.5	5.5
		(3.0)	(4.0)
1996–1998	5.7	9.4	4.5
		(2.5)	(3.2)
1990–1998	7.1	9.9	6.2
		(2.5)	(4.6)

Source: Central Bank and Ffrench-Davis (2018).

dictatorship. More than exports in 1990–1998, the decisive factor in the high record exhibited by the economy was the vigorous expansion of the non-exports economy, which grew at an annual average rate of 6.2% for the nine years covered.

Production for the domestic use is that part of the economy where SMEs and lower-skilled workers are overwhelmingly located and it explains the growth of jobs and wages and some improvement in income distribution during the 90s, reversing the regressive trend seen during the dictatorship.

Macroeconomic Disequilibria and Falling Productive Innovation, 1999–2013

It is commonly asserted that the Chilean economy has been characterized by macroeconomic equilibria. That is a very ill-informed or mistaken view of macroeconomics if it refers to the two recent decades or to the dictatorship. Inflation is one crucial component, but other components of macroeconomic equilibria also include the rate of utilization of labor and the stock of capital and the external balance. This set of macroeconomic balances prevailed only in 1990–1998; since then, inflation has remained low, but there have often been imbalances in the other components and, as was explained above, the dictatorship exhibited two extremely large macroeconomic disequilibria.

In contrast to Chile's situation in the face of the 1995 Mexican crisis, the Asian crisis found it in a vulnerable position (principally, a depressed exchange rate, more short-term liabilities, and a large external deficit). Since then, its economic performance has fallen markedly below that of the early 1990s, showing real macroeconomic instability and a decline in average economic growth (Figure 13.1). Slower growth has also been associated with slower progress on poverty, job quality, and the evolution of wages as well as a sharp drop in productivity improvements.

The relapse in the quality of real macroeconomic stabilization policies was aggravated since 1999 by the Central Bank's decision to liberalize the exchange rate and the capital account (thus leaving the exchange rate at the mercy of financial volatility) and the adoption of the *inflation targeting* approach, to the detriment of the external equilibrium, export development and the rate of utilization of potential GDP.

Two Economic Cycles in 1999–2013

The Asian crisis spread to Chile through two channels: a worsening of its terms of trade and a general decline in capital flows. In the latter case, there was a massive outflow of domestic capital, led by the private AFPs, which used the room for maneuver available to them as a result of successive liberalizations. In 1999, they accounted for a huge net outflow equivalent to 5% of GDP, naturally deepening the recessive adjustment.

In 1999, the economy contracted by 1% and remained strongly recessionary until 2003. The abrupt downturn in 1999 and the prolonged stagnation that followed occurred principally in non-export sectors (which now represented around 70%). Their annual growth dropped to a mere 1.9% (down from the 6.2% in the previous period). In terms of the quality of national policies, this meant that a negative external event had a far greater negative impact on what was produced in the domestic market for use in the domestic market than on the contribution of exports to GDP. Since 1999, Chile has handed over that part of internal management to international markets (principally, speculative financial markets and instability of the copper price).

The drop in GDP created a recessionary gap of around 6–7% with respect to installed capacity. This was, its level and its persistence, a decisive factor in the contraction of private investment in 1999–2003. Due to this and a drop in innovation, the average growth of potential GDP fell from 7% to 4% in this five-year period.

In addition, this recessionary gap meant a reduction in fiscal revenues. To address this, the government implemented a novel *structural fiscal balance* rule in 2001. This rule implies that spending is kept at a level consistent with structural fiscal revenues, calculated as the annual proceeds that the government would receive if *potential* GDP were being fully utilized and the price of copper was at its medium-term *equilibrium* level. As a result, the government saves when the economy overheats and, when it is depressed, uses those savings or borrows to maintain its level of spending. Albeit clearly an improvement on the pro-cyclical norm under which a government seeks to balance its spending and actual income on a year-by-year basis, this rule only went halfway since it only stabilized the fiscal expenditure trend. Additionally, a countercyclical approach would need to use tax and spending changes in order to contribute to stabilize private spending (Ffrench-Davis 2018, chap. IX).

In the case of the capital account, the Central Bank lifted not only restrictions on incoming capital but also most of the controls on financial transactions by residents of Chile with the rest of the world. In addition, it allowed the exchange rate to fluctuate freely in response to short-term market pressures, leading to intense exchange-rate instability.[2]

In the face of the Asian crisis, Chile missed the opportunity to apply vigorous stimulus measures, taking advantage of all the economy's accumulated strengths: high international reserves, outstanding fiscal discipline, and the wide recessionary gap that existed throughout the period between 1999 and 2003.

The economy's recovery was kick-started by a positive external shock. A boom in raw materials brought a marked increase in the price of copper and other exports, followed by a strong recovery of financial capital inflows. This positive external shock gave economic activity a decisive boost. Given the wide recessive gap between actual and potential GDP, domestic supply was able to respond with increases in output, without creating inflationary pressures. In parallel, the volatility of the exchange rate meant that it started to appreciate sharply, contributing to an important acceleration of imports. The recovery of GDP had been gradually so that, at the beginning of 2008, when the effects of the global crisis began to be felt, some recessive gap persisted. This was in sharp contrast to 1991–1997 when there was practically no gap.

The exchange rate has tended to be misaligned since 1999: either too high or too low, with a negative impact on growth, the value-added of exports, the competitiveness of SMEs, and employment. The price of the dollar fluctuated between USD 504 (3/00), USD 744 (2/03), USD 443 (08/03), and USD 652 (08/11), showing intense instability, with a predominance of excessive appreciation as from 2004 that eroded the contribution of trade to development.

To sum up, annual growth slowed from 7.1% to 4.3% in 1999–2007, a figure that, albeit still respectable, was well below that seen in 1990–1998. This represented a sharp reduction in the Chilean economy's rhythm of potential progress. Some analysts have argued that this was only natural as Chile moved closer to development. However, even at the end of this period, in 2007, per capita GDP in Chile was only a third of that in the United States in PPP perms (and, at market prices, the gap was far wider).

This situation reflected excessive concern about inflation, accompanied by exchange rate revaluation and a lack of concern that, for most of the time, the economy remained below its productive frontier, with all the depressive and regressive effects for growth and inclusion that this entailed. It occurred because different economic authorities slipped toward economic policies that often elicited support from neoliberal specialists and praise from the IMF for strict adherence to *inflation targeting* and a free exchange rate, and a state that was economically rather passive.

The global crisis brought a sharp contraction of world trade in 2008–2009, and a drop in commodity prices and financial flows. As from the third quarter of 2008, economic activity in Chile began to slow, causing a brief recessionary adjustment between the end of 2008 and 2009. However, by the last two months of 2009, there were already signs of reactivation, in contrast to the five long recessionary years between 1999 and 2003.

In 2008, the government implemented a strongly countercyclical fiscal policy,[3] at a time when the IMF, in a radical about-turn, had become a promoter of countercyclical policies. During 2009, the highly negative effects of the external shock were increasingly offset by the positive effects of fiscal policy. In 2009, the budget deficit reached 4.4% of GDP, with spending rising by 17% (principally on investment and subsidies for the most vulnerable sectors, including the cost of a reform of the private pension system to strengthen the government-funded solidarity pillar and temper the regressive nature of the private capitalization system introduced by the dictatorship in 1982). In addition, taxes on fuels, lending, and SMEs were temporarily reduced.

A significant part of the assets held in the country's sovereign wealth funds was repatriated (USD 9 billion, then equivalent to about 5% of GDP) to finance higher fiscal spending. These assets had been accumulated by the government in previous years (thanks mainly to fiscal savings in periods of high copper prices between 2004 and mid-2008). The government's countercyclical behavior coexisted with an outflow of private capital, principally on the part of the AFPs (whose assets under management were now equivalent to a huge figure close to 10% of GDP). In this case, as in 1998–1999, the liberalization of residents' capital flows once again played a negative pro-cyclical role.

The domestic market – supported by the countercyclical fiscal policy – accounted for practically all the increase in activity in the last four months of the government of President Michelle Bachelet (through to 02/10). Exports fell and it was not until 2011 that their volume exceeded its level in 2007. This reflected not only the intense contraction of world trade but also the weakness of Chile's supply of exportable products, which was a consequence of the pro-cyclical nature of exchange rate policy and a lack of productive development policies. Certainly, the return of copper prices to higher levels as from the middle of the year also made a decisive contribution to the recovery of private expectations which, in turn, boosted domestic demand.

The reactivation seen in these four months, when GDP grew by close to 4%, was temporarily interrupted by an earthquake on February 27, 2010. Following this serious setback, recovery resumed as from April 2010, supported by the high price of copper and a significant recessive gap between potential and actual GDP. Strong domestic demand, with its origin in the countercyclical measures implemented in 2009, was further boosted by fiscal spending on post-earthquake reconstruction. Despite the destruction, the earthquake caused – estimated by the Central Bank at between 1 and 1.5% of annual GDP – installed capacity continued to be underutilized and higher public spending was consistent with a move toward macroeconomic equilibrium as long as this recessionary gap persisted.

Economic activity continued to recover rapidly through to the beginning of 2013, with GDP growth averaging 5.3% in 2010–2013. However, to avoid the common mistake of ignoring what happened prior to the recovery, the economy's performance must be measured with respect to the previous peak. Taking the peak of 2007 as the base, annual growth through to 2013 averaged 3.8%. In other words, for 15 years, Chile's economic growth had plateaued at around 4%.

The recovery of economic activity was reinforced by the price of copper which, after a brief drop in part of 2008–2009, showed a persistent increase. Copper companies responded by investing vigorously, further supporting the recovery and an increase in capital formation. In 2012–2013, mining investment accounted for 29% of all capital formation (even though, despite copper's importance, the mining industry accounted for only 10% of GDP). The projects initiated in 2007–2008 – when the financial and academic world thought we would live in *an age of great moderation*, a fashionable slogan among the elite of academics and analysts – began to complete their investment processes in 2013.

Recovery continued until early 2013 and, during that year, the economy reached its production frontier, which naturally boosted employment and investment. On the other hand, export volume showed annual growth of only 1% in 2008–2013, reflecting the effect of the slowdown in international trade, the deficiencies of Chile's exchange rate policy, and the persistent absence of productive development policies, aggravated by the declining ore grades of Chilean mines.

As the recessionary gap closed, the peso once again showed a marked appreciation and some new permanent items of fiscal expenditure were created without the corresponding permanent revenues. After its marked depreciation in 2008, the peso strengthened gradually and, in April 2013, once again began to appreciate strongly. In response to the exchange rate disequilibrium, real imports continued to grow much faster than real exports, and the external deficit widened.

To conclude, productive capacity was created far more slowly than in the 1990s. A significant part of the increase in actual GDP was explained by the absorption of capital and labor that had been underutilized as a consequence of the global crisis. Using available capacity is praiseworthy but is very different from creating that capacity, which is difficult to accomplish sustainably in the face of fiscal and trade imbalances. As a result, when the recessionary gap was disappearing in 2013, two macroeconomic imbalances prevailed: an excessively appreciated peso and a fiscal budget based on a temporarily high copper price.

The Situation in 2013

The cycle that began in 2008 ended in 2013, giving way to a new cycle that, as of 2020, was still in full swing. When negative external shocks caused by a drop in commodity prices began in 2013, while the Chilean economy and the Treasury had accommodated to an exceptionally high price of copper and the exchange rate was clearly overvalued (the price of the dollar was very low).

Over the course of 2013, the Chilean economy – where a recessionary gap was already building – faced an important combination of positive and negative factors that were not only economic in nature but also social and political. On the positive side, the government had liquid assets, equivalent to 11% of GDP, which it could use if it opted to implement a countercyclical fiscal policy. In addition, the Central Bank had net international reserves equivalent to 15% of GDP. However, over previous years, the economy had also developed a number of vulnerabilities.

Here we examine four variables which indicate that, without the rapid implementation of vigorous countercyclical measures, a prolonged recessionary adjustment was likely.

First, fiscal responsibility had been relaxed. Since 2009, Chile had, in fact, been running a structural fiscal deficit. A structurally balanced budget would have required a reduction in the growth of fiscal spending and/or a tax reform to increase revenues.

Second, during most of the decade-long commodity price boom, the real exchange rate was undervalued, causing a widening imbalance in the external accounts. Between 2008 and 2013, the volume of imports expanded at an annual rate of 6% compared to just 1% for exports, leading to an external deficit equivalent to 4.1% of GDP (at current prices) in 2013, despite the year's high average copper price (USD 3.32/lb).

Export volume and its diversification had stagnated. After a volume that rose 9.9% in 1990–1998, and 6.4% in 1999–2007, in 2008–2013 it dropped to 1% in total exports and both traditional and non-traditional sales. Additionally, fewer products were exported in 2013 than in 2008 and the number of companies exporting had also dropped. In the meantime, many free trade agreements had been signed since the return to democracy; these agreements included 64 countries in bilateral deals or with groups of countries such as the European Union. It is a surprising outcome, with all those agreements and stagnated exports with less exporters and fewer firms. By 2013, there was a clear need for a sharp reform of the exchange rate policy and a sustained devaluation of the peso and to open the discussion on introducing production development policies.

Third, after its strong recovery from the effects of the global crisis, the Chilean economy was operating at full capacity in 2013, making it inevitable that GDP growth would converge to its potential level, which was closer to the economy's actual growth of 3.8% in 2008–2013 than the 5.3% seen during the 2010–2013 recovery.

Fourth, these vulnerabilities were also compounded by other factors: (i) A significant reduction in the price of copper, which was only to be expected since very high prices are usually followed by very depressed prices. Hence, the importance of the implementation of a stabilization fund in the use of the resulting income; however, it applies only to the fiscal accounts through the Structural Fiscal Balance. (ii) A sharp drop in mining investment in line with the natural evolution of the cycle that began in 2006. (iii) Ongoing uncertainty in international markets and its transmission to most of Latin America. (iv) Domestic uncertainty related to the implementation of a progressive program of structural reforms by the new government that took office in March 2014.

Pending Challenges

The promising advances toward development seen in the early years after the restoration of democracy, gradually, with ups and downs, lost momentum and consistency as people's aspirations gained in strength. One element in this phenomenon, observed in many parts of the world, is growing discontent with the prevailing economic models and their neoliberal bias as well as with the evolution of globalization and its regressive bias. These elements and others specific to Chile – such as the marked weakening of economic growth, the inequality that persists despite evident improvements (which have, however, lagged behind growing aspirations of the population), and the massification of access to education (with the associated aspirations) and a marked deterioration in its quality (with the resulting frustration) – have created a divide between voters and their representatives that is reflected in an important drop in election turnout and an increase in mistrust. On October 18, 2019, Chile experienced a social explosion that was followed by the globalization of COVID-19 and its spread to the country.

Careful and open-minded analysis of the almost half-century covered in this article can shed light on how, rather than repeating the past, more sustained progress toward development could be achieved. History of the recent past can teach for improving the near future.

Notes

1. In general, figures, more in-depth analyses, and references are available in Ffrench-Davis (2010) in English and (2018) in Spanish. I appreciate the research support of Sebastián Freed.

2. During a period of 20 years, it has only intervened twice, under intense pressure from analysts and exporters, when the price of the dollar has been very low, and twice when it has been very high, prompting concern about the impact on inflation.
3. At the end of 2008, when monthly changes in the CPI were already negative, the Central Bank's monetary policy interest rate (8.25%) was seven points above that of the United States. The action of the Bank was lagging quite behind the government.

Bibliography

Agosin, M. R. (1998). Capital Inflows and Investment Performance: Chile in the 1990s. In *Capital Flows and Investment Performance: Lessons from Latin America*, edited by R. Ffrench-Davis, H. Reisen. Paris: OECD Development Centre/ECLAC.

Büchi, H. (1993). *La transformación económica de Chile*. Bogotá: Grupo Editorial Norma.

CIEPLAN (1982). *Modelo económico chileno: trayectoria de una crítica*. Santiago de Chile: Editorial Aconcagua (confiscated by the dictatorship).

————(1983). *Reconstrucción económica para la democracia*. Santiago de Chile: Editorial Aconcagua.

Consejo Nacional de Innovación (2007). *Hacia una Estrategia Nacional de Innovación para la Competitividad, T. I.* Santiago de Chile.

Cortázar, R., Marshall, J. (November 1980). Índice de precios al consumidor en Chile: 1970–78. *Colección Estudios CIEPLAN 4.*

Cortázar, R., Vial, J. (eds.) (1998). *Construyendo opciones: propuestas económicas y sociales para el cambio de siglo*. Santiago de Chile: Dolmen Ediciones.

DIRECON (2009). *20 años de negociaciones comerciales*. Santiago de Chile: Ministerio de Relaciones Exteriores.

Edwards, S., Cox-Edwards, A. (1991). *Monetarism and Liberalization: The Chilean Experiment*. Chicago: University of Chicago Press.

Ffrench-Davis, R. (2006). *Reforms for Latin America's Economies: After Market Fundamentalism*. New York and London: Palgrave Macmillan.

————(2010). *Economic Reforms in Chile: From Dictatorship to Democracy*. New York: Palgrave Macmillan.

————(2018). *Reformas Económicas en Chile, 1973–2017*. Santiago de Chile: Taurus.

Ffrench-Davis, R., Stallings, B. (eds.) (2001). *Reformas, crecimiento y políticas sociales en Chile desde 1973*. Santiago de Chile: LOM Ediciones/CEPAL.

Fontaine, J. A. (1989). The Chilean Economy in the 1980s: Adjustment and Recovery. In *Debt, Adjustment and Recovery: Latin America's Prospects for Growth and Development*, edited by S. Edwards, F. Larraín. Oxford: Basil Blackwell.

Foxley, A. (1983). *Latin American Experiments in Neoconservative Economics*. Berkeley: University of California Press.

Huneeus, C. (2016). *El régimen de Pinochet*. Santiago de Chile: Editorial Sudamericana.

Larraín, F., Vergara, R. (2000). *La transformación económica de Chile*. Santiago de Chile: Centro de Estudios Públicos.

Magud, N., Reinhart, C. (2007). Capital Controls: An Evaluation. In *Capital Controls and Capital Flows in Emerging Economies: Policies, Practices and Consequences*, edited by S. Edwards. Chicago: University of Chicago Press.

Mahani, Z. A., Shin, K., Wang, Y. (2006). Macroeconomic Adjustments and the Real Economy in Korea and Malaysia since 1997. In *Seeking Growth under Financial Volatility*, edited by R. Ffrench-Davis. New York: Palgrave Macmillan/ECLAC.

Marcel, M. (June 1989). Privatización y finanzas públicas: el caso de Chile, 1985–88. *Colección Estudios CIEPLAN 26*. Santiago.

Marcel, M., Meller, P. (December 1986). Empalme de las cuentas nacionales de Chile 1960–85. Métodos alternativos y resultados. *Colección Estudios CIEPLAN 20*. Santiago: CIEPLAN.

Meller, P. (1996). *Un siglo de economía política chilena, 1980–1990*. Santiago de Chile: Andrés Bello.

Moulian, T. (1997). *Chile actual. Anatomía de un mito*. Santiago de Chile: LOM Ediciones.

Muñoz, O. (2007). *El modelo económico de la Concertación: 1990–2005*. Santiago de Chile: Catalonia/FLACSO.

Pinto, A. (October–December 1981). Chile: el modelo ortodoxo y el desarrollo nacional. *El Trimestre Económico 192* Mexico.

Pizarro, C., Raczynski, D., Vial, J. (eds.) (1996). *Social and Economic Policies in Chile's Transition to Democracy*. Santiago de Chile: CIEPLAN/UNICEF.

Ramos, J. (1986). *Neoconservative Economics in the Southern Cone of Latin America, 1973–83*. Baltimore: Johns Hopkins University Press.

Servén, L., Solimano, A. (1993). Economic Adjustment and Investment Performance in Developing Countries: The Experience of the 1980s. In *Striving for Growth after Adjustment. The Role of Capital Formation*, edited by L. Servén, A. Solimano. Washington, DC: World Bank.

Uthoff, A. (2001). La reforma del sistema de pensiones y su impacto en el mercado de capitales. In *Reformas, crecimiento y políticas sociales en Chile desde 1973*, edited by R. Ffrench-Davis, B. Stallings. Santiago de Chile: LOM Ediciones/CEPAL.

Valdés, J. G. (1989). *La Escuela de Chicago: Operación Chile*. Buenos Aires: Ed. Zeta S.A.

Vega, H. (2008). *En vez de la injusticia*. Santiago de Chile: Random House Mondadori.

Williamson, J. (2000). Exchange Rate Regimes for Emerging Markets: Reviving the Intermediate Option. *Policy Analyses in International Economics 60*. Washington, DC: Institute for International Economics.

Yaksic, I., Stefane, A., Robles, C. (eds.) (2018). *Problemas económicos. Historia Política de Chile, 1810–2010, T III*. Santiago de Chile: Fondo de Cultura Económica/Universidad Adolfo Ibáñez.

Zahler, R. (2006). Macroeconomic Stability and Investment Allocation by Domestic Pension Funds in Emerging Economies: The Case of Chile. In *Seeking Growth under Financial Volatility*, edited by R. Ffrench-Davis. New York: Palgrave Macmillan.

14 The Economic Development of Costa Rica Based on Public Policies from 1920 to 2020

The Model of Social Economy with a Sustainable and Cooperative Approach

Federico Li Bonilla and
Monserrat Espinach Rueda

Introduction

Costa Rica, since the constitution of 1920, the President of Costa Rica (1920–1924), Julio Acosta Garcia, restores the Political Constitution of 1887, leaving the need for cooperation regulated (article 58). For the first time in the constitution, cooperation is inserted as a means to develop wealth. In this period, Costa Rica created public policies giving advantages to cooperatives, solidarity associations, labor corporations (sales), development associations, and peasant associations, among other labor economy organizations. The state supported itself, creating social and economic development in all the territories of the country.

A study of the main events that frame the current situation in Costa Rica is presented, marked to create social economy models with democratic foundations based on the country's actions.

After a research of the different economic, political, social, environmental, and technological measures – with priority given to human rights – of the different governments established in Costa Rica from 1920 to 2020, an analysis of the contribution by social economy enterprises and cooperatives over the last 100 years of management by the Costa Rican State is highlighted. We finally arrived at the model focused on sustainable development, the current model contemplated by the government, in line with the United Nations Agenda 2030. This is the result of management policies established since 1919.

In its economic model, Costa Rica has implemented the Agenda 2030 of the 17 Sustainable Development Goals (SDG) enacted in 2015 by the United Nations Development Programme (UNDP). The country manages in all its public policy actions (social, economic, environmental, human rights, political democratization, and technological) that are the foundation of Costa Rican economic development (Gobierno de la República de Costa Rica y Programa de las Naciones Unidas para el Desarrollo 2017).

DOI: 10.4324/9781003045632-15

According to Costa Rica's Social Progress Index (SPI), results are among the leading countries in the Latin American region. These indicators are aligned with the fulfillment of the 17 SDG and seek to eradicate extreme poverty in the countries by 2030, based on empowering countries in democratic practices of territorial participation, Productive property, innovation, technology, supported by territorial development, cooperatives, and other social economy organizations. The aim is to continue contributing to economic democracy, employment location, and promoting fair and organized trade, caring for natural resources and the environment (Porter and Stern 2018).

The 1920s period is intended to rescue the plans that drove the country in social policies (Briones Briones and Li Bonilla 2015) and to culminate in management policies that promote cooperation as a model of development (Li Bonilla 2013), prioritizing the promotion of a culture embodied in Law No. 19. 654 of 2016 (La Gaceta 2016). This promotes action plans to fulfill the 17 Sustainable Development Objectives at a territorial level and decentralizing power to local governments (Espinach Rueda 2018a).

Theoretical Framework and Review of the State of the Art

The Costa Rican State since 1821 is sovereign; between 1870 and 1930, there was a state formed by large estates where the unequal distribution of land "led to movements led by peasant workers who fought for better living conditions" (Briones Briones and Li Bonilla 2015, 3), these conditions, in 1920 led to the first political movements, which consolidated the state bureaucracy and social reforms that benefit the country today and born, according to the authors, the wage-earning sectors that make up the Costa Rican middle class.

By 1922, with the International Bank creation, which later in 1936 became the current Costa Rica National Bank, the government declared itself a country's entrepreneurs benefactor, where loans were granted to the population to finance at that time, coffee crops, the main export crop of the time, later bananas, and in the thirties the cooperative model promoted empowering the territories. Due to the lack of food during World War II, several crops were promoted to not depend on imports, industry, crafts, and tourism were encouraged. The state apparatus issued credits for territorial development, which empowered the territories and improved their access to road infrastructure to achieve the entire country (León Sáenz 2012).

By 1936, Law 3087 created the Office of National Planning (OFIPLAN), which is now known as the Ministry of National Planning and Economic Policy (MIDEPLAN) and dictates the strategic planning of Costa Rica in annual plans, medium and long term (Ministerio de Planificación Nacional y Política Económica 2013).

In 1941, Law 17 established the Costa Rican Social Security Fund to protect the health of Costa Ricans. In that same decade, from 1941 to 1950, given the crisis generated by World War II and the careful questioning of not continuing with the economic model of having two export products (coffee and bananas), implicit in the 1948 revolution, several policies were strengthened about trade, road infrastructure, consolidation of human rights, education and health (León Sáenz 2012).

The revolution of 1948 marks the change of Costa Rica when its leader José Figueres Ferrer makes the abolition of the army. Figueres Ferrer leaves the law of work. With it, the judicial one is respected relative to the cooperatives' creation when nationalizing the bank.

It is decreed that the Costa Rica National Bank will create a cooperative promotion department, thus initiating many cooperatives and recovered enterprises that become cooperatives, which make a territorial development, wealth, and decent employment. Also, all state banks must allocate 10% of their profits to cooperatives' development and promotion. On the other hand, the army's budgets pass to health and education for the citizens. It strengthens the social system and creates an emblem of social democratic democracy.

> Costa Rica is a democracy, and democracy is a real art in social life. It is the people's government; that is, of the human beings that make up the nation, its present and future life, and not merely public or private business, the country's territory, or its natural resources. It is the government by the people; that is, the self-determination of national life, and the ordering of society exercised by voluntary delegation by the people [...] and not by a privileged minority, or by a particular social sector, or by a political grouping or any other kind.
>
> (Figueres Ferrer 1955, 12)

The 1950s, characterized by the social-democratic welfare state's rise, promoted land management regional development, consolidated primary and secondary education, and strengthened state universities generating professional staff required for the country's economic and social boom (Ministry of National Planning and Economic Policy 2013).

For the 1960s, the action's main lines were planning in public investment, agriculture, and manufacturing industry toward a regional scope where it was sought to

> achieve Administrative Efficiency of the institutions of the Public Sector in the different territorial spaces, to increase the efficiency and productivity of their activities and seek a better fulfillment of the national objectives.
>
> (Ministerio de Planificación Nacional y Política Económica 2013, 11)

The experience of the Irazú Volcano's eruption in 1964 awakens in Costa Rica the need to promote plans in risk management and the environment.

In the 1970s, the agricultural sector was diversified, improving the fishing and livestock plan. National planning was organized to promote new crops, tourism, craft, small industry programs, irrigation, and electric power projects, and establish the National System of Science and Technology. The national cooperative movement is strengthened by promoting Law 4179 on Cooperatives, which seeks to create a comprehensive cooperative and territorial plans. The country is regionalized, and the state apparatus is organized "in seven sectors: Housing and Human Settlements, Education, Health, Work and Social Security, Energy, Finance, Transportes" (Ministerio de Planificación Nacional y Política Económica 2013, 23).

In the 1980s, development was promoted from a rural perspective. A National Plan for Associative Enterprises was formulated, the Tourism General Law was promoted, and the construction of the System of Social Indicators of Costa Rica was initiated to determine the Social Development Index (SDI). By the 1990s, the country focuses on reducing the state, and issues in public investment, regional and sectoral planning disappear. The National System of Sustainable Development is promoted, the System of Sociodemographic, Economic, and Environmental Indicators is constituted to measure Costa Rica's indicators. The construction of environmental indicators is promoted. Since 1994, the software has been used in public administration. Establishing an "institutional culture based on programming, evaluation of results, and accountability" has been promoted (Ministerio de Planificación Nacional y Política Económica 2013, 31).

For the 2000–2010 period, after a decade of stagnation in public investment, the future vision of public investment is being rethought, especially in the road, port, and air infrastructure, environmental vulnerability, promoting regional decentralization by strengthening municipalities as managers of public service provision, supporting laws for the transfer of powers and resources from the executive branch to the municipalities. Sectoral planning is strengthened, services comptrollers are promoted, and the Digital Government is formulated with a long-term vision of development for Costa Rica, where the country focuses on sustainability, with topics such as Carbon Neutral Costa Rica 2021, technologies promoting digital society and geo-information, translated into citizen-friendly information platforms, facilitating communication and supporting a supportive and inclusive society that allows equal opportunities for people regardless of gender (Ministerio de Planificación Nacional y Política Económica 2013)

From 2010 to 2020, the government promotes the Social Economic of Solidarity as a motor for development. For 2016, Law 19,654 Framework

Law of the Social Solidarity Economy is enacted to strengthen all sectors of the country in strengthening actions of territorial empowerment under a sustainable, social, and solidarity approach (La Gaceta 2016), strengthening in the budgetary charges the budgets in education, focusing them on the technological field and the territorial development in the empowerment of the Local Government (INCAE 2019). With the proposal of the Agenda 2030 of the 17 SDG, the government of Costa Rica

Became the world's first country reaffirming a high-level collective commitment to achieving the ODS on September 9, 2016, after signing a National Pact in which the government three branches (Executive, Legislative and Judicial), Civil Society Organizations (CSOs), Faith-Based Organizations (FBOs), and public universities, local governments and the private sector together with honorable witnesses such as the Ombudsman's Office and the United Nations System (UNS) committed themselves to the realization of long-term structural changes under an inclusive development with environmental sustainability in order to "leave no one behind," thus laying the foundations for the construction of an inclusive, diverse and multi-stakeholder governance structure for the implementation of Agenda 2030 in the country. (Gobierno de la República de Costa Rica y Programa de las Naciones Unidas para el Desarrollo 2017, 1) Agenda 2030 promotes the social economy within an environmental management approach, quality of life, and humanity's protection. According to the United Nations Educational, Scientific and Cultural Organization (2019), the pillar of development is inclusive education, which generates progress. "The global action program is implemented in the context of the Agenda 2030 for Sustainable Development and within the framework of Education 2030" (UNESCO 2018, 3) and the premises of sustainable education promote that the universities of a country should generate models of strategic alliances with the members of the central government, local government, territorial organizations, communities, non-governmental organizations (NGOs) and private companies, as development strategies to empower the inhabitants in their territories, through sustainable public policies (Espinach Rueda 2018b).

The Social Solidarity Economy, the cross-cutting theme of the sustainable model (Espinach Rueda 2018b), together with the variables that make up the Costa Rican cooperative model (Li Bonilla 2013), managing the country with political actions that favor the fulfillment of the 17 SDG (Gobierno de la República de Costa Rica y Programa de las Naciones Unidas para el Desarrollo 2017), consolidates an economic model. This new economy bases its social, economic, social, environmental, and technological development on an investment in human capital, which comprises, according to Word Bank Group (2019), "the knowledge, skills, and health that people accumulate throughout their lives and which allow them to develop their potential as productive members of society. It brings great benefits to individuals, societies, and countries".

Technological innovation creates a disadvantage among countries where the new characteristics of citizen education must be focused on empowering people from childhood

> The socio-behavioral skills development, such as the ability to work in a team, empathy, conflict resolution skills, and relationship management [...] Globalized, and automated economies place a more excellent value on human capabilities that machines cannot fully emulate [...] [and mention that] health is an essential component of human capital. People are more productive when they are healthier.

(Banco Mundial, 2019, 50) Countries with liberal economic systems have competed and negatively influenced social, environmental, and economic welfare (Organización Internacional del Trabajo 2017). The sustainable development model promoted by the UN in the year 2015 where 193 countries signed the Agenda 2030 agreement, the 17 SDG, as a new economic model that generates a social change in the countries, under the premises of improving the quality of life of people in harmony with nature and eradicating extreme poverty (2020), the Social Economy is the instrument to safeguard food security, quality of life, well-being in human rights and opportunities for people in harmony with nature (CLAC and FAIRTRADE 2016).

Costa Rica is an example to follow as a promoter of the 17 Sustainable Development Objectives of the United Nations Organization. The country has voluntarily worked with the United Nations Organization to be the model country that manages its political actions for development: economic, social, environmental, and technological, seeking a balance between social classes that benefits the quality of life and human rights (Gobierno de la República de Costa Rica y Programa de las Naciones Unidas para el Desarrollo 2017).

The decentralized democratization policies allow territorial development, create the political basis for each territory's inhabitants, determine their needs and prospects for human development, social, economic, and affect the environment and technology that affect innovation. From the identification of the needs required by a community, of a territory, located within a region, plans of action to be executed are made, which will compensate the actions to be satisfied for each territory's critical needs (Naciones Unidas 2013).

Methodology

This research is a qualitative investigation of historiographic analysis, documentary, descriptive, diagnostic, reflexive, to identify the different historical moments of public policies or decision making to promote public policies and action plans generated by the different governments of Costa Rica from 1919 to 2020. Thus, the bibliographic review of regulations, policies, and management actions executed in that period allows for elaborating a theoretically based process of understanding and understanding the economic, social, environmental, and technological policy management incurred in Costa Rica, 1920–2020.

It is intended from the qualitative research, to give the support to the academic, economic and political community of the interested countries, with the presentation of the proposal of a model of "a new sustainable economy of associative base", detailing from a meticulous revision of the different action plans executed and materialized in the data base of different historical documents and of the Ministry of National Planning and Economic Policy (MIDEPLAN) of Costa Rica, competent organ to register and execute the annual, medium and long term action plans of the country, where this body establishes that its primary objective "is to contribute to national development by providing reliable and timely information on government commitments to generate higher quality public goods and services, which allow spaces for decision making" (Ministry of National Planning and Economic Policy 2019, 9), the contribution expected in this chapter, will be a threshold of knowledge on Costa Rican social democratic policy under a sustainability approach, in a Costa Rican cooperative model, where health, education, innovation, technology and environment are pillars of the system.

Results

Given the need to impact on improving the countries' policies in actions that generate an improvement in social, environmental, and economic indicators, as the innovation and technologies potential that create people's job opportunities, it is essential to measure "the basic needs of food, drinking water, housing, security for all people. It is about living long and healthy lives, protecting the environment, as well as education, freedom and opportunity" (Porter and Stern 2018, 10), that people have to enjoy a quality of life. Costa Rican policies, which have contributed to the last 100 years of social democracy, have their peak with the abolition of the army in 1948 when these budgets are allocated to free and inclusive Costa Rican education in all territories of the country (León Sáenz 2012).

In Costa Rica for more than 100 years, the economic system has based the cooperative model as a pillar of territorial growth, advocating for the protection of a social economy (León Sáenz 2012; Li Bonilla 2013; Ministry of National Planning and Economic Policy 2013, 2016, 2017, 2019; Briones Briones and Li Bonilla 2015).

The country since the 1920s, with the incipient cooperative promotion and the incipient strategic planning in annual action plans, short term and long term, the axes of action and operativity, supported by the joint promotion, to create development associations, peasant associations, solidarity, among other types of social promotion. During all this time, they are in accordance and executed with variables that currently measure the indicators of the SPI, these measurement systems serve "to provide databases [...] to execute action plans to implement sustainable development" (Espinach Rueda 2018a) and they are the basis for measuring the actions executed not only at the national level but also in each of the 82 cantons that currently make up the country and are measured by the Cantonal Social Progress Index (INCAE 2019).

Costa Rica's territory particularities are characterized by the division of six territorial regions divided by the people's idiosyncrasy and not by regional political division. As he explains (Fernández 2017, 1)

> "territorial approach to rural development" comprises the territory not as an "objectively existing" physical space, but as a social construction, that is, as a set of social relations that give rise. Simultaneously, express identification and a sense of purpose shared by multiple public and private agents. In short, the inhabitants and their collective construction dynamics are the central actors and, in turn, the territories' ultimate goal.

Costa Rica's each region characteristics affect the territories' life quality; the country's current economic policies seek to improve the situations of the territories located in coastal and border regions (Ministry of National Planning and Economic Policy. Evaluation and Monitoring Area. Costa Rica 2018), the strategy is currently coastal, and border regions are the poorest in the country with indicators of the SPI, lower in quality of life and lack of social development opportunities for people (Espinach Rueda 2017; INCAE 2019).

Costa Rica has based its policies on improving the quality of life of people in the national territories. It encourages the country to use teamwork methods, such as cooperation. It was possible to demonstrate that in the territories, cantons, and communities where cooperatives exist, poverty rates are lower, and social development rates are higher. With an average of 20% of its surpluses generated (Li Bonilla 2013), it promotes social development in management policies from a Digital Government approach that generates reliable databases, where in the last 20 years, the country has focused on implementing the Social Economy of Solidarity model promoted by the programs of the United Nations Organization. "The evaluation processes must be based on the sustainable development principles, which will show the progress and gaps in the implementation of the interventions" (Ministerio de Planificación Nacional y Política Económica 2018, 14).

Education, technological innovation, health, access to drinking water, electricity, and improvements in road infrastructure are aspects to be considered of importance in all the country territory (INCAE 2019), and these pillars of social development drive management in government plans that promote Social Economy of Solidarity policies (La Gaceta 2016).

Promoting the country's most vulnerable territories from the different activities developed in the state apparatus is a task that has been carried out for over 100 years and is reaffirmed in the global commitments that the country has taken on. Since 2000, Costa Rica has been allied to pursue first the Millennium Development Goals (MDGs), promulgated by the United Nations, and then, since 2015, the SDG, which is an improvement and continuation of the MDGs, where the externalities that affected their fulfillment are improved, so that the countries that implement them have the best results in their search for sustainable development (Ministerio de Planificación Nacional y Política Económica 2020; Naciones Unidas 2020)

Concerning the advance in innovation and technology, the technology use has changed humanity and therefore, the management policies of the countries according World Bank (Banco Mundial 2019, 12)

> There has never been a time when humanity has not felt fear of the fate to which its talent for innovation might lead it. In the nineteenth century, Karl Marx noted with concern that "[1] machinery, however, operates not only as a powerful, irresistible competitor, always ready to turn the wage-earner into a "superfluous" worker. [...]. It becomes the most potent weapon to suppress periodic workers' revolts" (Fisher and Taub 2017). In 1930, John Maynard Keynes warned about the widespread unemployment caused by technology (Desai and Kharas 2017). However, innovation has transformed the living conditions. Life expectancy has increased, education and essential health care services are widely provided, and most people's incomes have increased.

To be able to generate technological innovation implies having management policies that interact in actions that allow the generation of action plans that from the analysis that is made of the political state of the last 100 years of Costa Rica that promotes the Costa Rican cooperative model as a management system to follow (Li Bonilla 2013), generates information inputs for other countries to find a threshold of information that will promote the cooperative model and tertiary education as drivers of a country's development (Li Bonilla and Sandoval 2013) and facilitate the improvement of social and economic development, in harmony with nature, that allows the fulfilment of the United Nations Agenda 2030 (Espinach Rueda 2017), where the growth of the SPI is promoted in line with the premises of the Social Solidarity Economy to create a development model, which is aligned with the decentralization of power, territorial empowerment and highlights the cooperative model as a social work tool to improve the quality of life and opportunities of the people (Espinach Rueda 2018a).

Discussion

Costa Rica, characterized by more than 100 years of developing management policies based on cooperative models (Li Bonilla 2013), has developed rural and urban territories with satisfactory results in social, economic, and environmental development, the level of the population affiliated to cooperatives, the cantonal income, the level of education and regional variables, such as the degree of urbanization and the extension of the Costa Rican territory, positively affect a country. Empirical research conducted in 2013 in Costa Rica demonstrated the positive relationship between the degree of territorial development and the level of associative affiliation (cooperatives) of its inhabitants in the country's different territories (Briones Briones and Li Bonilla 2015).

On the other hand, Li Bonilla and Sandoval (2013) stated that a significant result is a correlation between education level and associative level. The results indicated that the higher the population coverage with secondary and tertiary education, the higher the territory's level of associativity. On the other hand, what is relevant in the design of Costa Rican public policies is that it empowers the Local Government and recently promotes and strengthens the country's cooperative model by enacting recently (the year 2016) the Law of Social Economy of Solidarity (La Gaceta 2016), which seeks to promote cooperation as an instrument of local development, given that empirical evidence in Costa Rica shows that in the cantons with the highest level of associativity and tertiary education. Factual information shows the importance of strengthening education and associative development for the territories as a generator of progress for a country. To be expected, the more affluent and more prosperous a canton or territory is, the higher its associative level will be (Li Bonilla and Sandoval 2013).

Since the French revolution that changed people's human rights, there have been substantive changes in society enacted by an increase in productivity, an effect of the use of machinery and technology (World Bank Group 2019), but gradually creates a dehumanization of society (Briones Briones and Li Bonilla 2015).

Rescuing innovation and technology at all times, as drivers of development and currently reaching a fourth industrial revolution, robotics benefits people with specialized education. It brings consequences in income inequality to populations that do not enjoy technological advancement (Bandholz 2016), characterized by economic development models, where continuous innovation and implementation of disruptive technologies prevail, to be the current drivers of nations' economic development, with a more significant boost to job creation (World Bank Group 2019).

The World Development Report (2019), with data from the World Bank's Attitudinal Survey on the Impact of Digitization and Automation on Social Life, shows that technologies have made a significant and very positive impact on the economy by 85%, on society by 64%, and on quality of life by 67%. According to the World Bank Group (2019, 2): "Innovation, technology generates new sectors and new tasks". It mentions that economies must give primacy to human capital and countries must manage policies promoting social protection practices in social assistance programs in education and health where equitable tax reforms are sought for all sectors that affect country management improving new Human Capital Index, which measures the political consequences of countries' practices, by neglecting nations' social investments, mainly in health and education that allow a nation to grow in innovation and technology where the virtual nature of productive assets limits governments' ability to raise revenue.

The political and economic development of countries, in the face of the current global panorama of disruptive technology development, requires the development of soft skills to enhance the use of disruptive technologies

> Three types of skills are increasingly crucial in labor markets: advanced cognitive skills, such as the ability to solve complex problems; socio-behavioral skills, such as teamwork; and skill combinations that predict adaptabilities, such as reasoning and self-efficacy. Developing these skills requires a strong foundation of human capital and lifelong learning.
>
> (Banco Mundial 2019, 3)

Consequently, current economic policies must be subject to digital platforms' development to improve business opportunities in the territories, accompanied by educational programs that promote innovation and technology. The findings for the last century of Costa Rica show that its socio-economic development has been since the 1930s to date supported by cooperatives, then development associations, farmers' associations, solidarity associations, SALES, to promote productive ownership in the most significant number of people, thereby promoting economic democracy, which in turn bases the Costa Rican democracy.

Conclusions

The strongest democracies have competitive advantages over undemocratic governments in innovation and technology as human capital management. The incorporation of government plans focused on incorporating disruptive technologies, in line with the degree to which continuous and permanent industrialization is the key to lowering the incessant imbalance between social classes. In recent decades, the Ginni index has been increasing among social classes, creating a differentiation between countries. With it, people who live in undemocratic countries prefer to migrate to countries with democratic systems in search of improving their quality of life (World Bank 2019).

Many factors make a country lose competitiveness, which is consistent with shortcomings linked to social aspects that create disadvantages in opportunities and quality of life in people; these factors contribute to their inhabitants to migrate to countries that have better living conditions, with access to opportunities that are very relevant to social democratic policies of the most developed countries on the planet (Brenes Rodríguez 2018).

The ranking among countries in the SPI is aligned with the fulfillment of the 17 SDG, implemented by the United Nations Organization as an economic, social, political, and environmental development model followed in the countries improving people's life quality, improve employment opportunities, and reduce problems due to social gaps, pollution, territorial impoverishment, citizen security, human rights, health, education, democracy, as well as improving gender equality in human rights, premises of the Social Economy of Solidarity that contributes to reducing and eradicating extreme poverty (Gobierno de la República de Costa Rica y Programa de las Naciones Unidas para el Desarrollo 2017).

The better the GPI among the countries, the better the compliance with the 17 SDG (Espinach Rueda 2018a). After Chile, Costa Rica is the region leader is the best in Central America (INCAE 2020), which indicates that the country. However, it must improve in several national road infrastructure management, education and innovation, and technology, especially in areas where there is more social gap (coastal and border). In general terms, the country is concerned about taking a planned course of its management policies. Public policies already in the country's development plans have always considered promoting cooperation to develop the country's socio-economic wealth in different territories.

Bibliography

Banco Mundial. (2019). Informe sobre el Desarrollo Mundial 2019: La naturaleza cambiante del trabajo.

Bandholz, H. (September 14, 2016). Las consecuencias económicas y sociales de la robotización.

Brenes Rodríguez, M. A. (2018). La política social vinculada con familias en el entramado capitalista: la identificación del quehacer estatal costarricense en el PANI, IMAS e INAMU (1990–2014). *Revista Espiga* 17(35).

Briones Briones, E. and Li Bonilla, F. (2015). *Organizaciones Sociales en Costa Rica*. San José: EUNED.

CLAC and FAIRTRADE. (March 2016). El Comercio justo y los Objetivos de Desarrollo Sostenible: Un compromiso de todos.

Espinach Rueda, M. (2017). Agenda 2030 del desarrollo sostenible promulgada por la Organización de las Naciones Unidas. Caso Costa Rica. *Revista Ágora de Heterodoxias* 3(2).

_____(2018a). *Desarrollo Sostenible Hacia el cumplimiento de la Agenda 2030 de la Organización de las Naciones Unidas.* San José: UNED.

_____(2018b). Desarrollo Sostenible para resguardar la seguridad humana, a partir de los resultados del Índice de Progreso Social y su viculación con la Economía Social Solidaria. Revista Espiga.

Fernández, Diego. 2017. *Situación del desarrollo rural territorial y priorización de territorios en Costa Rica.* San José, C.R.: IICA.

Figueres Ferrer, J. (1955). *Cartas a un ciudadano.* San José: Editorial Bloy Morúa Carrillo.

Gobierno de la República de Costa Rica y Programa de las Naciones Unidas para el Desarrollo (PNUD). (June 2017). Costa Rica: Construyendo una visión compartida del desarrollo sostenible. Reporte Nacional Voluntario de los Objetivos de Desarrollo Sostenible. Retrieved from https://sustainabledevelopment.un.org/content/documents/15846Costa_Rica.pdf

Grupo Banco Mundial. (2019). Informe sobre el Desarrollo Mundial 2019. La naturaleza cambiante del trabajo. Retrieved from https://www.bancomundial.org/es/publication/wdr2019#about

INCAE. (2019). Índice de Progreso Socail Cantonal 2019. Retrieved from https://www.incae.edu/es/clacds/proyectos/indice-de-progreso-social-cantonal-2019.html

_____(2020). Índice de Progreso Social 2019. Retrieved from https://www.incae.edu/es/clacds/proyectos/indice-de-progreso-social-2019.html

Instituto de Investigación de las Nacionaes Unidas para el Desarrollo Social. (2013). Potencial y Límites de la Economía Social Solidaria. Retrieved from http://base.socioeco.org/docs/01s_-_sse_event_span_spanish_for_web_.pdf

Instituto Nacional de Estadísticas y Censos. Costa Rica. (October 17, 2019). Pobreza por ingresos se mantiene en 21.0% respecto al año anteirior. Retrieved from https://www.inec.cr/buscador?buscar=pobreza+extrema+2019 (último acceso: 5 de abril de 2020).

La Gaceta. (April 27, 2016). Alcance 78. Retrieved from https://www.imprentanacional.go.cr/pub/2016/05/16/ALCA78_16_05_2016.pdf

León Sáenz, J. (2012). *Historia económica de Costa Rica en el Siglo XX.* San José: Universidad de Costa Rica, IICE, CIHAC.

Li Bonilla, F. (2013). *El modelo cooperativo costarricense.* San José: EUNED.

Li Bonilla, F. and Sandoval, J. F. (2013). Importancia y aporte del sector cooperaritvo en el desarrollo humano: un análisis empírico para el caso costarricense. Cooperativismo & Desarrollo.

Ministerio de Planificación Nacional y Política Económica. (2019). Informe Anual 2019. Balance de resultados del PNDIP del Bicentenacio 2019–2022. Retrieved from https://www.mideplan.go.cr/

_____(2017). Informe de Seguimiento de Metas Anuales 2018 y cierre de período 2015–2018. Retrieved from https://documentos.mideplan.go.cr/share/s/HeSTOBOwRJWhoQgKy184jg

Ministerio de Planificación Nacional y Política Económica. Área de Análisis del Desarrollo. Unidad de Análsiis Prospectivo y Política Pública. (2020). Cambio Climático y Objetivos de Desarrollo Sostenible. Retrieved from https://documentos.mideplan.go.cr/share/s/PN8hz5bXRTCcrICXera2sg

Ministerio de Planificación Nacional y Política Económica. Área de Evaluación y Seguimiento. Costa Rica. (2018). Política nacional de evaluación 2018–2030. Retrieved from https://documentos.mideplan.go.cr/share/s/Ymx1WmMJTOWe9YyjyeCHKQ

Ministerio de Planificación Nacional y Política Económica. Área de Mordenización del Estado. Unidad de Estudios Especiales. (September 2016). Comportamiento de la estructura organizativa de los Ministerios en Costa Rica 2007–2015. Retrieved from https://documentos.mideplan.go.cr/share/s/2YnlFvCERPuFq6YdPzkqlQ

Ministerio de Planificación Nacional y Política Económica. Costa Rica. (2013). Memoria institucional Mideplan 1963–2013. Retrieved from https://documentos.mideplan.go.cr/share/s/T2JiandzTMSYp_oxmodVYA

Ministerio de Planificación Nacional y Política Económica, Secretaría Técnica de los ODS. (2017). Objetivos del desarrollo sostenible: Indicadores de seguimiento Costa Rica. Retrieved from https://www.inec.cr/sites/default/files/archivos-descargables-pagina/reodsinec2016-2017-01.pdf

Naciones Unidas. (February 12, 2020). Objetivos de Desarrollo Sostenible. Retrieved from https://www.un.org/sustainabledevelopment/es/development-agenda/

Organización de las Naciones Unidas para la Educación la Ciencia y la Cultura. (2019). Programa de acción mundial para la Educación para el Desarrollo Sostenible (2015–2019). Retrieved from https://es.unesco.org/gap

Organización Internacional del Trabajo (OIT). (2017). El trabajo decente no es solo un objetivo-es un motor de desarrollo sostenible. Retrieved from http://www.ilo.org/wcmsp5/groups/public/—dgreports/—dcomm/documents/publication/wcms_470340.pdf

Porter, M. (April 9, 2015). Porque importa el progreso social. Project Syndicate. Retrieved from https://www.project-syndicate.org/commentary/economic-development-social-progress-index-by-michael-porter-2015-04/spanish?barrier=accesspaylog

Porter, M. and Stern, S. (2018). Social Progress Imperative. Social Progress Index 2017. Retrieved from https://www.socialprogress.org/assets/downloads/resources/2017/2017-Social-Progress-Index.pdf

Sustainable Development Goals Fund. (2020). De los ODM a los ODS. Retrieved from https://www.sdgfund.org/es/de-los-odm-los-ods

The World Bank. (2019). The World Development Report 2019. https://www.worldbank.org/en/publication/wdr2019

UNESCO. (March 2018). Educación para el Desarrollo Sostenible (EDS) despúes de 2019. Retrieved from https://unesdoc.unesco.org/ark:/48223/pf0000261625_spa

Word Bank Group. (2019). About the Human Capital Project [Text/HTML]. World Bank. https://www.worldbank.org/en/publication/human-capital/brief/about-hcp

Index

Page numbers in **bold** refer to tables.

9780367492595